Georges
Plays:

The Girl From Maxim's
A Flea in Her Ear, Jailbird

Feydeau was the most successful French dramatist of the *belle époque* and is now widely regarded as one of the greatest of farce-writers and a worthy successor to Molière and Labiche. His series of dazzling hits matched high-speed action and dialogue with ingenious plotting. Reaching the heights of farcical lunacy, his plays nevertheless contain touches of barbed social comment and allowed him to mention subjects which would have provoked outrage in the hands of more serious dramatists. This volume of new, sparkling translations by Kenneth McLeish contains three plays from the peak of his career, *The Girl From Maxim's*, perhaps his best known, *She's All Yours* (*La Main passe*) and *A Flea in Her Ear* (*La Puce à l'oreille*), together with an early work, *Jailbird* (*Gibier de potence*).

Georges Feydeau was born in Paris in 1862, the son of the novelist Ernest Feydeau. His first one-act play, *Love and Piano*, was performed when he was 18 and he had his first success with *Tailleur pour dames* in 1887, when he also married an heiress. Among his many plays his best known are perhaps *Le Système Ribadier* (1892), *Monsieur chasse!* (1892), *Un Fil à la patte* (1894), *L'Hôtel du libre échange* (1894), *Le Dindon* (1896), *La Dame de chez Maxim* (1899), *La Puce à l'oreille* (1907), *Occupe-toi d'Amélie* (1908), and *On purge bébé* (1910). He contracted syphilis and was committed to an asylum in 1919 and died in 1921.

by the same author

FEYDEAU PLAYS: ONE
(Heart's Desire Hotel, Sauce for the Goose,
The One That Got Away, Now You See It, Pig in a Poke)

GEORGES FEYDEAU

Plays: Two

The Girl From Maxim's
She's All Yours
A Flea in Her Ear
Jailbird

Translated and introduced by Kenneth McLeish

Methuen Drama

METHUEN WORLD CLASSICS

1 3 5 7 9 10 8 6 4 2

This collection first published in the United Kingdom in 2002 by
Methuen Publishing Limited
215 Vauxhall Bridge Road, London SW1V 1EJ

The Girl From Maxim's, *She's All Yours* and
Jailbird first published in 2002
Copyright © 2002 by the Estate of Kenneth McLeish
A Flea in Her Ear first published in 2000 by Nick Hern Books
Copyright © 2000 by the Estate of Kenneth McLeish

Collection and introduction copyright © 2002 by the Estate of Kenneth McLeish

The right of the translator to be identified as the
translator of these works has been asserted by him in accordance
with the Copyright, Designs and Patents Act, 1988

Methuen Publishing Limited Reg. No. 3543167

A CIP catalogue record for this book
is available from the British Library

ISBN 0 413 76920 8

Typeset by Deltatype, Birkenhead, Merseyside
Printed and bound in Great Britain by
Cox & Wyman Ltd, Reading, Berkshire

Contents

Chronology   vii

Introduction   ix

THE GIRL FROM MAXIM'S   1

SHE'S ALL YOURS   189

A FLEA IN HER EAR   337

JAILBIRD   477

Georges Feydeau
Chronology

1862	Born in Paris, December 8
1874	Death of father, Ernest
1871–9	Attended boarding schools
1879	Joined a law firm as clerk
1880	Began to write and recite monologues
1881	*Par la fenêtre* (*Through the Window*), first play to be professionally performed, produced by Rosendaël
1883	*Amour et piano* (*Love and Piano*), Théâtre de l'Athénée
	Took post as secretary to Théâtre de la Renaissance
1883–4	Military service
1884	*Gibier de potence* (*Jailbird*), produced by Le Cercle Volney
1887	*Tailleur pour dames* (*Tailor to the Ladies*), Théâtre de la Renaissance – his first hit
	La Lycéenne (*The Schoolgirl*), Théâtre des Nouveautés
1888	*Un Bain de ménage* (*A Household Bath*), Théâtre de la Renaissance
	Chat en poche (*Pig in a Poke*), Théâtre Déjazet
	Les Fiancés de Loches (*The Fiancés of Loches*), Théâtre Cluny
1889	Married Marianne Duran
	L'Affaire Edouard (*The Edward Affair*), Théâtre des Variétés
1890	*Le Mariage de Barillon* (*Barillon's Marriage*), Théâtre de la Renaissance
1892	*Monsieur chasse!* (*The One That Got Away*), Théâtre du Palais-Royal
	Champignol malgré lui (*Champignonl in Spite of Himself*), Théâtre des Nouveautés
	Le Système Ribadier (*Now You See It*), Théâtre du Palais-Royal
1894	*Un Fil à la patte* (*On a String*), Théâtre du Palais-Royal
	Le Ruban (*The Ribbon*), Théâtre de l'Odéon
	L'Hôtel du libre échange (*Heart's Desire Hotel*), Théâtre des Nouveautés
1896	*Le Dindon* (*Sauce for the Goose*), Théâtre du Palais-Royal

Les Pavés de l'ours (*A Little Bit To Fall Back On*), Théâtre Montpensier, Versailles

1897   *Séance de nuit* (*Night Session*), Théâtre du Palais-Royal
Dormez, je le veux! (*Sleep, I insist!*), Théâtre de l'Eldorado

1899   *La Dame de chez Maxim* (*The Girl From Maxim's*), Théâtre des Nouveautés

1902   *La Duchesse des Folies-Bergères* (*The Duchess From the Folies-Bergères*), Théâtre des Nouveautés

1904   *La Main passe* (*She's All Yours*), Théâtre des Nouveautés

1905   *L'Age d'or* (*The Golden Age*), Théâtre des Variétés

1906   *Le Bourgeon* (*The Bud*), Théâtre du Vaudeville

1907   *La Puce à l'oreille* (*A Flea In Her Ear*), Théâtre des Nouveautés

1908   *Occupe-toi d'Amélie* (*Look after Lulu*), Théâtre des Nouveautés
Feu la mère de Madame (*Madame's Late Mother*), Théâtre de la Comédie Royale

1909   Moved into the Hôtel Terminus, where he lived until 1919
Le Circuit (*The Circuit*), Théâtre des Variétés

1910   *On purge bébé* (*Purging Baby*), Théâtre des Nouveautés

1911   *Cent millions qui tombent* (*A Hundred Million Falling*), Théâtre des Nouveautés
Mais n'te promène donc pas toute nue! (*Don't Walk Around Naked!*), Théâtre Fémina
Léonie est en avance (*Léonie Is Early*), Théâtre de la Comédie Royale

1913   *On va faire la cocotte* (*We're going to play cocotte*), Théâtre Michel

1914   Divorced
Je ne trompe pas mon mari (*I'm Not Deceiving My Husband*), Théâtre de l'Athénée

1916   Suffered increasing bad health caused by syphilis
Hortense a dit: 'Je m'en fous!' (*Hortense said: 'I don't care!'*), Théâtre du Palais-Royal

1919   Committed to a sanatorium by his family

1921   Died June 5

Introduction

Feydeau's father, Ernest Feydeau, was a stockbroker and novelist, a friend of Baudelaire, Flaubert and the Goncourt brothers – who mocked him in their *Journals* for an interest in ancient Egypt so passionate that it was 'a form of adultery with him'. He died when his son was eleven, and his wife and her second husband (the drama critic Henri Gouquier) sent the boy to boarding school. At about this time young Feydeau first became fascinated by theatre, and – like his near contemporary Alfred Jarry – wrote skits and sketches to amuse his school friends.

From 1883 Feydeau worked as secretary to the Renaissance Theatre, and his first full-length play, *Tailleur pour dames* (1887), had a successful run there when he was twenty-five. At about the same time he met and married an heiress, and in 1892 he had a hit with *Monsieur chasse!* at the Palais-Royal, the theatre which had previously seen Labiche's greatest triumphs. In the same year, *Champignol malgré lui* opened at the Nouveautés, and it and *Tailleur pour dames* each ran for more than 1000 performances. Feydeau went on to write more than two dozen plays, ranging from one-act sketches to historical spectaculars, and including the *grands vaudevilles* for which he is best known outside France: these range from *Un Fil à la patte* in 1894 to his mature masterpieces *L'Hôtel du libre échange*, *Le Dindon*, *La Dame de chez Maxim* and *La Puce à l'oreille*.

Feydeau's public success was offset by private misery. He spent each afternoon writing or directing, each evening at the show and then at Maxim's (where he had a table permanently reserved); he returned home at three or four in the morning, and began again at noon the next day. His wife shared none of his interests, and eventually asked him to leave. He gambled on the stock exchange, and lost not only the fortune his plays earned but also his valuable art collection. In 1909 he moved to a suite in the Hôtel Terminus (near the Gare St Lazare), and spent ten years there, dividing

his time between the theatre, Maxim's and a succession of
whores, from one of whom he contracted syphilis. He
stopped writing in 1916; in 1919 he announced that he was
Napoleon III, and was committed to an asylum; he died in
1921.

This private anguish is occasionally reflected in the plays. A
bitter or bilious note sometimes darkens the hilarity, and
collapsing marriages and lonely bachelors are treated with
more savagery than the plots seem to warrant. But it hardly
impinged on his dazzling public success. He was the most
successful dramatist of his generation in France, and regularly
had two, three or even four plays running at the same time in
Paris. He was an actor and a director whose stage business
exactly matched the demonic ingenuity of his plotting and
dialogue. By his death he was regarded as one of France's
major comic dramatists, a worthy successor to Molière and
Labiche, and his work is still performed cyclically at the
Comédie Française, two different plays each year.

Feydeau's style

Feydeau was a highly self-conscious stylist. He learned his
craft as a schoolboy by writing parodies and imitations of
authors he admired, and in later life often wrote scenes and
sketches simply as stylistic exercises. He analysed the work of
his great forebears and successful contemporaries, borrowing
– in a way which can easily be traced – a plot-inflexion here,
a type of scene there, a turn of phrase or business somewhere
else. Until the late 1890s he regularly worked with collabora-
tors, in the manner favoured by all comic dramatists of the
time – not so much sharing the actual writing, as honing ideas
together before one or other set the results down on paper.
(In Feydeau's case the writing is clearly his own. Each
collaborator's role seems to have been mainly to give advice
and approval, and in any case by the time of *Le Dindon* he was
working, for preference, entirely on his own.)

Feydeau's main sources were Molière, and through him
the *commedia dell'arte*, Plautus and Terence. These provided a

repertoire of characters and situations, and above all an attitude to society and human nature, which are the basic stock of farce. His gulled husbands, scheming servants, pompous military men and vacuous idiots may wear the clothes and follow the social conventions of the *belle époque*, but they come directly from this tradition. From Molière, especially, he learned the power of farce to make barbed social comment: he particularly admired *Le Malade imaginaire* and *L'Avare*.

One of the most fertile strands in Molière's output, that of the *comédie-ballet*, had been devised initially as a court entertainment for Louis XIV. These works (*Le Bourgeois Gentilhomme* is typical) frame straightforward satirical farce with extravagant music numbers, often involving pantomime-like characters (such as genies and mad professors), and using an unlikely mixture of ballet skills and slapstick. This tradition was matched, in popular theatre, by the vaudeville, or *voix de ville*. This was satirical street entertainment, in which the manners and ideas of the pretentious were burlesqued in (often bawdy) verse set to popular tunes, and whose grotesque and slapstick action was sometimes – as in *commedia dell'arte* – totally unrelated to the words being said. In Britain, and later in the United States, the style evolved into 'music-hall' and 'vaudeville' respectively; the sketches were separated from the music-numbers (though both remained satirical) and the physical display was split between slapstick (for example drunk-scenes) in the sketches and displays of such skills as plate-spinning or eccentric dancing (and later, striptease) among the other items. In France, the vaudeville tradition was gentrified into a kind of pastoral opera with spoken dialogue (of which Rousseau, no less, wrote an early example), into operettas like those of Offenbach, and into farcical plays satirising the bourgeoisie, with interpolated songs set to popular tunes of the day.

Labiche was the great nineteenth-century master of this last form, and his *An Italian Straw Hat* (usually nowadays performed without the songs) is a characteristic example of the genre. He also perfected a kind of vaudeville without songs: plays using physical business and rapid crosstalk to satirise bourgeois manners of the time. They were called *grands vaudevilles*, and are the principal link between Molière and Feydeau, and the main influence on Feydeau's style. In his *grands vaudevilles*, Labiche worked consciously to develop character: the puppet-like figures of *An Italian Straw Hat* are the exception in his work. The comedy is motivated by each character's individuality as well as by the needs of the situation: obsession, irritation and obtuseness, and the misunderstandings they engender, motor every play.

Labiche's plots – and Feydeau's after him – were also crucially influenced by the then-current fashion for the 'well-made play'. In this, the plot (usually in three acts) begins with an exposition which tells us the background history of the characters and also that there is a secret whose discovery will change all their lives. It starts at normal pace, but gathers momentum irresistibly until the first-act curtain comes down on confusion (often caused by revelation of the secret in question). There follows a series of *quidproquos*: mistakes, ironies, deceptions, misunderstandings, which always lead to a reversal of the hero's situation, from heights to depths or vice versa. The third act then explores the way this reversal affects every other character, and tidies up loose ends. Thousands of serious 'well-made plays' were written in the late nineteenth century – Ibsen's prose tragedies are outstanding examples – and the style was a main theatrical form in France, seen at its best in the plays of Augier, Becque and Sardou and of course the farces of Labiche. It was particularly valuable to farce-writers, as its discipline corseted the raucousness of vaudeville, allowing slapstick and hilarity to co-exist with a sustained satirical assault on bourgeois morality and convention.

Although Feydeau's main debt is to Labiche, he also learned from three contemporaries in particular. Maurice Hennequin, in the 1870s and 1880s, had great success with lunatic-action farces, successions of non-sequitur dialogue and slapstick confrontation – the original 'doors' French farces and the models for many of Feydeau's second acts (such as that of *Le Dindon*). Henri Meilhac, 'the Marivaux of the boulevards', and his collaborator Louis Halévy, wrote, among other things, the books for Offenbach's mythological burlesques, and were masters of the difficult art of letting characters speak apparently airy, natural dialogue while actually articulating the most extravagant passions and bizarre ideas. Their scripts flow as evenly and seamlessly as Hennequin's are unpredictable, and their influence can be seen particularly in Feydeau's opening acts, and in the way he brings back dialogue-interest in his third acts, restoring of urbanity which, while never less funny, produces a welcome change of pace from the breakneck slapstick of the second acts.

Feydeau's mastery of the conventions of the well-made play – not to mention his audience's familiarity with the form – allowed him to ironise and parody both it and its component parts, to deal easily and farcically with subjects which, handled by serious dramatists at the same period, evoked howls of outrage and embarrassment. Impotence, for example, is a subsidiary theme in Act Three of *Sauce for the Goose* (where it arises, if that is the word, from Redillon's sexual exhaustion) and it motivates the whole plot of *A Flea in Her Ear* (where, because Chandebise is impotent, his wife suspects – quite wrongly – that he is 'spending himself' with a lover). Another serious subject which runs through all the plays, to the point of obsession, is the status of women: their equality with men and their 'power' within society and especially within marriage and the household. Feydeau's plots may revolve around adulterous intrigues (or, rather, would-be or mistakenly-suspected-to-be adulterous intrigues), but the meat of the plays is often the way a wife takes control, asserts her individual dignity, even sanity, in a lunatic world. Invariably, he gives his women more richness of character than his men; the men bluster, scheme and flail, while the women change and grow. This gives his plays a dimension lacking in other farces – even in such masterpieces as (in English) *The Rivals* or *The Importance of Being Earnest* – and links them with such later writers as Orton, who explores what

might be called the condition of psychological anarchy, or
Ayckbourn, in whose plays psychological inadequacy is a
recurring theme. It is the essence of farce that such serious
matters – indeed any serious matters – should not obtrude,
that silliness should rule. But audiences leave a Feydeau play
sated in a different way from most other farces, and I believe
one of the main reasons is the way he touches on the darkness
in human life and the unpredictable obsession not only at the
surface but deep down in human character.

Each of the plays included in these two volumes shows a
different aspect of Feydeau's art. *Jailbird* (*Gibier de potence*) is an
early work, first performed in 1883, at a semi-private theatre
club, organised by the twenty-one-year-old author and like-
minded friends. It was one item in a miscellaneous pro-
gramme of monologues, comic songs and daft poems;
Feydeau himself directed and took the part of Plumard. The
piece shows occasional apprentice touches: the inconsequen-
tiality of some of the jokes, for example, climaxing in the very
last line of all, suggests a group of students giggling together
rather than a single-minded artist fully in control of his
effects. But the themes of Feydeau's major works are all here,
and the misunderstandings and dazzle of the dialogue show
his mastery even at this early age. In particular, the
'unmasking' scene and the scene where Lemercier and
Taupinier try to outboast one another as assassins stand with
his most lunatic, most felicitous inventions.

   Pig in a Poke (*Chat en poche*) was first performed in 1888, a
year after Feydeau's first big 'hit', *Tailleur pour dames*. It is a
masterpiece of construction, not so much an arch as
continuous escalation of confusion – and the Meilhac/Halévy
influence is especially noticeable, in that the characters'
apparently ordinary dialogue (the kind of language you might
have heard in any drawing-room of the time) belies the
astounding content of what the people are saying or the
thoughts inside their heads. Examples of Feydeau's scintillat-
ing stagecraft in this play are his careful, almost Ibsenish

control over the escalation of the daftness in the first act, the counterpointing in Act Two of the Winstanley/Julie story with the main plot, and the way he keeps back the play's major surprise, the Sistine Chapel business, until the last act, just when we might think that the comic possibilities of the situation had been exhausted. *Pig in a Poke* may be chamber music compared to the grand symphonic structures of *A Flea in Her Ear* or *The Girl from Maxim's*, but it is also one of his most accomplished works.

Now You See It (*Le Système Ribadier*, written in collaboration with Hennequin in 1892), a darker comedy altogether, subverts the vaudeville tradition, even as it follows it, letting the men's obsessions turn them into mechanistic puppets – in a manner English readers may associate with Orton's characters in *Loot* or *What the Butler Saw* – while the heroine's character and personality flower before our eyes. It has one of the smallest casts and tightest constructions of any Feydeau farce. It was one of the author's own favourite plays and he revived it in 1909 under a new title, *Nothing Known*.

The One That Got Away (*Monsieur chasse!*, 1892) is a fine example of Feydeau's 'demented clockwork' style of plotting, an effect much heightened by the smallness of the cast. Act One sets up a dozen criss-crossing situations, and shows us a group of people each of whom has something to hide from at least two of the others. Act Two brings all these people together in a situation where they should never, ever, meet, and is a frenzy of mistaken identities, mock-tragic dialogue and slapstick action involving doors, a closet, a double-bed, a man in underwear and a police chase. (Feydeau, who directed his own plays, always made his actors perform the dialogue of such scenes with utmost seriousness, as if they were high tragedy; the action, by contrast, was speeded up, heightened and mechanistic. Dislocation between the two styles made for hilarity – a production-method still followed in France, where Feydeau's farces are performed in rotation at the Comédie Française, but curiously seldom observed in English-language productions, perhaps because our farce-traditions tend more towards the end of the pier in one direction or 'high comedy' in the other.) Act Three picks up all the dangling loose ends from Act Two, further twists them and then untangles them while at the same time resolving the 'serious' issues of the play: Duchotel's infidelity and the suspicions of Léontine which set the action spinning in Act One.

Sauce for the Goose (*Le Dindon*), which enjoyed a long run at the Théâtre du Palais-Royal in 1896, is a characteristically 'well-made' *grand vaudeville*, with a lunatic second act framed by gentler material. It is, however, driven by character. Each person is clearly individuated and the differences between Redillon and Potagnac or Lucienne and Clotilde make the point that two individuals can share the same approach to life, or the same response to unexpected events, but show it in entirely different ways. Both this play and *Heart's Desire Hotel* (*L'Hôtel du libre échange*), which dates from two years earlier, make use of the hotel setting in order to create a space situated halfway between the private and the public, a space where desires which cannot be spoken of in a polite bourgeois salon emerge and press for satisfaction. Both plays make hilarious use of rooms with several doors, some of which allow for escape, while others lead only into cupboards or bathrooms. And both plays benefit from the sense that hotel guests have of being constantly observed, even spied on, by people they hardly know. *Heart's Desire Hotel* is justly one of the most famous comedies of assumed identity in the repertoire; the fact that the only couple to achieve any satisfaction is the young Maxime and Victoire, while the older characters remain frightened and frustrated, is entirely in keeping with the traditions of farce going back to classical times.

In most of Feydeau's plays the characters are drawn from middle-class society, but the plot of *The Girl From Maxim's* (*La Dame de chez Maxim*, Théâtre des Nouveautés, 1899) turns on a liaison – or rather two liaisons – between representatives of the respectable middle classes and a show-girl named 'Shrimp' (*la môme crevette* in Feydeau's original). After a series of *quidproquo*s, all set off as usual by the terrified attempts of the respectable married man to find a way out of the embarrassing situation his sex drive, combined with a lot of drink, has landed him in, it is the show-girl who saves the day by her cool-headedness and lack of personal pretensions. In this respect, both this play and *She's All Yours* (*La Main passe*, Théâtre des Nouveautés, 1904) come close to the Naturalist plays of the period in which bourgeois hypocrisy, especially in sexual matters, was satirised in more serious dramatic form. The characters of *She's All Yours* are recognisable people, who might be part of a play by Galsworthy. They are trying to come to terms with the modern world (as the play opens Chanal is trying to record a message on a phonograph) and the dilemmas into which they get themselves are at least partly due to their chronic inability to communicate with one another that recalls Chekhov.

A Flea in her Ear (*La Puce à l'oreille*) was one of Feydeau's greatest successes with the Paris public. It was first produced in 1907 at the Théâtre des Nouveautés, which had become the favourite venue for Feydeau's larger-scale plays. It attracted rave notices, critics commenting on its dazzle of speed and movement (particularly in Act Two), and calling it a classic. It had to be taken off when the character actor Torin, for whom Feydeau had specifically written the role of Camille, died unexpectedly. But it had a triumphant revival in 1915 and has since travelled the world, being considered one of the most perfectly constructed of all Feydeau's farces, a model for the form. Its handling of the theme of impotence with such consummate comic flair made it particularly successful in Britain, the USA and Scandinavia – perhaps the puritan inheritance makes sexual impotence an especially embarrassing topic in these countries – indeed this play has, somewhat unjustly, all but eclipsed Feydeau's other plays.

Translation

Translating farce is risky. We are dealing not just with a foreign country, whose customs and manners are only superficially like our own, but with foreign slang, foreign preconceptions and foreign ideas of funniness. This is a major part of the appeal, but it can also give the plays, in translation, a kind of exotic, pseudo-literary gloss lacking in the original. Gogol's *The Government Inspector* is a case in point. Its humour depends on a clear view of Russian small-town society at a particular moment in time, and the attitudes of people of that place and time to each other, to visitors, dignitaries and servants, are vital to the jokes. But to go at it head-on, to assume that the audience will know, or pick up, every nuance, would be to produce a play in English whose oddness baffled as often as it seduced. The results might be funny, but would weight the play in a way quite different from the original: it would become first and foremost a literary work, a critique, rather than a piece of straightforward stage entertainment. I have seen foreign-language versions of Ben Travers which unwittingly give the same impression. An alternative method of translation, regularly followed in Britain until the 1960s, is to resite the farce in a local setting, to English it. (In 1896 *Now You See It* was performed in Drury Lane in a version resetting it among the English aristocracy; in 1959 Coward similarly reworked *Occupe-toi d'Amélie* as *Look after Lulu!*) This process of adaptation sanitises the foreignness, but it can also choke the original motor of the humour, replacing the original preconceptions and 'givens' with notions from entirely another place and time.

In this volume, I have treated each of the plays slightly differently, though my purpose has been the same each time: to try to recapture the effect I think Feydeau was aiming at, in a form instantly understandable by modern English-speaking audiences. The translation of *Sauce for the Goose* is ninety-eight per cent meticulous. The first exception is the title. *Le Dindon*, to a French audience, means not only 'the turkey' but also the standard farce fall-guy, the character on whom every indignity is dumped – including, in this case, the reversal of fortune on which a 'well-made' play depends. Potagnac's last line, in the original, is, 'It was written [in the stars]: I'm the dindon' – and so he is. The second exception is the characters of Brünnhilde and Soldignac. In the original they are English, and speak a kind of strangulated, invented English which must have been hilarious in 1890s France but doesn't work in 1990s Britain. I began by giving them the kind of plum-in-the-mouth English we are used to in farce, but found that this made them more complex than the simple 'volcanoes' Feydeau had in mind, overbalancing their scenes. In the end I made them German, or rather cod-German, as fake as Feydeau's original English.

Pig in a Poke combines farce and comedy of manners, and it seemed to me that a rigid but unspoken social framework ought to underlie the action. Although that of the original (bourgeois Paris of the *belle époque*) is remote from us, it is paralleled in Edwardian England, and I accordingly reset the play in Camberwell in 1909. Since this made nonsense of Pennyfeather's original home (southern France), I transposed him first of all to Wales and then, because this hardly seemed exotic enough, to South America. The play also depends, in part, on the absurdities and pretensions of 'polite language' (which is constantly undercut by the basic situation); for this reason I slightly formalised my English, leaning a little towards the style of Pinero, Grundy, or other farce-writers of the period. When I began work on *Now You See It*, I took notice of Shaw's criticism of the 1896 English production mentioned above. He said that the play would be strengthened if it were dovetailed from three acts to two, and if the action were 'rotated' so as to be seen from the wife's point of view rather than those of the husband or lover. When I tried this, I found that it highlighted Feydeau's exposition of her character, making its development central to the plot. I reinforced this by making Summersby (Ribadier in the original) not merely a pompous, hypocritical businessman but an MP working, officially at least, for female emancipation. I made Shaftesbury-Phipps (Thommereux in the original) come home from India, the British Empire, rather than from Batavia, the Dutch Empire. And finally, I replaced two tiny Feydeau characters, a maid and butler, with the invented character of Oriole. Satisfyingly, despite these shifts and redirections, it was possible to leave most of Feydeau's original dialogue intact.

Kenneth McLeish, June 1993
(with additional material by David Bradby)

Translator's note: the original French texts, prepared from the prompt script, were full of indications of the actors' moves in the first production ('he goes two steps up left'; 'she sits' and so on). I have pruned these to a minimum, keeping suggested blocking and business only when they seem integral to character or action.

Kenneth McLeish's great passion was for comedy, and he delighted in the skills it demanded from everyone involved. He intended that these plays should be dedicated to all those professionals and amateurs who worked with him over many years to make people laugh. I am very grateful to David Bradby for his work in completing the introduction.

Valerie McLeish, 2000

The Girl From Maxim's

La Dame de chez Maxim

Characters

Lucien Petypon, *a society doctor*
Gabrielle, *his wife*
Doctor Édouard Mongicourt
Étienne, *Petypon's servant*
Shrimp, *from the Folies-Bergère*
General Petypon du Grelé
Lieutenant Marollier
Varlin, *an insurance agent*
Captain Corignon
Roadsweeper
Curé
Clémentine, *the General's niece, engaged to Corignon*
Émile, *the General's batman*
Chamerot, **Guérissac**, *junior officers on the General's staff*
Dowager Duchess of Valmonté, *an aged aristocrat*
Duke of Valmonté, *her son*
Baroness, **Madame Claux**, **Madame Ponant**,
  Madame Hautignol, **Madame Virette**, *a clan of
  provincial ladies, intent on good breeding*
Vidauban
Madame Vidauban
Tournoy
Madame Tournoy
Lord Mayor
Lady Mayoress
Children, **Firemen**, **Footmen**, **Officers**, **Porters**,
  Wedding guests

The action takes place in the 1880s. Acts One and Three
take place in Petypon's Paris apartment, Act Two in the
General's château in Touraine.

Act One

Reception room of **Petypon**'s *apartment. R, door to the hall; window. L, door to* **Gabrielle**'s *rooms. Centre back, slightly at an angle, large curtained archway leading to* **Petypon**'s *bedroom. The archway should be large enough for us to see the bed and other bedroom furniture. Onstage, the usual furniture: tables, chairs, armchairs, sofa, pouffe covered with a tablecloth, office desk, sideboard, bookcase. One other chair is brought in during the action: the 'Ecstatic Chair' (see page 53).*

As the curtain rises, the stage is in darkness, so that we can't yet see the fantastic disorder of the room, as if after a wild party. Doorbell, off. Pause. Then we hear voices in the hall.

Mongicourt (*off*) You're joking. He can't be.

Étienne (*off*) But he *is*, Monsieur.

Enter **Mongicourt** *and* **Étienne**.

Mongicourt (*loudly*) How *can* he be still asleep?

Étienne Not so *loud*, Monsieur.

Mongicourt (*lower*) How *can* he be still asleep?

Étienne It's a *mystery*. He's always up at eight, and it's twelve already . . .

Mongicourt Fast living.

Étienne Pardon, Monsieur?

Mongicourt Not important.

Étienne I thought I heard Monsieur say 'fast living'.

Mongicourt You know what that is.

Étienne Well, *no*, Monsieur. But I do know Doctor Petypon. A perfect gentleman — I'd trust him with my wife.

Mongicourt *You*, married?

Étienne   Good heavens, no, Monsieur. And if *that's* fast living, the way Doctor Petypon lives . . .

Mongicourt (*interrupting*)   D'you think we could have some light in here? You can't see a thing.

Étienne   Of course, Monsieur.

He opens the curtains. The room is in chaos, the sofa overturned, chairs and tables all over the place. A squashed top hat; a collapsed umbrella.

Mongicourt *and* **Étienne**   Oh!

Étienne   What's been going *on*?

Mongicourt   Looks like an orgy.

Étienne   But what was he *doing*?

Mongicourt   Fast living.

Étienne   H'm. If you ask me, *drink* was taken.

Mongicourt   Étienne!

Étienne   No, Monsieur. Not Doctor Petypon. All he drinks is soda water . . . with a dash of milk to settle his stomach.

Mongicourt (*pointing to the pouffe*)   What on earth is that?

Étienne   A pouffe, Monsieur. It's temporary. Madame's embroidering a cover. Till then, we're using that tablecloth.

He fusses round the room.

What a mess!

He starts tidying. **Mongicourt** *picks up the remains of the top hat.*

Mongicourt   Whatever's this?

Étienne   A hat, Monsieur.

Mongicourt   Very stylish.

Étienne   I don't know *what* he was doing ...

Mongicourt   Never mind what he was doing. I need him. Now. Wake him up. It *is* twelve o'clock.

Étienne   You'll have to take the blame, Monsieur.

Mongicourt   I'll take it.

Étienne   And it'll have to be done by normal sounds.

Mongicourt . Pardon?

Étienne   Doctor Petypon insists, Monsieur. He *hates* it when people wake him up by, ooh, I don't know, firing pistols.

Mongicourt   I'm quite unarmed.

Étienne   He likes to come to consciousness gradually. Humming would be good. D'you think we could hum for him, Monsieur?

Mongicourt   If you say so.

Étienne   Quietly at first, then gradually louder.

Mongicourt   Any particular tune?

Étienne   No, no. What about – ?

He hums 'Frère Jacques'.

Mongicourt   Why that?

Étienne   Madame embroiders to it. I find it *haunting*.

Mongicourt   Well, if you say so ...

Étienne   Quietly at first, Monsieur.

Mongicourt   Yes, yes, whatever.

He and **Étienne** *begin singing 'Frère Jacques'. They start quietly, but end up shouting at the tops of their voices. After some time there is a deep groan. It is impossible to say where from.*

Mongicourt   Shh!

Étienne What is it?

Mongicourt Some kind of animal.

Étienne Ah. No. That's Doctor Petypon. He'll be waking up.

Mongicourt Thank God for that.

Petypon (*invisible*) Oh . . . oh . . . oh . . .

Mongicourt Petypon?

Étienne Monsieur?

Mongicourt Hey, Petypon.

Petypon (*still invisible*) Oh . . . oh . . . ergh?

Mongicourt Get up, for heaven's sake.

Petypon (*still invisible*) What time is it?

Mongicourt (*to* **Étienne**) Just a minute. That wasn't from the bedroom.

Étienne It seemed to be behind us.

Mongicourt (*looking all around*) Where are you?

Petypon (*sulkily; still invisible*) Where d'you think? In bed.

Mongicourt It's coming from there.

Étienne I think you're right.

They turn the sofa over. **Petypon** *is revealed in shirtsleeves, tie unfastened, sleeping.*

Mongicourt *and* **Étienne** Oops.

Mongicourt What are you doing down there?

Petypon *opens his eyes, stares blearily and yawns. They recoil.*

Mongicourt What a stink of drink.

Petypon Don't be ridiculous.

He turns over and goes back to sleep.

Mongicourt Hey, Petypon.

He slaps his feet.

Petypon Now what is it?

He sits up and bangs his head on the back of the sofa.

Ow. The bed's caved in.

Mongicourt Ha!

He and **Étienne** *right the sofa completely.*

Petypon This is the sofa.

Mongicourt So it is – and look, you're under it.

Petypon Under it? What d'you mean, under it? It *is* the sofa?

Mongicourt *puts the sofa back over him.*

Mongicourt Oh yes.

Petypon (*struggling angrily*) What are you playing at? Who planted this sofa here?

Mongicourt *lifts a corner of the sofa.*

Mongicourt God moves in a mysterious way . . .

Petypon Get it off me.

The sofa is lifted off. **Petypon** *sits up on the floor.*

Ow. My head.

Mongicourt That's right. They all say that.

Petypon Is it light yet?

Mongicourt Still a glimmer left . . .

Petypon Oh boy, oh boy, oh boy . . . (*To him.*) Oh wow.

Mongicourt Wow indeed.

Étienne Shall I help you up, Monsieur?

Petypon (*irritably*) Étienne, don't *bother* me!

Étienne Monsieur, you can't lie there all day.

Petypon And why not, pray? If I like it there? I lay down here on purpose ... minutes ago, *seconds* ago ... My decision. No one else's. Mine.

Étienne Yes, Monsieur. (*Aside.*) Oh dear, oh dear.

Petypon *gets up, helped by* **Mongicourt**.

Petypon And now I'm getting up. My decision. No one else's. If that's all right with you.

Étienne Of course, Monsieur. (*Aside.*) People get so *grouchy* under sofas.

Petypon (*to* **Mongicourt**) This is *highly* embarrassing. Ow. My head.

Étienne Shall I serve breakfast now, Monsieur?

Petypon Ugh. No. How do people *eat* breakfast?

Étienne I couldn't say, Monsieur.

Petypon Where's Madame?

Étienne Madame went out, Monsieur. To Father Dominic, Monsieur.

Mongicourt Still hoping for enlightenment?

Petypon You've no idea. Now she's *seeing* things. (*To* **Étienne**.) You: go.

Étienne Yes, Monsieur. (*Aside.*) We *are* in a mood today.

Exit. **Petypon** *cradles his aching head in his hands.*

Mongicourt Bad, is it?

Petypon (*throwing his eyes up to heaven*) Ee-ooooo ...

He drags himself to a chair and sits on it.

Mongicourt I warned you. His Lordship demanded to

see the world. Step out ... flutter his wings ...

Petypon You snake in the grass! You dragged me round those dens of vice.

Mongicourt Thanks very much.

Petypon D'you think I'd have *dreamt* of it, left on my own? No, no: you said to yourself 'There's a simple, purehearted man, a scholar. Let's take his innocence and snap it, like a butterfly on a wheel.'

Mongicourt All I said was, 'Lucien, I'm dying of thirst. We've just spent two hours in surgery. Complicated case. Before we go home, let's go for a little drink.'

Petypon So where did you take me? Maxim's.

Mongicourt 'A little drink,' I said. You were the one who ... When *did* you get home?

Petypon God knows.

Mongicourt The quiet ones are the worst. I tried to prise you loose. You wouldn't budge.

Petypon So you slithered away and left me. Snake in the grass.

Mongicourt I practise self-control. Ration myself. That's the secret – knowing when to stop.

He sits on the pouffe.

Look at us. Me – as you see me, now. You – asleep under the sofa.

Petypon Don't rub it in.

Mongicourt By eight o'clock I was visiting my patients. By eleven, I'd seen everyone on the list, including the man we operated on yesterday ...

Petypon How is he?

Mongicourt No further complications.

He takes out his cigarette case.

Petypon   Recovering?

Mongicourt   Dead.

He takes out a cigarette.

Petypon   Drat.

Mongicourt   What did you expect?

Petypon   I said it was profitless to operate.

Mongicourt   No operations are ever profitless. They may not profit the patient, but they always profit the surgeon.

Petypon   You're a cynic.

Mongicourt   A professional.

He strikes a match. **Petypon** *leaps to his feet and blows it out.*

Petypon   No, no. Pfffff.

Mongicourt   Now what?

Petypon   Don't smoke. Please, I beg you, don't smoke.

Mongicourt   That bad, is it?

Petypon   What a way to wake up ... My head. Ow. And my mouth. Mniam, mniam, mniam.

Mongicourt   Classic symptoms.

Petypon   You think it's *medical?*

Mongicourt   Fur-in-the-mouth.

Petypon   Ah.

Mongicourt   In Latin, *hangoveria.*

Petypon   Yes. Or in Greek ...

Mongicourt   No idea.

Petypon   Me neither.

He collapses on the pouffe.

Mongicourt   You really knocked it back last night.

Petypon   Say that again.

Mongicourt   The Curse of Drink.

Petypon   No, the Curse of Knowledge. I said to myself: 'A scholar should try everything.'

Mongicourt   He gave his all for Science.

Petypon   And now look at me.

Mongicourt   These are early stages.

Petypon   I'm limp. Legs, arms, limp. Quite useless.

Mongicourt   Classic *hangoveria.*

Petypon   It isn't *fair.*

Gabrielle (*off*)   Up at last! Thank goodness. Oh, Étienne, take this shopping. Mind that one, it's fragile. (*Etc.*)

Petypon   My God, my wife! Quick, tell me: can you tell that I've . . . ? Do I look as if I've . . . ?

Mongicourt   Hardly at all.

Petypon   Ah.

Mongicourt   You could tell her you were out at a funeral –

Petypon   What?

Mongicourt   Yours. She *might* believe you.

Petypon   Thanks. Just a moment . . . If I . . . (*He runs his hands through his hair, trying to look alert and awake.*) Does that . . . ? Is there any . . . ?

Mongicourt   I shouldn't bother.

Enter **Gabrielle**. *She runs to* **Petypon**.

Gabrielle   Ah there you are, darling. Up at last. You

really have slept in. Good morning, darling.

She frames his face in her hands to kiss him, and jolts his fragile head.

Petypon   Good morning, Gab ... oh ....

Gabrielle   Édouard, good morning.

Mongicourt (*with a flourish*)   Madame, your servant.

Gabrielle *turns* **Petypon** *to face her.*

Gabrielle   Let me look at you a moment ... No, you don't look yourself at all.

Petypon   Don't you think so? I don't know what's the matter. I feel ... oh, I can't *tell* you how I feel.

Gabrielle   You're green. (*To* **Mongicourt**.) What's wrong with him, Édouard?

Mongicourt (*with professional gravity*)   Gabrielle, I'm glad you asked. He's suffering from ... *hangoveria. Extensiva.*

Petypon (*groaning*)   Oh.

Gabrielle   Dear God, he hasn't ...?

Mongicourt (*sombrely*)   Gabrielle, I'm afraid he has.

Gabrielle   It's serious?

Mongicourt   He'll live: I can promise you that.

Gabrielle   Oh, thank you. (*To* **Petypon**.) Poor darling ... you've got *hangoveria*.

Petypon   If Édouard says so.

Gabrielle   We'll have to look after you. (*To* **Mongicourt**.) What can we give him? A pick-me-up? A glass of brandy?

Petypon (*a shout of anguish*)   No, no. (*With a shudder*.) Not alcohol.

Gabrielle (*returning*)   What would you recommend, Édouard?

Mongicourt (*importantly*) Ah, Gabrielle. The usual treatment is syrup-of-figs and vinegar.

Gabrielle Syrup of figs. Vinegar. Just a minute.

She makes to go out.

Petypon Hey, no. (*Aside to* **Mongicourt**.) What're you trying to *do* to me . . . ?

Mongicourt (*taking pity*) Fortunately, Lucien has already passed into the secondary stage, the abatement period . . .

Gabrielle Thank God.

Mongicourt A hot drink, perhaps. For us all, perhaps. Lemon tea, perhaps.

Gabrielle (*going upstage*) I'll ring for Étienne.

Mongicourt (*mocking, to* **Petypon**) That better?

Petypon (*to him*) You know I detest lemon tea.

Gabrielle (*cheerfully, to* **Petypon**) I'd never have believed you could wake up in this state. This morning you were sleeping so peacefully. You didn't even notice when I kissed you.

Petypon (*stunned*) What d'you mean? You . . . you . . .

Gabrielle Youyou? What do *you* mean, youyou?

Petypon You . . . you kissed me?

Gabrielle Yes.

Petypon In bed?

Gabrielle Well, naturally. You were fast asleep, rolled up in blankets. All I could see was the top of your head. I kissed it. You do seem surprised.

Petypon (*stunned*) What? No.

Gabrielle (*starting to go again*) Étienne's not coming. I'll fetch the tea.

Mongicourt (*going to the door with her*) I think he needs it.

Exit **Gabrielle**.

Petypon   She kissed me in my bed . . . and I was under the sofa.

Mongicourt   Baffling.

He sits down, to think better.

Petypon   Well?

Mongicourt   I said it was baffling.

Petypon (*collapsing on sofa*)   Sleepwalking? Can't have been.

Pause. Suddenly a long, noisy yawn is heard from the bedroom.

Voice   Aoooooahahahahaha.

Petypon   Pardon?

Mongicourt   I didn't speak.

Petypon   You went 'Aoooooahahahahaha'.

Mongicourt   No I didn't.

Petypon   You must have done.
Voice (*yawning again*)   Ahooo. Ooooaha.

Petypon (*getting up*)   Good God.

Mongicourt (*getting up*)   You said it.

Voice   Aaaaooooaaaah. Ah. Ooooah.

Petypon   It's coming from my bedroom.

Mongicourt   Entirely.
They rush to the curtains at the back.

Petypon   There's someone in there.

*They pull back the curtains. Lying on the bed in a shift and little
else is a girl with a fresh countenance and blonde hair cut short.*

Petypon *and* **Mongicourt**   Ooooops.

Shrimp (*sitting up*)   Hello boys.

Petypon (*thunderstruck, to* **Mongicourt**)   Who *is* she?

Mongicourt (*vastly amused*)   Well, well, old man. Well,
well, well, well, well.

Petypon (*beside himself*)   What? Not. Nothing of the kind.
Don't be ridiculous. (*To* **Shrimp**.) Mamzelle . . . who are
you? Where did you spring from?

Shrimp   Don't be silly. You know exactly where I
sprang from.

Petypon (*indignantly*)   I've never seen you before in my
life. Why are you in my bed?

Shrimp   Oh, come on. (*To* **Mongicourt**.) 'Why am I in
his bed . . . ?'

Mongicourt   He really wants to know.

Petypon   Of course I want to know. (*Furiously to*
Mongicourt.) Must you laugh like that? This isn't funny.
(*To* **Shrimp**.) Come on, who are you? And how did you
get here?

Shrimp   Who d'you think you are, a judge? I'm
Shrimp . . .

Mongicourt   The Folies-Bergère, that dancer . . .

Shrimp (*patting his cheek*)   Aren't you the clever one.

Mongicourt   I say.

Shrimp   Well, cleverer than *him*. He remembers nothing.
The champagne . . . the cab-ride home . . . the sofa . . .
the bedroom . . .

Petypon (*aghast*)   What . . . ? We didn't. You, me . . . We
can't have . . .

Shrimp   Nice place you've got here.

Petypon (*suddenly*)   Oh my God!

Mongicourt *and* **Shrimp** (*who has got out of bed*)   Now what?

Petypon   That kiss. On the head. In my bed. It was *her*.

Mongicourt (*in a sepulchral tone*)   That kiss . . . was *her*.

Petypon   Gabrielle kissed *her* head, in my bed.

Mongicourt   Well, well, well, well, well.

They stand as though transfixed. **Shrimp** *has meanwhile put on undergarments, and comes to look at them with mocking eyes.*

Shrimp   What a pair of bookends.

With a music-hall dancer's ease, she high-kicks over the back of a chair.

'Houp-la. This one's for me.'

She sits on the sofa and stretches out her legs. **Petypon** *rushes to her.*

Petypon   Get up. You can't do that. You have to go. Someone might come. I'm a scholar. You can't stay here.

Shrimp   Aren't you *sweet?* (*She chucks him under the chin.*)

Petypon   What are you doing?

Shrimp (*singing*)   'She was only a bird in a gilded cage . . .' (*She makes eyes at him.*)

Petypon   Stop that at once. Get dressed at once.

Gabrielle (*off*)   What? *I* don't know. Lemons. Try the vegetable market. You've got the money? Just a minute . . . (*Etc.*)

Petypon (*loudly*)   Good grief.

Mongicourt (*the same*) Good grief.

Petypon (*dragging* **Shrimp** *to the bedroom*) Hide. You have to *hide*.

Mongicourt (*helping him*) Come *on*.

Shrimp What's the matter?

Petypon (*pushing her into the bedroom*) Just hide.

He and **Mongicourt** *close the curtains and quickly turn, trying to look innocent, as* **Gabrielle** *enters with the tea on a tray. She fusses wih the tea, and doesn't look at them.*

Gabrielle Here's the tea. I've sent Étienne out for some lemon.

While she isn't looking, **Petypon** *and* **Mongicourt** *try to hiss the explanation through the curtain to* **Shrimp**.

Petypon My wife . . . Madame Petypon, my wife.

Mongicourt His wife . . . Madame Petypon, his wife.

Gabrielle *turns and hears.*

Gabrielle What are you doing? We don't need to be introduced. We know each other.

Mongicourt (*going to shake her hand*) Good morning again, Gabrielle.

Petypon (*to her*) You don't understand. You didn't let me finish. (*To* **Gabrielle**.) Madame Petypon, my wife . . . I mean, Gabrielle, darling, don't you find it hot in here?

Gabrielle No.

Petypon Yes it is, it is. (*He grabs her hand.*) We'll go for a walk. Yes, we'll go for a walk.

Gabrielle I've been for a walk.

Petypon So you're in practice. Come on!

But he loses his grip, and she staggers away, spinning round and holding, for support, the chair where **Shrimp**'s *dress is lying.*

Gabrielle   What's this on the chair?

Petypon   What?

Gabrielle   It looks like a dress.

Petypon   Oh God.

Mongicourt   Oops again.

Gabrielle   What's it doing in *here*? When did it arrive?

Petypon   No idea. Not last night. Definitely not last night. This morning. They delivered it this morning. Didn't they, Édouard? (*Irritated, to him.*) For heaven's sake, *speak!*

Mongicourt   What? (*Loudly.*) Oh, absolutely.

Petypon (*to* **Gabrielle**)   They made a mistake. It's the wrong house. They came to the wrong house. I'll send it back.

He grabs the dress and makes for the door. **Gabrielle** *still has hold, so he is pulled up short and dragged back to her.*

Gabrielle   No, no, it's right.

Petypon   Pardon?

Gabrielle   It shouldn't have come to *you*, that's all.

Petypon   What?

Gabrielle   I've just written her a note.

Petypon   Her a note? Who a note?

Gabrielle   My dressmaker. She was supposed to deliver it yesterday.

Petypon   Impossible. No, no, no. Not yours. Wrong style. I mean . . . Give it to me. *Give* it to me.

Gabrielle (*resisting*)   Let go. Of course it's my style. 'You choose,' I say to her. 'You know my style: you choose.' I agree it *is* a bit . . .

Petypon   Yes, yes. Entirely. (*Pulling the dress.*) I'll have it altered.

Gabrielle   It's all right. It's fine. (*She pulls it away from him.*) The way you handle clothes . . .

Exit with the dress.

Petypon   That's torn it.

Mongicourt   Phut. Gone, vanished, disappeared, removed, abstracted . . . phut.

Petypon   That's easy for you to say. What are we going to *do*?

Shrimp *sticks her head out.*

Shrimp   Has she gone? Coast clear?

Petypon   Oh God, now the other one.

He hurries up to her.

Shrimp   You never told me you were married. *Bad* boy.

She pinches his nose. He pulls himself free.

Petypon   I'b dot . . . I mean, I'm not having any more of this. Out this minute. Out.

Shrimp   Don't be nasty. You were much nicer yesterday.

Petypon   Well, today I'm nasty. Out. Go on, quick march.

Shrimp   You might at least say please.

Petypon   Don't be ridiculous. Get on with it.

Shrimp   I'm nice to you, why can't you be nice to me?

Petypon (*beside himself*)   For heaven's sake get on with it. Stop fiddling and faddling. Get on with it.

Shrimp I'm not ready.

Petypon Arrrgh. (*He points to the door and roars.*) OU-OU-OUT.

Shrimp *sits on the sofa, leans back, stretches her legs.*

Shrimp You're not very good at this. I'm used to people who treat ladies with respect.

Petypon (*thinking he understands*) Ah. Respect. Fine. Excellent. (*Taking out his wallet.*) How much respect?

Shrimp *Now* what are you doing?

Petypon (*pompously*) It's not what *I'm* doing, my girl. It's what *you're* doing. Or what you're *going* to do. How much to go away?

Shrimp (*mocking*) You really are bad at this. (*Getting up.*) Are you *trying* to insult me?

Petypon Me? Good heavens!

Shrimp Well, fortunately I'm not insulted. And I don't want paying.

Petypon Oh. Fine. (*Replacing his wallet.*) Excellent. (*He shakes her hand.*) You *are* a pal.

He starts pushing her towards the door.

See you around – perhaps.

Shrimp I mean, I don't want *paying*. Now, if you gave me a *present* . . .

Petypon Ah.

Shrimp I mean, we don't want *this* gentleman to think . . .

Mongicourt Oh, I don't think.

Petypon (*taking out his wallet again*) All I want is peace and quiet. Here. (*He gives money to* **Shrimp**.) Ten francs.

Shrimp Ten francs. Oh good, I can tip the cab-driver.

Petypon What cab-driver?

Shrimp The one with the horse. Hay-money.

Petypon Good heavens, ten francs are what *I* charge. My patients: one consulation, ten francs.

Shrimp You don't half fancy yourself.

Mongicourt (*laughing*) That's right, Lucien. You don't half fancy yourself.

Shrimp Hey, none of that. I can talk proper if I want to. (*She declaims:*)

'I wandered lonely as a cloud
That floats on high o'er vales and hills
When all at once I saw . . .'

Mongicourt By Jove, I think she's got it.

Shrimp I can go on like that for hours. (*To* **Petypon**, *in a pathetic, put-upon voice.*) I could have been a schoolteacher. Nearly was, if that inspector hadn't taken advantage. (*She is becoming melodramatic.*)

Mongicourt What inspector?

Shrimp (*brokenly*) He promised to marry me.

Petypon *takes her arm and leads her to the door.*

Petypon Yes, very interesting. But you can tell us your life story some other time.

Shrimp For ten francs, you want a *life* story?

Petypon (*annoyed*) For heaven's sake, how much *do* you want?

Shrimp Who said I wanted money at all? *Bad* boy! *Bad*! (*She pulls his nose.*)

Petypon (*pulling free*) *Will* you stop doing that?

Shrimp   You want me to go? I'll go.

Petypon   At last.

Shrimp   I mean, if your one and only came back and found me here . . .

Petypon   Exactly.

Shrimp   She wouldn't half give you a mouthful.

Petypon   She wouldn't half . . . I mean, precisely.

Shrimp   All right, I'm off. And if you *do* decide to give me a present . . . My dress. The dress I was wearing yesterday. I still owe the dressmaker. You pay the bill, and that'll be that.

Petypon (*dazed*)   That'll be what?

Mongicourt (*aside to him*)   Remember who *has* the dress.

Petypon   Ah. Yes. (*To* **Shrimp**.) What a good idea. I'll do it. (*He takes out his wallet.*) How much was it?

Shrimp   Five hundred francs.

Petypon   Fi . . . fi . . . fi . . . fi . . . fi . . . ?

Shrimp   Fifty patients' worth.

She pinches his nose. He pulls free angrily.

Petypon   Stop doing that. (*He counts out money.*) A hundred . . . two . . . three . . . four . . . fifty . . . twenty . . . ten . . . ten . . . five . . . one, two three, four, five.

Shrimp   Thank you.

Petypon   Are you sure you can carry it?

Shrimp   I'll manage.

Petypon (*at the door*)   Fine. Good. Goodbye.

But **Shrimp** *has gone to the chair where her dress was.*

Shrimp   Hang on. My dress. It's vanished.

Petypon   What dress?

Shrimp   *My* dress.

Petypon   Oh, that dress. You don't need it. You're fine as you are. Go on.

Shrimp   I'll catch my death of cold in my commies.

Petypon   What?

Mongicourt   She's wearing them.

Petypon   Oh, those. Good grief, what a baby. Put *this* on.

He snatches the tablecloth covering the pouffe and puts it round her shoulders. She throws it down.

Shrimp   I will not. It tickles. I want my dress.

Petypon (*losing control*)   You want your dress. Well, you can't have your dress. And why can't you have your dress? Because it's not here. D'you hear? Not here.

Shrimp   What d'you mean? Who swiped it?

Petypon   Pardon?

Mongicourt (*to him, enjoying the situation*)   Answer the question.

Petypon (*beside himself again*)   My *wife* swiped it. *You* were here. You *heard* her.

Shrimp   You mean that was *my* dress? Well, that beats all. You gave away my dress. If you think I had it made to give away . . . Five hundred francs, that cost.

Petypon   Don't remind me.

Shrimp   I need a dress to wear.

Petypon   So, buy one.

Shrimp   Till *you* gave it away, I had one.

Petypon   I didn't give it away.

Shrimp   It comes to the same thing.

Mongicourt   She's right. It does.

Petypon   Whose side are you *on*?

Gabrielle (*off*)   She's mad, that dressmaker, quite mad. I don't know whose measurements these are . . .

Petypon (*wildly, to* **Shrimp**)   Hide! Hide!

Shrimp   What now?

Mongicourt   Don't argue. Hide!

Shrimp   I wish you'd make your mind up.

Petypon (*holding the door shut against* **Gabrielle**, *hissing at* **Mongicourt**)   For God's sake hide her.

Mongicourt   Yes. Yes.

Shrimp   Where? Where?

Mongicourt *tries to push her under the desk.*

Mongicourt   There. There.

Shrimp (*on all fours*)   The pouffe's in the way.

Petypon   Get on with it.

Mongicourt   Don't keep *saying* that.

Seeing that **Shrimp** *is on all fours in front of the desk, he covers her with the tablecloth as though she is the pouffe, and then sits on her. All this time* **Gabrielle** *has been pushing at the door, and now she bursts in.*

Gabrielle   What are you *doing*?

Petypon *collapses in her arms, making inarticulate cries as if he's having a seizure. He steers her towards the sofa.*

Petypon   Aha. Aha. Aha.

Gabrielle (*terrified*)   What's wrong with him? Édouard! It's another attack. *Hangoveria.*

Mongicourt (*without getting up from* **Shrimp**'*s back*) Hold
on to him. Don't let him go.

Gabrielle (*to* **Petypon**, *who is still whimpering, and has
turned them round so that her back is to* **Mongicourt**) Lucien,
my darling. Oof, you're heavy. Édouard, come and take
over. I can't hold him any longer.

She tries to turn to **Mongicourt**, *but* **Petypon** *pulls her back
round to face him.*

Petypon No, you, you. Not him. Aha. Aha.

Gabrielle (*supporting him*) But you're *heavy*.

Petypon *turns to the audience in such a way that* **Gabrielle**,
who is behind him, must do so also. He speaks in a fading voice.

Petypon Turn me to the north. Aha . . . Turn me to
the north . . .

Gabrielle Which way is north?

She turns him to face **Mongicourt** *and* **Shrimp**. *He quickly
turns her back again.*

Petypon That's south. You have to face north. Aha . . .
Turn me to the north.

Gabrielle I don't know where north is.

Petypon It's opposite south.

Gabrielle We'll have to sit down. I'm exhausted.
Édouard, please bring me the pouffe.

Petypon Not the pouffe. Aee!

Gabrielle I want to sit down.

Petypon I want to stand up. Aha . . . Édouard, get rid
of the pouffe. Get rid of the pouffe.

Mongicourt Get rid of the pouffe?

Gabrielle Can't you see it's upsetting him?

Mongicourt (*crossly*)   All right, I'll get rid of the pouffe. (*Muttering.*) Get rid of the pouffe … Get rid of the pouffe …

He joins his hands under **Shrimp**'s *knees, picks her up and takes her into the bedroom.*

Petypon   Has it gone yet?

Mongicourt *leaves* **Shrimp** *in the bedroom and returns with the cloth that covered her.*

Mongicourt   Yes, all gone.

Petypon (*instantly recovering*)   Phew, that's better.

Gabrielle (*letting go*)   Thank God. You frightened me.

Petypon (*brightly*)   No, no, no, no, no. All over. These attacks are always the same. Very severe, then, all of a sudden, over. (*To* **Mongicourt**.) Isn't that right? … (*Hissed aside.*) *Say* something, can't you?

Mongicourt (*quickly*)   Yes, over. And then … er … over.

Petypon   Over and over again. That's it exactly. (*Hissed.*) *Isn't* it?

Mongicourt   Yes, oh, isn't.

Gabrielle *moves from the desk with a cup of tea.*

Gabrielle   I certainly hope so. (*Handing* **Petypon** *the tea.*) Here.

Petypon   Thank you.

Gabrielle   You know, I wonder if this attack wasn't heaven, punishing you.

Petypon   What for?

Gabrielle   For laughing at me yesterday … about the miracle at the Gare du Nord. Don't you remember? I told you: 'You're wrong to scoff. God's listening. No good'll come of it.'

Petypon Oh, that miracle.

Mongicourt What miracle?

Gabrielle Didn't you see it in the papers? Saint Catherine appeared last week, to a family of innkeepers, by the refreshment counter on platform seven in the Gare du Nord.

Mongicourt I hope she had a ticket.

Petypon I hope she was *trained* for it.

Gabrielle It isn't funny. Every evening since, the saint has reappeared. I've seen her too.

Mongicourt You're joking.

Gabrielle She spoke to me.

Mongicourt What did she say?

Gabrielle 'Gabrielle, my child, heaven has chosen you for a noble destiny. Soon you'll be visited by an archangel, who will explain the mission you are to undertake . . . (*With a wide gesture, both palms in the air.*) Begone.'

Petypon *puts his cup in her upraised hand.*

Petypon Oh, thanks.

Gabrielle *puts the cup on the desk.*

Mongicourt And has the archangel visited you?

Gabrielle (*simply*) Not yet. I'm waiting.

Petypon Don't hold your breath.

Suddenly, **Shrimp** *is heard from the bedroom. She sounds fed up.*

Shrimp Get on with it. Get *on* with it!

Petypon (*hissed aside to her, through the curtain*) For heaven's sake!

Shrimp I'm getting *bored* in here.

Petypon (*loudly, to* **Gabrielle**) Ah ... Hahaha. Visions. Fascinating subject. Édouard, don't you think so? Eh? Eh? (*Hissed aside.*) I keep telling you, *say* something.

Mongicourt Oh. Yes. Fascinating.

Both Really fascinating.

Gabrielle Be quiet, both of you. Someone said something in there.

Petypon Where? In there? I didn't hear anything. Did you hear anything?

Mongicourt Not a thing. Nothing.

Petypon A thing. Not. Nothing.

Gabrielle It was in *there*.

Petypon *and* **Mongicourt** No, it wasn't. It can't have been.

Shrimp (*in a faraway, other-worldly voice*) Gabrielle ... Gabrielle ...

Petypon (*jumping*) What's she *doing*?

Gabrielle That's me they're calling. *Now* we'll see ...

She moves towards the curtains, but **Petypon** *bars the way.*

Petypon You mustn't.

Gabrielle (*pushing him aside*) What's *wrong* with you?

She pulls the curtains, and falls back in amazement.

Good heavens.

Mongicourt Wow.

Shrimp *is kneeling on the bed with a sheet over her head. Under the sheet she holds an electric light, shining on her face. The rest of the alcove is in darkness.*

Gabrielle   Look. Look.

Petypon *and* **Mongicourt**   Where?

Gabrielle   There. Can't you see it?

Shrimp (*in the other-worldly voice*)   Stay where you are.

Gabrielle   What is it?

Shrimp   These sacrilegious beings cannot see me. It is only to you that I am manifest.

Gabrielle   I don't believe it.

Shrimp   My daughter, kneel and worship. The archangel speaks.

Gabrielle   The archangel!

She falls to her knees and hisses at the two men.

Kneel! Now! Kneel!

Petypon *and* **Mongicourt**   Why should we? Why?

Gabrielle   The archangel's here. You can't see him, but I can. He's speaking to me.

Shrimp (*aside*)   We've got a right one here!

Gabrielle   Kneel! Kneel!

The two men kneel. Enter **Étienne**.

Étienne   Here's the lemon you asked for.

Gabrielle   Shh!

Petypon   Étienne, not now.

Étienne *suddenly sees* **Shrimp**.

Étienne   What's that?

Gabrielle   Shh! Kneel!

Étienne   There's something on the bed.

Gabrielle   You see it too?

Étienne   A sort of bogeyman. *Very* fetching.

Gabrielle   It's an archangel. Give thanks to God, who has numbered you with the blessed. You can see it and I can see it, but neither of these gentlemen can see it at all.

Étienne   I don't believe it.

Gabrielle   Kneel, and harken to the message from on high.

Étienne   I'll put the lemon down.

He puts it on the desk, and kneels.

Gabrielle (*to* **Shrimp**, *in a different tone*)   I'm listening, O Archangel.

Shrimp   Gabrielle! I have come from on high to reveal the mission thou hast been chosen to fulfil.

Petypon (*aside*)   Oh wow.

Shrimp   O Woman, art thou listening?

Gabrielle   Oh yes!

Shrimp   Arise, at once! Without hesitating a moment, go to the Gare du Nord, platform seven, walk up and down five times.

Petypon (*aside*)   Brilliant.

Mongicourt (*aside*)   She knows what she's doing.

Shrimp   Then wait by the refreshment counter till a man comes up and speaks to you. Listen carefully to his words: for because of what he says, a child will be born.

Gabrielle   A child?

Petypon (*aside*)   Steady on.

Shrimp   All France awaits this child. He will lead all Europe, and found his dynasty anew.

Gabrielle   This is amazing.

Mongicourt (*aside*)   She believes it.

Shrimp   Go, my child. For *la patrie*! For France!

Gabrielle *gets up, inspired.*

Gabrielle   For *la patrie*! For France!

Shrimp   Begone! (*Pause.*) And take *ye domestique*!

Gabrielle   To platform seven?

Shrimp   No, no, the kitchen will suffice. Adieu! I go, evaporating into space and zooming back to heaven. Wheeoooooo!

She falls flat to the bed, turning off the light as she goes. Pause.

Gabrielle   He's gone. Did you hear what he said?

Petypon *and* **Mongicourt**   No. What? Hear what?

Étienne (*getting up*)   That's *really* weird.

Gabrielle (*exalted*)   Oh Lucien! Fancy missing such a message.

Petypon (*aside*)   Good God, it worked!

Gabrielle (*eagerly*)   Listen: every moment is precious. The archangel was here. He spoke to me. He told me what heaven requires of me.

Petypon (*exaggeratedly*)   And what is that? You alarm me greatly.

Gabrielle   The Gare du Nord. Platform seven. The refreshment counter. A man will speak to me.

Petypon (*feigning indignation*)   I beg your pardon?

Gabrielle   From his words a child will be born.

Petypon   Good heavens!

Gabrielle (*excited*)   Lucien, he's to be our leader. All France is waiting. Heaven's will. It must be so.

Petypon   Oh God, oh God.

Gabrielle   What a message! You mustn't be jealous.

Petypon   But he won't be mine!

Gabrielle   He won't be anyone else's either.

Petypon   Gabrielle! Excuse me?

Gabrielle   You'll be a leader's father.

Étienne   If I was in *your* place, Monsieur, *I'd* say yes.

Mongicourt   Your country expects it of you, old man.

Gabrielle (*to him*)   Yes! Help me to persuade him.

*She throws herself at **Petypon**'s feet.*

Gabrielle   Lucien, darling!

Petypon *puts his hand on her head. He speaks in a weak voice.*

Petypon   I say, my will is weakening. Hark! What voices are these, calling to me? What are these visions, all in white, holding out to me their suppliant hands?

Gabrielle (*radiant*)   You've seen it too!

Petypon   'Yield, yield,' they're saying to me. 'For *la patrie*! For France!'

Gabrielle   For *la patrie*!

Mongicourt *and* **Étienne**   *La patrie*!

Shrimp (*under the sheet*)   *La patrie*!

Gabrielle *and* **Étienne** (*devoutly*)   The archangel's voice!

Gabrielle (*to* **Petypon**)   You heard it?

Petypon   Yes. I hear. I see. Scales fall from my eyes.

He takes her arm and pushes her towards the door.

Hurry! I agree. For *la patrie*! For France!

Gabrielle   For *la patrie*!

She opens the door.

Petypon (*same tone*) Begone! And take *ye domestique*!

Gabrielle Sorry. Yes. Come on, Étienne.

Étienne (*lyrically*) For *la patrie*!

He picks up the lemon and saucer.

For France!

*He follows **Gabrielle** out.*

Mongicourt Well, I don't know.

Petypon Who'd have . . . ?

Mongicourt You just don't . . .

Shrimp *throws off the sheet, jumps out of bed and comes downstage.*

Shrimp 'Houp-la! This one's for me!'

Petypon You're *really* something.

Shrimp And *you're* out of trouble.

Petypon A child, in the Gare du Nord.

Shrimp I'm good at spooks.

Mongicourt How did you light the sheet like that?

Shrimp The bedside lamp.

Petypon And the halo?

Shrimp The frame out of the lampshade.

Petypon Oh, thanks! Now you've pulled my shade to bits!

Shrimp I left my own at home.

Petypon All right, all right. My wife's left. Now you do the same.

Shrimp Dress me.

Petypon   Pardon?

Shrimp   For heaven's sake! Dress me. Give me something to wear.

Mongicourt   You heard her: dress her.

Petypon   How d'you expect me to dress you? What in? My wife's clothes won't fit, for a start.

Shrimp   Well, think of something.

Petypon   I say, Édouard . . .

Mongicourt   Yes?

Petypon   Would you mind? Run down to the shops. A dress, a coat, whatever they've got . . .

Mongicourt   I won't be five minutes.

Exit.

Petypon   While you're waiting, I'll find you a dressing-gown.

Shrimp   Thank you.

Petypon   Just don't let anyone see you. If my wife comes back, or anyone else, get into bed and hide.

Exit.

Shrimp   Yes, Lucien.

High-kick over chair by sofa.

'Houp-la! This one's for me!' What a crowd. Anyone'd think I embarrassed them.

Voices off.

Someone's coming! More of them. Here we go again.

She hurries into the bedroom, and tries to shut the curtains.

Now what's the matter? These are stuck now. Arrg!

She throws herself flat on the bed and pulls the sheet over herself, remaining quite motionless. Enter the **General***, followed by* **Étienne**.

General Tell Doctor Petypon his uncle's here: General Petypon du Grelé.

Étienne (*from the threshold*) Yes, Monsieur.

General Well? What're you hanging about in the doorway for? Come in, dammit.

Étienne Not allowed, Monsieur.

General Not *allowed?*

Étienne By the archangel.

General What's that?

Étienne The archangel.

General What the devil d'you mean? What archangel?

Étienne I can't explain, Monsieur.

General Damn fool you, then.

Étienne Yes, Monsieur. If you want Monsieur, Monsieur, I suggest you look about, here in here, or there in there.

General What are you babbling about? Here in here? *Where* in here? Perfectly obvious he's not in here!

Étienne He sometimes hides under the furniture.

General Hides under the furniture! He's mad. Get out!

Étienne Yes, Monsieur.

Exit.

General Under the furniture. Chah! What furniture? (*Picking up a very small item.*) Not *this* furniture. Ha, what have we over here?

He goes to inspect the bedroom.

Nobody.

He goes further in, out of view of the audience. **Shrimp** *lifts the sheet and pokes her nose out.*

Shrimp   Coast clear ... ?

She gets up on hands and knees, still covered. The **General** *reappears, and thinking she's* **Petypon***, gives her a mighty wallop on the bottom. She jumps violently and sits upright.*

Shrimp   Ow! What the devil ... ?

General   I say. Most frightfully sorry.

He looks at her more closely.

No, I *say*. You *are* my niece.

Shrimp   Pardon?

General   Uncle ... niece ... all in the family. (*Holding out his hand.*) Pleased to meet you, Gabrielle.

Shrimp (*shaking his hand*)   Good morning, Monsieur.

General   I'm General Petypon du Grelé. We've never met. Realise that. Spent last nine years in Morocco. But you've heard of me. My nephew.

Shrimp   Nephew?

General   That's the fellow.

Shrimp (*aside*)   Does he think I'm –

General   Well, not to put to fine a point on it, back from Morocco. In person. Here. By Jove, congratulate my nephew on his taste in women! Some damn fool said he'd married a real old boot. We could do with old boots like these in the Foreign Legion, what?

Shrimp   Oh General ...

General   Blunt man, don't you know. Call spade a spade. Eh? Eh?

Shrimp   Oh General! (*Aside*.) This family are all the same.

General   I say, not ill are you? In bed at this hour?

Shrimp   I slept in, that's all. I'll get up as soon as they bring my dress.

General   That's the ticket. Dress, yes. Haha!

He sits.

Now then, d'you know why I'm here? You got my letter?

Shrimp   No.

General   Damn fool postmen. Never mind. It'll come. Not much use then, of course: I'll have told you what it said, myself. Tell you now, in fact. Clémentine.

Shrimp   Clémentine?

General   Got it in one. Gel I adopted when her parents died. Didn't my nephew tell you?

Shrimp   Oh, Clémentine.

General   Clémentine.

Shrimp   Now I remember.

General   Yes, yes. Needs a matron of honour for a day or two. Matron of honour. I was hoping you'd . . .

Shrimp   *I'd* . . . ?

General   First choice, and a first-class choice. Haha. I mean, me: a general – not built for it, d'you see?

Shrimp   You can say that again.

General   Specialist training, all that.

Shrimp   Oh, General.

General   No offence intended. Eh?

Shrimp   None taken.

General Good for you! Like women who're honest, call spade a spade ... Haarumph! Clémentine. You understand, if memsahib was still alive ... Fact is, one day she upped and ... phut! (*With a gesture he shoots his wife up to heaven.*) Sad loss, what? (*Changing his tone.*) So, memsahib having gone AWOL, said to myself: 'Well, only thing to do: get her a man.'

Shrimp General!

General A gel has to marry some time.

Shrimp Not a man, a husband.

General Not with you. What's the difference?

Shrimp None at all. Oh, none at all.

General There you are, then. That's why, in a week's time, she's to marry Captain Corignon.

Shrimp Corignon? Of the Twelfth?

General That's right. You know the fellow?

Shrimp Do I know him? Ha! Good heavens!

General Devilish odd! D'you see him often?

Shrimp (*without thinking*) Not since I gave him up.

General Gave him up?

Shrimp (*quickly*) Er, gave him back, back to his regiment.

General (*blankly*) I see! Back to his regiment! You mean, gave him back to his regiment.

Shrimp That's right, up, back, what's the difference? What you give back, you give up.

General See what you mean.

Shrimp And what you give up –

General You give back. (*Laughter.*) That's deep. That's *very* deep.

Shrimp (*roguishly*) Ehehay!

General Pardon? Oh, yes. Ehehay! (*Different tone.*)
Anyway, this fellow Corignon . . . had him under my
command in Morocco for years, till he was transferred
back to Paris . . . Fine soldier, don't you know, man with
a future in front of him.

Shrimp Ah.

General Man of judgement. Man who knows what's
what.

Shrimp Oh, he *does*!

General You do know him, then?

Shrimp Oh, yes. I know Corignon.

General (*rather blankly*) Hum. Yes. Wedding takes place,
eight days' time. Tomorrow, engagement party, my house
in Touraine. Here, quite simply, to ask you and my
nephew to go down there with me. As I said in the letter,
and mentioned to you just now, bride needs someone to
act as matron of honour, and *I* need someone to act as
hostess at the reception. How about it, hey?

Shrimp Me? That's a joke.

General You agree?

Shrimp (*hesitating*) I don't know. Doctor Petypon.

General Leave him to me.

Shrimp (*aside*) Ehehay! Shrimp, from the Folies-Bergère,
matron of honour at Corignon's society wedding! I can't
wait to see his face.

General Well?

Shrimp All right, General. I'll do it.

General My dear niece! Give me a kiss.

Shrimp (*over his shoulder*) It's not so bad after all, this family.

Enter **Petypon**.

Petypon Étienne! Where the devil's my dressing-gown — Aargh! *Now* what's happening?

General Ah, there you are.

Petypon Uncle Charles!

Shrimp (*aside*) Off we go again.

Petypon (*astounded*) Uncle. You're my uncle. Uncle Charles!

General I know that, confound you. What's the matter? Seen a ghost, or what?

Petypon No, no, I meant . . . (*Aside to* **Shrimp**.) Why are *you* still here? (*To the* **General**.) My dear Uncle Charles!

They shake hands effusively.

Shrimp What larks!

Petypon My dear Uncle Charles . . . after all these years.

General Surprised you, eh? Thought so. Said to myself, 'This'll surprise him.'

Petypon And it did, it did.

General You've hardly changed at all. Ten years older, naturally.

Petypon Thanks. I'm sorry, if I'd known you were coming . . .

General (*grumbling*) Don't harp.

Petypon Oh, am I harping? Sorry if I'm harping.

General Just arrived from Morocco. Came straight to

Paris. Brought your cousin Clémentine.

Petypon   If I'd known you were coming . . .

General   Point taken, don't you know? (*Aside.*) Don't know what she sees in him.

Petypon   Um . . . you won't be in Paris *long*, I take it?

General   No. Leaving today.

Petypon   Oh. Ah. Excellent!

General   Beg pardon?

Petypon   Not excellent. No. I meant . . . it's just a word.

General   Gave myself two weeks' leave. Spending it in Touraine, seeing to your cousin's wedding. Oh yes, you'd better be there. Got anything on these next few days?

Petypon   Nothing important. You know, patients.

General   There we are then. Do it for Uncle, hey? Be nice to Uncle, hey? And one day Uncle may be nice to you.

Petypon   Oh . . . er . . . no need to hurry.

General   Stout fellow. (*Command tone.*) Right, then: orders of the day. We leave for Touraine tonight.

Petypon   *All* of us?

General (*same tone*)   You, me, Clémentine. All of us.

Petypon   Ah.

General   And the memsahib too, of course.

Petypon   Gabrielle? She'll be delighted.

General   Of course she will. Told me so in person.

Petypon   She told you? Who told you?

General   Your wife did. *She* did.

Shrimp (*aside*)   Oops.

Petypon   Wife? Where? *Wife?*

General (*indicating* **Shrimp**)   There's the little lady, there.

Petypon (*aghast*)   What, her my wife? Ridiculous.

General   Ridiculous?

Petypon   Wife, her, ha! Ha, ha, ha! Never!

General   Damn peculiar. Never, hey? In *your* house, *your* marriage bed . . . Not your wife, who is she?

Petypon   She's . . . She's . . . She's someone else entirely.

General   Soon settle this . . .

He goes to the bellpull.

Petypon   What are you doing?

General   Ringing for Étienne. He'll tell me the truth. Not your wife! Pull yourself together.

Petypon   Don't do that!

General   Thought so! She *is* your wife!

Petypon (*aside*)   This is *not* my day. (*Aloud.*) Aha! Ahahahaha! Hahaha! Ha!

General   Now what's the matter?

Petypon   Aha! Ha! Just my little joke. She *is* my wife.

General (*victorious*)   Told you so myself. Knew it all the time.

Petypon (*aside*)   After all, just for a few hours, no harm in it.

General   'Not my wife,' indeed. Fellow's a fool. Never mind: a fool with taste. Charming gel, charming.

Shrimp   Oh General.

General (*to* **Shrimp**)   No, dash it. Always say what I mean. (*To* **Petypon**.) D'you know, someone told me you'd married a real old boot.

Petypon   No, did they? (*Aside*.) Sorry, Gabrielle.

Knock at the outer door.

General   Come in!

Petypon (*at the same time*)   Don't come in!

Étienne *enters with a large cardboard box. He stays carefully on the threshold of the room.*

Étienne   Monsieur.

Petypon   What is it now? You can't come in.

Étienne   I'm aware of *that*, Monsieur.

General (*to* **Petypon**)   Stout fellow. Sticks to his guns. If he won't come in, he won't. No use arguing.

Petypon   What d'you *want*?

Étienne (*holding out the box*)   Madame's dress has come.

General   Aha!

He takes the box.

Right, you: dismiss. (*To* **Petypon**, *while* **Étienne** *leaves*.) Yet another proof she's your wife. Her *dress* has come.

Petypon (*giving in to the inevitable*)   Oh. Yes.

General   She told me she was just waiting for her dress, to get up. Well, it's arrived. (*To* **Shrimp**.) Here you are, girlie. Go and get dressed now.

Shrimp   Thanks, Uncle Charles.

Petypon (*aside*)   This is the limit!

Shrimp *opens the box and holds up* **Gabrielle**'s *dress.*

Shrimp (*aside*)   Oh dear, oh dear ... Still, beggars can't be choosers. (*To the* **General**.) Uncle Charlie.

General   Yes, my dear?

Petypon   'Uncle Charlie' now!

Shrimp   Uncle Charlie, would you mind drawing the curtains for me?

General (*enraptured*)   'Would you mind drawing the curtains for me?' I say!

He draws them, and goes to **Petypon**.

General   She's charming, charming! Just think of her in Touraine. She'll knock 'em for six in Touraine.

Petypon   I think she might.

Enter **Mongicourt** *with a parcel.*

Mongicourt   This is all I could find. Oh, excuse me.

Petypon (*aside*)   He *has* to catch on. (*To the* **General**.) Uncle Charles, may I introduce my old friend and colleague, Doctor Mongicourt? (*To* **Mongicourt**.) General Charles Petypon du Grelé. My uncle.

Mongicourt   Glad to meet you. After all these years.

General   Ah. Hem. Yes. Know what you mean.

Mongicourt   Really? Oh. Splendid. Splendid.

Mongicourt, **General**, **Petypon** (*laughing*)   Splendid.

General   Well, well, well.

All three   Well, well.

Mongicourt   Well.

Petypon   Well.

Mongicourt   Are you staying in Paris long?

Petypon (*alone*)   I say, well, well. (*Seeing he is on his own.*) Well?

General   Leaving today for Touraine. Seeing to niece's

marriage. (*To* **Petypon**.) Never told you she was marrying, did I? You'll be amazed. Corignon, Captain Corignon.

Petypon (*indifferently*) Really?

General (*surprised*) Corignon. You know, Corignon!

Petypon Never heard of him.

General Course you have.

Petypon Have I?

General Your wife said you knew him well, both of you.

Petypon Ah! *She* said . . .

General Yes.

Petypon Ah. Good. Fine. Excellent. (*Aside.*) We'll never get out of this.

Mongicourt Gabrielle? Is she here, then?

Petypon (*signing urgently to* **Mongicourt**, *who unfortunately isn't looking*) O yes. Ahem! Ahem! Yes, she is!

General In there, just getting up.

Mongicourt Getting up?

Petypon (*through his teeth*) Getting . . . *up.*

Mongicourt (*aside*) *Now* what? (*Aloud.*) Excuse me, General. Would you mind if I had a private word with my friend Petypon?

General Not at all.

Mongicourt Medical ethics. You know. One of our patients. Professional consultation. You do understand?

General By all means.

Mongicourt (*in a low voice, to* **Petypon**) What's going on? Your wife's in there?

Petypon (*the same, to him*)   It's Shrimp! He found her in the bed . . .

Mongicourt   You're for it now.

Petypon   I'm enjoying myself!

He starts as he hears **Gabrielle**'s *voice upstage.*

Petypon   Erg, Gabrielle! Now what? (*As* **Gabrielle** *enters.*) She's here!

Gabrielle *comes in and speaks without looking round.*

Gabrielle   All done. Mission accomplished.

Abruptly she finds herself face to face with the **General**.

Gabrielle   Oh, excuse me.

They exchange wary smiles.

Petypon (*quickly*)   My dear, this is General Charles Petypon du Grelé, my uncle.

Gabrielle   General Petypon.

She hugs him.

What a lovely surprise!

General (*taken aback*)   I say.

Gabrielle   Lucien's told me so much about you.

She kisses his cheek.

General   Has he? Has he? (*Aside.*) I don't know who she is, but she's damned affectionate.

Gabrielle   You must excuse me, General, for being so out of breath.

General   Take your time, dear lady.

Gabrielle (*to the others*)   I went to the Gare du Nord. I've just got back. It's done. (*To the* **General**.) He spoke to me!

General   Who did?

Gabrielle   The Chosen One.

General (*aside*)   What's she talking about?

Gabrielle (*with emotion*)   How marvellous and mysterious
are the ways of Providence! I waited in the Gare du Nord
for half an hour, walking up and down platform seven,
then suddenly, at the refreshment counter, I saw him. A
first-class passenger. I thought – I was quivering with
emotion – 'That's him! That's the man heaven destines
to create with a word the child who is to save *la patrie*,
save France!'

The **General** *looks hard at her for a moment, then says with
conviction to the audience:*

General   Woman's barkin'.

Gabrielle   I wanted to throw myself at his feet. I was
about to rush towards him, when an arm held me back!
Like the wind, a train came into the station, and a crowd
of people passed by me, swirled by me, and *he* hurried
past without a glance! The train pulled out of the station.
And then . . . then . . . from the mouth of a simple soul,
the Word was vouchsafed, the word I'd been waiting for:
'All tickets ready, please. All tickets ready for collection.'
(*Pause.*) The Chosen One was a ticket collector!

Petypon *and* **Mongicourt**   How amazing.

General   Extraordinary.

Gabrielle (*exhausted*)   Today has worn me out.

Mongicourt, *seeing the opportunity, tries to lead* **Gabrielle** *to
her own room.*

Mongicourt   That's right, that's right. You have to rest.
You ought to lie down for an hour or two.

Petypon   At least.

Mongicourt   I'm sure the General will excuse you.

Gabrielle (*letting them lead her off*)   You're right. You will excuse me, General?

General   What? Certainly.

Gabrielle *stops, bringing up short* **Petypon** *and* **Mongicourt** *also.*

Gabrielle   I hope, while you're in Paris, we'll see lots more of you.

General   Unfortunately, no. Leaving for Touraine, tonight.

Gabrielle   Touraine?

General   Tonight. House closed for ages. Needs staying in. Locals say it's haunted.

Gabrielle   You're not afraid of ghosts?

General   Don't wait to find out. Haha!

Gabrielle   Well, goodbye for the time being, General.

General (*bowing*)   Dear lady.

Gabrielle   I leave you with my husband.

Petypon *and* **Mongicourt** (*aside, sombrely*)   No.

Exit **Gabrielle**.

General (*aside*)   Her husband?

Petypon (*aside*)   Problems!

The **General**, *after staring at the two men, moves towards them. When he reaches* **Petypon** *he brushes him aside and holds out his hand to* **Mongicourt**.

General   My dear fellow, I beg your pardon. No idea this lady was your wife.

Mongicourt   *My* wi...

General   My nephew's fault. Never said her name when he introduced us.

Mongicourt Eh? That's all right.

Petypon (*quickly*) No, no, no. It was outrageous, unforgivable. My uncle's entirely right. (*To the* **General**.) You're entirely right. I should have said, 'Madame Mongicourt.' Never mind, though, eh? No harm done. (*Aside to* **Mongicourt**.) No harm done at all.

Mongicourt (*aside to him*) That's easy for you to say.

General (*to him*) Monsieur, compliments. Charming woman.

Mongicourt (*through his teeth*) Thank you.

General (*nudging* **Petypon**, *aside*) For a real old boot, that is.

Petypon (*annoyed, aside to the audience*) He keeps on saying that.

Mongicourt (*to the audience, in the same tone of voice*) This is pushing friendship a wife too far.

Enter **Shrimp** *in* **Gabrielle**'*s new dress.*

Shrimp There, I'm ready.

General Ah. My niece.

Shrimp How d'you like me?

She high-kicks over a chair.

'Houp-la. This one's for me.'

Petypon *and* **Mongicourt** *are horror-struck, but the* **General** *is delighted.*

General I say.

He mimics her movement.

'Houp-la. This one's for me.' (*To* **Petypon**.) Y'know, Lucien, she makes me feel young again.

Petypon (*muttering*) How nice. (*Aside.*) That's all we need.

General (*looking at his watch*)   I say, getting late. Standing gossiping . . . errands to run, things to do. (*To* **Shrimp**.) You've got the time? Five past four at the station?

Shrimp   Yes, Uncle Charles.

The **General** *goes to kiss her, then turns to* **Petypon**.

General   Er . . . mind if I . . . ?

Petypon   No, no, no.

General (*to* **Shrimp**)   Your husband doesn't mind.

Shrimp   Why should he?

She offers her cheek, and he kisses it.

General   If time, meet here. That's the ticket. Here.

Petypon   *What?*

Shrimp   Yes, Uncle Charles, that suits me fine.

Petypon   No, no. The station. The station's better.

General   Far better here. That way, can't miss each other.

Petypon (*aside*)   Oh, that's the ticket all right.

General (*to* **Mongicourt**)   Goodbye, Monsieur. Pleased to have metcher. Say goodbye to Madame Whatsname.

Mongicourt   Mongicourt.

General   Pardon?

Mongicourt   Mongicourt. Madame Mongicourt. (*Through his teeth.*) My *wife*.

General   Well, of course she is. Odd fellow. Right. Till later, Lucien, Gabrielle.

Shrimp   Au 'voir, Uncle Charles.

General   Au 'voir, Gabrielle.

He imitates her high-kick.

'Houp-la. This one's for me.'

Shrimp 'Houp-la. This one's for me.' Bravo, Uncle Charles.

General Charming. (*To* **Petypon**.) D'you hear, Lucien? She's charming.

Shrimp D'you hear, Lucien?

Petypon I hear.

General (*as he exits*) Old boot, ha! Hehehay. Hahaha.

His voice dies away offstage.

Petypon Oh crikey.

Mongicourt Have I really got this right? You're going with *her*?

Petypon That's right.

Mongicourt With Shrimp?

Shrimp That's right. What larks.

Mongicourt I don't know what to say.

Petypon (*to* **Shrimp**) Why me? Why *me*? What have *I* done? I know nothing about you. It's not as if we –

Shrimp It certainly isn't. We certainly didn't.

Petypon So why can't you leave me *alone*? Now I'm married to you.

Shrimp Poor darling.

Mongicourt What about me? *I'm* married to Gabrielle.

Petypon (*to* **Shrimp**) How d'you think I feel?

Mongicourt (*through his teeth*) How d'you think *I* feel?

Petypon You could have said, 'Touraine? No thanks.' But you didn't. I mean, Touraine. What are you going to *do* there, with your 'What larks' and your 'Houp-la. This one's for me'?

Shrimp (*exaggerating the accent*)   No need to bite me 'ead off.

Petypon   See?

Shrimp   Cor, luvyou, don't you worry. I know 'ow to behave proper. You just watch me. Good and proper.

Petypon   Oh God. When we get there, just keep your mouth shut. Remember where you are.

Shrimp (*normal voice*)   I know how to behave.

Petypon   Just remember, that's all. All right: half past three, downstairs.

Shrimp   Right.

She runs to **Mongicourt**.

Goodbye, Monsieur.

She shakes his hand and high-kicks.

'Houp-la. This one's for – '

Petypon   Out. Now. My wife could come in at any moment.

Shrimp   I'm dressed, aren't I? Look at me.

She minces about respectably.

Anyone'd take me for a *neighbour*. By the way, about dresses. Your wife has no *idea*. (*Waving to* **Mongicourt**.) Bye, Édouard.

Mongicourt   Till we meet again.

Shrimp (*to* **Petypon**, *pinching his nose*)   Till this afternoon, you *bad* boy.

Petypon   Leave my nose *alone*.

Étienne *appears at the door, stopping faithfully at the threshold.* **Shrimp** *pats his cheek as she passes him.*

Shrimp   There, there. It might never happen.

Exit.

Étienne (*aside*)   Where did *she* come from?

Petypon (*irritably*)   What is it now?

Étienne   Two men have arrived with an armchair with a light on it. They say you ordered it.

Petypon   Tell them to bring it in here.

Mongicourt   Another armchair?

Petypon   Not 'another' armchair: *the* armchair. Doctor Slivovich's Great Ecstatic Chair. Don't you remember, that conference in Vienna? I bought one for the surgery.

Mongicourt   La-di-dah!

Petypon   You'll be getting one too. All doctors will have them. This is the future. No one knows what rays have in store for us.

Mongicourt   Still experimental, then.

Petypon   Ether, chloroform, things of the past. From now on, when you want to put someone to sleep ... Doctor Slivovich's Great Ecstatic Chair ...

Étienne *reappears. He stops on the threshold and draws back to allow the passage of two* **Porters** *carrying the Ecstatic Chair. Its back is folded down over the seat. On the back is a box containing a pair of green gloves.*

Étienne   In here. That's as far as I'm allowed to go.

Petypon (*indicating*)   Put it over there.

The **Porters** *put the chair near the desk.*

Petypon (*to* **Mongicourt**)   Just look at that. (*To the* **Porters**.) Did you bring the gloves?

Porter   Yes Monsieur. In this box here.

Petypon   Thank you. Here . . . Here's one franc. Divide it between you.

Exeunt **Porters**.

Mongicourt   What are the gloves for?

Petypon (*putting up the back of the chair*)   The radiation. You plug in the battery, down here. You pull this handle.

He pulls a brass handle. A glow of light and a low hum.

Voilà.

Mongicourt   Voilà?

Petypon   Voilà. You pull it the other way . . . it stops.

He does so. The chair stops glowing and humming.

I'll show you again. You ask your patient . . . um . . . Look, come over here. You'll get a better idea.

Mongicourt   Er, no. No, thanks. You try.

Petypon   I'm *demonstrating*. Besides, I'm a doctor, not a patient.

Mongicourt   Problem is: me too.

Petypon   I'm not going to put you to sleep, for heaven's sake. I'm only going to show you how it works.

Mongicourt   Whatever you say.

Petypon   You don't believe me.

Mongicourt   Oh, I do.

Petypon   Well then?

Mongicourt   All right, if you insist. But no funny business.

Petypon   Me?

Mongicourt (*without enthusiasm*)   All right, then.

He sits in the chair.

Petypon   There you are. Well?

Mongicourt (*settling himself*)   So far so good.

Petypon   Right. Now, with this lever here, I can adjust the patient's position.

Mongicourt   Patient's position?

Petypon   Patient's position. For example –

He works a lever. The chairback falls flat.

Mongicourt   Hey.

Petypon   Exactly.

He puts the back up again.

And this way, I can put you up again.

Mongicourt   Thank you.

Petypon (*reading from the manual*)   And if I want to put the patient to sleep, I pull this handle here.

Mongicourt (*hurriedly*)   Yes yes. You don't have to –

Too late. **Petypon** *has pulled the handle. The chair lights up and hums.* **Mongicourt** *freezes in his last position, a seraphic smile on his face.* **Petypon** *continues his demonstration, reading from the manual without realising what he has done.*

Petypon   'Immediately, under the influence of the rays, the patient falls into an ecstasy of delight and complete unconsciousness. You can take as long as you like: open the patient up, poke around, take bits out, close, stitch, as if you were embroidering in your living-room at home.' Amazing, isn't it? (*Pause.*) Say something. Édouard . . . Good lord, I've done it, I've put him out. Oh no. Oho. This Gabrielle *must* see.

He goes to the door of his wife's room.

Gabrielle. Gabrielle.

Gabrielle's voice   What is it?

Petypon   Come here, quickly.

Enter **Gabrielle**.

Gabrielle   What's the matter?

Petypon   Look at Édouard.

Gabrielle   What's he doing?

Petypon   He's asleep.

Gabrielle   You mean he came to see you, and went to sleep?

Petypon   No, no. Look closer.

Gabrielle   The Ecstatic Chair.

Petypon   Exactly.

Gabrielle   You mean you – ?

Petypon   Precisely.

Gabrielle   Doesn't he look silly?

She moves towards the chair.

Petypon   Careful. It'll put you out as well.

Gabrielle   It wouldn't.

Petypon   You'd think he was in heaven.

Gabrielle   Yes.

Petypon   Total ecstasy. Gabrielle, you see a man in ecstasy.

Gabrielle   Who'd have thought it?

Petypon   Well, he's had enough ecstasy for one day. We musn't wear him out. There.

He pulls the handle, and **Mongicourt** *wakes up with a start, still smiling seraphically.*

Mongicourt   Fair princess ... tell me that you love me ...

Petypon Don't act the fool.

Mongicourt (*gradually returning to reality*) Eh?

Petypon I said, don't act the fool.

Mongicourt What happened?

Petypon You went to sleep . . . that's what happened.

Mongicourt I didn't.

Petypon You did.

Mongicourt I don't believe you.

Petypon Well, it certainly wasn't *me*.

Mongicourt You put me . . . ? Well, amazing. Works like a charm. I didn't feel a thing.

Petypon There you are, then.

Mongicourt (*leaning back eagerly*) Let's have another go.

Petypon (*stopping him*) Ah no. Don't be greedy.

Mongicourt It's *astounding*.

Petypon So useful in emergencies.

Gabrielle You're a private doctor. You don't *have* emergencies.

Petypon As a matter of fact, I've got one right now. This afternoon. A long way out of town.

Gabrielle Ah.

Petypon Sorry, darling.

Gabrielle You'll have to stay the night. I'll get you a bag.

Petypon Would you, darling?

Exit **Gabrielle**.

Mongicourt   I like your nerve.

Petypon   What else can I do? I can't go to Touraine with two wives. This isn't Morocco.

Étienne *appears, stopping on the threshold. He has visiting cards on a salver.*

Étienne   Monsieur . . .

Petypon   What is it?

Étienne   Two gentlemen, Monsieur. They want to see you alone, Monsieur.

Petypon (*reading the cards*)   Never heard of them. What do they want?

Étienne (*as before*)   They say it's about . . . last night's business.

Petypon   Last night's business? Édouard?

Mongicourt   Lucien?

Petypon   They've come about last night's business.

Mongicourt   Last night's business?

Petypon   I've no idea. (*To* **Étienne**.) You'd better show them in.

Exit **Étienne**.

Mongicourt   Well, if it's about last *night's* business, excuse me . . .

Petypon   Oh, Édouard, if I could start last night again . . .

Mongicourt   I know what you mean.

Petypon   See you later.

Mongicourt   See you later.

He goes to the door, and meets **Marollier** *and* **Varlin** *coming in.*

Mongicourt Gentlemen.

Exit.

Petypon Well, gentlemen, what can I do for you?

Marollier You are Doctor Petypon?

Petypon Yes indeed.

Marollier Marollier, lieutenant in the Tenth Brigade. Monsieur Varlin.

Varlin Insurance agent . . . fire, life, accident . . . anything you like, really . . .

He offers several business cards to **Petypon**.

Varlin Please take a card.

Petypon Too kind.

Varlin If you're embarking on a lifetime of insurance, I'd recommend . . .

Marollier (*sharply*) Stop that. You didn't come for that.

Varlin Sorry. (*Meekly, to* **Petypon**.) Sorry.

Petypon Do please sit down.

Marollier No doubt, Monsieur, you know exactly why we're here.

Petypon Not the foggiest.

Marollier It's about last night's business.

Petypon Ah. Last night's business.

Marollier Exactly.

Petypon I'm sorry, but *what* last night's business?

Marollier What last night's business? You've *forgotten*?

Petypon I'm afraid so.

Marollier Hardly surprising, the state you were in.

Petypon   I ... Pardon?

Marollier   In any case, Monsieur, not here to *discuss* last night's business. Two names, that's all we want. Two friends who'll act for you.

Petypon   *Act* for me? Oh, a duel. Fine. But *why*? (*To* **Varlin**, *who seems lost in the clouds*.) I mean, you like to *know*.

Varlin (*far away*)   Not the faintest idea.

Petypon   Pardon?

Marollier (*turning on* **Varlin**)   What are you doing *now*? What a way to behave!

Varlin   I don't even know him. (*To* **Petypon**.) He was sitting next to me at the bar. You know how it is. He was *there* ... I was *here* ...

Marollier   He doesn't want to know where *he* was, where *you* were ...

Varlin   Next thing, that business happened. Just like that. Well, I pretended not to notice ...

Marollier   All right, no need to tell him your life story. (*To* **Petypon**.) Monsieur, after the insults that were exchanged last night, our principal has instructed us ...

Petypon   Look, for heaven's sake, *what* insults?

Marollier   What insults? I'd have thought that when someone says to someone else 'Are you grinning at me, pal?' ...

Petypon   Mepal? Oh. I'm terribly sorry. Oh God, Mepal. Please tell your principal that if I *did* call him Mepal, it was entirely by accident ... a slip of the tongue ... and from the bottom of my heart, I take it back.

Marollier (*icily*)   You can't take it back.

Petypon   Pardon?

Marollier   Because *you* didn't call *him* Mepal, *he* called *you* Mepal.

Petypon   Who did?

Marollier   Our principal.

Varlin   The man at the bar. I *told* you. He was *there*, and I was *here*, and –

Petypon   You mean, *he* called *me* Mepal, and now he's sent you here to . . .

Marollier   He admits you're the injured party.

Petypon   Kind of him. Well, Mepal . . . it was obviously a joke . . . (*To* **Varlin**.) Wasn't it?

Varlin (*as before*)   Not the faintest idea.

Petypon   Sorry I asked. (*To* **Marollier**.) You really think I'm going to fight your . . . principal because he insulted me?

Marollier   If you don't fight when you're insulted, when *do* you fight?

Petypon   That, Monsieur, is for me to decide.

Marollier (*coldly*)   Very well, Monsieur. We're clearly wasting our time. This whole conversation is *quite* irregular.

Petypon   I'm sorry: *you* came here. Someone calls someone Mepal, and then sends his seconds . . . D'you think I'm not used to this? I *am* a doctor . . .

Marollier   Affair of honour.

Petypon   You listen to me, pal . . .

Marollier   No, you listen to me, pal . . .

Petypon   I've had enough of this.

He pushes **Marollier** *into the chair and pulls the handle.* **Marollier** *assumes the ecstatic position.*

Petypon That's better.

Pause while **Varlin** *digests the situation.*

Varlin What's he doing?

Petypon Never mind. He was annoying me; I shut him up.

Varlin Now that *is* interesting.

Petypon A fine one . . . a fine one. (*Shouting under* **Marollier***'s nose.*) A fine one! If you think you can frighten me, pal . . . You and your principal. (*To* **Varlin***.*) Who the devil is your principal anyway?

Varlin An officer.

Petypon Oh, an officer.

Varlin Captain Corignon.

Petypon Of course, Captain Co – What? Corignon? Did you say Corignon? The Corignon who's getting married?

Varlin Not the faintest i –

Petypon The man's my cousin.

Varlin What man?

Petypon Or will be shortly. What a small world . . . What made him insult me in the first place? What was wrong with him?

Varlin You were with the woman he loved. Not the woman he's marrying, the other one, you know, the one *you* were with last night.

Petypon Shrimp!

Varlin Is that really her name? When he saw you with her – we were at the bar, *there* and *here* – he lost his temper. 'I'm going to smash that booby's face in,' he said.

Petypon Charming.

Étienne (*offstage*) Yes, yes, Monsieur. I'll tell him you're here.

Enter.

Captain Corignon.

Varlin *and* **Petypon** Mepal!

Corignon Doctor *Petypon?*

Petypon That would be me.

Corignon (*embarrassed*) Monsieur, I don't know what to say. Good lord, if I'd known it was you. What a way to indroduce myself. My dear cousin-to-be . . .

He holds out his hand. **Petypon** *shakes it, very man of the world.*

Petypon My dear fellow, think no more about it.

Corignon I don't know how to apologise. You see, when I saw the two of you last night, you and Shrimp . . . You know what it's like, the woman you love . . . you're at the bar, and suddenly you see your friend with someone else . . . you forget you're engaged to another, your heart's engaged to another, and you see red. That's what happened to me.

Petypon Perfectly understandable. (*Nodding at* **Varlin**.) This gentleman's been telling me.

Corignon *bows slightly to* **Varlin**, *as though to a complete stranger.*

Corignon How de do?

Petypon Varlin, Monsieur Varlin.

Corignon Pleased to meet you.

Petypon Your second.

Corignon *crosses to shake* **Varlin**'s *hand.*

Corignon I thought I'd seen you before somewhere.

Varlin Everyone says that.

Corignon Of course they do. (*To* **Petypon**.) I'm sorry: idiotic.

Varlin (*nettled*) What d'you mean, idiotic?

Corignon No, no . . . not you idiotic, me idiotic, for sending seconds.

Varlin Oh good.

Corignon (*to* **Petypon**) No need to fight a duel. Shake hands, be friends.

Petypon (*magnanimously*) My dear chap. Forget it ever happened.

Corignon (*shaking his hand cordially*) Phew! That's a relief.

Petypon I mean, for heaven's sake! We're reasonable people. Not like our friend here . . .

He indicates **Marollier**, *in the chair.*

Corignon Marollier. What's *he* doing here?

Petypon Sleeping.

Corignon You mean he came here on business, sat down, dozed off – ?

Petypon I'll give him back to you.

He pulls the handle. **Marollier** *jumps like a puppet, then says*:

Marollier Ah Adelina, you nightingale of song. (*Moving imaginary veils, he sings and dances.*) Tralalala . . . tralalala . . . trala . . . trala . . . lala . . . lala . . .

Corignon Marollier, what the devil are you doing? Shape up, shape up.

Marollier (*waking*) What . . . ? Captain Corignon. What are *you* doing here? At your opponent's house? That simply isn't done.

Corignon I've apologised. It's all cleared up. It's over.

Marollier *You've* apologised? You can't do that. Not up to you.

Corignon Oh, it's not?

Marollier *We're* the seconds. *We* apologise.

Corignon (*getting angry*) Not in my duel you don't. Clear out of it!

Marollier (*furiously*) Corignon.

Corignon Listen to me, pal. I've had enough of this. If you want to make something of it . . .

Petypon We've *done* this bit.

Marollier (*sharply, to him*) What did you say?

Petypon Me? Nothing. Talk to *him*, not me.

Marollier You've not heard the end of this.

Petypon Who, me?

Marollier No, him.

Petypon Ah, fine.

Marollier (*going round them in turn, frostily*) Monsieur, Monsieur, Monsieur . . . Good morning.

Corignon We'll meet again, Monsieur.

Exit **Marollier**.

Petypon (*to* **Varlin**) Who does he think he is?

Varlin Not the faintest id –

Corignon Never mind who he thinks he is. *I'll* deal with him.

Petypon I should think so, too. (*To* **Varlin**.) We know how to deal with *his* sort. (*He looks at his watch.*) Good heavens, half past three. Monsieur, Monsieur, I'm terribly sorry, but I've a train to catch.

Corignon   What a shame. We were getting along *so* well.

Petypon   I'm going to Touraine. Your wedding. I expect I'll see you down there.

Corignon   I couldn't get leave today, so I'm going down tomorrow. Fine then, see you down there.

Petypon   Fine.

Varlin   Fine.

Corignon   Cousin.

Petypon   Cousin.

They shake hands. **Petypon** *turns to* **Varlin**.

Petypon   Monsieur, delighted to have met you.

Varlin (*shaking his hand*)   Me too, entirely. If you ever need insurance ... One never knows ... Death is just around the corner.

Petypon   Thanks for reminding me. And after *you* ...

Varlin (*inching past*)   Sorry.

Exeunt **Corignon** *and* **Varlin**. **Petypon** *sees them out, then crosses to his wife's door.*

Petypon   Gabrielle. Gabrielle.

Gabrielle *hurries in.*

Gabrielle   What is it?

Petypon   I'm devilish late. My bag?

Gabrielle   In the hall.

Petypon   Thanks. (*He notices a letter she is holding.*) Is that for me?

Gabrielle   No, for me. I'll read it shortly.

Petypon   Good. My hat? Coat . . . ?

Gabrielle   In the cupboard.

Petypon   Right.

He hurries into his bedroom. **Gabrielle** *reads her letter.*

Gabrielle (*to him, off*)   This is very odd. The General's invited me to Touraine for his niece's wedding. Says he wants me to act as matron of honour. Why didn't he say so when he was here just now? I've nothing packed. Never mind . . . I'll come on later. You go ahead.

Petypon *returns. He hasn't heard a word.*

Petypon   There, ready.

Gabrielle   D'you want to see the letter?

Petypon   Not now. No time.

Gabrielle   What d'you make of it?

Petypon   I really haven't time.

General (*off*)   Are you *still* not ready?

Petypon   My God, Uncle Charles.

He hurls himself at **Gabrielle** *and drags her along.*

Petypon   Come in here. Your letter. We'll discuss it in the bedroom.

Gabrielle (*resisting*)   What's wrong with here?

Petypon   Come *on*.

Gabrielle   For heaven's sake!

She breaks free, and falls on the Ecstatic Chair.

Petypon (*inspired*)   Aha!

He leaps for and pulls the handle. **Gabrielle** *goes into ecstasy.*

Petypon   Sweet dreams.

General (*off*)   I tell you I'm going in.

Petypon   Quick ... hide her.

*He covers her with the tablecloth that originally covered the pouffe.
Enter the* **General**.

General   Come along, come along. Been waiting hours
downstairs.

Petypon   Won't be a moment.

General (*intrigued by the silhouette on the chair*)   What the
devil's that?

Petypon   Nothing. An anatomical model.

General   Not very lifelike ...

Petypon   Don't touch it.

General   Why not?

Petypon   I've had it repainted.

General   I say.

Petypon (*pushing him towards the door*)   Wait downstairs.
I'll fetch my coat and be right with you.

General   Don't be long, eh?

Petypon   I promise.

Exit **General**.

Petypon   I can't leave her here like this. We'll be away
for days.

Étienne *comes to the threshold, blocking the* **Roadsweeper**.

Étienne   Look, wait in the hall. I'll *tell* him you're here.

Sweeper   He's *expecting* me. (*To* **Petypon**.) 'Arternoon,
guvnor.

Petypon   What on earth ... ? Let him in.

Sweeper (*to* **Étienne**)   Told yer.

Étienne *goes, eloquently.*

Petypon What is it?

Sweeper It's me, the Place Pigalle roadsweeper.

Petypon What d'you want? We haven't any roads.

Sweeper I've come to dinner.

Petypon Pardon?

Sweeper You invited me to dinner.

Petypon I invited you to dinner?

Sweeper See, you remember. Bless yer. I was sweeping away last night, and you and your young lady came past, and you came and 'ugged me . . .

Petypon Ugged you?

Sweeper Yer. Like this.

Petypon Thank you.

Sweeper 'I like your face,' you said. 'Come and have dinner termorrer arternoon.'

Petypon You're joking.

The **Sweeper** *takes a visiting card from his pocket, wipes it and hands it to* **Petypon** *with a flourish.*

Sweeper Here, look: the card you gave me.

Petypon (*dumbfounded*) I . . . ah . . . oh . . . (*Aside.*) Well, never mind, a friend in need . . . (*To him.*) Look, here's fifty centimes.

Sweeper Fifty centimes?

Petypon Yes . . . and Étienne will give you dinner in the kitchen.

Sweeper Oh, I dunno . . .

Petypon Never mind dunnoing. *Do* something.

Sweeper   *Do* something?

Petypon   I have to go out. At once. As soon as I've gone, I want you to pull this handle here on the chair . . . and then completely ignore whatever happens next.

Sweeper   Pull handle, completely ignore. Fair enough.

General (*offstage*)   Come on, can't you?

Petypon   Uncle Charles again. (*To the* **Sweeper**.) You're sure you understand?

Sweeper   Course I do, bless yer.

Petypon   Thank you.

Sweeper   Give us an 'ug.

Petypon   What? Oh. There.

They hug. He goes.

Sweeper   Nah then, this handle 'ere . . . One, two, three . . .

He pulls the handle. **Gabrielle** *springs awake.*

Sweeper   Blimey.

Gabrielle   My God, I'm blind.

She fights her way clear of the cloth, slapping the **Sweeper** *in the process.*

Sweeper   Oi.

Gabrielle   Aah! Who are you?

Sweeper   I'm the sweeper you're 'aving to dinner . . .

Gabrielle *runs across the room to her own bedroom.*

Gabrielle   Help. Help. Lucien. Étienne. Étienne.

Sweeper (*following her*)   But I'm the sweeper you're 'aving to dinner . . .

Étienne *runs in.*

Étienne   What's the matter?

Gabrielle   Get rid of him!

Étienne *throws himself on the* **Sweeper** *and drags him out.*

Sweeper   But I'm the sweeper you're 'aving to dinner. I'm the sweeper you're 'aving to din . . .

Curtain.

Act Two

The **General**'s *château in Touraine. A large room on the ground floor. Three huge arched bays on to the terrace and formal garden beyond. Their doors are wide open. A baroque fireplace. Chandeliers. Vast mirrors in gilt frames. Tapestries, pictures on the walls. Doors L and R. Ornate furniture, including a grand piano. A buffet loaded with food and drink.*

Bright afternoon sun. As the curtain rises, a **Children**'s *choir and* **Soloist** *are performing, conducted by the* **Curé**. *Among the* **Guests** *grouped to listen are the* **General**, **Shrimp**, **Petypon**, **Clémentine**, *the* **Baroness**, *the* **Duchess**, **Chamerot**, **Guérissac**, **Madame Claux**, **Madame Hautignol**, **Madame Ponant** *and* **Madame Virette**. **Émile** *is at one end of the buffet, which is manned by* **Footmen**.

Soloist And our land will aye remember . . .

Children And our land will aye remember . . .

Soloist . . . this long-awaited day-ay . . .

Children . . . day-ay . . .

Soloist Which has fanned the dying ember . . .

Children . . . fanned the dying ember . . .

Soloist . . . and made October May-ay . . .

Children . . . October May-ay . . .

Soloist . . . With happy, smiling faces . . .

Children . . . aces . . .

Soloist We hymn their gentle graces . . .

Children . . . races . . .

Everyone (*in a flattering murmur*) Aah.

Soloist
Friends, all raise your glasses.
Before the moment passes,
On this their wedding day
Let's cheer and say . . .

(*Spoken.*) Hip, hip . . .

Children (*shouted*)   Hurray.

Guests (*a murmur of compliments*)   Delightful! Aah! How charming. Wasn't that exquisite? What a delightful surprise. (*Etc.*)

Shrimp, **Clémentine**, **Petypon** *and the* **General** *shake the* **Curé**'s *hand, embrace the* **Children**, *etc. The* **General**'s *voice dominates the surrounding hubbub.*

General   Clémentine. At the double now. These charmin' children . . . orange squash, cakes. Eat, drink, order of the day.

Clémentine   Yes, Uncle Charles.

Shrimp   This way, children.

She and **Clémentine** *lead the* **Children** *to the buffet, while the* **Guests** *surround the* **Curé** *to congratulate him.*

Baroness   My dear Ponosse, my compliments.

Curé (*flustered*)   Thank you, your ladyship.

Madame Virette   Father, that was *lovely*.

Curé   You really thought so?

Madame Ponant   Delightful.

Madame Claux   Exquisite.

Madame Hautignol   Heavenly.

Baroness   I wanted to cry.

Curé (*writing with embarrassed pleasure*)   No. Really? Oh . . .

Shrimp *and* **Clémentine** *take the* **Children** *off.*

Everyone   Quite delightful.

Duchess (*graciously joining the group*)   My dear Canon,
what can one say? Affecting, tasteful . . .

Everyone   Yes, yes.

Curé   Oh, your Grace, you overwhelm me. Oh, ladies
and gentlemen . . .

The **General** *comes from the buffet to shake his hand.*

General   Damn good show, Ponosse. Touchin', hey.
Affectin'. Well, nuff said. (*Calling.*) Émile.

Émile *comes up and salutes.*

Émile   Sir?

General   Fetch it, man. Don't stand gapin'.

Émile   Yes sir.

General   At the double.

Exeunt **Émile** *and* **Footmen**.

Curé (*to the* **General**)   General, I don't know what to
say.

General   Say nothing. Nuff said already. Words of your
song, dontcha know, straight to the heart.

Curé   Oh General.

General   Genuine, sincere, deeply moved. Said at once,
'Ponosse did this. Know it anywhere.' Someone said, 'This
that Shakespeare chappie?' 'No,' I said, 'Ponosse chappie
– can't you tell?'

Curé   General, really, I don't deserve . . .

General   That last bit: tears in the eyes. 'Let's cheer
and say, "Hip, hip, hooray".' Good, that. 'Say "Hooray".'
Like it.

Everyone   Yes, yes.

General   'Our land will aye remember.'

Curé (*singing*)   '. . . this long awaited day-ay.'

General   '. . . ay-ay.' Eh?

Curé   'Which has fanned the dying ember.'

General   'And made October . . .'

Curé   'October May-ay.'

General   Poets, eh? I've always called it 'May'.

Curé   Poetic licence, you know, the metre . . .

General   Knew it! Poetic licence, beyond me. Hunting licence, fishing licence, not the same thing at all.

Everyone *laughs.*

Guérissac   I say, sir, very good.

Chamerot   Very neat, sir, oh yah.

Enter a procession: **Émile,** *followed by* **Footmen** *carrying a large object on a small litter, carrying-poles on their shoulders.*

General   Aha! Here it is.

Guérissac   Gentlemen, to your places.

The **Officers** *form a ceremonial line, imitating bugle calls.*

Officers   Tara. Ta. Tara, tara, tara. Ta. Tata. Tara. Ta.

As the last note dies away, the **General** *removes the cloth to reveal a large, engraved and gilded bronze bell.*

Everyone   A bell.

General   Ponosse. Small token. Respect and thanks. Bell for the village church. Nothin' too good. Old, devilish old. St Mark's, Venice. Brought by Napoleon himself. Gave it to my grandfather, aide de camp.

Everyone   Ah.

General   Not over-large. Soldiers naturally chose smallest. Can't cart damn great bell all over countryside, especially when hiding it from natives. There. All yours. Stand easy.

Everyone   Bravo, bravo.

Curé   General, what can I say? I can't express ... Let me embrace you.

General   Steady on, Ponosse. Ladies, yes. But chaps of same persuasion? Still, man of the cloth ... Get on with it.

While he and the **Curé** *embrace, the* **Officers** *sound their fanfare.*

Officers   Tara. Ta. Tara. Tara. Tara. Ta.

Everyone *applauds. The* **General** *replaces the cloth on the bell and gestures to the* **Footmen**.

General   Down over there, then dismiss.

The **Footmen** *take the bell to one side, and exeunt. General party bustle. Enter* **Shrimp** *and* **Clémentine**, *followed by* **Petypon**.

General   Ah. Here come my nieces.

As soon as **Shrimp** *enters, the* **Ladies** *surround her in a flattering group.* **Petypon** *hovers anxiously.*

Madame Ponant   Delightful. Sweet.

Madame Hautignol   So stylish.

Madame Claux   So elegant.

Baroness   The Queen of Elegance.

Shrimp   Hey, your ladyness, spare a girl's blushes.

Baroness   Delightful.

Madame Virette   Exquisite.

Madame Claux 'Spare a girl's blushes'! How *very* Champs-Elysée.

Shrimp No, come on, ladies . . .

She talks to them. Meanwhile:

General (*to* **Guérissac** *and* **Chamerot**) Well, what d'you think of my niece, hey? Not that one, t'other one. Madame Petypon.

Chamerot Chic, sir. Parisian, yah? These old gels have seen nothing like her.

Shrimp No, go on: a glass of bubbly never did anyone any harm. Go on, spoil yourselves. You start, your ladyness. A glass of bubbly.

Baroness Well, perhaps a drop.

Shrimp One drop, coming up. (*Shouting as if she were a waitress.*) One glass of fizz-juice! One!

General I say! *I* say!

Clémentine (*coming up to him*) Would you like some . . . er, fizz-juice, Uncle Charles?

General Not now, m'dear. Ask the others first.

Clémentine Yes, Uncle Charles.

General (*to his* **Officers**) Wish she was more like t'other one.

Guérissac But why, sir? Mamzelle Clémentine is *charming*.

General Ha! Charmin', yes. Goose.

Guérissac I say, sir.

General Gave her advice, doncha know. Cousin here. Don't be ashamed. Pick up tips. *Savoir faire*. Few lessons, lick into shape. Won't recognise her. Nor will Corignon. Eh? Hey hey?

Officers   No, sir. Yes, sir. Excellent idea, sir.

Madame Hautignol (*to* **Madame Ponant**, *drawing her aside*)   My dear, that dress she's wearing!

General (*aside to the* **Officers**)   Listen to this, now.

Madame Ponant   I haven't been able to take my *eyes* from it.

General (*as before*)   Goin' on like this all day.

Madame Hautignol   It proves what I've always said: this season, *no one's* wearing bustles.

Madame Virette *joins them.*

Madame Ponant   You know how positive Madame Courtois was that *everyone's* wearing hoop skirts this season.

Madame Virette   Madame Courtois! I'd imagine Madame Petypon knows more about it than Madame Courtois. She *is* from Paris.

Madame Hautignol   Frankly, I find Madame Courtois rather a bore these days. She simply can't be bothered to keep up with fashion.

Madame Ponant   What's the point of having 'one's own little dressmaker' in Tours, if all she can do is the latest style from Poitiers?

Shrimp *joins the group, shadowed by the anxious* **Petypon**.

Shrimp   Not thirsty, then, ladies?

Madame Hautignol   Nothing for me, thanks, dear.

Shrimp   What about you?

Madame Ponant   Nothing, really.

Shrimp   You, then?

Madame Virette   No thank you. You're too kind, really.

Shrimp (*gaily*) I dunno, ladies. Will nothing persua
you to wet your whis –

Petypon (*quickly*) Wet your lips. Your lips.

Shrimp That's right.

Petypon (*aside*) Phew.

Shrimp Nothing tickle your fancy?

Madame Hautignol If you insist, a little orange
squash.

Shrimp One orange squash, coming up. Scuse me.
(*Shouting, as she goes upstage followed by* **Petypon**.) One
mauled orange! One!

As soon as she's gone, the **Ladies** *eagerly discuss her clothes.*
(Feydeau's note: the following dialogue should be adapted to whatever
styles are current. The ladies are in the latest fashion, and
Shrimp, *by contrast, is a little unusual.)*

Madame Hautignol You see that? The skirt without a
bustle, and fastened at the side.

Madame Ponant And the sleeves, my dear. Narrow
sleeves, padded shoulders?

Madame Virette I was *amazed* at her skirt. Cut
sloping, with a double pleat. I *said* so!

Madame Claux *joins them, all agog.*

Madame Claux You'll never guess, my dears.

Ladies What?

Madame Claux I've seen her petticoat.

Ladies Whose?

Madame Claux *Hers.* Madame Petypon's.

Ladies You haven't.

Madame Claux I promise you. Pink lawn. Cut wide
. . . wide . . .

Madame Ponant Wide?

Madame Hautignol I knew it! There you are. Madame Courtois says petticoats should be narrow, clinging.

Madame Ponant 'The latest style from Paris.'

Madame Claux You could take hers in each hand and stretch your arms wide, it would still hang loose. And panelled at the front, *panelled*. Yards of lace. It's gorgeous.

Ladies Really.

Madame Hautignol (*with curiosity*) But however did you *see* it?

Madame Claux Ah. I was subtlety itself.

Madame Ponant As always, as always.

Madame Claux I waited till there was no one near her. Then I went up and said, 'Dear Madame Petypon, I'm *dying* for a peek at your petticoat.'

Ladies (*admiringly*) Oh.

Madame Virette Just like that?

Madame Claux Just like that. Then . . . as graciously as anything . . . with the right hand like *this* . . . she took her overskirt . . . like *this* . . . and with a movement so . . . so refined – the leg as well as the arms, my dears – she *threw* it over her head like this . . . 'Houp-la!' (*She imitates the movement of a cancan dancer.*) I could see nothing but a *cascade* of rose and lace . . . and in the middle of it all, a leg drawing arabesques in the air.

Ladies You didn't.

Madame Claux I did.

Ladies (*almost swooning with rapture*) Oh my dear . . . my dear . . .

Madame Claux That's all there is to it.

Madame Ponant It's what I've always said. People only really *dress* in Paris.

Footman (*at the door*) Monsieur and Madame Vidauban.

This announcement is received with an excited murmur. The **General** *rises, trying to remember what the name means to him.*

General Vidauban? Don't remind me. Vidauban?

Madame Virette Our friend from Paris, General. The lady from Paris, who lends such an *air* to all our evening parties.

Enter **Vidauban** *and* **Madame Vidauban**, *she easy and smiling, he typical of men whose wives are acknowledged beauties.*

General Dear lady, pleased to meetcha. Vidauban, ha hey.

Madame Vidauban My dear General, the pleasure's ours. Ain't that so, Roy?

Vidauban Oh yes, my dear.

Madame Vidauban *descends on the four* **Ladies**.

Madame Vidauban My dears, good evening. (*To* **Madame Hautignol**.) What a *charming* ensemble. (*Expertly*.) It's a Paris gown. (*To* **Madame Ponant**.) Dear Madame, I missed you this morning. Market day. We *did* have an arrangement.

Madame Ponant I'm sorry, at the last moment something . . .

Madame Vidauban *Everyone* was there today. (*To the* **General**.) Now, *do* introduce me to that delightful Madame Petypon. Everyone tells me what a charming young gel she is.

General Meet people in the *market*?

Madame Vidauban The Wednesday market. Our

Champs-Elysées, you know. The whole *world* is there.

General   Harumph. Never mind. Allow me now, introduce, you know.

Madame Vidauban   We'll be delighted. Ain't that so, Roy?

They move with the **General** *to the buffet to meet* **Shrimp**.

Madame Claux   'Ain't that so, Roy?' *She's mortified.*

Ladies   Why?

Madame Claux   One minute she's the authority on Paris manners and fashions, the next, someone arrives who knows twice as much as she does.

Madame Hautignol   Well, it serves her right. All that 'In Paris, one *always* does this . . . In Paris, one *never* does that.'

Madame Ponant   She hasn't spent a *week* in Paris in her life. I always say Toulouse is the nearest she's ever *been* to Paris.

Ladies   You do. You always do.

Madame Hautignol *nods towards* **Shrimp** *and* **Madame Vidauban**, *who are greeting each other effusively*.

Madame Hautignol   She'll do herself an injury.

Madame Vidauban (*to* **Shrimp**, *gushing*)   Not at all, my dear. I *always* say exactly what I mean. I do.

Shrimp   Oh, so do I. I do. Oh blimey, yes.

Petypon (*gushing even more*)   Too kind. You really are too kind.

Shrimp (*exaggeratedly*)   No, *you* are.

Madame Vidauban   If you'd any *idea* how delighted I am to meet someone else from Paris. We're so cut *off* down here.

Petypon Ah. Cut off.

Madame Vidauban I mean, one is the *only* one down here who carries the torch of Paris in this *dreary* place.

Madame Virette (*to her clan*) Just *hear* her.

Shrimp So what part of Paris do you come from?

Madame Vidauban Oh, you know . . .

Madame Claux (*through her teeth*) The Toulouse part, naturally.

Madame Vidauban One *always* lived in Paris. One simply did.

Madame Claux (*to the clan*) One simply does.

Madame Vidauban Then of course, when one got married, you understand . . . one's husband has *business* interests . . .

She indicates **Vidauban**, *who bows.*

Madame Vidauban But even though one's self is here in the country, one's *soul* remains in Paris.

Madame Claux Oh, my *dear.*

Petypon You do pay it a visit now and then?

Madame Vidauban Eight days every autumn. But one keeps oneself *au fait* with the *salons.* It's as if one were there in person.

Émile *delivers a glass of orange squash to* **Shrimp**, *on a salver.*

Shrimp Ta. (*To* **Madame Vidauban**.) Please excuse me. I *must* deliver this.

Petypon (*quickly*) Yes, matter of life and death. Excuse me.

Madame Vidauban Not at all.

Shrimp *makes for the clan,* **Petypon** *dogging her heels.*

Shrimp *Will* you stop following me around?

Petypon What d'you expect? 'Wet your whistles.' You can't help coming out with them, can you?

Shrimp So what? 'Wet your lips', 'Wet your whistles', at least people know what I'm talking about.

She sucks from the straw, loudly.

Petypon I'd rather they didn't.

Shrimp *shrugs, takes a last suck, then holds out the rest of the drink to* **Madame Hautignol**, *swiping it out of range of* **Petypon** *who tries to snatch it.*

Shrimp Your orange squash, Missus.

Madame Hautignol Oh thank you, my dear.

Shrimp I recommend it. (*To* **Clémentine**, *who is coming towards her.*) I've been looking for you everywhere.

Madame Claux Did you know that our friend from Paris is really only from Toulouse?

Shrimp Well, knock me sideways with a feather duster.

She takes **Clémentine** *to join* **Petypon**.

Madame Claux (*to the clan*) There. I've told her, and I'm not sorry.

Shrimp *and* **Clémentine** *are intercepted by the two* **Officers** *and the* **General**. **Petypon** *skids up to intercept.*

General Dear nieces. There you are. Everything all right for you?

Shrimp *and* **Clémentine** Oh yes, Uncle Charles.

Petypon (*simultaneously, arriving*) Oh yes, Uncle Charles.

General What d'you mean, 'Oh yes, Uncle Charles'? Not talking to you. 'Dear nieces,' I said. *You're* not my dear niece.

Petypon Oh no. Sorry.

General *I'm* not sorry. Bad enough having you for a nephew. No thanks. (*To the* **Officers**.) Hey, hey?

Laughter. He goes to join **Shrimp** *and* **Clémentine**, *who are with the* **Curé**.

General So glad you get on, the pair of you.

Clémentine Yes, Uncle Charles.

General Breeding. Always shows. Clémentine, don't forget. Cousin here: tips, pick up tips.

Clémentine Yes, Uncle Charles.

General 'Yes, Uncle Charles.' 'Yes, Uncle Charles.' Sound like parrot. Say something else, God dammit.

Curé Oh.

Clémentine (*scandalised*) Uncle Charles.

General (*not at all put out*) ... as the padre's always sayin'.

Curé (*scandalised*) Oh, General.

He retreats upstage, making a faint sign of the cross.

General (*to* **Shrimp**) Needs you. Lick her into shape. Know what I mean?

Shrimp Uncle Charles, no trouble. In a moment or two I'll take her into a corner and show her how to be'ave in company.

General Bravo.

Petypon *That* I can't wait to see.

Shrimp *and* **Clémentine** *move away.* **Petypon** *goes to join them, but is blocked by the* **General**. *They try left and right, but still block each other, unintentionally.*

General Damn fool. Keep left. (*To the* **Officers**,

following.) Look at him. Jealous. Can't leave her for a moment.

He turns to find the **Curé**, *watching* **Petypon** *and* **Shrimp** *arguing animatedly in front of the buffet.*

Curé Such a pleasure to see such a *devoted* couple.

General Yes, yes.

He leaves them. The **Curé** *goes to* **Guérissac** *and* **Chamerot**, *who are so busy looking at* **Shrimp** *that they don't notice him.*

Guérissac D'you know: amazing. More I see of her, more I think I know her from somewhere.

Chamerot I say, yah, me too.

Curé Can't see it myself.

Chamerot But where? Simply can't place the woman. Where?

They rejoin the **General**. **Shrimp** *is the centre of attention once again.* **Petypon** *is at his wits' end.*

Everyone (*laughing*) Hahahahahaha.

Petypon (*tearing his hair*) Argh.

Madame Claux So witty.

Madame Hautignol So amusing.

Madame Ponant How well she puts things.

Everyone Hahahahahaha.

Shrimp (*innocently*) What's the matter? Something tickle your fancy?

Petypon *grabs her hand and pulls her away.*

Shrimp *Now* what?

Petypon '*Now* what?' Can't you see the effect you're having?

Shrimp   This is a bit bloody much, you know.

Petypon   *What?*

Shrimp   Just leave me alone.

Petypon   What about breakfast this morning? D'you think ladies in high society go around saying: 'Oho, Reverend, what's this? Footsy-footsy under the table, eh?'

Shrimp   For heaven's sake. He was trampling me to death.

Petypon   Oh really?

Shrimp   Yes. My feet. My plates of meat.

Petypon   I'm sure the poor man was quite oblivious.

Shrimp   Well, good for him. *I* wasn't, I can tell you.

Petypon   Fortunately they can't get enough of you. All I'm saying is, be *careful.*

Shrimp   Now look here: shut it.

Petypon   Shut what?

Shrimp   (*doing it for him*)   Your mouth. Oaf.

Petypon   Pfui.

Without pause, **Shrimp** *addresses the* **Curé***, who is approaching with a glass.*

Shrimp   That's right, Reverend, you fill your boots. (*To* **Petypon**.) Stop kicking me.

Curé   I must confess, even the cloth, dear lady, does not absolve us from human frailty. Alas, alas.

Petypon   Alas.

Shrimp   I didn't have a chance to say so before. That little song of yours, very nice. (*Aside to* **Petypon**.) That better, oaf?

Curé   Oh, really . . .

Shrimp   In fact, I'd like you to let me have it.

Petypon (*aside*)   Oh-oh.

Shrimp   I'll have a go at it.

Curé   Madame, too kind.

Petypon   You've no idea. She can't sing a note. (*Through his teeth to her.*) Can't sing.

Shrimp   Of course I can sing.

Curé (*archly*)   I said so, as soon as I saw you. 'She sings,' I said.

Shrimp   Blimey, Reverend, we all of us sing a bit.

Petypon (*aside to her*)   Watch what you're *saying*.

Curé   Of course you do. In Paris, *everyone* sings a bit.

Shrimp   Too kind, Reverend, too really kind.

Petypon (*trying to manoeuvre her away*)   Yes, yes, too kind, Reverend, too really kind.

Footman (*from the door*)   His Worship the Mayor and the Lady Mayoress.

General   Ah. (*Calling.*) My dear niece.

Shrimp *and* **Petypon** *go to him,* **Petypon** *arriving first.*

Shrimp *and* **Petypon**   Yes, Uncle Charles?

General (*pushing* **Petypon** *aside*)   Might have guessed *you'd* come rushing up. (*To the* **Mayor** *and* **Mayoress**.) Allow me ... er ... (*Introducing* **Shrimp**.) Niece. (*To* **Shrimp**.) Mayor ... Lady Mayoress.

Mayor   My dear young lady. I hope you'll be very happy.

General   No, no, wrong gel. (*Pointing to* **Clémentine**.) Bride: this one.

Mayor   Aha. My dear, the same to you.

General (*pointing to* **Shrimp**)   This one married already.
Husband: that fool there.

Petypon   Charming.

General   Petypon. Doctor. Nephew. (*To* **Shrimp**.) My
dear, d'you mind? Her Worship, buffet?

Shrimp   Glad to oblige. (*To the* **Mayoress**.) Over here,
your Highness.

Mayoress   Thank you. (*To her husband.*) You don't mind,
Camille?

Mayor (*indulgently*)   Nay, you run along. Oh, one
thing . . .

Mayoress   Yes, Camille?

Mayor (*drawing her aside*)   You remember. What I *told*
you?

Mayoress   No. What?

Mayor   Of course you do. (*To* **Shrimp**.) Excuse me,
would you?

Shrimp   Any time.

Mayor (*aside to his wife*)   I *said*, keep your eyes open, see
how the nobs behave. Learn a few manners. We may
need them later *on*.

Mayoress   Oh yes.

She starts away, then returns.

But everyone knows you're a butcher.

Mayor   Shh! Get on. She's *waiting*.

Shrimp (*at the buffet*)   What can I offer you, your
Highness? Mauled orange, glass of fizz-juice. Whaddyer
fancy?

Petypon   Oh God.

Mayoress   I really can't decide. Er . . . Whaddyer recommend?

Petypon *throws up his arms and leaves them to it.*

General   Nothin' to see in here. Just Michelangelo.

Mayor   Who? Oh, the statue. Think he'd do one for me?

General   Doubt it. Dead. So they tell me.

Mayor   Could be awkward, that.

Petypon *has come up behind them and is listening.*

General   Upstairs, doncha know, Watteau Room.

Petypon   They usually are.

General   What? Oh. No, Watteau.

Petypon   Watteau. Ah. What ho?

General   What're you babblin' about? Take his Worship upstairs. Show him Watteau.

Petypon   What Watteau?

General   Fool. In Watteau *Room*. Watteau.

Petypon   But my wife . . .

General   Not going to eat her. Jealous husbands! At the double.

Petypon   This way, your Worship.

Mayor   After you.

Petypon   No, after you.

Mayor   Entirely.

Petypon   There you are, then.

He ushers the **Mayor** *out, with a last aside to the audience.*

Petypon   What can go wrong? She's with the Lady Mayoress.

Exit. Moment of general conversation. Then a sudden burst of laughter from a group containing the **Duchess**, **Vidauban** *and* **Madame Vidauban**.

Duchess   The gardener said *that*? How rich!

Madame Vidauban   Your Grace, one heard it from the Cardinal's own lips.

Duchess   One just can't get the staff.

Madame Vidauban   After all, the *depths* of the countryside.

Duchess   You're absolutely right. (*Calling.*) Guy. Guy.

Shrimp (*going to her*)   Hey, Duchess, you just went 'Gee gee'.

Duchess   No, no. I was calling my son: glass of water.

Shrimp   Leave it to me. (*At the top of her voice.*) Émile! Oi, Émile! (*Politely to the* **Duchess**.) You have to catch their attention. (*Loudly.*) Chimp-features! Move it!

Émile (*coming up, frostily*)   Madame yelled?

Shrimp   A glass of water for her Ladyship. She's *parching* here. (*As he goes.*) These penguin-men are all the same.

The **Duchess** *gives a silvery laugh. The clan politely echoes her.*

Shrimp   Have I said something funny?

Duchess   'Penguin-man'. One's never heard *that* before.

Shrimp   You're joking. *Penguin*-man?

Duchess   One sees what it means, of course. One has simply never heard it.

Another silvery laugh, echoed by the clan.

Shrimp   Well, blow me down. She's never heard of a penguin-man. (*Heartily, nudging* **Madame Vidauban**.)

That's a good one. A Duchess, never heard of a penguin-man.

Madame Vidauban (*after a moment's pause, nudging the next lady along*)   That's a good one. A Duchess, never heard of a penguin-man.

Shrimp   I mean, what else would you call them?

Madame Vidauban   We call them that all the time, in Paris. Don't we, Roy?

Vidauban   Oh. Er, rather.

Émile *brings a glass of water on a salver.*

Duchess   Well, well, how very . . . (*Looking at* **Émile** *through her lorgnette.*) So *you're* a penguin-man? (*Taking the glass.*) One does see that.

Émile (*aside, as he leaves*)   'One does see that.'

Duchess   Paris seems so far away sometimes. But never mind. You must meet one's son. (*Calling.*) Guy.

The **Duke** *appears.*

Duke   Yes, Mama?

Shrimp   You're joking! This grown-up young man, your son?

Duke   One certainly is.

Duchess   He certainly is.

Shrimp   Well, well, well.

Duchess   One insists on one thing: he's to spend some time in Paris, find out where his talents lie.

The **Duke** *flashes the audience a roguish look: he thinks he knows.*

Madame Vidauban   Where do his talents lie?

Duchess   Without experience, one hardly knows.

The **Duke** *looks innocent.*

Duchess Unfortunately, he *has* no experience.

The **Duke** *makes a face.*

Shrimp (*aside*) Another half-wit.

Duchess One has a *glimmering*. He could be a writer.

Madame Vidauban Of course, a writer.

Shrimp He *looks* like a writer.

Duchess And after all, we *all* know how to *write*.

Shrimp Blimey, yes.

Duchess The only thing is . . . Paris. He's such an innocent, and in a year he comes into such an enormous fortune . . .

Shrimp *Does* he?

Duchess The poor boy's *delicate*. And not only that . . . (*Aside, so that the* **Duke** *can't hear.*) . . . one's afraid he's growing rather interested in . . . you do understand.

Shrimp Oh, yes.

Duchess They do, doncha know? Boys do.

Shrimp Oh, they do.

Duchess And if he should . . . I mean, the wrong sort of gel . . . *imagine* . . .

Shrimp (*affecting horror*) Phew. Blimey.

Duchess He'd be gorn, entirely gorn.

Shrimp Don't get in a state.

Duchess One *worries* so.

Shrimp Your glass is empty. Let me take it for you.

She ogles the **Duke**, *who has begun to hover.*

Duchess No, please, my dear. That's what *penguin-men* are for.

Shrimp   My pleasure. Really.

*She takes the glass and flirts her way outrageously past the **Duke**, who totters to lean on a chair-back. **Shrimp** goes to the buffet. The **Duchess** has missed all this byplay.*

Duchess (*to **Madame Vidauban***)   What a delightful young woman.

Madame Vidauban   Delightful.

Shrimp *returns from the buffet, and tickles the **Duke** in passing. He giggles, foolishly.*

Shrimp (*to him*)   Aren't you the sly one?

Duchess   And so refined.

Madame Vidauban   Oh yes.

Shrimp *returns to the group, the picture of innocence, leaving the **Duke** goggling.*

Shrimp   There you are, Duchess.

Duchess   My dear, how kind.

Shrimp   My treat. (*Looking sideways at the **Duke**.*) I enjoyed myself.

Duchess   Too kind.

*The **Duke** rushes out on to the terrace. **Shrimp** shrugs.*

Shrimp (*aside*)   Half-wit.

Duchess   One's overwhelmed.

*Enter **Mayor** and **Petypon**.*

Mayor   So *that's* a Watteau.

Petypon (*distracted, trying to find **Shrimp***)   Oh, yes. All of it, entirely.

*He sees her leaning over the back of the **Duchess**'s chair, talking animatedly.*

Petypon My God.

He rushes up and gives her a sharp slap on the bottom.

Shrimp (*starting up*) Pig.

Duchess (*astonished*) Pardon?

Shrimp No, no, my husband. Excuse me a moment.

Duchess Of course, my dear.

Shrimp (*to* **Petypon**) *Now* what?

Petypon You're mad. That Duchess is a *Duchess*.

Shrimp I know she's a Duchess.

Petypon What've you said to her? And how have you *said* it?

Shrimp What's that to you? I do what I like. And I say what I like. If you don't like it . . .

She does a high-kick over a chair.

'Houp-la. This one's for me.'

The room falls silent.

Petypon Oh.

Everyone Ah.

Shrimp (*realising what she has done*) Ooh.

Petypon Ah well, it had to happen.

General (*enraptured*) I say. Ain't she *marvellous*? (*Imitating her.*) 'Houp-la. This one's for me.'

Petypon *seizes the opportunity, and rushes from guest to guest.*

Petypon It's the latest craze. In Paris. Everyone's doing it. You see it everywhere. 'Houp-la . . .'

He tries, and fails.

Shrimp That's right. Everyone's doing it.

Everyone   They *are?*

Petypon   The Prince of Wales started it. The British Prince of Wales.

Shrimp   They're all at it now.

Everyone (*in a confused murmur*)   How strange. I say. What a curious idea. (*Etc.*)

Petypon (*suddenly inspired*)   Isn't that right, Madame Vidauban?

Madame Vidauban   Pardon? (*With conviction.*) Yes, that's right, that's right.

Petypon (*to the others*)   There you are.

General astonishment.

Madame Hautignol (*to* **Madame Vidauban**)   You *knew* about it?

Madame Vidauban (*unruffled*)   Well, naturally I knew.

Madame Ponant   *I've* never seen you do it.

Madame Vidauban   Never seen me . . . ? I never stop. I do it all the time. Don't I, Roy?

Vidauban (*with great conviction*)   Yes, m'dear.

Madame Vidauban   Never seen me do it? Well, well, well.

She does a high-kick over a chair.

'Houp-la. This one's for me.'

Everyone   Oh.

Petypon   Phew.

Shrimp (*hopping about, as delighted as a child*)   She did it, she did it.

Petypon (*catching hold of her*)   All right. That's enough.

Mayor (*aside to his wife*) There, Liliane. That's what I meant. Little things like that. Paris trifles. Learn them. Look carefully, and learn.

Mayoress Oh, yes, I will.

She takes a chair and practises. The whole room follows suit. Then there is a distant fanfare and brass band music. Everyone stops.

Everyone What's that? What's happening?

General Fire Brigade Band. Émile said they'd arrived. Ladies and gentlemen, outside. Terrace. Concert.

Everyone makes for the terrace. The **General** *goes up to* **Petypon**, *who is with* **Shrimp** *at the buffet, and takes his arm.*

General Come on, come on.

Petypon (*resisting*) The thing is, Uncle Charles, I . . .

General Yes, yes: your wife. Tell you one thing, she must be sick of this. Jealous husband. Sick of it. Come *along.*

He pushes him to the exit, and while getting his hat, notices the **Mayoress**, *still practising high-kicks. He starts clapping.*

General Bravo, hey, bravo.

Mayoress (*startled*) Oh.

She rushes out. The **General** *and* **Petypon** *follow. No one is left but the* **Duke** *and* **Shrimp**. *He's extremely apprehensive.*

Shrimp Kiss me.

Duke Eh?

Shrimp Kiss me, dummy.

Duke (*absolutely terrified*) Oh. Er. I.

After a moment's hesitation, he goes to peck her on the cheek, but at the last moment, she turns her head and delivers a short but passionate kiss full on the lips. He starts, at first with anguish, then with appreciation.

Shrimp There you are. That didn't hurt.

Duke Oh no.

Shrimp I could really *go* for you.

Duke You could?

Shrimp Come and see me in Paris.

Duke But your husband...

Shrimp Don't worry about him.

She leads him to a sofa, and sits.

It won't bite you.

Duke What won't?

She pulls him to sit.

Shrimp Sit closer, closer.

She rocks him like a baby.

See? You like it.

Duke Oh yes.

Shrimp Show me how much, then. Kiss me, dummy.

Duke Rather!

He kisses her neck greedily.

Shrimp I knew you'd like it.

Enter **Petypon**.

Petypon Arg!

Duke (*struggling to stand up*) It's your husband. Let go.

Shrimp (*holding on*) Never mind him.

Duke Let me *go*.

He jerks free. **Petypon** *confronts* **Shrimp**.

Petypon Suppose someone else had seen you?

Duke (*aside, astonished*) I say!

Shrimp Don't start again.

Petypon This is how to behave, is it? Sprawling with Dukes all over the sofa.

Shrimp Where d'you want us to sprawl?

Petypon Nowhere. Look, in Paris, do what you like. But for heaven's sake, down here, behave yourself.

Shrimp *shrugs.*

Duke (*aside*) Stand up to him. Be masterful. (*As* **Petypon** *approaches.*) Eek!

Petypon Your Grace, I understand. She's a woman, you're a . . . man. You're young, she's pretty. In Paris, there'll be nothing to stop you. But down here: suppose the General, or anyone else but me . . .

Duke What? Oh. Rather. Rather. (*To* **Shrimp**.) He has got a point.

Shrimp He's a gorilla.

Petypon That's not fair. Your Grace, I appeal to you. Am I a gorilla?

Duke (*to* **Shrimp**) That is a bit strong. I mean, a gorilla.

Petypon There, you see? The Duke agrees with me.

Shrimp He knows nothing about gorillas.

Petypon He knows everything about gorillas. Shh! Someone's coming.

He goes to look.

My God, Gabrielle. It's Gabrielle.

He rushes to **Shrimp** *and starts pulling her towards the terrace.*

Petypon Come on, come on. Come *on.*

Shrimp What's the matter now?

Petypon Never mind. Come *on*.

Shrimp (*blowing kisses to the* **Duke**) See you later, sweetie.

Petypon Never mind that. Come *on*.

Exeunt.

Duke Odd fellow. Never mind. Masterful, eh? I must tell Mama. 'Get in with the wrong sort of gel . . .' If she could see me now!

Enter **Gabrielle**, *preceded by* **Émile** *with her suitcase.*

Gabrielle Thank you, Émile. Put that in my room, will you?

Émile Which room, Madame? All the rooms are taken, Madame.

Gabrielle Of course they are. And one of them's taken by Madame Petypon.

Émile Oh yes, Madame.

Gabrielle Well, put the case in there.

Émile Whatever you say, Madame.

Exit.

Duke (*hugging himself*) One glance. They can always tell . . .

He sees **Gabrielle**.

Duke I say. Sorry.

Gabrielle No, no. *I'm* sorry. I've just got off the train. I haven't had time to change.

Duke Oh, not on *my* account.

Gabrielle The General's here.

The brass band music gets louder.

Duke Oh, is he? I mean, he is. Outside. But after he's been outside, he'll be . . . inside.

Gabrielle I'll go and change.

Exit.

Duke The thing is . . . oh, she's gone. What a funny woman.

*Outside, on the terrace, a line of **Guests** has formed, backs to the audience. We can see the **Firemen**'s helmets, and their banner, and nothing else. They are watching the **General**, out of our sight in the garden. The band music ends, and he clears his throat.*

General Errrrrhmph! Harrmmmph! Gentlemen. First, Second Auxiliary Volunteer Fire Brigades. Fine body of men. Old soldier, heart swells with pride. Flag, don't you know. Flag of honour, fluttering, band, er, banding. As Napoleon said, Battle of . . . wherever it was . . . No, never mind. Point is: pride, respect, gratitude. Brass bands, firemen, backbone of the country. Well done, hey? Keep up good work, and, um, carry on. That's the ticket. Carry on and as you were. What, hey?

Cheers and applause.

Firemen Three cheers for the happy couple! Hurrah, hurrah, hurrah.

General Beer, cider. In the kitchen.

Firemen Three cheers for the General! Hurrah, hurrah, hurrah.

General Later. Play again later. Now: kitchen. At the double.

*The company breaks up. The clan of **Ladies** moves indoors, followed by the **General** and his **Officers**, and the **Curé**.*

Madame Ponant That was charming.

Madame Virette Exquisite.

Madame Claux   Quite delightful.

She high-kicks over the nearest chair.

'Houp-la! This one's for me!'

Everyone   Bravo!

Madame Claux   If it's good enough for Paris . . .

General   Anyone seen my nieces?

Guérissac   Sir, in the rose-garden. Madame Petypon was walking with Mamzelle Clémentine.

General   Showing her ropes. Hey? Paris ropes?

Curé   General Petypon, I wonder . . . it did occur to me . . .

General   Occurred? What occurred?

Curé   Apparently Madame Petypon is an excellent musician.

General   That so, hey?

Curé   She tells me she often sings.

Madame Vidauban   Oh, we *must* ask her.

Madame Ponant   Delightful.

Madame Hautignol   Just a verse or two . . .

General   Good idea. Soon as she comes in, I'll ask her.

Everyone   Bravo, bravo!

They all talk animatedly. Enter **Gabrielle**. *She has changed out of her travelling clothes. She doesn't see the* **General**, *he doesn't see her.*

Gabrielle   That's better. Now, where's the General?

Madame Ponant   My dear General, *another* guest. Do introduce us.

General   Who to?

Madame Ponant That lady, there.

General Good Gad. *Her* again.

Gabrielle (*to the* **Officers**) Gentlemen, have you seen the General?

Chamerot The General?

General Why *here*?

Guérissac He's over there.

Gabrielle Ah, so he is.

General Invited? Never.

Gabrielle (*excitedly, running to him*) Oh, General.

General Kind of yer.

Gabrielle I'm sorry I'm so late. I had to change trains . . . I'd no idea it was *this* afternoon . . .

General Sorry, I'm sure.

Gabrielle I had them take my cases right up.

General *Pardon*? (*Aside, to the* **Ladies**.) She's not quite . . .

Gabrielle My husband sends his apologies. Some kind of emergency. Deep apologies.

General (*half to the* **Ladies**, *half to her*) Apologies, hey? Husband, hey? No one else available?

Gabrielle Who d'you mean?

General Ha ha! I think you know. (*To the* **Ladies**.) I think she knows.

Enter the **Duchess** *and the* **Mayor**.

Gabrielle I felt I had to come on ahead. To be at your side. Ghosts or no ghosts, my simple duty.

General Ghosts. Yes. You believe in ghosts.

Gabrielle   I'm here, that's the main thing. (*Drawing him to one side.*) General . . .

General   Madame?

Gabrielle (*in a low voice*)   Won't you introduce me?

General   What? Oh. Pleasure.

He goes towards the **Ladies**, *saying aside*:

Thing is, what's her *name*? Her *name*? (*To the* **Ladies**, *aside, while* **Gabrielle** *neatens herself, ready for the introduction.*) Ladies, like you to meet . . . Thing is, don't ask her name. Can't remember. Don't like to ask, some people annoyed to be asked. All I know is: friend of my niece, doncha know, my niece.

Madame Vidauban   A lady from Paris?

General   That's the fellah.

Ladies (*rising*)   We'd be delighted.

Madame Vidauban   Charmed.

The **Ladies** *line up to be introduced.*

General   Ladies, allow me . . . (*Quickly.*) Madame Whatever-her-wretched-name-is.

Madame Vidauban   Pardon?

General (*aside to her*)   I *told* you. (*Aloud.*) Madame Vidauban.

Madame Vidauban   Enchanted.

Gabrielle   Delighted.

Madame Vidauban *high-kicks over a convenient chair.*

Madame Vidauban   'Houp-la! This one's for me!'

Gabrielle   Good gracious!

The **General** *brings forward the* **Mayoress**.

General Lady Mayoress.

Mayoress (*timidly*) Madame, enchanted.

Gabrielle Delighted.

Mayoress (*high-kicking ineptly*) 'Houp-la! This one's for me!'

The line moves up one place.

Gabrielle (*meanwhile*) Two of them?

General Madame Hautignol.

Gabrielle Madame.

Madame Hautignol Madame, delighted.

Gabrielle (*aside*) Will she . . . ?

Madame Hautignol (*high-kicking*) 'Houp-la! This one's for me!'

Gabrielle (*aside*) It's an old country custom. (*Aloud.*) Thank you, Madame.

General Madame Virette, Madame Claux.

Gabrielle Mesdames.

Mesdames Claux *and* **Virette** (*together*) Madame.

They both high-kick over the same chair, from opposite sides, and land each other hefty kicks.

'Houp-la! This one's . . .' Ow!

Madame Virette I do beg your pardon.

Madame Claux My fault entirely.

Madame Virette I hope I didn't hurt you.

Madame Claux It was nothing . . .

Gabrielle (*aside*) You never see that in Paris.

General Last but not least, Canon.

Curé Madame, I'm honoured.

Gabrielle No Father, the honour's mine.

Curé (*high-kicking*) 'Houp-la! This one's for me!'

*He joins the **Ladies**, who congratulate him.*

Gabrielle (*aside*) Perhaps he started it.

*She crosses to the **Ladies**.*

Gabrielle You must excuse me, ladies. The train . . . I had to change trains . . .

General Yes, yes, we know.

*He notices the **Duchess**, talking to the **Mayor**.*

General (*aside*) Ha-hey. Duchess. (*Aloud.*) Your Grace, allow me . . . Madame . . . er . . . (*As before.*) Whatever-her-wretched-name-is.

Duchess I'm sorry? I didn't quite catch –

General (*aside to her*) Tell you later. (*To **Gabrielle**.*) Her Grace, Duchess of Valmonté.

Gabrielle Your Grace, enchanted.

She high-kicks like the others.

'Houp-la. This one's for me.' (*Aside.*) When in Rome . . .

Ladies (*whispering aside*) Did you see that? You can see she's from Paris.

Madame Hautignol Thank goodness she knows we *know*.

Duchess The thing is, my dear, one's great age doesn't quite permit . . .

Gabrielle I'm sorry?

*The **Duchess** picks up enough of her skirt to reveal her ankles, then sketches a gentle circle of her foot above the ground.*

Duchess 'Houp-la. This one is indubitably mine.'

Gabrielle Oh, your Grace. Your Grace.

She turns to the **General**.

Gabrielle Now, don't worry about a *thing*. I'll take charge right away.

General What was that?

Gabrielle (*passing round the guests*) Please do sit down, ladies. Madame, please take a seat. If you'd be kind enough, Madame. Over here, Madame ... (*To the* **General**.) There! We're ready. We *have* arranged some music?

General Soon as my niece comes in, askin' her to sing.

Gabrielle Your niece. Charming girl. I can hardly wait to meet her.

General Feels same about you, I'm sure.

Gabrielle (*to the guests*) Ladies and gentlemen, please do be patient. When the General's niece comes in, we're asking her to sing.

Guests We know. We know already.

Gabrielle You know already?

General Course they know.

Gabrielle Well, never mind.

General (*aside*) Where does she think she is?

Gabrielle Will you take some refreshment, dear lady? And you, Madame, some small refreshment? And you, Madame ... ?

General What's she playing at?

Gabrielle *has reached* **Madame Vidauban**.

Gabrielle Dear lady, some refreshment? No, I insist ...

She turns, to find herself facing **Émile**, *who is coming from the buffet with a tray of glasses.*

Gabrielle   Footman. Over here. Bring the drinks over here. Be quick about it.

Émile *looks at the* **General** *for guidance.*

General   Pass 'em round. Have to humour 'em.

Émile *bows and passes them round.*

General (*aside*)   Unbelievable.

Footman (*at the door*)   Monsieur and Madame Tournoy.

The **General** *moves towards them, but* **Gabrielle** *beats him to it.*

General   Ah.

Gabrielle   Monsieur Tournoy, Madame Tournoy. How kind of you to come.

She high-kicks, to the bewilderment of the couple.

'Houp-la. This one's for me.' I'm sorry to be so late. I had to change trains.

Monsieur *and* **Madame Tournoy**   That's quite all right. Think nothing of it.

General (*to* **Gabrielle**)   Excuse me. D'you mind?

Gabrielle   I'm sorry. (*To the* **Tournoys**.) You haven't met the General. (*To him.*) Monsieur and Madame Tournoy.

General   Past belief.

Gabrielle   Now, Madame, if you'd like to follow me to the buffet. This way. And Monsieur Tournoy too.

General   I say, I think I –

Gabrielle   No, please. Leave everything to me.

General   Beginnin' to annoy me.

Gabrielle There we are.

General Look here, dear lady –

Gabrielle (*coquettishly*) Oh, please. 'Dear lady.' Don't call me 'dear lady'.

General What, then?

Gabrielle (*flirting*) Well, that's up to you. For example: what do you call your niece?

General What? hey? 'Niece.'

Gabrielle All right, then, call *me* niece. That'll be perfect. And I'll call you Uncle Charles.

General What?

Gabrielle *shakes his hand.*

Gabrielle Good afternoon, Uncle Charles.

She kisses one cheek.

Dear Uncle Charles.

She kisses his other cheek, then goes to join the **Ladies**.

General (*aside*) Ought to be put away.

Clémentine *and* **Shrimp** *come in from the garden, arm in arm.*

General Ah, there you are. Where have you been?

Clémentine I was picking up tips, Uncle Charles.

Shrimp She was picking up tips, Uncle Charles.

General Hope they worked.

Clémentine Oh yes, Uncle Charles.

General Har. (*To* **Shrimp**.) Now then. Surprise for you. Real surprise.

Shrimp A surprise? What is it?

She sees **Gabrielle**.

Shrimp (*aside*) Ma Petypon. *That's* what was wrong with him.

The **General** *is introducing* **Clémentine** *to* **Gabrielle**.

General Dear lady, my niece. Bride: Clémentine.

Gabrielle How delightful. Congratulations, my dear. Congratulations.

She kisses her forehead. **Clémentine** *is confused.*

General Now: sure I don't need to introduce you. *Other* niece . . .

He makes an expansive gesture, which could indicate either **Shrimp** *or* **Gabrielle**.

General Madame Petypon.

Before **Gabrielle** *can speak,* **Shrimp** *seizes her hand and shakes it hard.*

Shrimp Introduce *us*? That would be a joke. The General wants to know if he need introduce us. What a joke. *What* a joke. Is it really you?

Gabrielle Pardon?

Shrimp What a lovely surprise. How are you? How are you?

Gabrielle (*bewildered*) Fine, thank you . . . er . . . and you?

Shrimp Well, well, well. Let me look at you. How well you look. How very well. (*To the room in general.*) Doesn't she look *well*?

General *Looks* well enough.

Shrimp Can you imagine, since I saw you last, I can't tell you . . . Jean-Jacques has been *so* ill.

Gabrielle Has he?

Shrimp Fortunately he was better in time for the wedding.

Gabrielle Oh, good.

Shrimp You know, Suzanne.

Gabrielle Suzanne?

Shrimp She married Frédéric.

Gabrielle Who?

Shrimp Frédéric. *You* know.

Gabrielle I do?

Shrimp The fat one.

Gabrielle That one.

Shrimp That's right. She married him. Who'd have thought it? 'Frédéric' – you know what she was like. And then she married him. Just shows, you can never tell. Is everything all right? You've gone all faint. Would you like something to drink? Mauled orange? Iced coffee? Lemonade?

Gabrielle Bee-ee-eer.

Shrimp Coming up. Just make yourself at home.

General She has already.

Gabrielle (*utterly bewildered*) Thank you. Er, thank you. Thank you.

Shrimp I'll fetch it. Just a moment.

Gabrielle Yes. (*Aside, as* **Shrimp** *goes.*) Who on earth was that? 'Madame Petypon' the General said. But that's *my* name. He never said hers. I'll ask. (*Taking the* **General** *aside.*) Excuse me, General. Would you tell me something?

General Only have to arsk.

Gabrielle What's that lady's name?

General   What lady?

Gabrielle   The one you introduced to me just now.

General (*thinking this is a joke*)   Eh? Oh, har har. Very good. That's a good one.

Gabrielle   Pardon?

General   That's very good.

Everyone laughs, and he goes to the buffet to tell **Shrimp** *the joke.*

Gabrielle   What's the matter with everybody? (*To* **Madame Vidauban**.) Madame, excuse me . . .

Madame Vidauban   Yes, my dear?

Gabrielle   Could you please tell me the name of that lady? The one the General's just introduced me to?

Madame Vidauban   Ah. Hahaha. Very good. Very good indeed.

All laugh again. **Gabrielle**, *discountenanced, moves away.*

Gabrielle (*aside*)   I don't see what's so funny. (*To the* **Curé**, *who is chatting to the* **Mayor**.) Excuse me, Father, could you tell me . . .

Curé   It's all right, I heard. Hahaha, very good. Really excellent. Hahaha.

Guests   Hahaha. Very good. Hahaha.

Gabrielle   Thank you. (*Aside.*) What a simple sense of humour. (*To* **Émile**, *who is passing with his tray.*) Excuse me, Émile. Tell me that lady's name: the one talking to the General just now.

Émile   That's Madame Petypon.

He continues collecting glasses, moving away.

Gabrielle   Madame Petypon? The General's remarried? Lucien never told me.

She runs to **Shrimp**, *seizes her hands, swings her round and takes her away from anyone else.*

Gabrielle   Oh, come here. Let me look at you. Let me look at you.

Shrimp   What's the matter?

Gabrielle   Can you imagine, I never knew. Émile's just told me. You're Madame Petypon!

Shrimp   Pardon?

Gabrielle   The wife of General Petypon.

Shrimp   What?

Gabrielle (*without stopping*)   Auntie!

She kisses one cheek . . .

Shrimp   *What?*

Gabrielle   Auntie!

  . . . and the other one.

Shrimp   Lord, what larks.

Everyone   What on – ?

Gabrielle   How marvellous. I'm delighted. It's so exciting.

She kisses one cheek again . . .

Auntie!

  . . . and the other . . .

Auntie!

She runs to **Madame Vidauban**.

Gabrielle   Imagine, she's my auntie.

General (*moving to* **Shrimp**)   What's she calling you? Her aunt?

Shrimp That's right.

General It never ends. Just now she was calling me her uncle.

Ladies Was she?

Shrimp She's just trying to be friendly.

General You mean she's crazy.

Curé (*going to* **Gabrielle**) Dear lady, did you find what you were asking?

Gabrielle Yes thank you . . . Father.

General I can't stand it. I'm her uncle, you're her auntie, and he's . . . her father.

He takes **Guérissac** *to* **Gabrielle**.

General Dear lady . . .

Gabrielle Yes, Uncle?

General Don't you want to meet your second cousin twice removed?

Gabrielle That's not my cousin.

General (*to* **Guérissac**) Oh, what a shame. You're not her cousin. Some other time.

Gabrielle Oh, I forgot. Upstairs, I . . . I won't be a moment. Do excuse me.

She makes her way apologetically through the crowd.

Excuse me . . . I won't be a moment . . . Do excuse me . . .

Exit.

General Quite, quite, mad.

Everyone Extraordinary.

The **Curé** *tries to catch his eye.*

Curé   Ahem . . . ahem . . . General . . .

General   What's wrong with *him*?

The **Curé** *makes signs in* **Shrimp***'s direction.*

General   Oh yes. (*To her.*) I say, my dear, I ought to warn you: we've all been plotting.

Shrimp   What d'you mean?

General   Against *you*, my dear. We'd like you to sing something for us.

Everyone   Yes, yes.

Shrimp   You're joking. I can't sing.

Curé (*roguishly*)   Oh, now, now, you can.

Everyone   You can, you can.

Shrimp   I can't.

General   If we asked *very* nicely?

Shrimp   I didn't bring any music.

Everyone (*disappointed*)   Oh.

Clémentine   No, cousin, you did. I saw you carrying it this morning.

Shrimp   Oh, how could you?

Duke   Dear Madame, please sing us something.

Shrimp   You'd like that, would you, Dukey?

Duke   Oh *yes*.

Shrimp   Well, if *you* ask so nicely . . .

Duke (*radiant*)   Oh, Madame.

Shrimp   All right. But I must have my music.

Clémentine   I'll fetch it. Where did you put it?

Shrimp   Silly, in the *music* room.

Clémentine   I won't be a moment.

Exit. The **Footmen** *start arranging chairs.*

General (*to the* **Officers**)   Come on, lend a hand, you chaps: save a bit of time.

Enter **Petypon** *breathlessly.*

Petypon   Phew. That's that.

Shrimp *drags him aside.*

Shrimp   Never mind 'that's that'. Your *wife's* here.

Petypon   I know that.

Shrimp   What?

Petypon   I've just locked her in.

Shrimp   Eh?

Petypon   I saw her going into the bedroom; the key was outside, so: flim, flam, double-locked.

Shrimp   What good will that do?

Petypon   It gives me time. And boy, do I need time.

Enter **Clémentine**.

Clémentine   Here's your music, cousin.

Everyone   Bravo, bravo.

Petypon   What now? What music? What're you doing now?

Shrimp (*as she opens her case*)   They want me to sing something.

Petypon   You're mad. You can't.

Shrimp   The Dukey asked *ever so* nicely.

She goes to the piano, **Petypon** *hard on her heels.*

Petypon   I don't care who asked you nicely. What're

you going to sing? Have you thought of that?

Shrimp (*leafing through sheet music*)   I don't know. What about 'She Was Only a Farmer's Daughter'?

Petypon   Have you gone raving mad?

Shrimp   I see what you mean. What about this, then?

Petypon   That's more like it.

Shrimp *waves the music.*

Shrimp   All right, who's tickling the ivories?

General   Er . . . Father?

Curé   No, no. I only . . . er, tickle the organ.

General   What d'you mean? If you can tickle one, you can tickle any of 'em.

Curé   I'd rather not.

General   Fair enough. (*To the assembled company.*) Does anyone here play the piano?

The **Duke** *indicates the* **Duchess**.

Duke   Mama *did* play for Caruso once.

Everyone   Ah.

General   Your Grace, you will oblige us?

Duchess   One will do one's best.

Everyone   Ah.

General   This way, your Grace.

Duchess (*taking his arm*)   Why, thank you.

Everyone   Bravo.

Patter of applause as they go to the piano. The **General** *sees* **Gabrielle**'s *travelling-case on it.*

General   Who left this here? (*Calling.*) Émile.

Émile   Yes, sir?

General   Take this away, confound it.

He throws him the case, and **Émile** *removes it. Meanwhile,*
Shrimp *has gone to the* **Duke**.

Shrimp (*huskily*)   You see, Dukey? See what I'd do for
you?

Petypon (*pulling her away*)   Yes, yes, all right, all right.

Duke (*to the whole room*)   Ain't she charmin'?

Thinking **Shrimp** *is still beside him, he turns to kiss her.*
Petypon *gets it.*

Duke   Oh.

Petypon   Thanks.

Duke   Ugh.

Petypon   Not *now*. People are watching.

Duke   I should think they are. (*Aside, as* **Petypon** *goes
with* **Shrimp** *to the piano.*) There's no other word for it,
she's charmin'. I say, she never gave me her address.

He goes to talk to **Shrimp**, *but* **Petypon** *is in the way. They
both step left and right to let the other pass, but remain in each
other's way.*

Duke   Oh, sorry.

Petypon   Did you want something?

Duke   No. That is, yes. You'll do just as well. What's
your address in Paris?

Petypon (*who has picked up a chair*)   My address? 66 *bis*
avenue Malesherbes. Why?

Duke   Why? Er ... (*Looking roguishly at* **Shrimp**.) I
thought I might call.

Petypon   Really? We'd be delighted.

Duke How kind.

He holds out his hand to be shaken. Absent-mindedly **Petypon**
holds out the chair. The **Duke** *shakes it and is left holding it.*
Petypon *returns to the piano.*

Duke (*aside, gleefully*) 66 *bis* avenue Malesherbes. She's as
good as mine!

Petypon I had a chair, just now.

Duke Oh, sorry. Thinking of something else.

He gives back the chair.

Petypon How generous.

The **Guests** *have taken their places, and* **Shrimp**, *having
finished giving instructions to the* **Duchess**, *faces them, music in
hand. She curtseys, and introduces the song.*

Shrimp 'My Little Pussy-cat'.

Everyone Oh. Sh. Aah.

Petypon (*aside*) Good grief. Not that.

The **Duchess** *plays an introduction.*

Shrimp (*singing*)
Alone in my attic room I sat.
I gazed at the twinkling stars above,
Stro-o-king my pussy-cat,
That looked up at me with eyes of love.
Stro-o-king my pussy-cat,
My darling little pussy-cat.

Everyone (*applauding*) Bravo. Charming. Delightful.

Petypon (*aside*) All right so far.

Shrimp (*like a music-hall chairman*) Sec-*ond*-ah Verse.
(*Singing.*)
Then my landlord, cruel and grim,
Came to see me one fine day,
To-oo-ook my cat with him,

Stole my pussy-cat away.
To-oo-ook my pussy-cat,
My darling little pussy-cat.

Everyone (*applauding*) Bravo, bravo.

Guérissac (*aside to* **Chamerot**) Are you thinkin' what
I'm thinkin'?

Chamerot If you're thinkin' what I'm thinkin', why yes
I am.

Madame Hautignol (*aside to* **Madame Ponant**) D'you
think this is Beethoven?

Madame Ponant Undoubtedly.

Madame Hautignol I thought it was.

Shrimp, *who has been spending this time conferring with the*
Duchess, *returns to her place.*

Shrimp *Last*-ah Verse.

Everyone (*pleased*) Ah.

Shrimp The sad one. (*Singing.*)
Lord, I pray you, from on high
Look down on my miseree;
Hee-hee-hear my piteous cry,
And send my pussy back to me.
Send me back my pussy-cat,
My darling little pussy-cat.

Everyone Aah. Bravo, bravo. What a delightful voice.
How well she sings. (*Etc.*)

General Well done, my dear.

Petypon Thank God that's over.

Duke (*low, to* **Shrimp**) That gave me a lot of pleasure.

Shrimp There's more where that came from.

Duke I say.

Shrimp You only have to ask, Dukey darling, you only have to ask.

Petypon That's quite enough of that.

Shrimp Can't you shut your cake-hole?

Petypon *collapses into a chair in despair. The* **Duchess** *comes up.*

Duchess Dear child, one can hardly put it into words. Your little song: so touching. That poor dear child with only her pussy-cat to love, and then to have it stolen away. So sad.

Shrimp (*trying not to laugh*) Oh, sad, yes, sad.

Duchess One was moved almost to tears. What colour was the pussy-cat?

Shrimp (*really not knowing where to look*) Pardon?

Guests Yes, yes. What colour was it? Her pussy-cat, what colour?

Shrimp I . . . (*She can't contain her laughter any longer.*) Hahahaha. That's a good one. What colour. Hahahaha.

Everyone (*astonished*) What's the matter? What's she laughing at?

Petypon (*aside, apprehensive*) Trouble brewing.

Shrimp Hahahaha. It's a good one. Hahahahaha. Hahahahaha. (*Carried away by her laughter.*) Stone the bloody crows.

Petypon Told you.

Stunned silence. **Everyone** *looks at everyone else, and murmurs can be heard: 'What did she say? What did she say?'* **Petypon** *tries desperately to save the day.*

Petypon It's the latest craze in Paris. Baroness Bayard started it.

Guests (*not convinced*)   Baroness Bayard? Really?

Petypon *is thinking fast. Suddenly, he says loudly*:

Petypon   All right. What next? We've had the singing, what else shall we have? What goes with singing?

General   Dancing, of course.

Shrimp   Oh yes, yes. Let's dance.

She runs for the piano.

A quadrille.

Everyone (*echoing*)   A quadrille.

Petypon (*grabbing* **Shrimp**)   Haven't you done enough?

Shrimp   I'm not going to dance. I'm going to play.

Petypon   Oh. Play.

Shrimp *goes to the* **Duchess** *at the piano.*

Duchess   Look, my dear: an album of dance music.

Shrimp (*sitting*)   You take the top end.

Petypon   Don't say another word.

Several guests   A quadrille. A quadrille.

Sets are formed as the **Guests** *prepare to dance. Most furniture has been cleared to the terrace.* **Chamerot** *suddenly slaps his forehead.*

Chamerot   Good lord, yes. Quadrille. Got it. I say, Guérissac.

Guérissac   Chamerot?

Chamerot   I've realised who she reminds me of: Shrimp, at the Folies-Bergère.

They glance quickly at her.

Guérissac   Good lord. Extraordinary.

Chamerot   You think so too?

Guérissac   It's impossible. Petypon . . . Shrimp . . . *married?*

Chamerot   But everything fits. The way she moves, the way she talks.

Guérissac   Well, Shrimp or no Shrimp, she's got what it takes.

Duke (*overhearing*)   Who has?

Chamerot   Madame Petypon. Don't you think she's a bit of a . . .

Duke (*coldly*)   I haven't the slightest idea.

He turns on his heel and leaves them as **Shrimp** *and the* **Duchess** *start to play.*

Chamerot   What's wrong with *him?*

Shrimp   Well, come on, everyone's waiting.

Guérissac *and* **Chamerot**   I say. Rather.

They run and join the other dancers. The introduction is played again, and the dancers pay respects to each other.

Shrimp   Ready, then?

Everyone   Ready.

The dancers are formed as follows: **Clémentine** *and the* **Mayor**, *with* **Guérissac** *and* **Madame Ponant**; **Chamerot** *and* **Madame Vidauban** *with* **Madame Claux** *and an* **Officer**. *Other quadrilles are on the terrace. The gentlemen, in the centre, promenade the ladies on their right arms. There follows an 'avant-deux' with* **Madame Claux** *and the* **Officer**, **Chamerot** *and* **Madame Vidauban**. *At this point,* **Émile** *enters, looking for someone. He sees* **Clémentine**, *and taking advantage as she begins her 'avant-deux', crosses behind her. He follows her steps at a respectful distance while addressing her loudly.*

Émile   The dressmaker's just brought the wedding dress, Mamzelle. Is there any message for her?

Clémentine *returns to her original position.*

Clémentine   No, that's all right.

Madame Ponant (*as she begins her 'avant-deux'*)   The wedding dress? Oh, could we have a look?

Ladies dancing the quadrille   Ooh yes. Yes please.

Clémentine (*on her 'avant-deux'*)   Of course. (*To* **Émile**.) When the dance is finished, fetch the dress and put it in there. (*She points offstage.*)

Émile   Yes, Miss.

Exit. The dance reaches the end of the first set.

Shrimp   Sec-*ond*-ah Set.

Everyone   Sec-*ond*-ah Set.

The new fours are: **Clémentine**, *the* **Mayor**, **Madame Claux** *and an* **Officer**; **Guérissac**, **Madame Ponant**, **Chamerot** *and* **Madame Vidauban**. *At the beginning of the second set they do an 'avant-quatre' in a stiff and wooden manner.* **Shrimp** *starts singing with the music.*

Shrimp   Tralala, tralala.

Petypon   That's enough.

Shrimp (*low voice*)   Shut up, you.

Petypon   Thanks.

Shrimp   Tralala. I used to *love* this dance. Not like them, though. Tralala. Come on, can't you. Liven it up a bit.

Petypon   Really.

Shrimp   Sh. (*To the dancers.*) You look as though you're at the dentist's, all of you. Have you swallowed your brollies, or something?

Petypon If you don't mind, less of the commentary.

Shrimp Can't I even talk now? Look at them. What a crowd of marionettes. (*To the* **Duchess**.) Go on by yourself. This is unbelievable.

She gets up to join the dancing. **Petypon** *grabs her wrist.*

Petypon No, no, *please*.

Shrimp Leave me *alone*.

She runs to the middle of the quadrille and until the end of the set, dances like a stage performer. **Everyone** *stops, astounded.*

Everyone Oh.

Petypon *rushes to her and tries to hide her, fanning the tails of his jacket to make himself broader.*

Petypon That's enough. Look, you . . . Er, darling, that's enough. For heaven's sake.

Shrimp *tosses her skirts over her head and goes upstage.*

Everyone Oh.

Petypon (*collapsing on a chair*) That's the absolute end.

He starts rushing round, as before.

It's the latest fashion in Paris. It was started by the Princess –

Ladies Not this time.

Petypon I know! A waltz. A waltz.

Shrimp *has returned to the piano.*

Shrimp All right, a waltz.

She leafs through the music.

Everyone A waltz.

General move as **Guests** *take their partners. The* **General** *goes to* **Petypon**.

Chamerot (*aside to* **Guérissac**) *Now* d'you believe me? *Now* d'you admit she's Shrimp?

Guérissac I'm stunned.

Chamerot It must be.

Everyone A waltz.

Shrimp *dances past* **Chamerot** *and* **Guérissac**.

Shrimp Don't you want to waltz?

Chamerot I say . . . Shrimp.

Shrimp (*instinctively*) Yes?

Chamerot Told you.

Shrimp Blast.

Guérissac Aha.

Shrimp Look, no tricks. For heaven's sake, no tricks. In Paris, anything you like, but not here, *please*.

Guérissac *and* **Chamerot** This isn't Paris, hey?

Shrimp Everyone, a waltz.

Everyone A waltz.

The two **Officers** *join the other dancers.* **Shrimp** *goes to the* **General**.

Shrimp Uncle Charles . . .

General No thanks. Bit past it.

He takes **Petypon** *by the arms and places him in the way.*

General Here, Lucien, you dance with her.

Shrimp (*taking* **Petypon**'s *wrist*) Good idea.

Petypon (*resisting*) I don't want to.

Everyone Go on.

Petypon *is forced to join in. The dance begins, and as the* *dancers head out to the terrace, the* **General** *follows and stops in the archway.*

General   Youth must have its fling! Enjoy yourselves.

He turns and sees **Corignon**, *who has entered.*

General   I say, the bridegroom.

Corignon (*saluting*)   General.

General   My dear fellow, bit late, aren't you? Your fiancée's just waltzed off into the garden.

Corignon (*clearly not that bothered*)   What a pity.

He goes to talk to the **Duchess**, *who is still playing. The* **General** *calls offstage*:

General   Clémentine ... I say, Clémentine ... It's no good. She can't hear me. (*To the* **Duchess**.) I say, your Grace, you can rest your fingers. There's no one left.

Duchess (*stopping*)   Good heavens, you're right.

General   Let's go and join the young ones.

Duchess   Gladly.

General   Corignon, you wait here. I'll send in your fiancée. I believe she's got a surprise for you. Won't say any more. No, no ...

Corignon   Sir, what do you mean?

General   Nuff said. You'll see. This way, your Grace.

He gives the **Duchess** *his arm, and exeunt.*

Corignon   A surprise. A pair of slippers she's embroidered. Something equally exciting. Oh, this marriage. *Why* did I have to see Shrimp again last night?

Enter **Clémentine**. *She stops on the threshold.*

Corignon   She's here. My dear Clémentine, I've been so longing to see you.

He kisses her hand gallantly.

Clémentine   Hallo there, er . . . cheeky.

Corignon   Beg pardon?

Clémentine (*embarrassed, lowering her eyes*)   Where the galloping gorgonzolas have you been all this time? What time d'you call this to turn up?

Corignon (*disbelieving*)   Good heavens.

Clémentine   Come here, let's have a look at you.

She sits on a chair, and pulls him on to her lap.

There we are. Isn't that comfy? Mmmmm.

She nuzzles his neck by the ear.

Corignon   I say, good gracious.

Clémentine   Likes that, does he? Well then . . .

She kisses him again. He breaks free.

Corignon   I've heard this before somewhere.

Clémentine   Who's a pretty boy, then?

She gets up and high-kicks over a chair.

'Houp-la. This one's for me.'

Corignon   I'm going mad. I'm seeing things. She thinks she's Shrimp now. Clémentine. Are you all right? Where did you pick all this up?

Clémentine   Aha. Mine to know and yours to find out, cheeky.

Corignon   You didn't learn *this* in Switzerland. Where did you get it from?

Clémentine   There. My cousin taught me.

She points to **Shrimp**, *who is standing in the doorway watching.*

Clémentine   Madame Petypon. She taught me.

Corignon   My God. Shrimp.

Shrimp   Well, cousin, how d'you like what she's been learning?

Corignon   You, here?

Clémentine   You've met her already?

Corignon   Yes. (*Quickly.*) No. (*Pause.*) That is . . .

Shrimp   We met at the photographer's.

Corignon   Please, darling, leave us alone for a moment. I've got to talk to . . . my cousin.

Clémentine   Go ahead, don't mind me.

Corignon   Thank you.

Clémentine (*high-kicking*)   'Houp-la. This one's for me.'

Corignon   Good grief.

Clémentine (*aside as she goes*)   I hope he likes the change in me.

Exit.

Corignon   What are *you* doing here?

Shrimp   What are *you* doing here?

Corignon   This is a respectable household.

Shrimp   Charming. I thought it would be fun to watch you getting married. In any case: you came down to be with your fiancée, I came down to be with the man who said he loved me.

Corignon   That's quite enough.

Shrimp   What's the matter? You're not embarrassed?

Corignon   Of course not. Embarrassed? Ha! Fact is, I was . . . er, fond of you once, and for that reason, if nothing else, if you'd the slightest –

Shrimp   But I haven't. Not the slightest. Not the slightest at all.

Corignon   How true that is!

Shrimp   I mean, what *is* the slightest? Have *I* ever flaunted my other lovers in *your* face? Have I? And today you don't feel ... 'er, fond' of me any more.

Corignon   I do. I mean I don't. I just don't know.

Shrimp   You're getting married, and you just don't know?

Corignon   Stop reminding me I'm getting married. You don't know what it feels like.

Shrimp (*low*)   'Houp-la. This one's for me.'

Corignon   I say, do you still love me?

Shrimp   I might.

Corignon   Just say the word, I'm yours.

Shrimp   I say. And what about Clémentine?

Corignon   D'you really think she loves me? She'll marry me for the same reason she'd marry anyone else ... because Uncle Charles said she had to.

Shrimp   That's true.

Corignon   How do *you* know?

Shrimp   She told me.

Corignon   Charming.

Shrimp   I asked her if she loved you, and she said, 'Oh no. Love doesn't come into it. It's just ... "Houp-la. This one's for me."'

Corignon   You're joking.

Shrimp   You must be the first husband in history who gets cross with his wife because she says he's hers.

Corignon Tell me: how can any marriage be happy when he doesn't love her and she doesn't love him?

Shrimp Say what you like, it's marriage.

Corignon Isn't it better – more *moral* – for two people who love each other to unite in freedom, than for two people to shackle themselves in a loveless marriage?

Shrimp All I am and all I've ever been: your answer.

Corignon We could be so happy together. Don't stop to think. No more discussion. Let's follow fate wherever it leads us. Will you be mine?

Shrimp You really mean it?

Corignon Mine for ever.

Shrimp It's a very long time.

Corignon Then don't let's waste it. Now! Let's go. Let's elope.

Shrimp All right: I'm game.

Corignon Ah.

Shrimp A coat, a shawl to hide my hair, we're off.

Corignon I'll write a note to the General, and tell him it's over.

Shrimp I'll tell Petypon to forward my luggage.

Corignon Have you seen a pen?

Shrimp Over there.

Corignon In a moment, I'll be yours for ever. Ah! With Clémentine that was just an empty phrase, with you it's . . . it's . . .

Shrimp Don't be long.

Corignon I won't.

Shrimp (*aside, with a high-kick*) 'Houp-la. This one's for me.'

Exit.

Corignon   God's will. He can't have sent me this
temptation to *resist*. No, he knows me too well for that.

He is about to leave, when **Gabrielle** *hurries in. They collide.*

Corignon   Frightfully sorry.

Gabrielle   I'm having a *ghastly* time.

Corignon (*trying to get past*)   I say. Oh dear. No, really.

Gabrielle   I went into my room. I shut the door. I
never even touched the lock.

Corignon   And quite right too, if I may say so. Now, if
you'll . . .

Gabrielle   And when I tried to get out, the door was
locked. Double-locked.

Corignon (*humouring her*)   Of course it was.

Gabrielle   The key turned on its own. I've been in
there for half an hour. No one heard. Then someone
came.

Corignon *suddenly snaps, and barks an order.*

Corignon   Ten . . . *shun!*

She comes bewilderedly to attention, he salutes and exit. Pause.

Gabrielle   He really wasn't interested. It's all very well
for the General to say ghosts don't exist. The whole
thing's . . . You can't tamper with the supernatural. Stay
calm, stay calm. What did you come in here for? Keys,
keys, the keys of the case.

She looks for her bag on the piano.

I'm sure I put my bag on the piano. Perhaps it's on the
floor.

She scrabbles. Enter **Petypon***.*

Petypon My *God*, what an evening. Erg, it's her!
Someone's let her out.

He leaps to put out all the lights.

Gabrielle (*startled*) What's happened?

Petypon (*aside*) Hide, hide . . . My God, bright
moonlight . . .

He ducks out of sight.

Gabrielle I can't see a thing. What are these shadows
so suddenly surrounding me?

Petypon If I duck behind the piano, I'll be invisible.

Gabrielle Don't be silly, Gabrielle. It's just a fuse. No
need to panic.

Petypon *trips and falls on to the piano keys.* **Gabrielle**
screams.

Gabrielle Aaaaaah.

Petypon Damn that piano stool.

He hides.

Gabrielle Who's there?

Silence.

Who's at the piano? No answer. I heard you. (*Pulling
herself together.*) Come on, Gabrielle, go and see.

Petypon *hits more chords.*

Gabrielle Aaaaah.

Petypon *starts playing 'chopsticks'.*

Gabrielle It's playing itself. It's haunted.

*She goes to the door, to be met by what looks like a tall white ghost
– in fact a mannequin wearing the wedding dress and carried by*

Émile. *He is followed by a string of dancing* **Guests**, *who go round her in formation and disappear out into the garden again.*

Gabrielle   Have mercy, spirits. Oh, have mercy.

Petypon *rushes to the bell, removes the cloth and places the bell over her head.*

Petypon (*in an other-worldly voice*)   Gabrielle ... Gabrielle ... This is your guardian angel. Harken to my voice, and obey my commands.

Gabrielle (*from inside the bell*)   The archangel.

Petypon   Under this protective shield you can brave the spirits. But to avoid disaster, leave this enchanted castle immediately. Take your bags and go, without a backward glance.

Gabrielle   Oh, thank you, thank you.

Petypon   Begone, and give *ye* thanks to God.

General (*off*)   Yes, yes. I'll see what's going on.

Petypon   Oh my God, not him now.

He hides behind the piano. Enter the **General**.

General   Who switched the damn lights off?

He switches them on again. **Gabrielle**, *with the bell on her head and its tasselled cover hanging down over her outstretched arms, is stumbling about.*

General   What the devil? Oh, the madwoman. Hey. What're you doing under there?

He tries to remove the bell.

Gabrielle   Leave me alone. Leave me alone.

General   Don't be ridiculous.

Gabrielle   Leave me alone.

General   This bell is *mine*. *Will* you give it back?

Gabrielle No. The archangel . . . the archangel . . .

She and the **General** *go out, struggling.* **Petypon** *emerges.*

Petypon At last I'm rid of her. That's one less precipice to fall over. Now, where's the other one?

Enter **Mongicourt**.

Mongicourt Ah, there you are.

Petypon What are *you* doing here?

Mongicourt Thank God I'm in time. My dear fellow, I've come all the way from Paris. I've come to warn you: catastrophe.

Petypon Really. Tell me. I'm ready for anything.

Mongicourt (*portentously*) Your . . . wife . . . is . . . here.

Petypon Don't ever do that again.

Mongicourt Pardon?

Petypon If that's all you came for, you really needn't have bothered.

Mongicourt You mean you knew?

Petypon Of course I knew. She's been here for hours. I've had the devil's own job getting rid of her.

Mongicourt You mean she . . . ? You mean you . . . ? Thank God. But how could I have *known*? She said she was leaving. I said to myself: 'I have to warn him.' I ran to the station. Caught the first train down. Jumped in. 'Thank God,' I thought, 'I'll get there before her.' Unfortunately, the first train down was a stopping train, so the second got here first. I should have known. As the Bible says, the first shall be last, and the last shall be –

Petypon For heaven's sake, not the Bible now.

Mongicourt But it's turned out all right?

Petypon You're joking. This is Shrimp. Every time she

opens her mouth she drops a clanger. Only you can help me now. Go and find the General. Tell him you've come to fetch me for an urgent operation, an emergency, and that no delay is possible. I'll tell him I'm sorry, whisk Shrimp away, and it'll all be over. (*Pushing him out.*) Go on, hurry up. You can still save me.

Mongicourt   Where's the General?

Petypon   In the garden, with the guests.

Mongicourt   All right, stop pushing. The trouble you get into . . .

Exit into the garden. Enter **Corignon**.

Corignon   Where the devil's Émile? There's a letter to deliver.

Petypon   Ah, Corignon.

Corignon   Ah, Petypon.

Petypon   I think I ought to warn you. (*Portentously.*) Shrimp's here.

Corignon (*entirely relaxed*)   Shrimp's here?

Petypon   Shrimp's here.

Corignon   I say, what larks.

Petypon   *Larks*? I wish she was *anywhere*.

Corignon   Very soon, she may be.

Petypon   I do hope so.

Corignon   Love to stop and chat. Fact is, in rather a hurry. I say, since you *are* here . . . wonder if you'd do a chap a favour.

Petypon   Me?

Corignon   Have to leave, dashed urgent. Would you mind . . . er, when you next see the General, would you give him this?

Petypon (*taking the letter*)   With pleasure.

Corignon   Dashed good of you.

Enter **Shrimp**, *dressed for travel, with a veil over her face.*

Corignon   Ah, there you are. Let's go.

Shrimp (*aside*)   My God, it's 'im!

She bends double, tottering like an old lady, taking **Corignon**'s *arm.*

Shrimp   Good afternoon, young man.

Petypon (*bowing*)   Good afternoon, Madame. (*Aside, as they leave.*) What a charming old lady. His grandmother, I expect.

Exeunt **Shrimp** *and* **Corignon**.

Petypon   How odd, sending the General a letter when he's staying in the same house. Army stuff, top secret, that'll be it.

Enter the **General**.

General   Dashed odd. You see Corignon? Fellow's disappeared.

Petypon   Ah, ha! Uncle Charles, this letter, top secret, nod and wink, nuff said, eh what?

He hands over the letter and steps out of range as the **General** *unseals it.*

General   For me? Well, if you say so. (*He glances through it.*) Good Gad!

Petypon   Gad?

General   Confound the fellow.

Petypon   What's the matter?

The **General** *loses control. (Feydeau's note: from here until the end of the act, he plays in a towering rage, at the top of his lungs.)*

General   The bounder. Elopes with his mistress, sends a
note to *tell* me. On his wedding day. Thunder and
lightning. Who does he think he is? My godson? Stuff and
nonsense. Émile!

Émile (*hurrying in*)   Yes, sir?

General   Captain Corignon. Have you seen the fellow?

Émile   Yes, sir, just now, getting into a carriage with
Madame Petypon.

Petypon   What was that?

General   What did you say? Madame Petypon? You
sure it was Corignon? Oh, never mind. Get out.

Exit **Émile**. *The* **General** *goes to shout at* **Petypon**.

General   Did you hear that? He's eloped with your
wife.

Petypon (*airily*)   If you say so.

General   If I say so? Is that all you can say? Not up to
me to say so. Up to you. Dash it, no cuckolds in this
family. And you're not going to be the first. Stuff and
nonsense. If I say so. Émile.

Enter **Émile**.

Émile   Yes, sir?

General   Quick. Pack bags. Mine, Doctor Petypon's.
Bring 'em. Now.

He turns him on his heel and shoos him out.

Émile (*as he escapes*)   Yes, sir.

Petypon   What are you doing?

General   What am I doing?

He grabs his lapels and shakes him.

D'you think I'm letting them get away? D'you think we're

not going after them? Wait here. Don't move. I'll see if I
can catch them. If I can't, you're coming with me.

He makes for the door, meets **Gabrielle**. *She is terrified.*

Gabrielle   Oh! General.

General (*without stopping*)   You leave me alone. No time
for madwomen now.

Exit.

Gabrielle   Lucien.

Petypon   You again.

Gabrielle   Thank God you're here.

Petypon   I'll explain later.

Gabrielle   Lucien, don't leave me. The house is
haunted.

Petypon (*pushing her towards an exit*)   Yes, yes, all right.
We'll be going in a minute. Calm yourself. Go on ahead,
I won't be a minute.

The **General** *returns.*

Petypon   Oh my God.

General   Too late, they've gone. Lucien, your wife's a
trollop.

Gabrielle   I *beg* your pardon?

She goes to the **General**, *turns him to face her and gives him a
resounding slap.*

Gabrielle   There.

General   Thunder and lightning.

Petypon   Ow.

Gabrielle   Trollop indeed!

Exit, furiously.

General   D'you know, that's the first time in my life a woman's ever done that to me. For no reason at all, at least.

Enter **Mongicourt**.

Mongicourt   Ah, there you are, General.

General   Yes, here I am. And you're responsible for the behaviour of your wife. You are? In that case, here!

He slaps him.

Mongicourt   Ow.

General   I expect you'll want satisfaction. Well, at your service. (*To* **Petypon**.) Come on, Lucien, we'll catch 'em yet.

Exit.

Petypon   I'm done for. Done for. Done for.

Exit.

Curtain.

Act Three

*Scene as for Act One. Enter **Gabrielle** in travelling clothes, followed by **Étienne**, who is carrying her bag.*

Gabrielle My husband *isn't* here?

Étienne He was, Madame, but he went out again. Just a moment ago. With his *hat* on.

Gabrielle He might at least have waited.

Doorbell, off.

That's probably him now.

Étienne I'll see, Madame.

Exit, leaving the door open.

Gabrielle What's he *doing*? Doesn't he care any more? He was there. He saw what happened. He could have raged, fumed, demanded satisfaction. Instead, he leaves me standing and goes off with the General on the earliest train.

*Enter **Étienne**.*

Gabrielle Was it my husband?

Étienne No, Madame. A young man who –

Gabrielle Oh, see what he wants. Unless it's urgent, I'm not at home.

Étienne Yes, Madame.

*Exit. **Gabrielle** goes towards her room.*

Gabrielle Visitors, now! The last thing I want.

*Exit into her room. At the same moment, **Étienne** and the **Duke** enter by the main door. The **Duke** is bright and eager, with a bunch of flowers. **Étienne** is vainly trying to keep him from coming in.*

Étienne   I'm sorry, Monsieur. Madame's only just arrived. She's exhausted. Unless it's really urgent –

Duke   Of course it's urgent. Tell her I'm here: the Duke of Valmonté.

Étienne   The Duke of . . . ?

Duke   Valmonté.

Étienne (*impressed*)   Ooh. I say.

Duke   What did you say?

Étienne   Nothing.

Duke   Madame's expecting me.

Étienne   Oh, no, Monsieur.

Duke   I'm sorry?

Étienne   She's expecting no one. She said so.

Duke   Exactly. (*Patiently.*) No one. That means *me*.

Étienne   I don't understand.

The **Duke** *gives him money.*

Duke   There.

Étienne   *Now* I understand. I'll tell her no one's here.

Exit.

Duke   That's the way to do it.

He walks about a bit, and admires himself in a hand-mirror.

H'm. Not bad. Pretty good, in fact. Oh, another spot. How did that get there?

He hears voices off, hurriedly puts the mirror away and picks up the bouquet.

Be *masterful!*

Gabrielle (*off*)   I thought I told you to say I was out.

Duke (*in eager anticipation*)   Rrrrr . . . (*As* **Gabrielle** *comes in with* **Étienne**.) Rats! It's the other one.

Étienne   He did say it was urgent, Madame.

Exit. **Gabrielle** *recognises the* **Duke**.

Gabrielle   Good heavens!

Duke (*frostily*)   Madame.

Gabrielle   The Duke of Valmonté?

Duke   Madame, in person.

Gabrielle   Oh good. Yes. Good.

They sit, nonplussed with each other.

You were at the reception.

Duke   Was I? Oh yes, I was. So were you. Er . . . I hope Madame Petypon is well.

Gabrielle   Very well, thank you. A little tired by the journey. Unpacking. Well.

Duke (*gazing at her closed door*)   How irritating.

Gabrielle (*aside*)   What's he looking at?

Duke   Er . . . she really is all right?

Gabrielle   Who is?

Duke   Madame Petypon.

Gabrielle   Ah. (*Aside.*) How annoying to be talked about as if I wasn't there. (*Aloud.*) Of course. Thank you for asking.

Duke   How kind.

Gabrielle (*after another embarrassed silence*)   I'm sorry, Monsieur. I really am rather busy.

Duke   You carry on, Madame. Don't mind me. Carry on, do please.

He turns and ignores her completely.

Gabrielle   No, I mean . . . I didn't . . . I can only spare a few moments.

Duke (*coldly*)   Kind, I'm sure. One mustn't waste one's time.

Gabrielle   I couldn't have put it better.

Duke   Exactly. (*After another awkward silence.*) Charming reception, hey?

Gabrielle   Oh, charming.

Duke   Delightful place, Touraine.

Gabrielle   Delightful. Yes.

Duke   The garden of *la France*.

Gabrielle   Is it?

Duke   Oh yes. (*Aside.*) I hope *she's* enjoying this. (*To her, holding out his bouquet.*) Excuse me, Madame.

Gabrielle (*thinking he is offering her flowers*)   Oh, thank you.

He snatches them back.

Duke   No.

Gabrielle   What d'you mean?

Duke   I was gesturing.

He gestures.

Gabrielle   Ah.

Duke   Does it take long, unpacking?

Gabrielle (*losing her temper*)   I've no idea. It depends. When you're not interrupted. I'm sorry, Monsieur, but I can't believe you came here simply to talk about unpacking.

Duke   Naturally I didn't.

Gabrielle Étienne said it was urgent.

Duke It is.

Gabrielle Well, what is it?

Duke I can't tell *you*.

Gabrielle *What?*

Duke No, no, I'm sorry. We'll talk about anything else, but it's no use expecting me to tell you what I came for.

Gabrielle I see. (*Aside.*) A lunatic. (*Aloud, humouring him.*) But in that case, Monsieur . . . why *are* you here?

Duke That, Madame, is *my* business.

Gabrielle Oh.

Duke It's getting late. Madame Petypon is obviously busy. I'd hate to disturb her. I'll come again some other time.

Gabrielle Really?

Duke Goodbye, Madame. Till another time. (*Aside.*) What a peculiar woman.

Exit.

Gabrielle What was all that about? He comes to tell me, urgently, that Touraine is the garden of *la France*. A lunatic. Raving.

Petypon *hurries in from his own room.*

Petypon Who was that at the door just now?

Gabrielle Lucien.

Petypon When did *you* arrive?

Gabrielle Ten minutes ago. Étienne said you'd gone out.

Petypon Well, I hadn't. Just to post a letter. (*Frostily.*) Aren't you ashamed of yourself?

Gabrielle   Why should *I* be ashamed?

Petypon   For what you did to Uncle Charles.

Gabrielle   *Me*, ashamed?

Petypon   Slapping your own uncle. Even if it is by marriage.

Gabrielle   You wanted me to *let* him insult me?

Petypon   It was an accident.

Gabrielle   He was paying me a compliment?

Petypon   What did he call you?

Gabrielle   Never mind what he called me. And what about Édouard? What had *he* done? You should've seen him on the train home. He was fuming, absolutely fuming. I suppose the General meant *his* slap to be a compliment?

Petypon   Of course he didn't. It's human nature, when someone slaps you, to want to slap someone back. It's natural.

Gabrielle   *You* were there. He could have slapped *you*.

Petypon   Why me?

Gabrielle   Well, obviously: Édouard's not my husband, you're my husband, so you get slapped.

Petypon   Thanks. I suppose I should have offered him my cheek.

Gabrielle   I wish I'd never gone there. All that way, just to be called a . . . well, called a . . .

Petypon   What made you think it was you he meant? You're not the only Madame Petypon.

Gabrielle   Which other one was it, then?

Petypon   How on earth should I know?

Gabrielle Unless . . .

Petypon What?

Gabrielle Unless he meant your *aunt*. He can't have been calling *her* a . . .

Petypon Of course he could. (*Aside, eyes to heaven.*) Sorry, Auntie!

Gabrielle She was *charming*. (*Pause.*) I mean, I did find her a little *odd*.

Petypon You've never met her.

Gabrielle Of course I've met her.

Petypon When?

Gabrielle Yesterday.

Petypon *What?*

Gabrielle The General introduced us.

Petypon He intro . . . (*Aside, trying to work it out.*) I don't follow this at all. She saw Auntie. Auntie died eight years ago. And the General introduced them. (*To her.*) Are you *sure* he . . .

Enter **Étienne***, carrying the* **Duke***'s flowers and a note.*

Étienne A letter and some flowers, Madame.

Gabrielle For me?

Petypon It's your birthday?

Gabrielle I don't think so.

Étienne It was the young man who was here just now. No one. He asked me to give these flowers to Madame Petypon in person. *And* the note.

Gabrielle What is it he *wants*?

Petypon Who is he?

Gabrielle Some lunatic.

Étienne The Duke of Valmonté.

Petypon *turns sharply, slapping him with the flowers.*

Petypon Good God.

Étienne That *hurt*.

Petypon *shoos him out, bundling the flowers into his arms.*

Petypon Get out. Go, now. Go.

Étienne (*huffily*) I'll put these in water.

Exit with the flowers. **Petypon** *tries to get to the note first, but* **Gabrielle** *has already opened it.*

Petypon *I'll* read that.

Gabrielle No, *I* will.

Petypon Now we're in trouble.

Gabrielle Oh.

Petypon What's the matter?

Gabrielle He *is* a lunatic. Look what he's written.

Petypon Tell me.

Gabrielle (*reading*) 'Dearest Madame, since your sorceress' voice enthralled my listening ears with those words of love, my heart thinks of naught but you.'

Petypon I say.

Gabrielle A love letter. To me. What does he *want?* (*Reading.*) 'Alack and alas! Why must shyness paralyse my tongue? It's not as if you didn't encourage me.'

Petypon (*snatching the letter*) Let me see that.

Gabrielle I've hardly met him.

Petypon (*reading*) 'I write to you to burn my boats. I'll return in a trice, and when I do, you'll find eloquence in my heart to match your passion for me. I kiss you, kiss you, kiss you . . .' (*Scandalised.*) I *say*.

Gabrielle Who does he think I am?

Petypon (*melodramatically*) Really, Gabrielle. At your age.

Gabrielle What did you say?

Petypon Turning the head of a boy like Valmonté. I'm ashamed of you.

Gabrielle I only said two sentences to him at Uncle Charles'. 'The General's not here? I'll see if they've taken up my luggage.' I can't see how *that* . . .

Petypon It's the way you say these things. Did you encourage him at all? (*Seductively.*) 'I'll see . . .' (*Wink.*) '. . . if they've taken up my luggage.' You can do *anything* with the way you say things.

Gabrielle But I didn't.

Petypon You can tell me. No smoke without fire.

Gabrielle I'm a non-smoker.

Petypon (*with a gesture*) That's as maybe. Haarumph! I won't have it, d'you hear? I'm putting my foot down. I forbid you to see him, ever again. When he comes again, I insist that you see him and tell him you won't be seeing him.

Gabrielle I *won't* be seeing him.

Petypon So I should think. Er, not. Haarumph. (*Aside.*) I think that was masterful enough.

Enter **Étienne**.

Étienne Doctor Mongicourt.

Petypon Here we go again.

Enter **Mongicourt**. *He's not pleased.*

Mongicourt Lucien, about time too.

Petypon What's the matter *now*? Just a moment. (*To* **Gabrielle**, *sweetly*.) Darling, excuse us, would you? A professional consultation . . .

Gabrielle Darling, of course. (*To* **Mongicourt**.) Édouard, I'll talk to you later.

Mongicourt (*furiously*) You most certainly will.

Exit **Gabrielle**. **Petypon** *escorts her to the door, all smiles, then closes it and rounds on* **Mongicourt**.

Petypon What are you *playing* at?

Mongicourt Me, playing at? *He's* your general. Have you forgotten what he did to me?

Petypon Oh, that.

Mongicourt 'Oh, that'? 'Oh, that'? He slapped me across the face. For nothing. Twice.

Petypon No, once. You do exaggerate.

Mongicourt I do *not* exaggerate.

Petypon Of course you do.

Mongicourt What does it matter how many times? D'you think I'm taking it lying down?

Petypon Oh, not a duel . . .

Mongicourt Of course a duel.

Petypon Oh, God.

Mongicourt What's that supposed to mean, 'Oh, dear'?

Petypon Not 'Oh, God', 'Oh, God'. I mean, he's my uncle. I can hardly . . . I can't be your second.

Mongicourt I don't want you to be my second.

Petypon You can't fight without a second.

Mongicourt Who said I was going to fight?

Petypon How can you have a duel without fighting?

Mongicourt *I'm* not having a duel. *You* are.

Petypon You want *me* to fight the General?

Mongicourt Naturally.

Petypon Because *he* slapped *you*?

Mongicourt She's *your* wife.

Petypon But he thinks she's *yours*.

Mongicourt And I'm fed up with it. I'm going to find him and tell him the truth.

Petypon Thanks. Just what I need.

Mongicourt Pardon?

Petypon Just when I'm almost out of it. Just when there's been no trouble so far.

Mongicourt You think there's been no trouble so far?

Petypon No trouble for *me*. Gabrielle suspects nothing. The General's happy. I've just written him a letter saying I've forgiven my wife, and we're off to Baden Baden this evening.

Mongicourt Pardon?

Petypon Baden. Baden Baden. We're going to get a telegram.

Mongicourt How d'you know you're going to get a telegram?

Petypon I wrote it.

Mongicourt What?

Petypon You have to make these things *convincing*.

Mongicourt I don't believe this.

Petypon Baden Baden. And you want to spoil it by blurting out the truth.

Mongicourt   I'm to put this slap in my pocket and forget about it?

Petypon   If you'd be so kind.

Mongicourt   I go all the way to Touraine for a slap in the face.

Petypon   How far d'you usually go?

Mongicourt   Don't be ridiculous.

Petypon   Good job you're not superstitious.

Mongicourt   What?

Petypon   It's uncanny. France is hardly *small*. Paris is here . . . Touraine's *here* . . . The middle of nowhere . . . You go all the way to the depths of nowhere, at the very moment there's a slap in the face flying about. Probably not meant for you at all. Some people are just unlucky. I mean, if you'd stayed at home . . .

Mongicourt   Have you quite finished?

Petypon   Now you want to betray your best friend. And all to avoid a little bit of fencing.

Mongicourt   I hate fencing.

Petypon   You're afraid he'll hit you. That's typical. If you thought *you'd* hit *him*, wild horses wouldn't stop you.

Mongicourt   I don't believe this.

Petypon   Trust me. They wouldn't.

Mongicourt   Phooey.

Petypon   Just because it's *your* skin that might get a hole in it. You're supposed to be my friend. There's nothing more to say. In fact, don't say *anything* to *anyone*.

Mongicourt   We'll see about that.

Petypon (*suddenly*) Shut up!

Mongicourt Now what?

General (*off*) My nephew's at home, is he? At the double, man!

Petypon It's him. Hide. It's him.

Mongicourt I'll tell him.

Petypon No, *I* will. Hide. I'll *tell* him.

Mongicourt You promise you'll fix it?

Petypon Trust me. Come *on*.

They both go into the bedroom. **Étienne** *shows in the* **General** *and* **Shrimp**. *The* **General** *carries duelling swords in a case.*

General Thank you. Now tell Doctor Petypon I'm here.

Étienne And Madame?

General Don't mention Madame. Just tell him the General's here.

Étienne (*glancing at the sword-case*) There'll be tears before bedtime.

Exit.

General Trust me. Know the fellah. Sort it out.

Shrimp He'll *throw* me out.

General Tell you what: I'll have a word before he sees you. Go in there. Time comes, I'll call you.

Shrimp Thanks, Uncle Charles.

Exit into another room.

General Big surprise in store.

Knock at **Gabrielle**'*s door, off.*

Come in.

Gabrielle *half opens the door and puts her head through.*

Gabrielle Have you finished your private talk?

General (*aside*) Good Gad, her again.

Gabrielle (*aside*) The General.

General (*aside*) Why is she always *here*?

Enter **Gabrielle**.

Gabrielle My dear Uncle Charles –

General Oh, no. Don't start. After last time.

Gabrielle Uncle Charles, it's not important.

General Have you *no* idea of the effect you have on people?

Gabrielle Uncle Charles, of course I do.

General And no more 'Uncle Charles'. From now on, *Mon général.*

Gabrielle You don't want me to be your niece any more?

General No, I don't. Once, might have considered it. But now: never.

Gabrielle If you only knew how sorry I am.

General About time, too.

Gabrielle I was upset. All those ghosts.

General Don't start again.

Gabrielle I'm not starting again.

General Look, bit of advice. Next time you see a ghost, pick up great big stick and thrash the fellow. Soon see the back of it. Nuff said.

Gabrielle Don't mock the other side.

General Other side, cha! You see things, and when you

see things, you do things, and then you're sorry.

Gabrielle   Oh, I am. I said I am.

Pause. The **General** *softens.*

General   All right. No offence taken. Nuff said.

Gabrielle   Thank you.

General   One condition, mind. Husband has to be sorry too. Own lips: has to say he's sorry.

Gabrielle   Don't worry, he will, he will.

General   *I* slapped *his* face, doncha know. Your husband.

Gabrielle   He didn't mention that.

General   Hardly something to boast of. Haarumph. Nothin' against the fellow . . .

Enter **Petypon**.

Petypon   Uncle Charles. (*Aside.*) Blast. Gabrielle.

General   Come on, come on. Been keeping me waiting.

Gabrielle   Lucien, darling, I've apologised to Uncle Charles. He's forgiven me.

Petypon   Oh yes?

General   Har, husband has to say sorry too.

Petypon   No question.

General   What say? *His* business, ain't it?

Petypon   Gabrielle, d'you mind if I have a word with Uncle Charles in private?

Gabrielle   No, no . . . (*As she goes.*) You never said he slapped you.

Petypon   Pardon? When?

Gabrielle   He's just told me so himself.

Petypon   You mean, when I was little.

Gabrielle   No, yesterday.

Petypon   What? Yesterday? The merest tap.

Gabrielle   Ah.

Petypon   I mean, he *is* my uncle.

Gabrielle   H'm.

Petypon   Come on, come on.

He shuts the door behind her. The **General** *has been watching, in some amusement.*

General   I don't believe it. Not possible. You're in love with her.

Petypon   Me? Her? Why?

General   Good heavens, man, every time I come I find her here. You know, if she was a little less ... ugly, she wouldn't be too bad.

Petypon (*not liking this*)   Uncle Charles.

General   Never mind. Lucien, come to talk to you of reconciliation.

Petypon   Pardon?

General   Nothin' between your wife and Corignon.

Petypon (*feigning doubt*)   I'm not so sure.

General   I am. Certain. So, come to tell you: forgive and forget.

Petypon   Aha. Uncle Charles, I agree with you entirely. So much so, I wrote this morning telling you I'd forgiven my wife, and we were leaving for Baden Baden this very evening.

General   I say. Good news. Just a moment ...

He goes to the curtains of the bedroom.

Petypon   Now what?

General   Won't be a moment.

Exit.

Petypon   Thank God I've got my health and strength.

Enter **General**, *ushering in* **Shrimp**.

General   This way, my dear. Don't be afraid.

Petypon   Argh!

General   Throw yourself into your husband's arms. He forgives you.

Shrimp (*going to embrace* **Petypon**)   Lucien!

Petypon   Not again. I never want to see her again. Take her away.

General   What're you talkin' about?

Petypon   Take her away. Away!

General   You gone raving mad?

Shrimp   Ah well, if that's how you feel ... I did it to please the General. But now I've had it up to here. You can keep your old bag, and bloody good luck to the pair of you.

General   Good Gad.

Petypon   Good grief.

Shrimp   Goodbye.

She makes to exit, but the **General** *stops her.*

General   No, child. Heaven's name. You'll be sorry later.

Shrimp   I fall over backwards to save his precious skin.

Petypon   Shhh, shhhh.

Shrimp   Never mind 'Shhh, shhhh'.

General   My child . . .

Shrimp   Count yourself lucky I'm respectable. Cause if I wasn't . . .

General   Look, I say, go back in there a moment, d'you mind?

Shrimp   Course I mind. I'm sick of going back in there.

General   Time comes, I'll call you.

Shrimp   Oh, all right. Just for you. I dunno. Why do people drink when they don't know what they're doing?

Exit.

General   What's the matter with you? Damn fool. Are you crazy or something? One minute you've forgiven her, on your way to Baden Baden. Then this.

Petypon   I'm sorry, Uncle Charles. After all that's happened. It just came over me.

General   All that's happened? Nothing's happened.

Petypon   You're absolutely right. Call her in, let's get it over and done with.

General   Funny way of putting it.

Petypon   Oh, entirely.

General   Well, then . . .

He makes to fetch **Shrimp**, *but* **Petypon** *pulls him back.*

General   What's the matter now? Let go, damn it. What're you *playin'* at?

Petypon   Nothing.

General   Damn fool way of goin' on.

Petypon   You don't . . .

General   Damn lucky you've got *me* to sort things out.

Étienne *appears at the door.*

Étienne   Monsieur, those two gentlemen are here again.

Petypon   Which two?

Étienne   Lieutenant Marollier, Monsieur Varlin. Something to do with Captain Corignon.

General   Aha.

Petypon   What?

General   I know all about it.

Petypon   All about what?

General   Your duel.

Petypon   What duel?

General   With Corignon. Told him you'd challenged him.

Petypon   I've done nothing of the kind.

General (*to* **Étienne**)   Ask 'em to wait. In the waiting-room. No, just a minute. That woman's in there. In the dining-room.

Petypon   Oh boy. Oh boy.

General (*to* **Étienne**)   Er . . . and tell Madame Petypon . . . (*Repeating the name with emphasis.*) Tell Madame Petypon that the General would like to see her in Doctor Petypon's examination room.

Petypon   You can't do that.

General   Do what I damn well please. (*To* **Étienne**.) Well? At the double.

Étienne   Oh, *yes.*

Exit.

Petypon   That's the giddy limit.

General (*picking up a sword*)   Soon get this sorted.

Petypon (*trying to dodge the sword-point*)   Pardon? Ow.

General   Careful, can't you? Get yourself killed before you start. That's *his* job.

Petypon   Look, Uncle Charles, it's nothing to fight about.

General (*feinting and parrying with the sword*)   Nothin' to fight about? Bounder needs a lesson. Superior officer: can't fight him. But *you* can. Injured husband, *you* can.

Petypon   Why does everybody keep trying to make me fight?

Mongicourt *sticks his head in.*

Mongicourt   Lucien.

Petypon (*rushing to him, hissing aside*)   I'm *dealing* with it. Get back in, I'm *dealing* with it.

Mongicourt   Get a move on.

Petypon   Get in. I'll tell you when.

He pushes him in, as the **General** *turns.*

General   Who was that?

Petypon   No one. A patient . . . getting impatient. He can wait. It's a waiting-room.

Gabrielle (*off*)   In my husband's examination room? Thank you, Étienne.

General   Someone's coming. Your wife. Now, none of that like last time.

Petypon (*aside, as* **Gabrielle** *enters*)   I knew this would happen.

General   Madwoman again.

Gabrielle   Uncle Charles, you wanted to see me?

General Quite the opposite.

Petypon That's right, the opposite. Go away. I mean, please. Darling . . .

General (*aside*) Now he calls her darlin'?

Gabrielle Étienne said Uncle Charles wanted to see me in your examination room.

General Course I didn't. Fellow's a fool.

He sits in the Ecstatic Chair.

Me, want to see Madame Mongi –

Petypon (*seeing him in the chair*) Aha.

Gabrielle What's he saying?

General – court. I told him to fetch Madame *Pety* –

He is rooted, as **Petypon** *pulls the handle.*

Petypon Phew.

Gabrielle What's happened?

She rushes to him.

Petypon What d'you mean?

She touches the **General** *and freezes also.*

Gabrielle Eek.

Pause.

Petypon I said, what d'you mean? Gabrielle! What are you doing?

He rushes forward, seizes her arm and freezes. Pause. **Étienne** *appears at the door.*

Étienne Lieutenant Marollier.

He waits three or four seconds for a response, then looks with astonishment at the group.

What are they *doing*? Monsieur . . . Madame . . . Oh!

Shock; ecstasy. He has touched **Gabrielle** *and is frozen. Pause. Enter* **Marollier**.

Marollier It's ridiculous, standing around in the hall. This isn't a dentist's. Good lord, there's someone here. I say, the General.

He salutes, talking to him.

Sir, frightfully sorry. Coming to see my uncle. Floor above. Wrong apartment. Sorry, I . . . Pardon? Sorry. Thought you said something, sir.

Pause. He goes closer.

What's wrong with them all? Statues. My God, they've turned to stone.

He runs to the door, shouting:

Help. Police. Help. Catastrophe. Police. Help.

Enter **Mongicourt**.

Mongicourt What's the matter? What on earth's the matter?

Marollier I don't know. Look at them.

He seizes **Gabrielle**'s *arm, and freezes.*

Mongicourt Good heavens, they forgot to put the gloves on. If only I'd a camera.

He pulls the release handle.

Come on. Upsy-daisy.

They jerk awake at the same instant, each one in ecstasy. The following five speeches are spoken and performed simultaneously:

Petypon (*dancing and singing*) London bridge is falling down.

Marollier My beloved is mine, tralala.

General   *Allons, enfants de la patrie* . . .

Gabrielle (*to* **Étienne**, *embracing*)   My dearest love, come
to my arms.

Étienne (*to* **Gabrielle**, *embracing*)   My dearest love, come
to my arms.

*All at once, they awake fully. The following four speeches are spoken
simultaneously:*

Petypon (*aside*)   What happened?

Gabrielle (*aside, in* **Étienne**'s *arms*)   Where am I?

Marollier (*aside*)   I'm going crazy.

General (*aside*)   What's goin' on?

Suddenly, they see each other.

All   Aargh!

Étienne, *still under the influence, is still holding* **Gabrielle**.

Étienne   My dearest love, my sweet . . .

He kisses her.

Gabrielle   Étienne, what are you doing?

Étienne   My God, it's a woman! My God, it's Madame!

He rushes for the door, pursued by **Gabrielle**.

Marollier   The General hasn't seen me. Get out of
here . . .

He pushes past **Gabrielle** *and escapes.*

Gabrielle   Oh, the brute.

Mongicourt (*to* **Petypon**)   Well, Lucien.

Petypon   How did *he* get here?

Mongicourt   Never mind. The General's here. (*To the*
General.) General . . .

Petypon   Later. Not now.

General (*coldly*)   Nothin' to say to *you*, sir. Seconds callin', say everythin'.

Mongicourt   This is ridiculous.

Petypon   No, it isn't. He's right.

General   Lucien, wait here. Let me fetch your wife.

Petypon (*trying to cover his utterance of 'wife'*)   Yes, yes. Go, go. Ha, ha.

General   Back in a moment.

Exit. **Gabrielle** *goes to* **Petypon**.

Gabrielle   *Who* did he say he was fetching?

Petypon   Not who, what. His pipe, his pipe.

Gabrielle   He distinctly said 'your wife'.

Petypon   That's right. *Yoorwife.* It's an African pipe. *Yoorwife.*

Gabrielle   Oh, really?

Petypon   You say: 'I'm just going to light up my *yoorwife.*'

He tries to hustle them off.

Come on, through here . . . this way . . . this way.

Mongicourt (*resisting*)   You haven't told him yet.

Petypon   You can't rush into these things.

General (*off*)   I promise he won't this time.

Petypon (*aside*)   Ye gods. (*Pushing the others out.*) This way. Come *on.* This way.

The following three speeches are spoken simultaneously:

Gabrielle   Why? Why?

Mongicourt No. No.

Petypon Go. Go.

*The **General** appears at the curtain.*

General Lucien...

Petypon Just a *minute*. (*To the others*.) Get *on* with you.

They all three disappear through the door, which closes.

General Now what? *We* come in, *he* rushes out.

*He ushers in **Shrimp**.*

General Come in, my child, come in. Promise he'll be kind. Affectionate. Back to normal.

Shrimp Oh, Uncle Charles, if it weren't for you...

*The **General** hugs her affectionately.*

General Now, now, no sentiment. Haarumph.

Shrimp You're so kind ... you always understand...

General What? Hey? Har. Oh, the devil! Give your old uncle a kiss.

Shrimp Oh yes, Uncle Charles.

She kisses him.

General (*overcome*) Oh, by Jove. By Jove, by Jove. By Jove, by Jove, by Jove. If only you weren't ... if I wasn't ... Oh, by Jove, by Jove, by Jove.

Shrimp That was fun.

General Oh, yes. If only ... By Jove, by Jove.

Shrimp I've always wanted a man like you. A man who really understands.

General What was that? He doesn't *understand*? I say!

Shrimp I'm nothing to him.

General   I *say*! Another woman, is there?

Shrimp   I don't want to talk about it.

General   I say, I say. No *wonder* you lost your head.

Shrimp   If I'd realised what it would lead to . . .

General   Poor innocent child. (*Taking her in his arms again.*) Happy homes. Broken up. Husband's heartlessness. Happens all the time.

He kisses her.

Shrimp   Oh, Uncle Charles.

She kisses him.

General   I say, by Jove, I say . . .

He breaks free reluctantly.

If only you weren't . . . Poor, dear child. Husband indifferent, another man's arms . . . I say, I say . . .

He kisses her.

We can't have that. (*Kiss.*) No, no, no, no, no, no. (*Kiss.*) This is what we'll do . . .

He leads her to the Ecstatic Chair.

Sit down here, will you?

She sits.

I'll talk to him. See what happens. If only you were . . . Thunder and lightnin'!

With this last, he thumps the back of the chair, and **Shrimp** *is transfixed. The* **General** *doesn't notice, goes to the door, turns.*

General   Don't move.

Exit. Pause. Enter **Étienne**.

Étienne   His Grace the Duke of Valmonté.

He shows in the **Duke**, *and exit. The* **Duke** *has a new bouquet.*

Duke   I hope I'll have more luck this time. It's bafflin'.
She asked me to come, and when I do she refuses to see
me. Absolutely bafflin'.

Suddenly he sees the ecstatic **Shrimp**.

Duke   Ooh! There she is. You were there all the time. I
was afraid you'd refuse to see me. You've no idea how
happy you've made me. Thought of nothing but you since
the minute I saw you. Told Mama I was coming to see
you. She told me to give you her regards. 'Give the gel
my regards,' just like that. What's the matter? What are
you looking at? What's she looking at? Madame . . . It's a
game. I warn you, Madame . . . if this is a game, two can
play at it. Madame, I *may* kiss you. Oh, you can smile.
Not joking. Masterful. Games of my own. Count to three.
One . . . two . . . You still won't answer? Fine then,
coming, ready or not. Three!

He kisses her and freezes in situ. The door is opened.

General (*off*)   In here, Lucien. Dammit, *in* here. (*As he
enters, backwards, beckoning* **Petypon**.) See sort of wife you
married. Picture of innocence . . . picture of . . .

He turns and sees the couple.

Oh.

Petypon   Who started the chair?

General   What the devil now?

Petypon   It's nothing. Watch.

He pulls the release lever. The **Duke** *and* **Shrimp** *awake.*

Duke } *simultaneously* { I'm a Duke, and I'll do as I please.
Shrimp }   { What a man. What a cutie-pie.

They kiss.

General (*loudly*)   WHAT IS GOIN' ON?

They separate in embarrassment.

Duke   I say.

Shrimp   Now what's happening?

Duke   The General!

He rushes into the bedroom.

General   Where did he spring from?

Shrimp   What happened?

Petypon   Nothing. It's the chair. When the handle's down and you sit in it, you go to sleep.

General   You don't say. Everyone?

Petypon   Everyone.

General   Heh. I wouldn't.

Petypon   You would.

General   Well, some other time. Children, brought you together again. As you oughter be. No explanations. No recriminations. Kiss and make up.

Petypon (*aside*)   There's nothing for it. (*Aloud.*) Oh darling, come to my loving arms.

General (*pushing* **Shrimp**)   Go on. Lovin' arms.

Shrimp (*exaggerating*)   Lu . . . cien.

She holds out her arms to him, huge. Enter **Gabrielle**.

Gabrielle   Oh.

Petypon (*aside*)   My God, my wife.

General (*aside*)   The madwoman.

But **Gabrielle** *goes to* **Shrimp**, *arms outstretched.*

Gabrielle   How *kind* of you to call.

Petypon (*aside*)   Eh?

Shrimp Yes, er, dearie.

Gabrielle I'm so happy to see you.

Petypon (*aside*) She's happy?

Gabrielle *kisses* **Shrimp**.

Gabrielle Auntie.

Petypon (*aside*) What was that?

Gabrielle Dear, dear Auntie.

General Completely potty.

Gabrielle What a lovely surprise. (*To* **Petypon**.) It's Auntie. (*To* **Shrimp**.) We *must* talk about what happened in Touraine.

Shrimp Ah.

Petypon We mustn't. No, we mustn't.

Gabrielle Auntie'll want to know.

Petypon She won't. And *I* certainly don't.

Gabrielle Oh, don't be so grumpy. (*To* **Shrimp**.) Come into my room. We won't disturb him there.

Petypon *bounds to stop them leaving.*

Petypon You can't!

Gabrielle Of course we can. You stay with Uncle Charles, I'll talk to Auntie. What's wrong with that? (*Eagerly*.) This way, Auntie. I've so much to tell you.

Petypon Wait a minute.

Shrimp I have to talk to my niece.

Exeunt.

Petypon I've had enough of this.

General Wants to make everyone a member of her family. Deuced peculiar.

Petypon Yes.

General Escaped loony. Never mind. Who cares about her?

Petypon (*aside*) Charming.

General You we're talkin' about. Don't know how glad I am ... you, your wife, in each other's arms at last.

Petypon My wi ... ? Oh, my wife.

General Damn fool you if you don't appreciate her. Pretty ... no, exquisite ... adorable ... Adorable, you fool.

He pokes **Petypon** *in the ribs.*

General Exquisite, you oaf. (*Poke.*) Delightful. (*Poke.*) And you go chasin' after someone else.

Petypon Uncle Charles, you seem quite fond of her yourself.

General Me? Hah. No secret. If she wasn't your wife ... or my niece ... 'Houp-la. This one's for me.' What, what?

Petypon Yes? What?

General What d'you mean, what? Oh, what? You mean if I ... if you ... I say! Make you my sole heir, in a flash, that's what.

Petypon What?

General What, what?

Petypon (*aside*) To think it's been so easy all along. (*Aloud.*) All right, Uncle Charles. I'll tell you. She isn't my wife.

General Ha, ha, ha.

Petypon Pardon?

General Damn funny. Ha, ha, ha. You are a card.

Petypon But Uncle Charles . . .

General You never stop. Ha, ha, ha. You never stop.

Étienne *appears.*

Étienne Monsieur . . .

General (*inspired*) Not your wife, eh? We'll see, we'll see. (*To* **Étienne**.) I say, chappie. Whose wife is Madame Petypon? (*To* **Petypon**.) Don't prompt the fellow.

Étienne The Doctor's wife. Doctor Petypon's wife.

General There. Told you.

Étienne (*aside*) *I* don't understand it.

Petypon (*aside*) What a man! Never believes a word you say, unless you're lying.

Étienne Monsieur, the gentlemen who arrived some time ago want to know if you've forgotten them.

General Course we haven't. Send 'em in.

Exit **Étienne**.

Petypon (*aside*) This is all I need.

General Piece of advice: keep your wife out of it.

Petypon Well, naturally.

General What d'you mean, 'Well, naturally'? You don't even know what I was going to say. Corignon's agreed. Keep reasons for the duel hush-hush.

Petypon Hush-hush? Good, good.

General Even seconds'll know nothin' about it.

Petypon Yes, yes.

General We'll tell 'em nothin'.

Petypon No, no.

General Reasons for duel: anything you like.

Petypon   Fine, fine.

General   *He* said ... *you* said ... doesn't matter.

Petypon   No, no.

General   General harassment ... annoyance ... no need to be precise.

Petypon   Good, good. (*Aside.*) Doesn't bother me. *I'm* not fighting.

General   I say!

Petypon   What's the matter now?

General   You've only got one second.

Petypon   Oh no.

General   Can't be both seconds myself.

Petypon   Oh, no. We'd better call it off.

General   Won't hear of it.

The **Duke** *appears, sees the* **General** *and tries to escape.*

Duke   Golly.

General   He'll do. I say, d'you mind?

Duke   You see, General, I –

General   All right. Won't eacher. You can be second second.

Duke   Second – ?

General   Second. Second *second*, man.

Duke   But.

General   No need to worry. Let me do talkin'. You agree.

Duke   Oh, I agree, I do agree. (*Aside.*) Why did I *come*.

Étienne (*at the door*)   Lieutenant Marollier and Monsieur Varlin.

General   Gentlemen . . .

They come in. **Petypon** *introduces them to the* **General** *and the* **Duke**.

Petypon   My seconds.

Marollier (*stiffly*)   *Mon général*, it was with pride that I learned I was to defend my principal's interests against a second of your importance. Sir, I shall be punctilious.

General   Should hope you will. And lookee here, while this duel's happenin' none of that '*Mon général*' rubbish. Equal gentlemen, each serving his principal . . .

Marollier   Yes, *mon général*. Trouble is, afterwards, you'll be a general again and I'll be a lieutenant.

General   Well spotted that man. But till then: equal. Equal.

Marollier (*introducing* **Varlin**)   Monsieur Varlin, the second second.

General   The Duke of –

He gestures to the **Duke**, *and accidentally slaps him.*

Duke   Ow.

General   Get out of the way, dammit.

Duke   I agree.

General   The Duke of Valmonté.

Duke   I do agree.

General   For heaven's sake put those flowers down.

Duke   Pardon?

General   Fightin' a *duel*, not flower bazaar.

Duke   Oh, I agree.

Varlin   Perhaps his Grace thinks he's the second at a marriage?

Marollier   Don't you start. Control yourself.

General   Please be seated, gentlemen.

Marollier   Thank you, *mon général*.

He and the **General** *sit.* **Varlin** *looks for a chair. The* **General** *gestures at the Ecstatic Chair.*

General   There's one. Arms open to greetcha.

Varlin   No thanks.

He finds a chair and sits. Only the **Duke** *is now standing.*

General   Gentlemen, sure you know ... (*To the* **Duke**.) Sit down, can't you? Damn fool.

The **Duke** *sits, sulkily.*

General   Now, gentlemen, sure you know how all this started. Nothin' serious. Know the kind of thing. 'Krug's best champagne money can buy.' 'No it ain't.' 'Yes it is.' That kind of thing.

Marollier   Exactly. Your principal goes for Krug, ours swears by Veuve Clicquot.

General   Does, does he?

Marollier   Ev-er-y time.

Petypon   Do I?

General   There you are, then. Seems to me my chappie's injured party. No question.

Marollier   Quite right. Except ...

General   Except?

Marollier   It's entirely different.

General   Quite right *and* different? Explain yourself.

Marollier   *My* principal is the injured party.

General   *Your* principal?

Marollier   He was the one offended by what your principal said.

General   More fool him, then. Remark wasn't even addressed to him. Looking for an excuse to insult *my* principal.

Marollier   But *my* principal . . .

General   *My* principal . . .

Marollier   *Mon général* . . .

General   Never mind '*Mon général*'.

Marollier   But . . .

General (*getting up*)   As you were! How dare you? Lieutenant contradict a general?

Marollier (*getting up*)   I'm sorry, *mon général*.

General   Have you cashiered. Damn fool.

Petypon   None of it matters, in any case. I take it back, whatever I said. No need for a duel.

General   Mind your own business.

Marollier   Quite right, *mon général*. (*To* **Petypon**.) Mind your own business.

Varlin (*getting up*)   Mind your own business when you're told.

Petypon (*aside*)   Charming. My duel, my head, my . . . charming.

Duke   What's she *doing* all this time?

The **General** *sees that he is still sitting.*

General   Get up, can't you? Damn fool.

Duke (*getting up sulkily*)   Oh, fiddle.

General (*as they all sit again*)   Gentlemen. *My* principal
. . . (*To the* **Duke**, *who is still standing.*) Sit DOWN, for
heaven's sake.

The **Duke** *sits down abruptly, on his flowers.*

Duke   My roses.

General   I insist: *my* principal, injured party.

Marollier   Yes, yes, *mon général.* Of course.

General   And *as* injured party, choice of weapons. Rules
out swords – damn good job. Not man for swords.
Corignon would spit him like a chicken.

Petypon   Nasty.

Marollier   Of course, of course.

General   Don't you agree, Duke?

Duke (*to himself*)   I can't give her this *now*.

General   Duke.

Duke   Eh?

General   Asked you, what d'you think?

Duke   Me? (*Blowing through his lips, idiotically.*) Prrrrfffffft.

General   Thanks. (*To* **Varlin**.) What about you,
Monsieur?

Varlin   Nothing to do with me.

Marollier   You're doing it again.

General   Bad as each other. Never mind. So long as *we*
agree. Pistols.

They all rise.

Marollier *and* **Varlin**   Pistols.

Petypon   Don't be ridiculous.

Everyone What?

Petypon Pistols? I'm not having this. It's out of the question.

Everyone Eh?

Petypon This is *my* quarrel, *my* duel, *I've* got choice of weapons, and *I* choose ... scalpels.

General That *is* ridiculous.

Marollier This isn't a farce, you know.

Enter **Gabrielle**.

Gabrielle What's all the shouting?

Petypon (*who hasn't seen her*) It's my duel and those are my weapons.

Gabrielle Lucien. You're fighting a duel? Darling, no. They'll hurt you.

Petypon Leave me alone.

General She never stops.

Gabrielle Lucien, darling, please say you won't do it. Think of me. I love you.

General AhHA!

Marollier Madame, madame, no one said anything about a duel.

General Hey? What?

Marollier Just a friendly chat.

General Ah.

Gabrielle But I heard you. Lucien. Darling.

General Darling, hey? That's it! No wonder she's always here. (*To the* **Duke**.) Take a good look: this is the kind of woman men put above their homes and marriages. Gentlemen ...

He bundles the **Duke** *and* **Varlin** *together to push them out. The* **Duke***'s flowers are crushed again.*

Duke   My roses.

General   (*pushing them to the door*)   Continue this conversation some other time.

The others   Yes, General.

General   Another time.

He pushes them out, then rounds on **Petypon***.*

General   Plain as daylight. Nuff said. Your *mistress*.

Petypon   Pardon?

Gabrielle   *What* was that?

Petypon   Uncle Charles . . .

General   Don't speak to me.

Gabrielle   His mistress?

Petypon   Don't get involved.

Gabrielle   What do you mean, his mistress?

The **General** *fetches* **Shrimp***.*

General   Poor child, come in. See how best friend's betrayed you. Husband's mistress.

Shrimp   (*aside*)   Oo-er.

Gabrielle   I am not his mistress. I'm his wife.

General   Wife? What d'you mean?

Petypon   I'll explain.

General   *Here's* wife, here.

Gabrielle   No, she's *your* wife.

Petypon   Don't get involved.

Shrimp   (*aside*)   Someone's for it.

General My wife? Her? Ha, ha, ha. That's a good one.

*He collapses, to **Petypon**'s glee, into the Ecstatic Chair.*

Petypon (*aside*) The chair.

*He rushes and presses the handle, but the **General** gets up.*

General Ha, ha, ha, ha, ha.

Petypon Missed.

Gabrielle Uncle Charles, will you please explain?

Petypon No! He mustn't!

*Enter **Mongicourt**.*

Mongicourt General, I have to talk to you.

Petypon Too late!

He falls into the Ecstatic Chair, which is still on, and is frozen.

General Refuse to listen.

Mongicourt I insist.

General Not a word, Monsieur. After what your wife has done.

Mongicourt What wife?

General (*pointing to **Gabrielle***) This wife.

Gabrielle Me?

Mongicourt She's not my wife.

Gabrielle I'm Lucien's wife.

Shrimp (*who has meantime crept to the door*) Well, byebye all.

She escapes unnoticed.

General Don't be ridiculous. I *know* his wife. *Met* the woman. He brought her to Touraine in person.

Gabrielle Oh, he did, did he?

General   In any case, know perfectly well you're wife of Monsieur Whatdyemacallit here. Mangycur.

Mongicourt *and* **Gabrielle**   What?

General   What is this? New fashion, is it? Everyone pretending wife belongs to someone else? Even try an' tell me Lucien's wife is *my* wife. Goin' a bit far, what, goin' a little far.

Gabrielle   What's he talking about?

General   Nuff said. His wife *my* wife. Where is she? Gabrielle . . . Gabrielle . . .

He goes looking for **Shrimp**. *The others follow him.*

Gabrielle
Mongicourt } *simultaneously* { But Uncle Charles . . .
General, for heaven's sake.

General   Stand out of the way, God dammit! Gabrielle . . .

Exit.

Mongicourt   This is getting beyond me.

Gabrielle (*to* **Petypon**)   You . . . you . . . passing off your mistress as your wife. (*To* **Mongicourt**.) Just look at him. He's laughing at me.

She rushes to slap him.

Mongicourt   Don't do that! You haven't got the gloves.

Gabrielle   Where are they?

Mongicourt   Don't bother.

She rummages on the desk until she finds them.

Gabrielle   Of course I'll bother.

She puts them on and moves back to the Ecstatic Chair.

You cheated me. I trusted you and you, you . . .

She slaps him, hard. He doesn't move.

You took a mistress.

Slap.

And now you sit there *laughing.*

Slap. **Mongicourt** *hurries and presses the release handle.*

Mongicourt You've made your point.

Petypon (*as he wakes up*) Cuckoo.

Gabrielle What?

Petypon Cuckoo, my beloved.

Gabrielle Cuckoo, now?

She slaps him again.

Petypon Ow.

Gabrielle Uncle Charles has told me everything. Everything's over between us. I'm going back to Mother.

Petypon Gabrielle, please.

Gabrielle Don't try to smarm round me. My mind's made up. Nothing you say will ever change me.

Petypon Oh, all right.

Gabrielle I'm leaving.

Petypon If you like.

Gabrielle We're getting a divorce.

Petypon Whatever you say.

Gabrielle I'm taking back my dowry.

Petypon Of course you – What?

Gabrielle It's over. (*She points to the door.*) Never darken my door again.

Petypon Yes, dear.

He drags his steps to the door, turns and says, pathetically:

I'm going back . . . to Nanny.

Exit.

Mongicourt You *were* a bit hard.

Gabrielle Playing around at his age. One wife not enough for him. Well, now he can have as many as he likes.

Enter **Étienne**.

Étienne The Duke of Valmonté.

Gabrielle Couldn't be better.

Enter **Duke**. *Exit* **Étienne**.

Duke Not again.

She grabs him.

Gabrielle Come here, darling. You couldn't have come at a better time.

Duke *and* **Mongicourt** What?

Gabrielle You sent me a letter, said you loved me.

Duke Did I?

Gabrielle Don't deny it. I won't make you suffer.

Duke What's she talking about?

Mongicourt You'll soon find out.

Gabrielle (*taking a flower from the* **Duke***'s bouquet*) First, this flower from your bouquet for my corsage.

Duke Don't do that.

Gabrielle A token of our love.

Duke You'll *ruin* them.

Gabrielle And now, Duke . . . take me!

She throws herself into his arms, crushing his bouquet again.

Duke No. Aaargh! No.

Gabrielle Take me, take me. Let me slake my vengeance in your loving arms.

He drags her to the door, unable to free himself.

Duke Let me alone. Help. Mama.

He breaks free and exit.

Gabrielle What's wrong with him?

Mongicourt Don't ask.

Gabrielle Men are all the same. All talk, and if you take them at their word . . .

Petypon's *voice is heard from upstage, distant and ethereal.*

Petypon Gabrielle . . .

Gabrielle Who's that?

Petypon Your angel.

Mongicourt (*aside*) Now what?

Gabrielle *kneels.*

Gabrielle I recognise your voice.

Mongicourt *pulls the curtain to the bedroom.* **Petypon** *is there, with sheet and lamp, like* **Shrimp** *in Act One.*

Mongicourt (*aside*) Lucien.

Petypon Shhh.

Mongicourt This is ridiculous.

Petypon Gabrielle . . .

Gabrielle I'm listening.

Petypon You're making a terrible mistake. Your husband is the best of men.

Enter the **General**.

Petypon   Oh, for heaven's sake.

He hides his face.

General   Laughin' at me. Laughin'.

He sees the apparition.

I say.

Petypon   That's torn it.

He starts waving his arms, trying to frighten the **General**.

General   What the devil . . . ?

Gabrielle   Uncle Charles. In the nick of time. Dear Saint Michael, forgive me in advance for what I'm going to do. It's to convince a heretic.

She picks up a sword and waves it about.

Petypon   What's she doing?

Gabrielle   Watch this, Uncle Charles, and believe in God.

She goes towards the bed, waving the sword.

Mongicourt   You mustn't. I can't stand it. Ha. ha, ha.

Petypon   Gabrielle, not the sword. No! No!

Gabrielle (*recognising him*)   Oh.

Petypon   Now don't do anything silly.

Gabrielle (*rushing at him*)   You've been doing this on purpose.

Petypon *jumps off the bed, keeping it between them. She tries to get at him.*

Petypon   Gabrielle!

Gabrielle   Stay exactly where you are.

Petypon (*breaking for it*)   Help.

Gabrielle (*chasing*)   I'll teach you.

Mongicourt (*as* **Petypon** *interposes him between them*)   Oh.
Ah. Oh.

He gets out of the way. **Petypon** *dodges round the* **General**
and exit, followed by **Gabrielle**. **Mongicourt** *collapses in
laughter.*

Mongicourt   Hahahaha. Poor old Petypon.

General   Ha, ha, ha. Ghosts, eh? Ha, ha, ha.

Mongicourt   Ha, ha, ha. What am *I* laughing at?

General   Nephew wants to fool the world. Can't be
done. Nuff said. By the way, Monsieur, must offer you
humble apologies.

Mongicourt   *Me*, General?

General   Know everythin' now. Dear child told me
everythin' out there. Dear, sweet child . . . Can you
imagine, never been to Morocco? T'other one: *not*
Madame Mongicourt.

Mongicourt   She's Madame Petypon.

General   Know that. Now. Yesterday, mind, when I
thought . . . when I gave you . . .

He gestures a slap.

Mongicourt   Oh, yes.

General   Admittedly, only a slap. But insult in intention.
Slap meant for you only so long as you were your wife's
husband.

Mongicourt   Ah.

General   But since you're not, slap's not yours. Not to
keep. Just for delivery.

Mongicourt   Pardon?

General   Belongs to Lucien. So, deliver it.

Mongicourt   Oh, yes.

Enter **Petypon**.

General   Ha! Nick of time.

Petypon (*aside*)   Please, God forgive me. One last lie, to convince my wife. (*To* **Gabrielle**, *off.*) Gabrielle, come on.

He takes her hand and leads her in.

General   There you are. Warn you, know everything now. You lied to me.

Petypon   I did?

Gabrielle   What now?

General   Dear child you called your wife ain't wife at all. This lady: wife.

Petypon   That's what I've been killing myself trying to tell you.

General   Made a fool of me. Nuff said. Chap's heir. Nothin' changes that.

Petypon (*overjoyed*)   It doesn't?

General   But everything's over between us. Never see you again, as long as I live.

Petypon (*aside*)   Better and better. (*Aloud.*) Oh, Uncle Charles.

General   No, never.

Gabrielle   Uncle Charles, please forgive him. When he pretended she was his wife he was doing a good deed. He knew she was Corignon's mistress, and it was to avoid a scandal, to prevent the cancelling of the marriage, that he told this holy lie.

General   That's as maybe. Fact remains, made a fool of *me*.

Shrimp *comes to the door, stopping at the threshold.*

Everyone   Oh.

Shrimp (*to the* **General**)   Come on, Charlie. What's keeping you?

General   Won't be a moment, darlin'.

Everyone   Oh.

Mongicourt (*to* **Petypon**)   The General and I have made up our quarrel.

Petypon   Oh?

Mongicourt   He found a way to solve it. We decided he gave me the slap just for delivery.

Petypon   Really?

Mongicourt   That's all right with you?

Petypon   No skin off my nose.

Mongicourt   If you say so.

He slaps him, hard.

Petypon   Ow.

General   Touché.

Petypon   That *hurt.*

Gabrielle (*running to him*)   Lucien!

Mongicourt   A present from the General.

General (*to* **Shrimp**)   Ready when you are.

Petypon (*mistaking him, worried about another duel*)   When *I* am?

General (*indicating* **Shrimp**)   No, when *she* is.

Shrimp   'Houp-la.' (*Patting the* **General**'s *cheek.*) 'This one's for me.'

Tableau as the curtain falls and we reach

The End.

She's All Yours

La Main passe

Characters

Alcide Chanal
Francine, *his wife*
Hubertin
Coustillou, *a politician*
Émile Massenay
Sophie, *his wife*
Inspector Germal
Inspector Planteloup
Belgence
Lapige
Auguste, **Étienne**, **Madeleine**, **Marthe**, *servants*
Police constable
Porters

The scene is Paris, at the start of the twentieth century. The first three acts take place in March, Act Four a year later, in June.

Act One

Sitting-room in the **Chanal** *household, comfortably furnished in the latest style. To one side are glass doors leading to the hall, to the other side* **Chanal**'s *office, partitioned off with door and large windows allowing us to see what happens inside. Double doors at rear to the rest of the house.*

At the start of the act **Chanal** *is fiddling with a cylinder phonograph. He gets everything ready, then picks up a piece of paper with a message written on it, starts the machine, clears his throat and declaims.*

Chanal 'My dearest sister . . .' (*Cough.*) Cahum! 'So the deed is done. From today you'll be a married woman: this afternoon in the sight of the law, this evening in the bed of your husband.' Not bad at all. 'A sobering thought indeed – especially for me, because I know exactly what's involved.'

Enter **Francine** *from the hall: she's been out and wears gloves and a fur stole.*

Francine Ready when you are.

Chanal *silences her with an imperious gesture, then gets back to his recording.*

Chanal 'Unfortunately, I can't be at your side at this crucial time. An ocean stands between us. But at least my voice will wave across the waves, advising you.'

Francine *explodes with laughter. He silences her with the same imperiousness, and declaims again.*

Chanal 'You'll discover a secret, penetrate a mystery, the one on all young women's minds . . .'

Francine What are you *doing*?

Chanal For heaven's sake be quiet.

Francine No need to shout.

Chanal Sh! I'm recording.

Francine How stupid you are –

Chanal (*exasperated*) Oh!

He stops the machine, gestures her to be quiet, and starts it again.

Francine (*continuing serenely*) – to record in here.

Chanal Don't be ridiculous. And keep your mouth shut. That's a cylinder wasted.

Francine 'A cylinder in time . . .'

Chanal Don't tell me. Don't you ever *listen* to yourself?

Francine Pardon?

Chanal You could *see* I was recording.

Francine What were you recording?

Chanal Nothing. A message for Caroline. For New York: the wedding. And you come in and . . . It hasn't got a brain, you know. Doesn't sort things out. It records everything it hears.

Francine You mean, everything, exactly . . . ?

Chanal Listen.

He plays the cylinder back.

Phonograph ' "My dearest sister . . ." (*Cough.*) Cahum! "So the deed is done. From today you'll be a married woman: this afternoon in the sight of the law, this evening in the bed of your husband." Not bad at all. "A sobering thought indeed – especially for me, because I know exactly what's involved." ' 'Ready when you are.'

Chanal (*over it*) How nice! You're ready.

Phonograph ' "Unfortunately, I can't be at your side at this crucial time. An ocean stands between us. But at least my voice will wave across the waves, advising you." ' 'Ha, ha, ha.' 'Shh! "You'll discover a secret, penetrate a

mystery, the one on all young women's minds ..." '
'What *are* you doing?' 'For heaven's sake be quiet.' 'No
need to shout.' 'Sh! I'm recording.' 'How stupid you
are – '

He switches it off.

Chanal Satisfied?

Francine That wasn't me on there.

Chanal What?

Francine It wasn't.

Chanal It made you up?

Francine I didn't say 'How stupid you are –'. I said,
'How-stupid-you-are-to-record-in-here.' Totally different.

Chanal I stopped it.

Francine That's how gossip starts.

Chanal It's a machine!

Francine Put another cylinder in, and start again. You
can get rid of that stupid stuff about the ocean.

Chanal What stupid stuff about the ocean?

Francine 'My voice will wave across the waves.'

Chanal It was a joke.

Francine A joke, at your sister's wedding.

Chanal Really.

Francine 'From today you'll be a married woman: this
afternoon in the sight of the law, this evening in the bed
of your husband.' What a thing to tell a bride on her
wedding day.

Chanal It's not exactly a secret.

Francine So why remind her? Voice waving across the
waves, a smutty cylinder – what are you *doing* to her?

Chanal   Smutty?

Francine   Are you sending full instructions? You're like those people, you say you're going to a play, they say, 'Ah, you'll really enjoy it. Especially the bit when *he* says *this*, and *she* goes . . .' You sit there watching, and all the time you're thinking, 'I know what's going to happen!' Let them find out for themselves. Caroline may not enjoy it, but at least it'll come as a surprise.

Chanal   How d'you know she won't enjoy it?

Francine   What?

Chanal   What proof d'you have?

Francine   Experience.

Chanal   You know nothing about it.

He removes the cylinder and puts in a new one.

Never mind. Your lunch is getting cold. Ring for Étienne. I've had mine. It's no way to run a household, the husband having *his* lunch and then, some other time, the wife having *her* lunch.

Francine   Why didn't you wait, then?

Chanal   Oh, fine. It's my fault!

Enter **Étienne**.

Chanal   Madame would like her lunch.

Étienne   Yes, Monsieur.

Exit.

Chanal   What do you *do* out there? Every day it's the same. You've been out since nine this morning.

Francine   That's why I'm back early.

Chanal   Early!

Francine (*confronting him*)   What is it? What d'you think's going on? Admit it: you think I've got a lover.

Chanal (*quizzically*) Do I now?

Francine You're always the same. Always think the worst. So now it's a lover.

Chanal *shrugs*.

Francine What's that supposed to mean?

Chanal Darling, don't be silly. Of course you haven't a lover.

Francine What?

Chanal It's obvious.

Francine Really?

Chanal Some women are born to have lovers, others . . . aren't.

Francine *Aren't* they?

Chanal I've lived five years with you. I *know* you. A lover? Don't be silly. You were born to be a wife, a mother – it's not our fault we don't have children. It's just not you, a lover. It isn't: trust me.

Francine Well, I didn't want to tell you, but you've made me. (*With force.*) I . . . have . . . a . . . lover.

Chanal Of course you have.

Francine A lover. He loves me, and I love him.

Chanal I congratulate you both.

Francine I've a lover. A lover, a lover, a lover.

Chanal And I want you to give him my regards.

Francine Oh!

Chanal Darling, you're trying too hard. You're pulling my leg. A lover? You're . . . out of your league.

Francine What?

Chanal The league of honest women. I'm sorry.

Francine How dare you say that to me?

Chanal I'm right.

Francine You're not.

Chanal Am.

Francine Not.

Chanal Don't be silly.

Doorbell, off.

Look me in the face and tell me you've a lover.

Francine You are so . . . *annoying*!

Chanal See? What a silly, what a silly!

He pats her cheek. She pulls away. Enter **Étienne**.

Étienne Monsieur, a gentleman.

He hands **Chanal** *a visiting card on a salver.*

Chanal Hubertin! What does he want? Show him in.

Exit **Étienne**.

Francine Who's Hubertin?

Chanal From the club . . .

Étienne *shows in* **Hubertin**.

Étienne Monsieur Hubertin.

Exit.

Hubertin Morning.

Chanal Morning. Allow me: Monsieur Hubertin from the bridge club, Madame Chanal.

Hubertin Madame . . .

Francine   Monsieur . . .

Hubertin   I say, haven't we met before?

Francine   I don't think so.

Hubertin   Don't you know someone in my building?

Francine   I don't even know your building.

Hubertin   21 rue du Colisée.

Francine (*quickly*)   No. Sorry. You're mistaken.

Hubertin   Mm?

Chanal   Of course you are. We don't know *anyone*.

Hubertin   Ah well, no harm done. I'm sorry.

Francine   No harm done.

She sits.

Chanal   What can we do for you? Do sit down.

Hubertin   It's all right, it won't take a moment. You know the club rules: all debts must be paid within twenty-four hours. I've come to settle up.

Chanal   Oh, no need. Rules are for professionals . . . not people who know each other.

Hubertin (*taking out his wallet*)   No, no. Neither a borrower nor a lender be. Many a mickle maks a muckle.

Chanal   The thing is . . . last night . . . you were at something of a . . .

Hubertin   What d'you mean?

Chanal   *You* know.

Hubertin   You mean I was squiffy.

Chanal   I wasn't implying –

Hubertin   It's all right. I don't mind. (*To* **Francine**.) The thing is, you know what it's like, when the sun is over the yardarm . . .

Francine   What yardarm?

Hubertin   No, no, it's a habit. The colonies, don't you
know?

Francine   The colonies.

Hubertin   Out there for years. And when in Rome, as
the saying goes. Sun over the yardarm, glass in the hand.
You have to do it. Picked up the habit. And even now
I'm home . . . don't seem to lose the taste for it. Colonial
manners, don't you know. Not soaking it up, just . . .
colonial manners.

Francine   I see.

Chanal   When in Rome . . .

Hubertin   I said that, didn't I? Trouble is, my wife
can't see it.

Francine   Ah. Well, she . . . Yes.

Hubertin   It's all right for her. She's from *out* there.
Half a dozen cocktails, she's got the head for it. But me?
Try to keep up with her – well, you do, don't you – fall
flat on my face each time. Embarrassing.

Francine, **Chanal**   Oh, very.

Hubertin (*in a different tone, holding out a banknote*)   So, here
we are. Nine hundred and eighty francs. Here's a
thousand. No, don't worry: all's fair and square. I find a
glass or two keeps me up to the mark, clears the head,
steadies the hands . . . and for bridge, it's unbeatable. I
see everything double.

Chanal   How d'you tell the cards?

Hubertin   Perfectly simple: I divide by two.

Chanal   Of course.

Doorbell, off.

Hubertin   Clever, eh?

Chanal   Nine hundred and eighty francs. I'll get your change.

He goes towards the office. Enter **Étienne**.

Étienne. Monsieur Coustillou.

Chanal   Show him in.

Exit **Étienne**.

Hubertin   Did he say Coustillou?

Chanal   Oh yes. The MP. Leader of the Opposition. The orator. Coustillou.

Hubertin   You don't mind if I stay, do you? I'd love to meet him.

Chanal   I'll introduce you.

Enter **Coustillou**, *shown in by* **Étienne**. *He is the picture of a glossy, successful public figure, well-dressed, superbly coiffeured, sleek and elegant. But he is desperately ill-at-ease and embarrassed and is holding a bunch of asparagus.*

Chanal   My dear chap, come in. We were just talking about you.

Coustillou   Were you?

He tries to close the door behind him. But his hands are full: one with asparagus, one with his hat. He dithers, then puts first the asparagus and then the hat on his head. He then shuts the door, just as **Étienne** *shuts it from the outside. His hand is trapped.*

Coustillou   Ow.

Chanal   Étienne can shut it.

Coustillou   Mooah, mooah.

He frees his hand, puts down the hat and goes to shake **Chanal**'s *hand, the picture of suaveness.*

Coustillou   How are you?

Chanal *is sitting on a low stool, which means that the handshake is impossible to manage.*

Chanal   Fine, thanks.

Coustillou   Ah. Mooah.

He goes, suavely, to shake **Francine**'s *hand, and falls over the stool.*

Coustillou   Ow.

He rubs his shin.

Chanal   You do that every time you come. (*To* **Hubertin**.) You'd think he'd remember.

Coustillou *has meantime picked up the stool to straighten it, and stands irresolute with it dangling from his hand.*

Coustillou   It's . . . the thing is, I . . . Mm . . . Mooah . . .

Chanal   Don't get so flustered.

Francine (*taking pity*)   *You* fluster him. Monsieur Coustillou, ignore my husband. Come and say hello.

Coustillou (*eagerly*)   Ah!

He hurries forward, contriving inadvertently to hook the legs of the stool he's carrying round a standard lamp and bring it crashing down. He scrabbles to reassemble the pieces.

Coustillou   Mooah.

Chanal (*aside*)   Exactly: a bull in a china shop.

Coustillou *tries to recover his savoir-faire, standing up and extending his hand with a politician's smile. Unfortunately he's still draped in the stool.*

Francine   Put the stool down first.

Coustillou   Sorry.

He looks for somewhere to put it.

Chanal (*aside*) This can go on all night.

Coustillou *goes man-to-man to* **Francine** *and pumps her hand, then smirks up to* **Chanal** *and kisses his hand flirtatiously.*

Coustillou Old fellow . . . my dear . . .

Chanal Start again.

Coustillou Sorry.

He starts back towards **Francine**.

Coustillou Only joking.

Chanal *steers him towards* **Hubertin**.

Chanal Monsieur Hubertin. He's very anxious to meet you.

Coustillou Ah. Aha?

Hubertin A fervent admirer.

Coustillou Aha? Mm . . . ooah.

Chanal Do put that down.

Coustillou What down? (*Realising he still has the asparagus.*) Oh, this down. Mooaaah.

He dithers, trying to find the right place for it, finally gives it to **Hubertin**.

Chanal He doesn't want it.

Coustillou What? It's a branch . . . um, bouquet . . . um, it's asparagus.

Chanal We didn't think it was candyfloss.

Francine Are you fond of asparagus, Monsieur Coustillou?

Coustillou Oh no.

Chanal So why d'you carry it?

Coustillou (*completely thrown*)   I . . . um . . . you see . . .
it's . . . I thought . . . it's to . . .

Chanal   To break the ice.

Coustillou   Exactly.

Chanal   Ah, fine. Just what you need. A brilliant idea.
You're the clumsiest man in the universe, so you make
things easier for yourself by carting round asparagus.

Coustillou   Mooah.

Chanal   Put it in the hall.

Coustillou   Yes! Yes! Thank you!

*He makes for the door. On the way he sees in his path the stool
which he fell over earlier, and makes a last-minute, matador's swerve
to avoid it.*

Chanal   Very good.

Coustillou (*nervously*)   Ha, ha.

Exit.

Francine   Leave him alone.

Chanal   What a clown.

Hubertin   That's Coustillou the orator? Voice like
thunder, brings tears to every eye . . . ?

Chanal   He does to mine.

Hubertin   What a tragedy.

Chanal   He makes *me* cry.

Francine   You don't have to make him worse.

Enter **Coustillou**, *without asparagus. He is very ill at ease.*

Chanal   Thought what to do with it, then?

Coustillou   What? Oh. I . . . Yes.

Chanal   Feel better now?

Coustillou   Well, I . . . No, I . . . You see I . . . moo . . .

Enter **Étienne** *with a card on a salver in one hand and the asparagus in the other. He takes them to* **Francine**.

Étienne   For Madame.

Francine   Pardon?

She takes them. Exit **Étienne**. **Coustillou** *is on the rack. She looks at the asparagus, then reads the card.*

Francine   'From the office of Alphonse Coustillou.'

She looks at **Coustillou**. *He tries to lean nonchalantly on the back of the sofa, but misjudges the angle and prevents himself falling only by vaulting right over it and sitting with a bump. He sits bolt upright, clutching his knees and grinning nervously.*

Francine   Monsieur Coustillou, you shouldn't have.

Coustillou   Oh, you know . . .

He gets up.

Chanal   You brought it for *us*. Why didn't you say so? Asparagus, in March. Where did you get it?

Coustillou   Oh, you know . . .

He tries to look man-of-the-world.

Francine   I'll tell cook to serve it for dinner. And you must stay and help us enjoy it.

Chanal (*to* **Hubertin**)   I'll get your change.

Exeunt. **Coustillou** *waits till they've gone, then releases his pent-up frustration by punching the back of the sofa in a fury. This only works him up even more, and he suddenly whirls on* **Hubertin** *and wags his finger threateningly in his face.*

Coustillou   Mmmoo . . . mmooo . . . You think I'm an idiot.

Hubertin   No I don't.

Coustillou   Oh yes you do. Well, you're wrong.

He goes and peers longingly off in the direction **Francine** *exited, then returns to the charge.*

Coustillou I may look like an idiot, but I'm not an idiot.

Hubertin I never said –

Coustillou I'd like to see someone call me an idiot. (*Gazing abstractedly off again.*) Just let them try. I'll show them. Idiot!

Hubertin Don't be silly. Everyone knows –

Coustillou That I'm an idiot?

Hubertin Yes. I mean, no. You're flustering me. You, an idiot? How could anyone think so?

Coustillou (*gazing off*) Well, then.

Hubertin Exactly. You're the leader of the opposition. You could bring down the government.

Coustillou Any time I want. An idiot! I'll show them.

Hubertin It's all right . . .

Coustillou I'll stand up in the Assembly, I'll look them in the eye, I'll say (*In a huge voice.*) 'In the name of the République . . .'

Enter **Francine**, *by the door he's been gazing at.*

Francine There we are. All ready.

Coustillou (*struck dumb by her arrival*) Eugh . . . Erghh . . . Moooooo.

Francine Did I hear someone shouting?

Hubertin He was.

Francine Monsieur Coustillou? Is anything the matter?

Coustillou I . . . Wheeee . . .

He picks up **Francine**'s *hat from where she put it down earlier,* *and is about to cram it on his head when he realises what he's doing.*

Coustillou Meeooo.

Francine Monsieur *Coustillou*, shouting. I don't believe it. No.

She beams at him. He is transfixed.

Coustillou Ooooaaaaah . . .

Hubertin (*aside*) The people's choice.

Enter **Chanal** *with change.*

Chanal Twenty francs. Thanks very much.

Hubertin No, thank you. If you'll excuse me . . .

Chanal You have to go?

Hubertin Afraid so. Business. Much better now, in the morning –

Chanal (*joking*) Than when the sun's over the yardarm, eh?

Hubertin (*serious*) Oh yes. Monsieur Coustillou, I –

He goes to shakes hands with **Coustillou**, *but is disconcerted to find him staring at him absolutely fixedly, lost in a world of his own.* **Chanal** *snaps his fingers.*

Chanal Coustillou. Hey, Coustillou.

Coustillou (*like a man startled out of sleep*) Wha . . . ? Whey!

Chanal Time to go. Monsieur wants to shake your hand.

Coustillou Oh. Sorry. Monsieur . . .

Chanal Thank you.

Hubertin Madame.

Francine   Au revoir, Monsieur.

Chanal   I'll see you out.

Exeunt **Chanal** *and* **Hubertin**. **Coustillou** *and* **Francine** *are left. She goes to the door to see the others off. He wriggles and writhes round the room, trying, without being embarrassed, to inch his way to the table where he left his hat. After a moment, enter* **Chanal**.

Chanal   That's that, then. Time for lunch, Francine.

Francine   I'm ready.

Chanal   Take Coustillou with you. I want to finish my recording.

Francine   Monsieur Coustillou, if you don't mind putting up with *me* . . .

Coustillou   Wheeooaaaaaaah.

He hurtles towards her.

Chanal   Mind the sofa.

Coustillou *swerves just in time, and exit with* **Francine**. **Chanal** *goes back to his phonograph. Doorbell, off.*

Chanal (*declaiming into the machine*)   'My dearest sister, so the deed is done. From today you'll be a married woman. Tonight you'll discover a secret, penetrate a mystery, the one on all young women's minds . . .'

Enter **Étienne** *with a card on a salver. We can see* **Massenay** *waiting in the hall.*

Étienne   Monsieur . . .

Chanal (*stopping the phonograph furiously*)   *Will* you be quiet?

Étienne   But Monsieur . . .

Chanal   Can't you see I'm talking?

Étienne   Who to, Monsieur?

Chanal   Mind your own business. Obviously not you. It's a conspiracy. First Madame, then you. What? What is it?

Étienne   There's a gentleman, Monsieur.

Massenay *is now at the open door, and can hear everything.* **Chanal** *is aware of this.*

Chanal   A gentleman. Who needs him? I don't need him.

Étienne   This is his card.

Chanal   I don't need his card, and I don't need him. I'm busy. I'm out. Tell him.

Massenay (*from the door, affably*)   Monsieur, so sorry to disturb you.

Chanal (*jumping*)   Erg! (*Instantly recovering; with overwhelming affability.*)   Not at all. My dear Monsieur.

Massenay   If you're busy, I can come back.

Chanal   Not at all. I wouldn't hear of it. Please do come in.

Massenay   How kind.

He comes in. Meanwhile, in dumbshow, **Chanal** *and* **Étienne** *exchange opinions. 'This is preposterous.' 'Oh, Monsieur.' 'Get out of here.' Exit* **Étienne**. **Chanal** *comes down to* **Massenay**.

Chanal   What can I do for you? Do please sit down.

Massenay   You *are* Monsieur Chanal?

Chanal   Entirely.

Massenay   You own this building?

Chanal   Technically, my wife does. But as manager . . .

Massenay   It comes to the same thing. Your ground floor apartment's empty.

Chanal   Indeed it is.

Massenay   I need a *pied-à-terre*. It would be perfect.

Chanal   You've seen it?

Massenay   No need. It's perfect.

Chanal (*baffled*)   Ah.

Massenay   The rent is . . . ?

Chanal (*sizing him up*)   Well now . . . three thousand . . . eight . . .

Massenay   That's settled then: four.

Chanal   Pardon?

Massenay   I said, 'That's settled, four.'

Chanal   Settled. I was . . .

Massenay   Four's good. Four quarters in the year, a thousand a quarter, cash down, no shilly-shallying. Well?

Chanal   Whatever you say, then. Four.

Massenay   Thank you. As for maintenance, repairs . . .

Chanal   My responsibility.

Massenay   Excuse me: mine.

Chanal   Ah. Fine.

A thought suddenly strikes him. He proceeds carefully.

Just one thing . . . You're so accommodating . . . I ought to mention . . .

Massenay   Yes?

Chanal   A young man like yourself . . . the apartment does belong to my wife . . . a matter of . . . Oh, for heaven's sake, the lease has a morality clause.

Massenay   No problem.

Chanal (*once again baffled*) Ah.

Massenay Bring women off the streets? Not me.

Chanal No, no. We're men of the world. I mean, now and then . . . We wouldn't hold you to it absolutely.

Massenay No question of that whatever.

Chanal I wasn't implying . . . We wouldn't want you to . . . I mean, now and then: your mother, your sister . . .

Massenay Not with my mother, not my sister.

Chanal I didn't mean . . .

Massenay I promise you. This building . . . the front hall . . . your concierge . . . No women will call for me.

Chanal Splendid, Monsieur. Thank you. If all tenants were like you, a landlord's life would be –

Massenay No sense making obstacles.

Chanal Whatever you say.

He goes to fetch documents from his office, grimacing to the audience:
'This is a strange one.'

I've got agreements drawn up ready. We just fill in the details.

Massenay Excellent.

Chanal We'll start with your name.

Massenay It's on my card.

Chanal Ah. You mean . . . ? Of course. (*Reading the card.*) Émile Massenay. You're not . . . ?

Massenay No, no, no. Coincidence.

Chanal I don't mean that. I mean . . .

Massenay Everyone makes the same mistake.

Chanal (*lost in his thoughts*) Massenay. Massenay. You didn't go to school in Saint-Louis?

Massenay   Till I was seven.

Chanal   So did I! What a coincidence! Don't you remember? Chanal . . . Chanal . . .

Massenay   Chanal . . . (*He turns away, thinking it out.*) Chanal . . .

Chanal *thumps him in the middle of the back, schoolboy fashion.*

Chanal   Snotnose.

Massenay   Pardon?

Chanal   Sorry.

Massenay   No, no. You took me by surprise. Now I remember . . .

He pushes him in his turn, schoolboy fashion.

Snotnose yourself.

Chanal   I knew you'd remember. Chanal. Chanal?

Massenay   That's right. The one who kept crying. The one whose mother was a . . .

Chanal   No, no. Me. *I'm* Chanal.

Massenay   Of course you are. Sorry. Monsieur Chanal. I didn't put two and two tog – Unforgivable.

Chanal   Better late than never. Snotnose!

He drapes his arm round **Massenay**'s *neck.*

Chanal   *Now* d'you recognise me?

Massenay *drapes his arm round him, so that they're attached like three-legged racers. They prance across the stage, this way then that way.*

Chanal   That's better.

Massenay   Oh yes.

Chanal   When you've flicked ink-pellets at each other
... there's nothing to beat it. You make friendships later,
but not like that.

Massenay   At our age, especially.

Chanal   That's right. Oh, what times they were!
(*Businesslike tone.*) Do please sit down.

They sit side by side. He goes all sentimental again.

Well, well. Good old Massenay. Well, well, well, well,
well. D'you remember Bourrache, the one who was
always pulling faces?

Massenay   That's right.

Chanal   I still bump into him.

Massenay   Really?

Chanal   Hasn't changed a bit. Same old faces.

Massenay   You're joking.

Chanal   Bursting with cheerfulness. Full of the joys of
life. These days he's an undertaker.

Massenay   Stands to reason.

Chanal   Poteau, remember Poteau?

Massenay   No.

Chanal   The one with that sister. She kept looking,
remember? Sideways. What a squint that was! 'Two for
one', don't you remember?

Massenay   Not remotely.

Chanal   Anyway, he's dead.

Massenay   Poteau? Poor fellow.

Chanal   Absolutely.

Massenay   What did he die of?

Chanal   He went just like that.

Massenay   Oh, not like that.

Chanal   Just like that. Anyone could have told him. If you must have a lady friend who ... and who ... the *last* thing you do is, after a five-course meal ... literally, the *last* thing you do ...

Massenay   You don't mean ...?

Chanal   At least he died with a smile on his face.

Massenay   Poor old Poteau.

Chanal (*new tone*)   Just a minute. You never knew a Poteau. He was at senior school.

Massenay   I *thought* I didn't ... Why are you upsetting me for nothing? What do I care if he's dead? Poteau!

Chanal   After all, we all have to go.

Massenay   I never meet anyone I was at school with. You know what it's like. You think you'll be friends for ever. You grow up, you drift apart ... I only meet one these days. *He's* done very nicely. They're the only ones you *do* meet. Except the ones who ask you for money. I don't know if you remember him: Coustillou, the MP.

Chanal   You're joking. He's here.

Massenay   Here?

Chanal   In there, with my wife. He's one of my oldest friends. He's *always* here.

Massenay   Amazing. He's one of *my* oldest friends. He's never mentioned you.

Chanal   They can't mention *everyone*.

Massenay   Coustillou, eh? Poor old Coustillou. The state he's in.

Chanal   What state he's in?

Massenay   Because he's in love.

Chanal   In love?

Massenay   Hasn't he told you?

Chanal   No.

Massenay   He talks of nothing else. His hopeless grand passion.

Chanal   Hopeless? Who for?

Massenay   He never says. Someone's wife, that's all I know. He's discretion personified. Tells me every detail, but never names names.

Chanal   He never said a word to me. Secrets, from me! Well, it's hopeless anyway.

Massenay   That's what upsets him.

Chanal   I could have given him a few tips, told him what to do. I know this woman.

Massenay   You don't.

Chanal   Well, not *this* one specifically. I know women, in general. 'What are you waiting for?' – that's what I'd have said. 'Shoulder arms, quick march, allez-oup! What are you waiting for?' Words to that effect. I wanted to spare your blushes.

Massenay   You think *I* haven't encouraged him?

Chanal   So what's stopping him? The husband?

Massenay   That's one reason.

Chanal   You're joking! One more cuckold?

Massenay   Oh, he'd get over the husband. The main reason is, his problem. He's terminally shy. He falls for a woman, doesn't stand a chance. Until he gets her, he falls over his own feet, can't get a word out – and the more he does that, the less he gets her. Passion, brush-off, passion, brush-off: it's a vicious circle.

Chanal   He's had it, then?

Massenay   That's the whole point, he hasn't. And he
never will, unless someone takes pity, makes the first
move, the kindness of her heart . . .

Chanal   It doesn't work that way.

Massenay   Especially not with *this* one. She's no idea,
he claims. And she never will have: every time he sees
her he stutters, he blushes, falls over furniture, he's useless.

Chanal (*vastly amused*)   I know, I've seen him.

Massenay   What?

Chanal (*double take*)   Just a minute . . .

Massenay (*getting there ahead of him*)   It isn't.

Chanal   It is! (*Amused again.*) *My* wife.

Massenay   Your wife?

Chanal   The wife in question: *my* wife. Whenever he
sees her, all that . . . and that . . . It's obvious.

Massenay   No, no, no, no, no, no. It isn't. I didn't.
You mustn't. He isn't. They can't be. Oh God.

Chanal   I think it's very funny. In any case: he's in love
with my wife. What's wrong with that? So long as that's
all he is. And it *is*. My wife's an honest woman.

Massenay (*fervently*)   Oh, she is. Yes, yes, yes, yes,
yes . . .

Chanal   You're just saying that. You've never met her.
But I have. I know her very well. No problems with her
– and none from Coustillou.

Massenay   Oh, no, no, no, no, no.

Chanal   So long as he's falling over furniture, I sleep
easy in my bed.

Massenay   Oh, do that, do that.

Chanal   Even so, it's funny. Coustillou! I have to tell her. Francine!

Francine (*off*)   What is it?

Massenay   What are you doing? Don't breathe a word to Coustillou. He'll kill me.

Chanal   Trust me. Ha! He'd have a heart attack!

Massenay   Like Poteau did.

Chanal   What? Oh. Poteau. Ha! No, this would be *before* . . .

Massenay   Exactly.

Chanal   Ah. (*Calling off.*)   Francine!

Francine (*off*)   What *is* it?

Chanal   I want to tell you something.

Enter **Francine**. *She doesn't see* **Massenay**.

Francine   What's the matter?

Chanal   You'll never guess. You and your high horse.

Francine   What are you talking about? (*Seeing* **Massenay**.) Monsieur.

Chanal   Sorry. My friend Massenay. Émile Massenay.

Francine   Pleased to meet you. Just a minute, you're not —

Massenay (*to* **Chanal**)   It's always the same.

Francine   You're not related?

Massenay   Unfortunately. He's E.T. and I'm A.Y.

Francine   What bad luck.

Massenay   It can't be helped. A.Y.

Chanal   Never mind A.Y. This is Massenay from school!

Francine   I'm sorry. I hardly know anyone.

Chanal   Never mind that. D'you know what someone's just told me? (*For maximum effect.*) Coustillou's in love with you.

Francine   Who told you?

Chanal   *He* did.

Francine (*to* **Massenay**)   *You* did?

Massenay   How could I? I didn't even know. All I said was, Coustillou's in love with someone's wife, but whenever he sees her he goes all . . . goes all . . . That's all. *You* said, 'My God, my wife!' *I* didn't.

Chanal   It comes to the same thing. (*To* **Francine**.) Well? Well? Aren't you amazed? Isn't it a revelation?

Francine (*calmly*)   I've known for ages.

Chanal   What?

Francine   Of course I have.

Chanal   He *told* you?

Francine   Just as well he didn't. When a man tells you he loves you, don't believe him. But when he *hides* it, it's obvious.

Chanal   I never even noticed.

Francine (*with gentle irony, no edge*)   You're a husband. You can't be expected to *notice* things.

Massenay   Touché, Madame.

Chanal   She's right. Now I think about it . . . it's obvious. I mean, for a start, all that asparagus.

Massenay   Asparagus.

Chanal   Today, yes. Pears, yesterday. My wife just has

to say, quite casually, 'Pears look good this morning', or 'I really fancy some asparagus', and bam! Two hours later, there's Coustillou, panting at the door with a bunch of asparagus or a pair of pears.

Massenay   You're joking.

Francine   I have to think what I'm saying.

Chanal   It's not as if it was anyone else. The other day I had indigestion, he was there, I said, 'I wish I had a peppermint' – nothing! If my *wife* had said it, he'd have brought her a shopful.

Francine   You are silly.

Chanal   You'll see, yourself. Now we're going to be neighbours. (*To* **Francine**.) Massenay's just rented the flat downstairs.

Francine   You're joking.

Chanal   I was just fetching the papers. (*To* **Massenay**.) Excuse me a moment . . .

Massenay   Of course.

Chanal   Get to know each other. I won't be long.

Exit into his office. Pause. **Francine** *is watching* **Chanal** *leave.* **Massenay** *is fiddling with a vase from the sideboard, pretending great interest in it. This continues till* **Chanal** *closes the door. Then*:

Francine   Darling! The flat downstairs!

Massenay   Oh yes.

Francine   (*running into his arms*)   Oh darling, darling . . .

Massenay   Wasn't it brilliant? You were so worried yesterday, at the rue du Colisée, afraid someone had seen you . . .

Francine   I was right. A friend of my husband's lives there. He saw me arrive, he saw me leave. Fortunately, my husband didn't notice. But he could've . . .

Massenay   Don't! It's all right now. No risk of being seen, no need to go out. Your own building, you can . . . we can . . . in our own building. So much more *convenient*!

Francine   For all three of us: you, me, my husband . . . Oh, darling.

Massenay   Oh, darling.

They are in each other's arms. Knock, off. They spring apart, looking nonchalant as they were when **Chanal** *went out.*

Francine   Come in.

Enter **Coustillou**, *timidly*.

Massenay (*as if finishing a remark begun earlier*)   . . . *quite* unlike the Eiffel Tower . . .

Coustillou   Hoohoo. I was just . . .

Francine   Monsieur Coustillou. Come in.

Coustillou   Sorry.

He goes to the piano stool and sits. He hasn't seen **Massenay**.

Massenay   Afternoon, Coustillou.

Coustillou *jumps back and flattens himself against the wall.*

Coustillou   Erg! What are *you* doing here?

Massenay   Visiting an old friend. An old school friend. Chanal.

Coustillou   Arg. Harg.

Massenay   He introduced me to Madame Chanal.

Coustillou (*in a panic*)   Oh, mooah . . . Monsieur Massenay, Madame Chanal.

Massenay   No, he's done it already. It's been done.

Coustillou   Mooarg.

Massenay   What's wrong with you?

Coustillou   You can't. It isn't. Whatever they say. It isn't her.

Massenay   What d'you mean?

Francine   Not me that what?

Coustillou   Not, erg, hoo, arg, nothing.

He hunches up on the piano stool.

Francine (*after a moment*)   Shouldn't you be going, Monsieur Coustillou?

Coustillou   No, me, no.

Francine   Didn't you say you had an appointment?

Coustillou   I can put it off.

He tries to look casual, leaning back nonchalantly and forgetting he's on a piano stool. He falls, recovers himself, puts his hat on, whips it off, puts it on his knee (still trying to look lackadaisical), then concentrates hard on the succeeding dialogue, frowning as if it's a philosophical discussion, turning his head hungrily to each speaker as if it's a tennis match.

Francine   Monsieur Massenay, what were we talking about?

Massenay   Just a minute. It was . . . no. It was . . . the Eiffel Tower. The second storey. The bookstall. You were saying there was a newspaper you liked the look of.

Francine   Was I?

Massenay   The *Stockholm Tidningen*, didn't you say it was?

Francine   That's right.

Massenay   I said I'd –

Before he can continue, **Coustillou** *is on his feet, darting to the door like arrow from bow.*

Francine   Going, Monsieur Coustillou?

Coustillou   I won't be a moment! A moment! Whey!

Exit, fast. Pause.

Massenay   It's really too easy.

Francine   You're inspired.

Massenay   By love.

Francine   Oh, darling.

Massenay   Darling.

Francine   If you knew how I feel! Since we ... I want to tell everyone. People in the street, the servants, my husband ...

Massenay   Careful.

Francine   It's all right, I won't *do* it. It's just ... keeping a secret ... and if I'll tell him, he'd be furious, and if he was furious he'd make a scene, and if he made a scene he'd have to say your name ... your beloved name ...

Massenay   It's not a good idea.

Francine   I know. We mustn't be selfish. If he knew he'd be so sad, and he doesn't deserve ... it's not his fault we ... he didn't ... Better not.

Massenay   Better not.

Francine   It's such a shame, I can't have a lover without cheating my husband.

Massenay   You've doubts?

Francine   Doubts? Oh, look in my eyes!

Massenay   Oh, darling.

Francine   All I meant was ... I was just saying it. I don't mean it. (*Fiddling with the things on the piano.*) You

know how it is. They teach you in school ... Morality ...
I mean ... Fortunately, you were strong. You ignored all
that.

Massenay (*smugly*) Well.

Francine When you set your heart on something ...

Massenay (*the same*) *You* know.

Francine If you hadn't insisted, I'd have been so
sad ...

Massenay Why shouldn't I have insisted?

Francine I mean, if you hadn't, I'd have ... forgotten
my wifely duty ... run after you ...

Massenay I say! If I'd only known.

Francine You're shocked.

Massenay Good heavens, shocked!

Francine It's the very first time I've –

Massenay I *say*! You've never betrayed him before?

Francine No, never!

Massenay Promise you'll be faithful always.

Francine Oh, I do, I love you.

Massenay Oh, darling.

Francine Oh, darling.

*In her ecstasy she accidentally, and without noticing, jogs the
phonograph, which starts to record.*

What did people do before they fell in love?

Massenay They waited for the day.

Francine How soon can we – ?

Massenay You decide.

Francine Tonight.

Massenay We *could*.

Francine I've managed to get away. I'll tell my
husband I'm going to the theatre with my mother. A
whole evening, just for you and me.

Massenay Wonderful. But, just for tonight, we'll have
to make do again with 21 rue du Colisée.

Francine Doesn't matter. I'm used to it now.

Massenay And in love, so much in love.

Francine Oh, darling.

They clinch. **Chanal** *opens his door. They spring to their former
positions.*

Massenay No, really, the Eiffel Tower.

Enter **Chanal**, *papers in hand.*

Chanal One thing . . .

Massenay What?

Chanal How long? The lease?

Massenay (*gazing at* **Francine**) As long as life is in me.

Chanal Don't be silly. Three years? Six years?

Massenay Not nearly enough.

Chanal Fine, twelve. Reviewable every three, at your
discretion. Your discretion . . . ?

Massenay Rely on it.

Chanal Excuse me again.

Exit. He leaves the door open. Pause. **Massenay** *goes to embrace*
Francine.

Francine Shh! He'll hear you.

Massenay Right.

They sit on the sofa. Gaze into each other's eyes. Are magnetically drawn together in a deep, long kiss. **Chanal** *is talking over his shoulder from his office.*

Chanal Have you run out of conversation, the two of you?

Francine (*quickly*) No, no.

Chanal Don't mind me. You carry on.

Massenay We didn't want –

Chanal I won't be a moment.

Francine (*hissing at* **Massenay**) Say something.

Massenay What?

Francine Anything. (*Aloud.*) Tell me about your primary school.

Massenay (*lyrically: he's talking about his school, but he's proposing love*) It's amazing. The Hubert Harcourt School. (*Kiss.*) Founded by Hubert Harcourt. (*Kiss.*) Hence the name. (*Kiss.*) 1813. (*Kiss.*) You climb the imposing steps ... (*Kiss.*) The hall, its statues, its polished parquet ... (*Kiss.*) Portrait of the fou – (*Kiss.*) – nder, that he sat for in person at the time ...

These rhapsodies are interrupted by a huge burst of mocking laughter from **Chanal**. **Massenay** *has just time to hurl himself away from* **Francine** *when* **Chanal** *comes in.*

Chanal Why are you in such raptures? It's only a primary school.

Massenay I wasn't.

Chanal You were. You should have heard yourself. (*Imitating.*) 'You climb the imposing steps ... (*Pause.*) The hall, its statues, its polished parquet ... (*Pause.*) Portrait of the fou – (*Pause.*) – nder, that he sat for in person ...' All those pauses for emotion. It's ridiculous.

Massenay   I'd no idea.

Chanal   You really love that school.

Massenay (*making sheep's eyes at* **Francine**)   Oh, yes.

Chanal   Here's the lease. Two copies. I've signed one, all you have to do is sign the other and we keep a copy each.

Massenay   Fine. Have you got a pen?

Chanal   Don't be ridiculous. Have you never done this before? Take it away, read it carefully, then sign and return one copy.

Massenay   If you say so. (*Gathering his hat.*) Well, I won't impose any longer.

Chanal   You, imposing? Never. Delighted to see you again.

Massenay   Me too. Madame, honoured to have met you.

Francine   I hope, Monsieur, now that we're neighbours, that we'll see much more of you.

Massenay   Oh, I do agree. Good afternoon, Madame. (*To* **Chanal**.) Bye, you.

Francine, *unseen by* **Chanal**, *blows a kiss.* **Chanal** *feels the wind of it on his neck. He looks round for the source of the breeze. Then sees that* **Étienne** *has opened the door.*

Chanal   Ah, Étienne. Show Monsieur out. (*To* **Massenay**.) Bye, snotnose.

Exeunt **Massenay** *and* **Étienne**.

Francine   What a nice man, your friend.

Chanal   Yes, isn't he? (*Pause.*) Had you thought of . . . getting closer to him?

Francine   What d'you mean? Oh. Yes.

Chanal No problem. Just requires organisation.

Francine Oh, yes.

Chanal I'd be really delighted. I mean, if you hadn't liked him . . . Women, one never knows. You're wonderful.

Francine You don't need to thank me.

Chanal (*going to the phonograph*) Now, for heaven's sake, let me finish my cylinder.

Francine I'm going out. I'm taking Mama to the theatre.

Chanal (*kissing her*) Good night, darling. Don't be too late home.

Francine As soon as it's over. I'll take a cab.

Chanal Go on, go on.

He shoos her out. Then fiddles with the phonograph.

Now, where were we?

Phonograph 'My dearest sister, so the deed is done. From today you'll be a married woman.'

Chanal That's the place.

Phonograph 'You'll discover a secret, penetrate a mystery, the one on all young women's minds . . .'
(*Continuing with* **Francine** *and* **Massenay**.) 'What did people do before they fell in love?' 'They waited for the day.'

Chanal Francine's voice.

Phonograph 'How soon can we – ?' 'You decide.' 'Tonight.' 'We *could*.' 'I've managed to get away . . .'

Chanal What did she say?

Phonograph 'I'll tell my husband I'm going to the theatre with my mother. A whole evening, just for you and me.'

Chanal   My God, my God!

Phonograph   'Wonderful. But, just for tonight, we'll have to make do again with 21 rue du Colisée.'

Chanal   Got them!

Phonograph   'Doesn't matter. I'm used to it now.'

Chanal   That's enough!

He stuffs a hanky into the bell. The machine continues, muffled but remorseless.

Phonograph   'And in love, so much in love.' 'Oh, darling.'

Chanal   Treachery!

He hurls himself to the door.

Étienne! Étienne!

Étienne (*hurrying in*)   Yes, Monsieur?

Chanal   Where's Madame?

Étienne   She went out, Monsieur. Just now, Monsieur.

Chanal   Fine. Go! Go, go!

Exit **Étienne**.

Chanal   Went out! She couldn't wait. Her lover, she couldn't wait! If I knew who it was . . . He must have been here. Which one?

Doorbell, off.

It was him! My God, the swine! Pretending, and all the time he . . . Coustillou! That asparagus business. Coustillou! Grr, the swine.

Étienne *shows in* **Coustillou**, *with an enormous bundle of newspapers.*

Coustillou   I couldn't remember the name, so I got them all.

Chanal   Get out!

Coustillou   Pardon?

Chanal   Get out, get out, get out.

Coustillou   But I've got the papers.

Chanal   See what I think of them!

He grabs them and starts trying to tear them wildly. They're too strong for him. He throws them away in a fury – right in **Étienne***'s face.*

Étienne   Ow!

Chanal   I'm sorry. An accident. (*Advancing on* **Coustillou***.*) You. Don't just stand there. 21 rue du Colisée.

Coustillou   Pardon?

Chanal   She's waiting.

Coustillou   Who is?

Chanal   My wife, you fool! Go to her! Make love to her! Go on, go on!

Coustillou   Make *love* –

Chanal   Traitor! Viper! Earthworm! Out, out, out!

He bundles him out.

Étienne, you see that swine? If he so much as darkens this door again, kick him downstairs. D'you hear? Go on! Go on!

He storms round the stage, turning at the last moment to say to the audience:

This feels so *good!*

He sweeps into his office and slams the door, as the curtain falls.

Act Two

Massenay's *love-nest in the rue du Colisée. The usual ornate, rococo style: the cupids and harlequins framing the mirror over the fireplace are typical. Apart from the entrance door (which needs a serviceable lock), a second door opens into the inner room. There is a window, lavishly curtained. The principal furniture is a four-poster bed; other items — sofa, chairs, tables — ad lib. There is a speaking-tube with the usual whistle attached, to attract the attention of the person at the other end.*

When the curtain rises, the day clothes of **Francine** *and* **Massenay** *are on separate chairs;* **Massenay**'s *long-johns and top hat are also there. The two love-birds are fast asleep in the bed.* **Francine** *is peaceful, but* **Massenay** *is having disturbed dreams, which culminate in him sitting bolt upright, pointing into the darkness of the room and shouting:*

Massenay   Further left! Further left, you fool!

Francine *(starting awake)*   What's the matter? What is it?

Massenay   He's going to land on us.

Francine *(shaking him)*   It's just a nightmare.

Massenay   Look out! Look out!

Francine   Émile! Wake up!

Massenay   What? Hoo. *(Awake.)* What's the matter?

Francine   You frightened me half to death.

Massenay   What? Me? How?

Francine   Dreaming out loud like that. My heart's really thumping.

Massenay   I'm sorry.

Francine   Feel it.

Massenay   Darling, I'm sorry. *(Jumping out of bed, in his* *long nightgown.*) I'll fetch you a glass of water.

Francine   You never told me you had nightmares.

Massenay   I don't. I usually just sleep with a sheet. You insisted on the quilt. They always give me nightmares. I thought it was a hot-air balloon.

Francine   Oh, darling, it's my fault. I'm sorry.

Massenay   No, no, it's my fault. My nightmare. Mind you, nightmares: they're worth having, just to wake up from.

Francine   You are clever.

Massenay   It was unforgivable of me, having a nightmare in someone else's arms. Your arms. We went to sleep in each other's arms.

Francine   Oh, Émile, afterwards! Just like the husband and wife in a fairy tale. Going gently off to sleep together, duty done . . .

Massenay   Oh, darling.

Francine   I completely forgot my husband.

Massenay   I should think so.

Francine   I was transported to Paradise.

Massenay   Naturally.

He is putting on his long-johns.

Francine   Falling asleep in each other's arms. That's what love is. If you don't do that, you can't be in love. No satisfaction at all.

Massenay   Well, I'm not so sure –

Francine   It's in all the stories. I mean, immediately afterwards, there's a moment or two of . . . of . . .

Massenay (*in his best Latin accent*)   *Animal triste.*

Francine   Pardon?

Massenay   It's Latin. *Animal triste*. It means . . .

Francine   Never mind, if it's Latin it proves it. Asleep in each other's arms – if you don't have that, it's like going out to dinner in a station.

Massenay   I say! *You* said *I* was clever.

Francine   No, I mean it. Going to sleep afterwards makes it seem . . . domestic, married, not an affair. Respectable.

Massenay   You know everything.

Francine   It was in the stars, we were made for each other. Some things are fated before we're even born. I mean, in the ordinary way, it should have been Coustillou. He's been standing there for weeks. In the ordinary way, he could say he got here first – but no! Brr! I couldn't.

Massenay   Poor Coustillou.

Francine   You think I ought to – ?

Massenay   No, I don't.

Francine   The moment I saw you . . . we'd never met, didn't know each other . . . I knew, right away, 'He's the one who'll . . .' – and you must have known, at the same moment, 'She's the one who'll . . .'

Massenay   Must I?

Francine   Don't say you didn't. It's like Morse code. Tap tap tap at one end . . . tap tap tap at the other. You were in the stalls, I was in the gallery, your eyes met mine, and something inside me knew at once –

Massenay   'He's the one who'll . . .'

Francine (*falling back luxuriously on the pillows*)   It's wonderful. If we were married, it'd be like this every morning.

Massenay   Oh, yes.

Francine   You're lucky, you're free. If I was free too, would you marry me?

Massenay   Like a shot.

Francine   It would be so wonderful. Happiness, any time we chose, for as long as we chose. No clock-watching, ever.

Massenay   No clock-watching! I mean ... the theatre must be finishing. It feels like midnight.

Francine (*lazily*)   So soon! Oh ... what time *is* it?

Massenay (*looking at his watch, on the bedside table*)   Oh, just ... My God!

Francine (*still yawning*)   What?

Massenay   There's something wrong with it.

Francine (*sitting up*)   It's not midnight?

Massenay   Six o'clock in the morning.

Francine   What d'you mean, six o'clock in the morning?

Massenay   Six o'clock in the morning.

Francine   It's stopped. We can't have slept all night.

Massenay   It's going. Listen. Tick, tock, tick, tock ... It's going.

Francine   If it is, it's fast. You lose all sense of time when you're asleep.

The clock on the mantelpiece gathers itself to chime.

Ah! Listen!

They count the chimes.

Both   Two ... three ... four ... five ... six ...

Massenay   Seven.

But the clock has stopped chiming. It's like treading on a stair that isn't there.

Francine   Six! Six! It's six!

Massenay   Six is bad enough.

Francine   Six is a disaster.

She leaps out of bed and starts pulling on her clothes.

Massenay   Oh God, oh, God, oh God, oh God . . .

Francine   It's all right for you. You aren't married.

Massenay (*forgetting*)   Of course I'm married.

Francine (*jumping*)   Married?

Massenay   No, no, no, no, no, no, yes.

Francine   Married! That's disgusting. You said you were a bachelor.

Massenay   Of course I said I was a bachelor. If you say you're married, you get nowhere.

Francine   Married!

Massenay   My God! What will I tell my *wife*?

Francine (*raging*)   Never mind your wife! No one asked you to be married. What am *I* going to tell my husband?

Massenay   We're done for, done for.

Francine   Don't be ridiculous. I can't tell him that.

Massenay   You're the one that said, 'Let's go to sleep.'

Francine   I did not say, 'Let's go to sleep.' I said, 'I feel so sleepy.' Entirely different.

Massenay   And look where it's landed us. What am I going to do?

Francine   You're so selfish. *You're* going to do? I'm at my wits' end.

Massenay Well, so am I, twice over: once for you and once for me.

Francine What are we going to *do*?

Massenay There's one way. You're supposed to be at your mother's. Perhaps your husband hasn't gone there yet. Hurry to her, tell her everything –

Francine *What?* Tell my mother I . . . ? Don't be ridiculous.

Massenay Mothers are women. They must've *all* –

Francine How dare you? *My* mother – ?

Massenay I didn't say she had. I didn't say mothers have lovers. Ridiculous. I mean, mothers have friends who have . . . In any case, they understand. It's what they're there for. Tell her everything. She'll send your husband a message: you're not well, you had to stay the night, she insisted . . .

Francine The sky's black, black, black!

Massenay It isn't: look, dawn.

Francine A comb, quick. Give me a comb.

Massenay In here!

Francine If I get out of this, I'll give up lovers for ever.

Massenay Me too! Oh, me too!

They jostle their way into the inner room and shut the door. Pause. Then we hear a key in the lock, and the door opens to reveal **Hubertin**. *He is completely drunk, his evening wear is slightly dishevelled and he is carrying a light-coloured overcoat, upside down so that the arms drag on the floor, and a pocket torch held the wrong way round so that it illuminates his stomach. (Feydeau's note: It's important that this is not a vulgar drunk-scene –* **Hubertin** *is a man of distinction, and his drunkenness is not so much a matter* *of falling down as of owlish overemphasis and exaggerated, clumsy care over his movements. The intoxication is mainly in his head: his eyelids droop, but his speech is finicky and self-aware rather than slurred.) He goes up to the bed as quietly as he can, trying to whistle gently to attract attention. The whistling takes all his attention before he finally gets it, more or less, right.*

Hubertin Fweep! It's all right. It's me. Gaby, c'est moi. Dark in here. What's wrong with this torch, shines backwards.

He looks hard at the torch, gradually loses his balance and takes a step or two backwards.

See what it's making me do.

He notices the audience, smiles at them confidentially.

I'm a lil bit ... not a lot, just a lil bit ...

He goes upstage a bit. He talks to himself, taking both parts.

What was I going to do? Hubertin, think. That's it. The door. What about the door? Oh, shut it. Yes, shut it. I will.

He sashays towards the door, but loses his balance, steps backwards, round, back to the door, down again ...

It's the devil of a way ...

He finally gets there, drapes himself against the door and shuts it.

Foof. No, just a minute. (*To the door.*) Don't go away.

He fishes the key out of his pocket, tries several times to fit it into the lock.

This key keeps growing. The keyhole's shrunk. (*To the keyhole.*) Behave yourself!

He succeeds in locking the door.

There we are. Much more comfy. Odd, isn't it, when you've had a few, amazing things happen.

He has made his way to the chair where **Massenay**'s *hat and coat and trousers are draped so that in the gloom they look like a person. He talks to them.*

What? You agree. Good evening. Bonsoir. I mean, amazing . . . I live on the fifth floor, but I come up one flight and here I am. Can *you* explain it? I've had a skinful. Head heavy. Ow . . .

He palpates his head through his hat.

Much too heavy. Seems *enormous* . . .

He lifts off the hat, to reveal a table lighter perched on his head.

That's better. No it isn't. (*Feeling it.*) It's hard! It's loose! It's coming off!

He catches the lighter as it falls, and looks at it owlishly.

A lighter. How did that get there? Amazing things happen.

He goes to put the lighter on the table, sees **Massenay**'s *clothes again.*

See what I mean? Amazing. Been here long? (*To the audience.*) Sh! Shhhh! Can't you see he's sleeping? Dark in here. Where did I put my matches?

He starts trying to find the pockets of his coat. It's still trailing on the floor, still upside down.

Someone's stolen the sleeves. They've put in legs.

He walks it about on the sleeves, then bundles it up and throws it into a corner.

Thing is, I'm a lil bit . . . So go to bed. What? Go to *bed.* Don't stand there saying you're a lil bit . . . Who's arguing? Who's arguing?

He starts undressing.

Take your clothes off.

*He sees **Massenay**'s clothes again.*

No, there they are. So drunk you dint even notice. You undressed and you dint even notice. That's right. So get into bed. Into bed? You'll catch your death of cold. So I will. So get into bed. I'll get into bed.

He gets into the bed, but in such a way that his head is below the pillows and his feet stick out at the bottom.

S'funny. I've got longer.

*He dozes. Pause. Enter **Francine**, talking over her shoulder to* **Massenay**.

Francine   Well, *I* don't know! Perhaps it's on the bed somewhere.

*She feels up and down the bed – and finds **Hubertin**.*

Hubertin   Gaby, no. I've got a headache.

Francine   Émile! Émile!

Hubertin (*sitting bolt upright*)   Gaby? Gaby?

Massenay (*rushing in*)   Francine! Francine!

Francine   There's a man in the bed.

Hubertin   There's a man in my wife's bedroom.

*He jumps out of bed, rushes to **Massenay**'s clothes on the chair, and starts pulling them on over his own clothes.*

Massenay   Monsieur, who are you?

Hubertin (*huge*)   I'm the husband.

Massenay   Pardon?

Hubertin   The husband! I'm the husband!

Massenay   My trousers. What are you doing with my trousers?

*He leaps at him. **Francine** restrains him.*

Francine Émile!

Massenay (*breaking free*) Let me get at him.

Hubertin (*over all this*) Yours, are they? We'll see about *you.*

He bundles them up and goes to the window.

Massenay (*still struggling*) Where are you going with those?

Hubertin (*throwing open the window*) I'll teach you to be my wife's lover.

Massenay What's he doing!

Hubertin (*throwing the clothes out of the window*) Ha-HAH!

Massenay (*breaking free and rushing to the window*) No!

Francine Émile!

Massenay He's thrown my clothes into the street.

Hubertin (*turning from the window, with immense dignity*) Now, sir, begone.

Massenay You're mad.

Francine A madman! Help!

Massenay Stop shouting. You'll wake the whole building.

Francine Please. Let's do what he says. Let's go.

Massenay Dressed like this?

Hubertin Sirrah, I'm waiting.

Massenay Wait all you like. *I'm* not leaving.

Francine Please!

Massenay The speaking tube. Call the concierge.

Francine Oh. Yes.

She rushes for the speaking tube and starts frantically blowing the whistle. **Massenay** *advances on* **Hubertin**.

Massenay Now for you.

He rolls up his sleeves. **Hubertin** *ignores him, goes to* **Francine**.

Hubertin Gaby . . .

Francine Émile! He's attacking me.

Massenay Never fear! I'm here!

He hurls himself between them, knocking **Hubertin** *off balance.*

Hubertin Ho-HO!

Massenay I'm not scared of you.

Francine Why doesn't the concierge answer?

She whistles even more frantically. **Massenay** *advances on* **Hubertin**, *pointing dramatically at the door.*

Massenay Out! Now!

Hubertin *just looks at him.*

Massenay Like that, is it? Shift yourself!

Hubertin *stays where he is.*

Massenay Right.

He tries to push him. A man pushing against an oak tree. **Hubertin** *doesn't budge.* **Massenay** *leans into his work. Then stops, panting.*

Massenay This is a heavy one.

Francine Get on with it.

Massenay (*furiously*) Don't tell *me*, tell *him*!

The struggle begins again. Same result. To **Hubertin**:

Massenay You're doing this on purpose.

He is bending down, putting all his effort into pushing, like a man trying to budge a train. **Hubertin** *looks down, amused, then bends with drunken dignity and kisses the back of his head.*

Massenay Stop that!

Another kiss.

Don't keep *doing* that.

Francine Stop playing silly games and throw him out.

Hubertin *has begun remorselessly to move forwards.*
Massenay, *still bent double and heaving mightily, is carried backwards by the sheer bulk of* **Hubertin**, *until he is hard up against the end of the bed.*

Massenay I'm doing the best I can.

Hubertin *puts his arms round his thighs, picks him up like a parcel and throws him on the bed.*

Massenay Hey!

Francine Oh my God.

She rushes to the figure in the bed.

Is that him?

Massenay (*struggling to get up*) No, it's me.

He jumps off the bed and advances like a boxer on the mountainous, motionless **Hubertin**.

Massenay *This'll* shift him.

He throws a punch. **Hubertin** *parries, as calmly as a boxing Buddha.* **Massenay** *tries another punch, with the same result. He pummels, to no effect. Then* **Hubertin**, *slowly, calmly, bops him and sends him spinning across the room.*

Massenay Ow-ooh!

Francine Now what are you playing at?

Massenay This! Can't you see? I'm playing at this!

Fetch a candle. How can I see to hit him, unless you fetch a candle?

Francine   Where are they?

Massenay   *I* don't know. Find one!

Francine   In the inner-room cabinet!

She hurries into the inner room. **Hubertin** *stands there, a delighted child.*

Hubertin   When it comes, are we going to fight again?

Massenay   You wait! You just wait! You'll see!

Hubertin   I'll like that.

Enter **Francine** *with a candle. She passes* **Hubertin**, *and the flame lights up his face.*

Francine   My God, it's Hubertin.

Massenay   What's Hubertin?

Francine   He's a friend of my husband.

Massenay   He's a warthog.

Hubertin (*who has been looking round*)   Oops.

Francine *and* **Massenay**   Now what?

Hubertin   I don't live here.

Francine *and* **Massenay**   What?

Hubertin   This isn't the fifth floor.

Francine (*beside herself*)   No it is *not* the fifth floor.

Massenay   It's the first floor.

Hubertin   I shouldn't be here.

Massenay   Ah.

Hubertin   Who the devil are you? I don't know you.

Massenay (*beside himself*)   Oh, we just thought we'd fetch you and play with you.

Hubertin   Well, go away.

Massenay   You go away! This is our apartment.

Francine   Creeping in here, attacking people . . . it's outrageous.

Hubertin (*a huge cry*)   Oooo-eee!

Francine *and* **Massenay**   Now what?

Hubertin (*advancing on her, beaming, with his hand outstretched*)   Madame Chanal!

Francine (*turning her back swiftly*)   Ha-h'm.

Massenay   Golly.

Hubertin (*with a drunkard's exaggerated politeness*)   What a delightful surprise. How are you?

Francine (*hiding behind* **Massenay**)   I'm not. I'm someone else.

Massenay   She's someone else.

Hubertin   Monsieur Chanal: how *is* he?

Francine   Never heard of him.

Massenay   Never heard of him. We've never heard of him. We aren't Madame Chanal.

Hubertin   I say.

Massenay   She's *my* wife.

Hubertin   Oh, I'm terribly sorry. You know how it is, when you've had a lil bit . . . not a lot, a lil bit . . . You see things you shouldn't. I mean, you . . . (*Confidingly to* **Massenay**.) You look like . . . (*Sketching it.*) a cucumber.

Massenay   Cucumber?

Hubertin (*delighted that he's got it*)   Entirely.

Massenay   Listen, you: when you've had a lil bit . . . you don't burst into other people's apartments.

Hubertin   But you took my door.

Massenay   What d'you mean, we took your door?

Hubertin   My key fitted it. (*Getting his mouth round this with difficulty.*) Fit-ted-it.

Massenay   This is ridiculous.

Francine   We'll discuss it tomorrow.

Hubertin   But Madame Chanal . . .

Massenay (*taking him by the arm*)   First, will you stop calling her Madame Chanal?

Hubertin   I don't know her first name.

Massenay   And second, will you go down to the street and fetch my clothes?

Hubertin   What clothes?

Massenay (*between his teeth*)   The ones you threw out of the window.

Hubertin   You really want them?

Massenay   Of course I want them. I can't go out like this.

He opens the window, leans out.

Hubertin   Whatever you say.

Massenay   Hey!

Hubertin *and* **Francine**   What?

Massenay   They've gone.

Francine   What d'you mean?

Massenay   Someone's stolen them. If they hadn't, they'd *be* there. They can't have stolen themselves.

Hubertin (*highly amused*) 'Stolen themselves.' That's very funny.

Massenay What are we going to do?

Hubertin (*sudden cry*) I know.

Massenay *and* **Francine** What?

Hubertin Let's play a game of poker.

Francine No!

Massenay How much more of this. Get out of here.

Hubertin Hey, mind your manners. I'm not being rude to you, you camel.

Massenay Camel! Now you've gone too far. I've taught you some manners once tonight already, and now you need some more.

Francine Go and fetch the concierge. He'll deal with this.

Massenay You're right. (*To* **Hubertin**.) You leave me no alternative.

He puts on his top hat and strides to the door. **Hubertin** *grins and goes to* **Francine**.

Francine Émile!

She hides behind **Massenay**. **Hubertin** *continues to advance. At the last moment he takes out a pack of cards.*

Hubertin Are we playing or aren't we?

Massenay NO WE ARE NOT PLAYING POKER!

Hubertin In that case, I challenge you.

Massenay Don't be ridiculous.

Hubertin I'm ready when you are.

Francine Émile! He's got a gun!

Massenay   Aee!

The two of them scramble down on to all fours, and make for the door.

Hubertin   Where have you gone? I can't aim straight when I've had a lil bit . . .

Massenay   Thank God, the door.

Francine   Well, open it. What are you waiting for?

Massenay   I can't. It's locked.

Francine   Aee.

Massenay   And my key's in my trousers, out the window.

Francine   We're at his mercy.

Massenay   Oh my Go-o-od.

Hubertin   Where are you?

Francine *and* **Massenay** *hide behind furniture.*

Massenay   Oh no you don't.

Francine   Have mercy. Monsieur, over here. (*She waves a hand.*) We'd love a game of poker. Especially with you. But I have to get dressed. You're wearing a poker-suit. I'm . . . in my nightie.

Hubertin   *I* don't mind.

Francine   It's not comfortable.

Hubertin   So take it off.

Francine   What?

Hubertin   In fact, that's a very good idea. We'll all take them off. Manners. If the lady undresses, so does the gentleman.

He takes off his jacket and waistcoat.

Francine   Émile! Now he's taking his clothes off.

Massenay (*rushing at him*)   You can't do that!

Hubertin (*throwing him the jacket and waistcoat*)   You always do that, for poker.

He undoes his trousers. He is still holding the gun.

Massenay   Stop it! D'you hear me, stop it! (*Defeated.*) Hoooo.

He puts the clothes down on a chair. **Hubertin** *takes off his trousers.*

Francine   Are you just going to stand there?

Massenay   What d'you *want* me to do?

Hubertin   There.

He tosses his trousers across the bed on to the floor, and stands in his long-johns. Delighted with himself, he dances a little jig, and fires the revolver accidentally into the air.

Massenay *and* **Francine**   Help!

Francine   Save me!

Massenay   And me! Save me!

They rush in all directions, like frightened rabbits.

Hubertin (*meanwhile*)   I say, I'm tired.

He sits on an upright chair, then collapses very slowly on it in a heap, cradling the revolver as if it were a baby. Meanwhile, oblivious to this, **Francine** *has been shaking and banging the door, and* **Massenay** *has thrown up the window and is trying to attract attention in the street. Eventually, he turns.*

Massenay   No one'll come.

Francine   The door won't budge.

Hubertin (*muttering*)   'S very draughty.

Voice (*off*)   What's going on in there? Who's shooting guns?

Francine (*running to the window*) It's God.

Massenay It's the people upstairs.

Hubertin Shut that window. 'S draughty. (*He covers himself entirely with the bed-quilt.*)

Massenay (*leaning to shout out of the window*) Help us, please help us! Tell the concierge. Call the police. There's a maniac in here.

Voice (*off*) A maniac, did you say?

Massenay That's right, a maniac.

He mimes a maniac, out of the window. **Francine** *sticks her head out to add her voice.*

Francine Hurry, please. Call the police.

Voice (*off*) Don't go away.

Massenay *closes the window.* **Francine** *is emotionally drained.*

Francine Harg, harg.

Massenay Where's he gone?

Francine What's the matter?

Massenay He's vanished.

Cautiously, on all fours, they search the room, looking under chairs, picking up vases, moving cushions. Eventually they creep up on the bed-quilt from opposite sides, lift it gingerly, and find **Hubertin** *asleep.*

Massenay Look at him!

Francine He's asleep. Let's go.

Massenay We haven't got the key.

Francine The police'll be here any minute.

She starts dressing.

Massenay   What am *I* going to wear?

Francine   *His* clothes. *He's* not using them.

Massenay   That's right. Why should I care what *he* wears?

He searches for the clothes.

Francine   Be quick. My skirt . . . my skirt?

Massenay *has put on* **Hubertin***'s trousers, which are short in the legs but big enough round the waist for three of him.*

Massenay   My, he's a big one.

Francine   Stop parading up and down. This isn't a fashion show.

Massenay   My shoes. I need my shoes.

Francine   Under there.

Massenay   Thank God he didn't throw *them* out the window.

Francine   Will you get on?

Massenay   All right, all right.

He starts struggling to put his shoes on, muttering at them.

Will you get on?

Francine   Now what's the matter?

Massenay   I always use a shoe-horn.

Francine   Well, use one.

Massenay   I haven't got one.

Francine   You haven't got anything!

The speaking-tube whistles.

Eek!

Massenay   Idiot!

Francine What did you say?

Massenay Not you, the concierge. In the speaking-tube.

Another loud whistle.

Francine Make him shut up. He'll wake the drunk one.

Massenay (*hobbling to the tube as fast as he can, his heels hanging out of his shoes*) Shut up, shut, up, shut up!

He snatches the tube, whistles, then speaks in a furious whisper.

You idiot. Where have you been? Call the police. Yes, police! We're in here with a maniac. Well, I don't know. *Find* some. Get on with it.

He hangs up the tube.

He says where's he to get police from at this time of night. *I* haven't got any. Ow, these shoes.

Francine How ridiculous, wearing evening shoes at a time like this.

Massenay What d'you want me to wear?

Francine I don't know. Boots, like me.

Massenay Thanks.

Francine This'll teach me to betray my husband.

Loud knocking at the door.

What's that now?

Massenay *I* don't know.

Germal (*off*) Open up, in the name of the law!

Massenay The police.

Francine Saved.

Massenay (*hobbling as fast as he can to the door*) Inspector, at last!

Germal Open up.

Massenay (*to* **Francine**) I can't. The key.

Germal I said, open up.

Massenay (*fawning through the door*) The thing is,
Inspector, the key. It's in my trousers pocket.

Germal Well, take it out then.

Massenay Ah! You see, my trousers are in the street
outside.

He hobbles towards the window, gesturing.

Germal A likely story.

Francine They are, they are.

Germal Just open this door.

Massenay Nothing would give me greater pleasure. But
. . . Just a minute.

He starts slapping and banging **Hubertin**'s *trousers, still bagging
round him.*

Massenay (*to* **Francine**) The drunk has a key. (*To the
door.*) Just a minute . . .

He tries it in the lock.

It worked for him, it should work for . . . ah. (*Opening the
door.*) Inspector, do come in. *This* is the problem.

He gestures at **Hubertin**.

Germal One moment, *if* you please.

He gestures to someone outside.

This way, Monsieur.

Enter **Chanal**.

Francine My husband!

She jumps into the bed and covers herself entirely with the sheet.

Chanal *hasn't seen her.*

Massenay   My God!

Chanal   Massenay! It was Massenay!

Germal   No use hiding, Madame.

Chanal   It wasn't Coustillou.

Germal   Madame, you can come out now.

Francine (*uncovering herself*)   Did someone call me?

Chanal (*beside himself*)   You! You!

Francine (*with an air of the utmost innocence*)   'Youyou', darling? What *is* the matter?

Chanal   What?

Francine   You don't imagine . . . just because I'm . . .

Chanal   Don't try to . . . Inspector, do your duty.

Francine   Inspector! Did you hear that, Monsieur Massenay? An inspector! He really imagines I . . .

Massenay   Unbelievable.

Francine   Inspector, I won't lower myself by denying it. You have your evidence.

Massenay   Now what are you doing?

Germal   Madame, you admit you're Madame Francine Chanal, wife of Monsieur Chanal?

Francine   Inspector, of course I do.

Germal   And you, Monsieur.

Massenay   Inspector, of course I do.

Germal   No, no, Monsieur: *your* name.

Massenay   Émile Massenay, at your service.

Germal   Massenay? Not – ?

Chanal Don't be ridiculous. Does he *look* like – ?

Massenay Age thirty-seven. Private income. 28, rue de Longchamp.

Germal Both of you admit being caught here *in flagrante delicto* –

Francine Of course. That . . . and more. Throw the book at us.

Germal That *would* be strict. *Flagrante*'ll do nicely. (*To* **Chanal**.) You agree, Monsieur?

Chanal *makes a gesture of baffled agreement.*

Francine (*as if firmly in charge*) Excellent. Now, Inspector, I do have to finish dressing. If you'd be so kind . . . ?

Germal Madame, of course. We've all we need. If you, Madame, and you, Monsieur, would be so kind as to call at my office between one and two this afternoon, I'll have the statements prepared for signing. Monsieur Chanal, if you'll come with me . . .

Chanal Inspector, at your service.

He prepares to go. He has to pass **Massenay***, who is still struggling with his shoes.*

Chanal You too, Monsieur.

Massenay (*crossly*) In a minute.

Chanal What *do* you mean, a minute?

Massenay You haven't a shoe-horn on you?

Chanal A shoe-horn?

Massenay No, sorry. Sorry.

Chanal This is no time for foolery.

Massenay No, no. Sorry.

Chanal Please remember your appointment: one o'clock

in the inspector's office. (*At the door.*) After you, Inspector.

Germal   No, no, after you.

Chanal   No, no, I insist.

Germal   Make yourself at home.

Chanal   What?

Germal   Sorry. Force of habit.

Exeunt.

Francine   Now what?

Massenay   Now what?

Francine   I hope you're satisfied. This is your fault.

Massenay   Darling, I'm heart-broken.

Francine   'Darling, I'm heart-broken.' What good does that do?

Massenay   I know. But what *can* I do?

He struggles with his shoes.

Francine   A gentleman would know what to do. In a perilous situation, a gentleman would gallop to protect his lady's honour.

Massenay   How? These shoes . . .

Francine   For heaven's sake, those shoes! If you can't find a shoe-horn, use a fork!

Massenay   A fork. How clever!

Francine   Thank you.

Massenay   There'll be one in there.

He goes to the inner room. She harries him.

Francine   What a lover you are! Doesn't even know how to use a fork!

Massenay *goes.* **Hubertin** *stirs.*

Hubertin This chair's not comfy.

He hitches himself up, still wrapped in the quilt, and flops face-down on the bed.

Francine I should have known! I should have known! (*At the door.*) What on earth is he *doing*? (*At the inner-room door.*) Aren't you ready?

Massenay (*off*) I'm coming.

Francine I'll wait downstairs.

She turns to the door again, and bumps into **Coustillou***, who has burst in.*

Coustillou You!

Francine Oh, you gave me such a fright.

Coustillou (*with a sob in his throat*) You, you, you.

Francine Yes, me, me, me. Who told you I was here?

Coustillou Your husband. He sent me. He gave me the address. He was downstairs. He said, you were up here with ... with your fancy man.

He sobs.

Francine For heaven's sake don't you start.

She goes.

Coustillou Wait! Ow!

She's slammed the door in his face. He turns broken-heartedly into the room.

A fancy man! I can't bear it! I just can't bear it! No! No! No!

With each 'No', he pounds his fist on the bed — and on **Hubertin** *sleeping under the quilt.* **Hubertin** *surges up.*

Hubertin   What the devil – ?

Coustillou   Hubertin! Her fancy man! Take that!

He slaps him.

Hubertin   That does it!

He fires.

Coustillou   No! Help! No!

He rushes out. **Hubertin** *fires a second shot after him, then crouches on the bed, en garde, like a hunter aiming at his prey.* **Massenay** *appears from the inner room.*

Massenay   He's shooting now. Help! Help!

He snatches **Hubertin**'*s hat, and stumbles out as fast as he can, dodging the non-existent bullets.*

Act Three

The sitting-room of **Massenay**'s *apartment. Window (with balcony) opening on the street below. Main doors to hall, centre back; doors R and L to the servants' quarters and other rooms of the apartment. The furniture, in the latest style, includes a sofa high enough to hide underneath. There is a writing-desk and a telephone.*

When the curtain rises, **Marthe** *is on the balcony, leaning over to look down the street. It's broad daylight.* **Sophie** *is beside the window, trying to see out. She is agitated.*

Sophie   There's a carriage.

Marthe   There is, Madame, you're right. That I can't deny.

Sophie   Is it Monsieur?

Marthe   That might be.

Sophie   No, it's going past.

Marthe   That is, Madame, you're right. That I can't deny.

They come into the room.

Sophie   It's awful, it's awful.

Marthe   Try to be calm, Madame. Don't upset yourself so.

Sophie   What if something's happened?

Marthe   That won't bring him home any sooner.

Sophie   Thank you. Anyone can see he's not your husband.

Marthe   Now Madame, 'No news, good news.' You know what they say. That could be good news.

Sophie   You mean I should be *glad* he's not home?

Marthe　You should not, Madame. You're right. That I can't deny.

Sophie　I could call someone. On the telephone. Who? His club. He told me he had a club. I'll get the operator, you get the number.

Marthe　Yes, Madame.

While **Sophie** *does all that old-fashioned-telephone business,* **Marthe** *searches through the directory.*

Sophie　What do they do all day? Why don't they answer?

Marthe　That's a bad time of day, Madame. The women arriving for the day shift, the night-shift men going home.

Sophie　They could surely find someone else. Little boys, for example.

Marthe　They could, Madame. You're right. That I can't deny.

Sophie　What's the number?

Marthe　There isn't one, Madame.

Sophie　What d'you mean, isn't one?

Marthe　Not under 'Club', Madame.

Sophie　It's 'Touring Club', 'Touring Club'.

Marthe　That it is, Madame. You're right. That I can't deny.

Sophie　You're doing this on purpose. Listen! Wheels! A vehicle!

Marthe (*on the balcony*)　That it is, Madame.

Sophie　Is Monsieur inside?

Marthe　I don't think so, Madame. That's a fish-cart.

She stays out there during what follows.

Sophie   This is too bad!

The phone rings.

At last! Hello. I'm sorry, I've nowhere else to turn. My husband, I've lost my husband. No, mislaid. He hasn't come home. I *know* it's early. It's never happened before. You don't know where he – ? No, of course. Oh, please. Thank you Monsieur.

She hangs up.

Now what are we going to do?

Enter **Auguste***, agitated.*

Sophie   Auguste, thank goodness? Yes?

Auguste   No, Madame.

Sophie   No?

Auguste   I went everywhere you asked, Madame. Restaurants, bars. All closed. Maxim's . . . waiters putting out the rubbish; the drunk they were putting out . . . No, not Monsieur. The police station, Lost Property Office . . .

Sophie   He isn't lost property.

Auguste   They do Missing Persons as well. Saves money. The morgue . . .

Sophie   No!

Auguste   They hadn't seen Monsieur.

Sophie   Thank God.

Auguste   They said not to worry, though, it was early. I left Monsieur's description: average height, medium nose, hair nondescript, speaks three languages fluently . . . I left the telephone number, in case he . . .

Sophie   Thanks, Auguste.

Doorbell, off.

Auguste   Perhaps that's Monsieur.

Sophie   No, he took his key. It must be Monsieur
Belgence. Let him in.

Auguste   Yes, Madame.

Exit.

Sophie (*to* **Marthe** *at the window*)   Still no one, Marthe?

Marthe   No, Madame. You're right. That I can't deny.

Auguste *ushers in* **Belgence**.

Sophie   Ah. You – ?

Belgence   My dear, what's wrong? Whatever's the
matter?

Sophie   Thank you for coming. I'm sorry I rang you so
early . . .

Belgence   That doesn't matter. You know I –

Sophie   I don't know what to do. I need someone to
help me. My husband still isn't home.

Belgence   You said, on the phone just now. It's
appalling.

Sophie   What can have happened to him? It's never
happened before. Oh, he's had an accident.

Belgence   No, he hasn't. Accidents aren't like this.

Sophie   Don't spare me. He's dead. I know he's dead.

Belgence (*comforting her*)   There, there. There, there.

Sophie   Still nothing, Marthe?

Marthe   No, Madame.

Sophie   You see? I didn't tell her to say that.

Marthe   That's true, Madame. Nothing. That I can't
deny.

Belgence (*playing it like a Dutch uncle*) Come on, now.
We're human. It's not all lost. While there's life, there's
hope. We must do something.

Sophie What do you suggest?

Belgence I don't know, something. In fact, I've done
something already. On my way here, I passed the police
station. The inspector's a friend of mine: Planteloup. I
said to him, 'Planteloup, no time to lose. A friend of
mine's just lost her husband ... mysterious circumstances
...' He said, 'I'm on my way' – he won't be long. He's
not brilliant, but he is a policeman.

Sophie He's dead, oh my God, he's dead.

She flings herself sobbing on to the sofa.

Belgence Now, now, there's no need to put yourself in
such a state.

He sits and tries to comfort her.

Please. My dear. I can't bear to see you. Oh, Sophie ...
(*Down on one knee.*) Sophie, you know I've always loved
you.

Sophie (*indignantly*) *What?*

Belgence I'm devoted to you. I didn't speak out,
because you're married. But now I can say, with all my
heart –

Sophie How dare you?

Belgence What?

Sophie Make declarations like that at a time like this!

Belgence I'm not making declarations.

Sophie Enough! You've said quite enough already.
What d'you take me for? Why should I listen to
proposals, with my husband not even cold?

Belgence You haven't. I didn't. All I meant was, I'm your slave, I'll do anything you want, you can count on me for anything.

Sophie Ah. (*Leaning her head on his breast.*) Thank you. I thought . . . When he was hardly . . . he was always so fond of you.

Belgence (*touched*) Dear Émile!

Sophie Only yesterday he was saying, 'Good old Belgence. Not much up top, but a dear, dear friend.'

Belgence, *moved, blows his nose, wipes away a tear.*

Sophie That was yesterday, and now today he's –

Belgence Alas.

They sigh together. Pause. Doorbell, off.

Sophie The bell! Marthe!

Belgence Marthe!

Sophie (*yelling*) Ma-a-a-a-a-arthe!

Marthe *arrives, fast.*

Sophie Someone at the door.

Marthe Yes, Madame.

She hurries to the hall door.

Belgence It's probably Inspector Planteloup, from the police.

Just as **Marthe** *gets to the door,* **Auguste** *throws it open from the other side.*

Auguste It's Inspector Planteloup, from the police.

Sophie Show him in.

She composes herself. Enter **Planteloup** *and* **Constable**.
Belgence *goes to greet* **Planteloup**.

Belgence My dear Planteloup, you're as welcome as flowers in spring. This is the unfortunate Madame Massenay.

Planteloup Madame, Monsieur Belgence has told me everything. You've no idea how pleased I am.

Sophie Pardon?

Planteloup For a police inspector, a major crime is manna from heaven. Often, it means promotion. Alas, you see, we don't all start on a level playing field. I've colleagues, in Belleville and Charonne, for example, fate smiles on them quite unfairly. Crimes, crimes, crimes, they hardly have to *stir* out of bed.

Sophie Inspector –

Planteloup I, on the other hand ... this *dreadful* area ... a drunk singing in the street is major crime.

Sophie Inspector, I really –

Planteloup Now at last, perhaps ... the fickle finger of destiny, smiling on me, on *me* ... Monsieur Massenay, a blameless, upright citizen, vanished overnight ... dark doings at dead of night ... this could be *magnificent*. (*To the* **Constable**.) Sit you down there, laddie. Make detailed notes. Now, Madame, in the Massenay Affair (as I think it will soon be called), the simplest theory to begin with is: murder.

Sophie I don't *know* that.

Planteloup (*benignly*) Of course you don't. That's what we have to prove. Our simple duty.

Sophie (*furious*) Oh!

Planteloup Now, d'you have, by any chance, a photograph?

Sophie Of poor Émile?

Planteloup Of poor Émile. Exactly.

Sophie   Just one. On his seventh birthday.

Planteloup   He'll have changed since then. How vexing. Our first setback.

He muses. Doorbell, off.

All except Planteloup   Someone's there! Someone's there!

Planteloup   Did you scream, Madame?

Sophie   Someone rang the bell. Auguste, go and see.

Auguste   Yes, Madame.

Exit.

Sophie   I'm sorry, Inspector. I'm not myself . . .

Planteloup   That's quite all right. We don't lose our husbands *every* day.

Sophie   Ah.

Planteloup   One question, Madame . . . of a delicate nature. If you wouldn't mind.

Sophie   No, no.

Planteloup   Did he have any little habits?

Sophie   Who, little habits?

Planteloup   Poor Émile.

Sophie   What little habits?

Planteloup   Drink, sex, gambling . . .

Sophie   Of course he didn't.

Planteloup   Oh, what a shame.

Sophie   What?

Planteloup   From the inquiry point of view.

Sophie (*aside to* **Belgence**)   Stop me before I slap him.

Belgence (*aside to her*) Better not.

Enter **Auguste**.

Sophie Well? Who is it?

Auguste A roadsweeper.

All Roadsweeper?

Auguste With Monsieur's clothes.

All Eh?

Sophie What do you mean, his clothes?

Auguste They were in the street.

All No!

Sophie In the street?

Belgence Just the clothes?

Sophie And Monsieur?

Belgence *and* **Planteloup** And Monsieur?

Auguste He wasn't in them.

Planteloup Not in them, eh?

Sophie He must have been.

Auguste That's what the sweeper said. At least if I understood him.

Sophie He doesn't speak French?

Auguste Yes he does. Except when he's barking.

All Barking?

Auguste Barking. It's hard to follow.

Sophie Oh, show him in.

Auguste Yes, Madame.

Exit.

We'll see about this.

...loup We will indeed.

Sophie His clothes. In the street. What's he doing?

Belgence Walking round stark naked, by the sound of it.

Planteloup (*rubbing his hands*) This gets juicier by the minute.

Sophie (*aside to* **Belgence**) He's *enjoying* this.

Belgence (*aside to her*) They lead very quiet lives.

Auguste *fetches in* **Lapige**, *a man at peace with the world, with his street-sweeper's hat in his hand.*

Auguste In here.

Sophie Quickly! You found the clothes?

Planteloup Excuse me. *I'll* ask the questions.

Sophie I just asked him –

Planteloup Excuse me. This is police business.

Sophie This is *my* business.

Planteloup Madame, are you obstructing our inquiries?

Sophie (*beside herself*) That does it!

She leaps for him, but is caught by **Belgence** *in the nick of time, and taken, muttering, to sit on the sofa.*

Planteloup Over here, my man.

Lapige *advances to stand in front of him.*

Planteloup You found the clothes?

Lapige *is about to answer, when* **Planteloup** *turns to* **Sophie**.

Planteloup That *was* what you wanted me to ask, Madame?

Sophie (*ironically*)   It'll do, it'll do.

Planteloup   These things must be done officially, in the official manner. An amateur might let something slip, which would seriously damage the whole inquiry.

Sophie *throws her arms in the air. He returns to* **Lapige**.

Planteloup   My man: you may answer the question.

Lapige   Um . . . (*Barking.*) Ruff, ruff, ruff.

Sophie   What's he doing?

Planteloup (*warningly*)   Madame, please! (*To* **Lapige**.) What are you doing?

Auguste   I told you.

Lapige (*who has been barking throughout the above*)   Ruff, ruff, ruff. It's all right, Madame, Messieurs. When I'm nervous, it happens, and then . . . (*Growling like a dog.*) rrrr, rrrr . . . it passes.

Belgence   Fascinating.

Sophie   There's nothing to be nervous about.

Planteloup   One more bark, and let's have no more of it.

Lapige   It isn't *like* that.

Planteloup   Well. Give your evidence.

Lapige   This morning, I was on my patch, rue du Colisée . . .

Sophie   Where?

Lapige   Outside number 21.

Planteloup   21 rue du Colisée. Have you got that, constable?

Lapige   I found some clothes. They belong to Monsieur Massenay, 28 rue de Longchamp. The address was in his wallet. In his pocket.

He hands **Planteloup** *the things.*

Planteloup   The pockets!

He, **Sophie** *and* **Belgence** *fall on the clothes and start going through the pockets, putting the items they find on the table.*

Sophie   Here's the wallet.

Planteloup   Peppermints.

Belgence   Purse. Keys.

Sophie   Gloves, clean hanky.

Planteloup   Bus timetable.

Belgence   Change.

Planteloup   Ow!

All   What?

Planteloup   A toothpick. That's sinister.

Belgence   A revolver.

Sophie   That's his.

Planteloup   It's not been fired. (*To the* **Constable**.) The deceased was taken by surprise.

Sophie   No!

Planteloup (*laying the revolver on the table*)   Now, my man, how did these garments get into the street?

Lapige   How should I know? All I know is they were lying in the . . . ruff, ruff, ruff.

Planteloup   He's doing it again.

Sophie   We noticed.

Belgence   He was doing so well.

Planteloup   Take it calmly. There boy, there boy. Lying in the . . . ?

Lapige In the ruff, ruff.

Sophie (*trying to help him*) The gutter?

Lapige Rrr . . . ruff . . . yes.

Planteloup 'In the gutter.' That wasn't so hard. Madame said it, and *she* didn't bark. It's quite . . . When did you begin?

Lapige Last night.

Planteloup Not finding the clothes, barking.

Lapige The day I was born.

Planteloup Ah.

Lapige Mama was frightened by a greyhound.

Planteloup A greyhound. (*To the* **Constable**.) A greyhound.

Lapige He climbed all over her.

Planteloup Aha! You claim that this greyhound and your mother . . .

Lapige No, no. Mama was . . . long before he . . . ruff, ruff, ruff.

Planteloup Yes, yes. Don't start again. I understand. A fixation . . . (*To the* **Constable**.) a retrospective fixation.

Sophie Never mind all that!

Planteloup Excuse me, Madame. All evidence could be vital. (*To* **Lapige**.) Apart from the clothes, you found nothing else? Nothing that might suggest who left them there?

Lapige *does one of those elaborate French shrugs.*

Planteloup Excellent. Go and sit over there. And don't bark unless you're spoken to.

Auguste *shows* **Lapige** *to a chair, out of the way.*

Planteloup   Constable, take this down. 'Conclusion after preliminary investigation of roadsweeper, in the mysterious Massenay affair . . .'

Sophie   Shh!

All (*whisper*)   What?

Sophie   I heard a key.

All   A key?

Sophie   Someone's coming.

She switches off the light. They freeze where they are. Pause. Then the door opens surreptitiously, and a hand holding a candlestick comes in.

All (*whisper*)   A candle, look, a candle.

The hand is followed by **Massenay***, dressed in top hat, long-johns and* **Hubertin***'s outsize trousers. He creeps towards one of the inner rooms, making as little noise as possible. He is interrupted by a huge shout.*

All   It's him! It's him!

Light on. General rejoicing (not shared by **Planteloup***). Consternation of* **Massenay***.*

Sophie   Émile!

Belgence   Massenay!

Marthe *and* **Auguste**   Monsieur!

Lapige   Ruff, ruff.

Planteloup   Now then, now then.

Massenay   Good heavens, you're up already.

Sophie   You're not dead.

Massenay   Oh. Yes. How are you? My goodness, it's late.

Sophie Late? What d'you mean? Coming home at this hour?

Planteloup (*striding forward*) Monsieur, explain yourself.

Sophie It's him. It's my husband. (*To* **Massenay**.) Oh, darling.

Belgence (*to* **Planteloup**) She's right. It's him.

Planteloup Irrelevant. Monsieur, this is highly irregular. You disappear, you're murdered, the police are called in . . . You can't just spring up again out of nowhere.

Massenay Who is this man?

Sophie A police inspector. We thought something had happened to you.

Belgence They were opening an inquiry.

Massenay (*highly amused*) I don't believe it. (*To* **Planteloup**.) Good news, Monsieur: you can close it again.

Planteloup Just one moment. We're not puppets, you know. We don't dance just because you pull our strings.

Belgence Planteloup, old man –

Planteloup Stay out of it. (*To* **Massenay**.) This is a most unusual case . . . extremely rare . . .

Massenay I'm sorry. But for me it's a matter of . . . life or death.

Sophie What did happen?

Planteloup (*aggressively*) That's what we'd all like to know. Explain yourself.

Massenay Excuse me, if I explain myself to anyone, it'll be to my wife.

Sophie Go on, then. Why are you back at this hour, and dressed like that?

Massenay   You noticed the clothes.

Sophie   Of course I noticed the clothes.

Planteloup   Highly irregular.

Massenay   D'you know, this candle . . . I think it's light enough to see by.

He blows out the candle.

Planteloup   It's been light enough to see by for three whole hours.

Massenay (*sarcastically*)   Thank you *so* much.

Sophie   Well? *Well?* Explain yourself.

Massenay   Fine. First of all: these aren't my clothes.

Planteloup   You're joking.

Sophie   For heaven's sake!

Massenay   You don't believe me?

Sophie   What's the *explanation*?

Massenay   Ah, the explanation. It's . . . you see . . . the railway company.

All   The railway company?

Auguste (*slightly out of phase with the others*)   – way company?

Massenay   Auguste, you've got it: the railway company. (*To them all.*) I must have dozed off. Forgetting the compartment was full of people. Next minute, I'm awake, and paf! They've stolen my clothes. Chloroform. They left me these . . . I was wearing these. They don't fit, do they?

Sophie   What rubbish! What line?

Massenay   Line, line? Oh, line. Didn't I tell you? (*To* **Belgence**.) I forgot to tell her. (*To* **Sophie**.) You'll never believe this. Calais. I've been to Calais. In these clothes, to Calais.

All   Calais!

Auguste (*as before*) – alais!

Massenay (*to him*)   Exactly, Calais. I went to the station to see some people off . . . for Calais.

Planteloup   Highly irregular.

Massenay   What d'you mean, irregular? I bought a platform ticket. They said, 'It won't be going for ages. Come and sit down inside.' 'Oh, right. *Gut, gut.*' – one of them was German, the youngest one, hardly more than a boy really . . .

Sophie   Get on with it.

Massenay   Next minute . . . D'you know, they don't come round and warn you . . . They used to come round and warn you . . . The train started, and whoof!

Sophie   Whoof!

Planteloup   Amazing.

Belgence   Incredible.

Massenay   Unfortunately, it wasn't a stopping train. So: Calais I went to, Calais I came back from, paf!, these clothes . . . and here I am.

Planteloup   What *is* the world coming to?

Sophie   Poor darling.

Massenay   That's just what I kept thinking. 'Poor darling. She'll be watching. She'll be waiting . . .' But there was nothing I could do. None of it was my fault.

Planteloup   We believe you.

Massenay   I was asleep. The carriage was full of people.

Planteloup   Not to mention choloroform.

Massenay   How do *you* know?

Planteloup   You said so.

Massenay   There you are then. It hangs together perfectly.

Sophie   It's unbelievable.

Belgence   Unbelievable.

Planteloup   Unbelievable.

Massenay (*venting his rage on him*)   What d'you mean, unbelievable? What are you, an atheist?

Planteloup   Now, then. I'll be the judge of that. One other thing . . .

Massenay   What 'other thing'?

Planteloup   It's extraordinary. Your clothes were stolen on a train somewhere on the way to Calais, and they were picked up on the pavement of the rue du Colisée.

Massenay   Oh God.

Sophie   He's right, you know.

Belgence   So he is.

Massenay   You mean, someone . . . ?

Planteloup   My friend, exactly.

Massenay   On the . . . on the . . . ?

Planteloup   Exactly: on the.

Massenay   Well, well, well, well, well, well.

Planteloup   Weren't expecting that, were we?

Massenay   What d'you mean, 'were we'?

Planteloup   And the explanation?

Massenay   I . . . It . . . it's obvious. The train . . . the robbers . . . communication cord . . . it was a stopping train!

Planteloup   And there we have it.

Massenay   Are you calling me a liar?

Belgence   Émile, keep calm.

Massenay   He's getting on my nerves.

Planteloup (*equally cross, squaring up to him*)   Now, then!

Belgence, **Sophie** (*trying to calm* **Massenay**)   Émile!

Massenay   How should I know how my clothes got into the rue du Colisée? I wasn't in them, was I?

Planteloup   Precisely.

Massenay   In any case, who found them?

Planteloup, **Sophie**, **Belgence**   He did.

Massenay (*to* **Lapige**)   You did. Fine. You can tell them. Was I in them?

Lapige   Um . . . ruff, ruff, ruff, ruff, ruff.

Massenay   Pardon?

Lapige   Ruff.

Massenay   What are you barking for? I didn't ask for barking. I asked if I was in them.

Lapige   Rrrr . . . rrrrr . . . No.

Massenay (*triumphant*)   You see? Rrr, no. We were separated. Not my responsibility. In any case, who cares? Your business, not mine. Police business, not my business.

Planteloup   Just you wait. (*To the* **Constable**.) Mark this one 'Urgent'.

Massenay   Mark it any way you like. Now, if you'll excuse me, since you've found my clothes . . .

He starts gathering them up.

Planteloup   Leave those alone.

Massenay   They're mine.

Planteloup   They're evidence. Not to be tampered with.

Massenay (*tugging*)   Excuse me.

Planteloup (*tugging*)   Excuse *me*.

Mêlée. **Massenay** *is left with nothing but his hat and his hankie.*

Massenay   Well, thanks. Not content with sticking his nose in where it doesn't belong, he snaffles my best suit.

Planteloup (*huge*)   What did you say?

Belgence (*trying to calm* **Massenay**)   Émile, calm down.

Massenay (*turning him and pushing him away*)   You stay out of it.

Belgence (*trying to calm* **Planteloup**)   Planteloup, calm down.

Planteloup (*same gesture as* **Massenay**)   *You* calm down.

He turns his back and sulks.

Massenay   What idiot brought him here in the first place?

Planteloup (*turning, furious*)   What did you say?

Belgence (*pacifying, penitent*)   *I* did. Sorry.

Massenay   I should think you're sorry. Take him back where you found him.

Planteloup   What did you say?

Massenay   I wasn't talking to you.

Planteloup   Well, I'm talking to you, and I'm telling you your behaviour has been most suspicious from start to finish.

Massenay   From start – ?

Planteloup – to finish!

Sophie Belgence, stop them!

Belgence Planteloup, old chap, listen . . .

Planteloup I will *not* listen! I am *not* an old chap. I'm an officer of the law. You, sweeper, follow me.

Lapige *tags at his heels like a faithful hound.* **Planteloup** *rounds on* **Massenay**.

Planteloup And you: hold yourself at the disposition of the law.

Belgence Planteloup!

Planteloup Not listening! Come on, you!

He whirls to summon **Lapige**, *not realising that* **Lapige** *is right behind him. He treads hard on his foot.* **Lapige** *retreats, whimpering like a dog.*

Lapige A-hoo, a-hoo.

Planteloup Oh, never mind your paw . . . your foot. Get out of the way.

Lapige A-hoo, a-hoo. A-hoo.

Massenay Throw him a bone, why don't you?

Planteloup *storms out, pushing* **Lapige** *and followed by the* **Constable** *and* **Belgence**. **Massenay** *sees them to the door, slams it behind them, then comes downstage, still raging.*

Massenay What a brute! What a total brute!

Sophie Never mind him. Only one thing matters: you're here, you're back.

Massenay (*taking her in his arms*) Darling.

Auguste Ahem. Monsieur . . .

Massenay Ah. Fetch me something to wear. Marthe, a cup of tea, with rum.

Marthe   Yes, Monsieur.

Exeunt **Auguste** *and* **Marthe**.

Sophie   Oh darling, I thought I was going mad. I couldn't know about Calais, could I?

Massenay   Oh no.

Sophie   I'm *glad* I was so worried. It's *good* for you. You don't know the value of the husband you have till you haven't got him.

Massenay   Seems a bit hard.

Enter **Auguste** *with clothes.*

Auguste   Here you are, Monsieur.

Massenay   Thank you.

He starts changing, behind the sofa, helped by **Auguste**. *Enter* **Marthe**.

Marthe   Your tea, Monsieur.

Massenay   Put it over there.

Marthe   Yes, Monsieur.

She puts it down and exit. The phone rings.

Sophie   Auguste . . .

Auguste   Yes, Madame. (*Answering the phone.*) Hello. Yes. Ah, yes. Mm.

Massenay   Who is it?

Auguste   The morgue, Monsieur.

Massenay   The morgue?

Auguste   Oh yes, Monsieur. (*On the phone.*) Beg pardon? Fished him out?

Massenay   Fished who out?

Auguste   Monsieur, Monsieur.

Massenay Me?

Auguste In an advanced stage of decomposition.

Sophie Darling, no!

Massenay They're out of their minds.

Auguste What shall I tell them?

Massenay Tell them they're mad. No, just a minute. (*Taking the phone.*) Good morning. My manservant tells me you ... Ah. No, it can't be. This is me, here. In person. What? How d'you mean, can you get rid of it? *I* don't know. So far as *I'm* concerned. Do what you like with it. Pardon? No, no, a pleasure. Thank you. (*Hanging up.*) They're so polite. 'At your service, any time, day or night.' They're so polite.

Sophie What an adventure.

Massenay Ab-solutely. (*Stretching luxuriously.*) It's so nice to be home again. Catch your breath, relax ...

Noise of someone clumping in the hall, nearer and nearer.

Massenay *and* **Sophie**. Now what?

Marthe (*off*) You can't! Stop that! Don't put your hands on me.

Hubertin (*off*) Don't be shilly.

Massenay It's a nightmare.

Marthe (*off*) What are you *doing*?

Sophie (*rushing to* **Massenay**) Émile, what is it?

Massenay No idea.

Marthe *bursts in.*

Marthe Monsieur! Help! A drunk, Monsieur.

Sophie What d'you mean, a drunk?

Marthe He ... Oh Madame, he ...

Sophie   What?

Marthe   He grabbed my . . .

Sophie   Did he?

Marthe   That I can't deny, Madame.

Massenay (*to himself, pacing*)   Not Hubertin. Not him again.

Sophie   Émile. Go and see. Throw him out.

Massenay   Ab-solutely.

He braces himself to stride to the rescue.

Sophie   Not by yourself. Auguste! Au-guste!

Enter **Auguste**, *fast.*

Auguste   Yes, Madame?

Sophie   Quick. There's a drunk.

Auguste   A drunk?

Sophie   Help Monsieur.

Massenay   This way.

He strides out. **Auguste** *follows.*

Auguste   Whatever next?

He's gone.

Sophie   What a day. What a dreadful day.

Marthe   Yes, Madame. That I can't de –

Hubertin *bursts in, by an inner door.*

Marthe   Aah!

She rushes out, R.

Sophie   Aah!

She rushes out L. **Hubertin** *stands there. He is wearing his* *mackintosh and a top hat, but apparently nothing else.*

Hubertin Don't be frightened, lil turtle doves. It's me. It's Hubertin. Women are such babies.

He finds the teacup.

How thoughtful. With a head like this, just what I need.

He picks up a spoonful of sugar, then pours it back.

No, no. You take tea neat.

He drains the cup, smacks his lips.

My, that was neat. (*Pause.*) Cold, mind . . .

Auguste *and* **Massenay** *burst in.*

Auguste In here, Monsieur.

Massenay (*very high horse*) In here, are you? Fine. Get out.

Hubertin Now, now, now, now, now. No need to shout.

Massenay I'll set my man on you.

Auguste *makes a deprecating gesture, moves out of range.*

Hubertin Émile.

Massenay How dare you? 'Émile' – how dare you? We haven't been introduced.

Hubertin (*twisting with embarrassment*) I'm *sorry*.

He collapses on the sofa.

Massenay For heaven's sake!

Hubertin I say . . .

Massenay Don't bother.

Hubertin (*putting up his hand like a schoolchild*) Please, sir.

Massenay You *can't*.

Hubertin   One question, then I'll go.

Massenay   Oh. Get on with it.

Hubertin (*getting up and lurching towards him*)   Why did you take my clothes?

Auguste   What did you say?

Massenay (*quickly*)   How dare you? *Me*?

Hubertin *collapses on* **Massenay**, *who holds him up like a man propping up a collapsing building.*

Hubertin   When I looked for them, they'd gone.

Auguste   Those clothes were *yours*?

Massenay (*struggling to keep* **Hubertin** *upright*)   Don't be ridiculous. Mind your own business. Of course they weren't his. They came from Calais.

Hubertin   Don't be nasty. Gaby said I had to come. 'Get out,' thass what she said, 'and don't come back till you've found them,' thass what she said.

Massenay   Fine. I'll give you clothes. No problem. If you just go away.

Hubertin *signs that he will.*

Massenay   Cross your heart?

Hubertin (*with enormous, drunken force*)   An . . . hope . . . to . . . *die*! Spit . . . in . . . your . . . *eye*!

He takes one of **Massenay**'s *hands, spits in his own, and shakes it.*

Massenay   Thanks very much.

He pushes him off. **Hubertin** *falls back on the sofa.*

Hubertin   Time for bed again.

Massenay   Who told you this address?

Hubertin   Shh! The con-ci-erge.

Massenay   I'll have a word with him later.

Enter **Sophie**.

Sophie   Has he gone?

Massenay   My wife, now.

Hubertin (*getting up and attempting a bow*)   Madame, I –

Sophie   Him!

Massenay (*pushing* **Hubertin** *back down*)   That's enough.

Hubertin   Ow.

Sophie   You're all alone with him? He hasn't hurt you?

Massenay   He's perfectly tame. It's all right. Go.

Sophie   And leave you alone with him? I won't.

Hubertin (*surging to his feet again, very man-of-the-world*)   Forgettin my manners, entirely. Still wearing hatancoat.

Massenay   Don't start.

Hubertin   Not in a sittin room.

He takes off the hat and starts unbuttoning the raincoat.

Massenay   It's quite all right.

Hubertin   No, no, no, no, no. Manners.

He takes off the coat and is revealed in long-johns.

Sophie   My God.

Massenay   For heaven's sake.

Sophie   He's undressed.

Massenay   And *well* away.

Hubertin (*throwing the hat and coat at* **Auguste**)   Be kind enough to deal with these, my man.

Auguste (*as they fall all over him*)   Yerk.

Massenay (*at the top of his voice*)   What are you *playing* at? My *wife's* here.

Hubertin (*matching him for volume*)   Where is she, then?

Massenay   She's there.

Hubertin   That's not your wife. I met your wife last night.

Sophie   Pardon?

Hubertin   What are you, a serial husband?

Massenay (*aside*)   Trouble brewing.

Sophie   What's he talking about? What's he mean, 'I met your wife last night'?

Massenay   Don't listen to him. He's drunk. He doesn't know what he's saying. Fantasy, feverish fantasy . . . (*To* **Hubertin**.) Pig, sot, oaf, will you shut your mouth and get out of here?

Hubertin   You sound just like my wife.

Massenay   If you're always like this, I'm not surprised.

Hubertin (*hugely contrite*)   You're absolutely right. I'm unworthy. A walking disaster. Not fit to lick your boots.

Massenay   I should think you aren't.

Hubertin (*tearfully*)   I drink. I come home late. I murder.

Massenay, **Sophie**, **Auguste**   Arg!

Hubertin   I should never have killed him.

Sophie   No.

Auguste   You?

Massenay   Who?

Hubertin   A bigshot. An MP. A Coustillou.

Sophie He murdered Coustillou.

Massenay No, he didn't.

Hubertin I did. And you. I murdered you.

Massenay You didn't.

Hubertin (*breaking down completely*) I did. You're just being polite, you don't want to embarrass me, but I know you're dead. I'm sorry!

He flings himself, sobbing, on **Massenay**, *who staggers.*

Massenay Thanks. No. It's quite all ... (*Aside, as he manoeuvres him to a chair.*) Now we'll never get rid of him.

Hubertin I was lying in bed. He smacked my bottom. I reached out my arm, like this ...

He stretches out his hand, and finds **Massenay**'s *gun on the table.*

Hubertin I fired. Bang ... bang ... bang ... bang ...

With each 'bang', he fires a real shot. Total panic. Everyone ducks behind furniture for cover.

Sophie He's shooting!

Massenay Take cover!

Auguste Help!

Marthe *rushes in.*

Marthe What's happening?

Hubertin Bang!

He shoots again. **Marthe** *and* **Sophie** *panic, rush for safety to the same place, collide, then rush out in opposite directions, waving their arms and panicking.*

Hubertin I'm finished. Done for. I don't deserve to live.

He slumps and sobs. His arm droops over the arm of the chair.

The gun falls to the ground, unnoticed. Pause. Then **Massenay** *gingerly cocks an eye from his hiding place, round the corner of the sofa.*

Massenay   Has he finished?

Auguste (*popping his head round the piece of furniture he's hiding behind*)   Who *is* he, Monsieur?

They approach each other, on their knees, for a whispered conference.

Massenay   I've no idea. It's bad he's here, that's all I know. Very, *very* bad.

Auguste   He mustn't stay here. Too dangerous. He'll have to be dealt with.

Massenay   Do *you* know how?

Auguste   The gun. He's dropped the gun.

Massenay   Pass it over.

Auguste *hurries over on his knees and passes it, unseen by the sobbing heap that is* **Hubertin**.

Auguste   There, Monsieur.

He gets up and starts shaking **Hubertin**.

Auguste   Come on, you. Stop sobbing on our sofa.

Hubertin (*lifting his tearful face*)   Leave me. I'll sob myself to death.

He drops his head as before.

Massenay   No one's stopping you. But you're not doing it here. Out, now, or take the consequences.

Hubertin   That's right. Show no mercy. I deserve it.

Massenay (*waving the revolver about*)   This gun is loaded, and I'm not afraid to use it.

Hubertin   Use it. I beg you. End me. It won't hurt: when I've had a lil drink, I don't feel pain.

Massenay (*to* **Auguste**)   *Now* what? I can't just shoot him.

Hubertin   Pull the trigger.

Massenay   Oh, don't worry. I intend to.

Hubertin   What are you waiting for?

Massenay (*raging*)   None of your business. *I'm* in charge. I'll shoot when I'm good and ready. It's not for *you* to tell me when to shoot.

Hubertin   I haven't the patience. You, footman, a brandy and soda. I'm thirsty here.

Massenay   That does it. Now you've gone too far. Auguste, take this . . . specimen and throw him down the stairs.

Auguste   Me, Monsieur?

Massenay   Yes. You.

Auguste (*aside to him*)   I can't. He's big.

Massenay (*aside*)   I'll help you. When I say 'piccolo' grab his shoulders. I'll get his legs.

Auguste (*aside*)   'Piccolo'?

Massenay (*aside*)   Yes. (*Huge.*) 'Piccolo!'

They grab **Hubertin**.

Hubertin   What are you doing?

Massenay   Mind your own business. (*To* **Auguste**.) You see? It's easy.

Auguste   Easy for you, Monsieur. You've got the easy end. (*Staggering.*) I don't think I can hold him.

Massenay   Don't be such a baby.

Auguste   I can't. It's no good.

He drops his end.

Massenay   We were so *close* . . .

Hubertin (*on the floor*)   Upsy-daisy, all fall down.

Massenay   *Will* you be quiet?

Sophie *nervously puts her head in.*

Sophie   All right?

Massenay   We're seeing to it. Don't worry.

Sophie   He's here, still here? Oh no.

Massenay   We're *seeing* to it.

Sophie   He hasn't hurt anyone?

Massenay   Of course he hasn't. (*To* **Auguste**.) There's nothing for it: fetch removing men.

Hubertin   And a brandy and soda while you're at it.

Auguste (*to* **Massenay**)   Monsieur . . . ?

Massenay   Yes, yes, anything.

Auguste   Yes, Monsieur.

He ducks round the table, and appears before **Hubertin**, *very formal.*

Auguste   Ahem. Monsieur's brandy and soda.

Hubertin (*getting to his feet, eyes fixed ahead, like a dog on the scent*)   A-ha!

Massenay   Genius, Auguste.

Hubertin   Where is it, then?

Auguste (*opening the door to the kitchen*)   This way, Monsieur. No, no, after you, Monsieur.

Hubertin   One brandy and soda, any minute now.

Exit.

Auguste   Hey presto.

Massenay, **Sophie**   Auguste, you're wonderful.

Auguste   It's just a knack.

Massenay   Get his hat and his coat on, and throw him down the backstairs.

Auguste   Of course, Monsieur.

He takes **Hubertin**'s *hat and coat, and exit.*

Massenay   Boy oh boy oh boy oh boy oh boy.

Sophie   What a morning.

Massenay   Whatever next?

Doorbell, off.

Sophie (*starting*)   A visitor.

Massenay   More disaster.

Sophie   Don't say that.

Marthe (*putting her head nervously round the door*)   Is that . . . has he . . . ?

Massenay   What is it?

Marthe   Nothing. Just . . .

Massenay   Just what?

Marthe   Monsieur Coustillou's here.

Massenay *gazes aside at the audience: stunned bewilderment.*

Sophie   Show him in.

Massenay (*snapping out of it*)   What? No! You can't.

Sophie   Why not?

Massenay   I . . . we . . . he . . . Sorry. (*To* **Marthe**.) Show him in.

Marthe (*off*)   This way, Monsieur.

Massenay (*aside*)   He knows!

Coustillou *enters, strides over to him with furrowed brow and agitated manner.*

Coustillou   I've got to talk to you.

Massenay   Have you?

Sophie   What on earth's the matter?

Coustillou   Nothing. I . . . Madame.

He recovers his poise, shakes her hand.

Madame, good morning. I'm sorry, I was rather . . .

Sophie   And so are we! Imagine, a drunk, here in the –

Coustillou   Oh, I do agree, Madame. (*To* **Massenay**, *urgently.*) You've got to help me. I'm fighting a duel.

Massenay   You are?

Sophie   You, Monsieur?

Coustillou   I can't tell you why. Later . . . if the press get to hear of it . . . It doesn't matter why. A fellow called Hubertin.

Massenay (*without thinking*)   Not him again.

Coustillou   You know him?

Massenay (*firmly*)   Never heard of him.

Sophie   I don't think we've ever met a Hubertin.

Coustillou   You're lucky, let me tell you. He's a . . . he's an absolute . . .

Sophie   Like our drunk. The drunk we had in here just now.

Coustillou (*not taking this in at all*)   I'll show him. Oh, I'll show him.

He paces, nervously and furiously.

Massenay   Calm down.

Enter **Auguste**.

Auguste   All right so far, Monsieur. He's in the kitchen. He's got his clothes on.

Massenay   Oh, God. Shh! Shh!

Auguste (*who hasn't noticed*)   He told me his name. It's Hubertin.

Massenay (*trying to drown this out*)   *Allons, enfants de la pat* –

But **Coustillou** *has grabbed* **Auguste** *by the lapels and is shaking him like a plum tree.*

Coustillou   *What* did you say?

Auguste   Monsieur, Monsieur.

Coustillou   Did you say Hubertin?

Massenay   Don't be ridiculous. You're besotted. You're dreaming. Vertin. He said Vertin.

Coustillou   Vertin?

Massenay   Exactly. Monsieur Hugh Vertin. (*To* **Auguste**.) Didn't you? *Didn't* you?

Auguste   Yes, Monsieur.

Coustillou   Who is this Vertin?

Massenay   Nobody. Nobody at all. A drunk, a tramp. We give him clothes. In the kitchen. Doesn't everyone have tramps?

Coustillou   *I* don't.

Massenay   Well, *we* do.

Coustillou   It's very odd.

Massenay   Not in the least. Auguste, send the poor, dear fellow on his way. (*Aside to him.*) And tell me *when*.

Auguste (*to him*)   The thing is, Monsieur, he wants to play poker.

Massenay   Fine. Play.

Auguste   I don't know how to.

Massenay   You can play snap, can't you? Let him play poker, you play snap. He's so drunk he won't know the difference. Get on with it.

Auguste   If you say so, Monsieur.

Doorbell, off. He goes.

Massenay   Someone else, now.

Coustillou   Look, before they . . . I mean, I . . .

Massenay   In a *minute*. Can't you see I'm busy?

Sophie   What's happening now?

Massenay   Nothing. An appointment. Take Coustillou in there. I'll deal with them. (*To* **Coustillou**.) Five minutes. I'll deal with them.

Coustillou   I suppose so.

Sophie   *This* way, Monsieur.

Coustillou (*to* **Massenay**, *as he passes*)   Just get on with it, that's all.

Massenay   Of course. (*Aside to* **Sophie**.) Don't mention the drunk.

Sophie   Don't worry. (*To* **Coustillou**.) *This* way, Monsieur.

Exeunt.

Massenay (*almost beside himself*)   What else can go wrong?

Enter **Chanal**.

Chanal   I'm not disturbing you?

Massenay   What? No . . . no . . .

Chanal *turns back to the door.*

Chanal This way, Francine.

Enter **Francine**. *She is formal and distant with* **Massenay**.

Massenay Madame.

Chanal Oh, call her Francine. If I wasn't here, you'd call her Francine. Don't not call her Francine on my account.

Massenay (*highly embarrassed*) Look, Alcide, I know what you're saying. I know you're angry. I mean, I want to –

Chanal *Me*, angry? Whatever for? Because you and my wife . . . ? Why should I be angry? I mean, because you like her? Why shouldn't you? *I* like her.

Massenay I . . . we . . . hum . . .

Chanal No, no, no, no, no. We must be pliable. *Pliable.* Especially when there's no alternative. (*To* **Francine**.) Do sit down, my darling. There's absolutely no need to stand.

Massenay Alcide, I . . . you . . . I don't know what to say.

Chanal Don't say a word. I won't deny, when I first heard about this, I saw red. If you'd been there, the pair of you, I'd have wrung your necks. But you weren't there. I could hardly wring necks that were somewhere else. So I started thinking. 'My dear old boy,' I said to myself, 'it's happened. You've become a –'

Francine Alcide!

Massenay Don't say it!

Chanal No, no, no, no, no, no, no, no. These things *must* be faced. 'My dear old boy, it's happened. Nothing you can do about it. Put a good face on it.'

Massenay Oh!

Chanal 'After all, they didn't do it to *annoy* you.'

Massenay, **Francine** (*quickly*)   Of course not.

Chanal   And if you didn't do it to annoy *me*, it must be because you're in love. And who am I to say no, when heaven says yes?

Massenay   Oh Alcide!

Chanal   So. I'll tell you what I've decided. (*Sharply to him.*) Sit down there. (*Back to his first tone.*) I'm going to court.

Massenay   What?

Chanal   I mean, I have to think of my own position.

Massenay   Oh. Yes.

Chanal   It won't be a *big* case. A little one. Domestic. Nothing *cosmic*.

Massenay   Happens all the time.

Chanal   We'll leave you out of it. I'll have to name Francine, naturally, but we'll leave you out of it. Asterisk asterisk asterisk, that's what you'll be.

Massenay   How kind you are.

Chanal   Come on! Just because I have a tiny domestic disaster, doesn't mean I have to be vindictive. This isn't about my happiness. It's about you! Your happiness. Your dear wife's happiness.

Massenay   How kind you are.

Chanal   If two people want to be happy, who am I to shatter their dream for ever?

Massenay   You're a saint, a saint. (*To* **Francine**.) Isn't he a saint?

Francine   A saint.

Chanal   No, really, I'm not. Marriage, to me, is like standing on the bridge of a great ocean liner. Putting into harbour. You've piloted across the swelling ocean, and now you're putting into harbour. The pilot comes aboard, and you stand there, smiling benignly. You show him the wheel, and say, 'There you are, old boy. She's all yours. Take her.'

Massenay What d'you mean, 'She's all yours, take her'?

Chanal My wife, for heaven's sake. She's all yours. Take her.

Massenay What?

Chanal After all, you *are* going to marry her.

Massenay Me? Your wife? You're crazy.

Chanal (*innocently*) I'm sorry – ?

Massenay I can't marry your wife. I'm married already.

Chanal (*feigning utter surprise*) You're *not*! You? Married?

Massenay Of course I'm married.

Chanal How very *awkward*.

Massenay Cha!

He paces. **Chanal** *goes imperturbably to* **Francine**, *taps her shoulder.*

Chanal How *very* awkward.

Massenay (*coming down to him*) I mean, if I wasn't, she'd be the first I'd ... I mean, I'd ...

Chanal This *is* very awkward. Married, eh?

Massenay (*trying to shrug it off with ruefulness*) What can one do?

Chanal I know what you mean. (*New tone.*) Still, none of my business.

Massenay What?

Chanal I mean, you were married already, when you
. . . when you and my wife . . . You should have thought
of this then.

Massenay (*nettled*) What d'you mean, this then? What
d'you want me to do? I'm not a bigamist.

Chanal So where does that leave us? I know: divorce.

Massenay I don't believe this.

Chanal It's only polite. If a chap breaks up another
chap's marriage, he marries the wife. It's simply what one
does.

Massenay I'm married already! What am I to tell my
wife?

Chanal Truth's always best.

Massenay (*beside himself*) I will not tell my wife the
truth.

Chanal Awkward, is it, for you? Would you like *me*
to . . . ?

Massenay (*furious*) No I would *not* . . . (*Controlling
himself.*) No, thank you.

Chanal It's up to you. The choice is yours. Behave like
a gentleman, look the world in the eye and say, 'I
honoured the Code', or be taken to court and show
everyone you're a crocodile.

Massenay This is blackmail.

Chanal I say, so it is. Well? Have you decided?

Enter **Marthe**.

Marthe Monsieur . . .

Massenay What is it now?

Marthe The porters are here with the bags.

Massenay   What bags?

Chanal   It's all right. I know. (*To* **Marthe**.) Tell them to bring them in.

Exit **Marthe**.

Chanal   My wife's bags.

Massenay   WHAT?

Chanal   They're bringing her bags. So tell me. Which way is her bedroom?

Massenay   She hasn't got a bedroom!

Marthe *throws open the double doors, and a stream of* **Porters** *starts fetching in bags of varying sizes.*

Massenay   Get these out of here! Out! Out! Out!

Chanal   It's all right. Leave them.

Massenay   What d'you mean, leave them? (*To the* **Porters**.) Take them out!

Chanal   Leave them.

He gives the **Porters** *money, shoos them out and closes the doors.*

Massenay (*completely walled in by bags*)   What are you *playing* at?

Chanal   What are *you* playing at?

Massenay   Don't take that tone with me!

Enter **Sophie**.

Sophie   What's all the noise about?

Massenay (*aside*)   My God, my wife.

Sophie (*taking in the scene*)   What's happening?

Massenay   Monsieur Chanal, my wife. (*Introducing* **Francine** *and* **Sophie**.) My wife . . . Madame Chanal. (*Smiling like a maniac.*) Well, *isn't* this nice?

Sophie   Whose are all these bags?

Massenay   What bags?

Sophie   Those bags.

Massenay   Oh, these? They're . . . bags.

Chanal (*calmly*)   They're my wife's bags.

Massenay (*aside*)   Help me!

Sophie (*to* **Massenay**)   His wife's bags?

Massenay   Good heavens, so they are.

Chanal (*aside to him, charmingly*)   Shall I tell her now?

Massenay   No! Don't!

Chanal   Up to you, then.

Sophie   What's happening?

Massenay   Ha, ha. Nothing at all. Nothing much at all.

Sophie   What?

Massenay   Well. My friend Chanal. My dear old friend, Chanal. My old school friend, Chanal. (*Giving him one of those schoolboy mock-punches.*) Good old Chanal. He's here in Paris for a day or two, with his . . . with his . . . with his bags.

Chanal   No I'm not.

Massenay   You *are*.

Chanal   I'm not.

Massenay   I say you *are*.

Chanal   You're completely mistaken. (*To* **Sophie**.) The thing is: Madame –

Massenay   Will you shut up?

Chanal   What d'you mean?

Massenay   You know exactly what I mean.

Chanal   Don't be ridiculous.

Massenay   Me, ridiculous?

Sophie   Just a minute . . .

A huge row develops, all three talking at the tops of their voice.
Francine *sits aside from it all, as she's done ever since she came
in. At the height of the argument, enter* **Coustillou**.

Coustillou   I say. I am still here.

Massenay (*rounding on him*)   *You*, now! Get out of here!
Get *out*!

He pushes him down on the sofa next to **Francine**, *indeed almost
on top of her. Extreme embarrassment of* **Coustillou**.

Coustillou   You. Madame, I . . . you . . . hoo . . .
harg . . .

Massenay *grabs him to his feet and bundles him out by the
servants' door.*

Massenay   I told you to get *out* of here!

*Huge row and clatter from the next room. Shouting, breaking
crockery, clanging pots and pans.*

My God, I put him in the kitchen. With Hubertin!

The row escalates, until **Coustillou** *is projected into the room, his
clothes torn, his hat in ribbons.* **Hubertin** *follows him, fully
dressed, pummelling and pushing him like a whirlwind.*

All   Ah!

Coustillou   Stop it! Help! Help!

Hubertin   Rat! Camel! *Politician*!

He yanks **Coustillou**'s *hat down over his eyes, gives him a last
kick in the pants, and stalks to the door.*

Hubertin   You've not heard the end of this!

Exit.

Sophie (*going to* **Coustillou**)   Monsieur Coustillou!

Coustillou (*panting, exhausted*)   Harg, harg, what *was* that?

Sophie   It's all right.

Coustillou   It was worse than Parliament.

Auguste (*at the door, announcing*)   Inspector Planteloup.

Sophie   So soon?

Massenay   What does *he* want?

Planteloup *bursts in in a fury.*

Planteloup   Monsieur Massenay, you played fast and loose with me.

All   Eh?

Planteloup   Your trip to Calais was a blind. You were arrested last night in the rue du Colisée, in bed with the wife of someone called Chanal.

Coustillou   You mean it was *him* . . . ?

Sophie   What did you say?

Chanal   It had to happen.

Sophie (*confronting* **Massenay**)   Arrested? Last night? In bed with . . . ? Ha!

She slaps him so that he falls on the sofa.

Massenay   That hurt.

Sophie   Don't talk to me. All's over between us.

Massenay   Sophie!

Sophie   Don't ever speak to me again. Inspector, this way.

Planteloup   Certainly, Madame.

Exeunt.

Massenay (*getting up and going to* **Coustillou**) It's not what it seems.

Coustillou The lover . . . was you!

Massenay What of it?

Coustillou *This,* Monsieur.

He slaps him.

Massenay What's it got to do with . . . *you*?

He slaps him back.

Coustillou That does it. I challenge you.

Massenay No, I challenge *you*.

Too late. **Coustillou** *has stalked out.*

Chanal So there we are, old man. She's all yours.

Act Four

The same setting as for Act One. It is a year later, and all the furniture has been moved round slightly, is subtly different. When the curtain rises, **Chanal** *is sitting formally in a chair, turning over the pages of a magazine like someone in a waiting-room. He looks at his watch after a while, gets up, rings, then goes back to his reading. He is irritated about something, stares fixedly at a small side-table.*

Chanal What are you *there* for? That's not where you belong.

He moves the table somewhere else, sighing with indignation.

Dear oh dear oh dear.

Enter **Étienne**.

Étienne Did you ring, Monsieur?

Chanal Yes.

Pause.

Are you sure Madame's coming back?

Étienne Yes, Monsieur, for lunch. She said you were coming. 'My ex-husband's coming,' she said. 'Make sure he waits.'

Chanal You mean she said, '*I'll* make sure he waits.'

Étienne (*not realising the irony*) No, Monsieur.

Chanal (*looking at his watch*) Quarter past two. I thought, 'I'll say I'll be there at one, I'll turn up at half past, that should be just about . . .' I should have known. Madame and time! I could have added another hour.

Étienne (*dusting*) Madame and time! Even in the old days –

Chanal H'm.

Étienne   And still! The way Monsieur goes on.

Chanal   Me?

Étienne   No, Monsieur. The new Monsieur.

Chanal   Ah.

Étienne (*throwing his arms in the air and casting his eyes to heaven, melodramatically*)   Like that, Monsieur.

Chanal   Well, I'm not sorry it's someone else these days.

He looks at the top of **Étienne**'s *head, as* **Étienne** *has bent to dust a side-table.*

Chanal   Étienne, you've been tearing your hair.

Étienne   No, Monsieur. It does that by itself.

Chanal   Just a minute ... Shouldn't that table be in the hall?

Étienne   Madame prefers it here.

Chanal   Everything has to be different.

Étienne   We say that all the time, Monsieur. In the kitchen. Among ourselves.

Chanal   We *bought* that table for the hall. Ah well. Étienne ...

Étienne   Yes, Monsieur?

Chanal   Apart from the furniture, how *are* things?

Étienne (*not getting the point*)   Not too bad, Monsieur.

Chanal   Really?

Étienne   The wife and I, we've had a little boy.

Chanal (*taken by surprise*)   Oh. Congratulations. (*Driving on.*) No, I meant, how *is* Madame?

Étienne   Not too bad, Monsieur.

Chanal   Good.

Étienne (*still dusting*)   I mean, it wasn't an *easy* pregnancy.

Chanal   Whose pregnancy?

Étienne   Madame my wife's.

Chanal   Ah.

Étienne   I mean, it was premature. Five months.

Chanal   Oh, Étienne, I'm so sorry.

Étienne   No, Monsieur. He's fine. He weighed eleven pounds.

Chanal   And he was premature?

Étienne   The doctor said we were very lucky. Who could know how big he'd have been if he'd gone nine months?

Chanal   You counted wrong.

Étienne   No, Monsieur. My wife had spent six months with Madame's cousins in the country, and she'd been back six months. So –

Chanal   I understand.

Étienne   You know, Monsieur: the Captain.

Chanal   I guessed it would be.

Étienne   He looks just like me.

Chanal   The Captain?

Étienne   The baby.

Chanal   A dutiful son. I mean, no one *forces* him . . .

Étienne   Would you like to see him, Monsieur?

Chanal   Well, I came to see Madame . . .

Étienne   So you did, Monsieur. And here she comes.

Enter **Francine.**

Francine My dear Monsieur Chanal, I'm so sorry to keep you waiting. Étienne, make me a sandwich, would you? I'm absolutely –

Étienne Yes, Madame.

Exit. At once her tone towards **Chanal** *lightens.*

Francine Alcide! I'm so sorry! Have you been waiting long?

Chanal Three-quarters of an hour.

Francine That's a relief. I thought I'd kept you waiting. It's an awkward day, that's all. *Hours* at the dressmaker, and then the funeral. I couldn't put them off.

Chanal Especially the funeral.

Francine All those Duchaumels!

Chanal What, all of them?

Francine Don't be silly. Just the granny. The rich old granny. Eighteen million francs . . .

Chanal They took it hard?

Francine Singing, dancing, the food, the drink, the fireworks . . . I mean, not in *church* . . .

Chanal Not even Roman candles?

Francine Sorry?

Chanal Blessed by the Pope.

Francine Alcide!

Chanal Anyway, she had a good send-off.

Francine Oh yes.

She sits and wriggles a little with pleasure.

It *is* good to see you.

Chanal You too.

Francine   You know what it's like. When people have been married . . . they're *attached*.

Chanal   Unbreakably. Unbreakable bonds. All Nature cries, 'Never break those bonds.'

Francine   Oh, Alcide.

Chanal   The first husband's always the real one.

Francine (*flirting*)   Shh! *He* could have heard you.

Chanal   If *he* could have heard, I wouldn't have said it. (*Passionately*.) Unbreakable! I'll prove it. I'm here. I shouldn't be here, I've no business to be here. The ex-husband, yesterday's business. (*Change of tone*.) Business, that reminds me. A year since the divorce, we have to sign some papers. Both of us, sign. I've got them with me. (*Passionate*.) But I'd have come anyway. I had to. It's bigger than both of us. I've only got three days in Paris. I thought, 'I *must* see how they are.'

Francine   Alcide.

Chanal   I know it's not done. Good heavens! But if the wife, the husband, the ex-husband . . . if none of them object . . . If an ex-husband and an ex-wife . . . they can still be *friends* . . .

Francine   Oh, darling.

Chanal (*loving this, but pretending mock seriousness*)   I say! Tut, tut!

He sits on the stool at her feet, passionately.

Francine   It just slipped out.

Chanal   But Massenay – don't you think you should ask his permission to call me darling?

Francine   He didn't ask *your* permission, before he –

Chanal   That's right, he didn't.

Francine   And that was *much* more serious.

Chanal   You're telling me.

Francine   Well, then.

She goes to sit on the piano stool.

I wish he *had* asked your permission. Because if he had, you'd have said 'Out of the question'.

Chanal   Ab-solutely.

Francine   And *we'd* still be married.

She sighs. He sighs. She goes to him, rueful.

Oh darling, I never knew what I had. If wives have lovers, just now and then, and their husbands gave permission, marriage would be *so* much happier.

Chanal   Of course. But people! (*He shrugs at the stupidity and rigidity of the world. Then changes tone.*) You *are* all right?

Francine   Not really.

Chanal   Massenay?

Francine   You should hear him. When *he* was cheating *you*, that was fine. Now *he's* the husband, he shouts, he rages, he tears his hair. Jealous. No reason. I'm a loyal wife. I don't have lovers. I mean, *you'd* know, wouldn't you? I wouldn't not tell you.

Chanal   Thank you.

Francine   There are times when he . . . when we . . . when I could throw myself into the arms of the first man who came along. Give him good reason to be jealous.

Chanal   Francine, darling . . .

Francine   You don't know what he's like. None of his old friends are allowed to call. Men friends, I mean. As if *that* ever stopped a wife from . . . Except Coustillou. He's not afraid of Coustillou.

Chanal   Well, *Coustillou* . . .

Francine   Ever since that fight they had, they've been like *that*. Coustillou was best man at our wedding. He still falls over the furniture. Émile trusts him. It's crazy.

She is fiddling with her hair in front of the mirror.

Isn't he here? Émile? Didn't he stay to see you?

Chanal   He had to go out. So Étienne said. (*Change of tone.*) So that's what it's like!

Francine   You sound as if you're pleased.

Chanal   Good heavens, no.

Francine   Oh!

Chanal   What am I saying? I'm sorry for your sake. But what d'you think I'd think, if I asked how you were and you said, 'Darling, much happier than when *you* were here'?

Francine (*affectionately*)   Selfish!

Chanal   Just human.

Enter **Étienne** *with a plate of sandwiches on a salver. He goes to the piano.*

Francine   Put it on the little table. Where's it gone?

Chanal   Where's what gone?

Étienne   It's all right. It's here.

Francine   Someone's moved it?

Chanal   I did. Sorry. It was in the wrong place.

Francine (*affectionately*)   You never change.

Chanal   I've a tidy mind.

Étienne *puts down the salver, brings the table, spreads a cloth and starts laying out the lunch things.*

Francine   Did Monsieur go out?

Étienne He waited to have lunch till you came home, Madame, and when you didn't he put his hat on and went out. No lunch. He said, 'We'll see what she's up to *this time.*'

Francine Did he?

Étienne He didn't seem pleased.

Francine Ah well. Étienne, you remember Monsieur?

Étienne Oh, yes, Madame. We're delighted to see him.

Chanal Thanks, Étienne. Who's we?

Étienne Myself and Madeleine, Monsieur.

Chanal Your wife.

Étienne If she could say hello, she'd be so pleased, Monsieur.

Chanal Of course she can. You don't mind, darling – ?

Francine Of course not.

Étienne Oh, Monsieur, she'll be so happy. (*At the servants' door, talking as if to a pet.*) Come in. It's all right. Madame says you can. (*To them.*) She was just outside. In case she caught a glimpse as Monsieur passed by . . .

Enter **Madeleine***, wiping her hands on her cook's apron.*

Madeleine Oh, Monsieur.

Chanal My dear Madeleine. How nice to see you.

Madeleine How are you, Monsieur? I hope . . . I hope you're well.

Chanal Fine, fine. And you?

Madeleine Not bad, Monsieur. Oh, but it's not the same! I'm sorry, Madame. It's not that Monsieur isn't . . . but *this* Monsieur . . . Oh, Monsieur, you *spoiled* us.

Chanal Spoiled you?

Étienne   That's the word, Monsieur.

Chanal   You think I *spoiled* you?

Madeleine, **Étienne** (*in chorus*)   Oh yes, Monsieur.

Chanal   Oh, come on . . .

Francine   Yes, Madeleine. If that's . . .

Madeleine   Yes, Madame.

Francine   You can't stand chattering here all afternoon.

Madeleine   No, Madame. It's just . . . Madame . . .
When *Monsieur* . . .

Francine   The kitchen. Thank you.

Madeleine   Yes, Madame. Goodbye, Monsieur.

Chanal   Goodbye, Madeleine.

Francine   Oh, Madeleine?

Madeleine   Yes, Madame?

Francine   Tell Marie I need her.

Madeleine   Marie went out, Madame.

Francine   In that case, you do it. My sitting-room . . .
the dress I was wearing yesterday. Bring it in here, please.

Madeleine   Yes, Madame.

Exit.

Francine   I must change out of this. It's all right for a
funeral, but . . . (*The dress is remarkably festive.*)

Étienne   Here's Monsieur, Monsieur.

Enter **Massenay**, *in a foul mood.*

Massenay (*seeing* **Francine**)   I should *think* so, too.

He thrusts his coat and hat at **Étienne**.

Massenay   Bring me a sandwich.

Étienne   Yes, Monsieur.

Exit. **Massenay** *strides down to* **Chanal** *as if complaining to him, man to man.*

Massenay   Half past two and still no lunch.

Chanal   Good to see you too.

Massenay (*changed tone*)   Sorry. (*Shaking hands.*) Good afternoon. (*Back to his grouch.*) I don't know what it was like when *you* were here. All I ask is, Madame lets me know when exactly I can expect some *lunch.*

Francine   You could have had it any time you liked.

Massenay   I didn't get married to eat a private lunch!

Francine   In any case, if you'd *been* here ... I've been back for ages.

Massenay (*marching to confront her nose to nose*)   That's a lie. You came back fifteen minutes ago. The concierge told me.

Francine   You take evidence from *him* these days?

Massenay (*huge*)   Where have you been?

Francine   Ask the concierge.

Massenay (*as if about to leap at her*)   Francine.

Francine (*scornfully; demurely*)   Yes?

Massenay (*controlling himself, furious with himself*)   Ohh.

Chanal   Children. Little ones. Don't argue today of all days. Today *I'm* here.

Francine   Today's no different from any other day.

Massenay   Exactly! You'll tell me in a minute you had lunch with your mother. Well, you didn't. I've been there and you didn't. I wanted cards on the table. You haven't had lunch there since Saturday.

Francine   You went specially to ask her? You could have stayed at home. I could have told you, I've had lunch here every day this week. Or d'you think I eat two lunches?

Massenay (*sulky*)   Don't be ridiculous.

Francine   Today, for example. Look: a sandwich. Waiting. If you'd *looked* before you roared . . .

Massenay   Fine. One lunch, two lunches, what does it matter? What matters is where you are till the middle of the afternoon.

Francine (*losing her own temper*)   I've had enough of this.

Chanal   Little ones –

Massenay   Stay out of it.

Francine   I'm at my lover's. Satisfied?

Massenay   Oh, I believe you.

Francine   *What?*

Massenay   Well, it wouldn't be the first time.

Francine   What did you say?

Massenay   You heard.

Chanal   Er . . .

Francine   I've had other lovers?

Massenay   Of course you have.

Francine   Name one.

Massenay   Good heavens: me!

Francine, **Chanal**   Ah.

Massenay   You see?

Francine   I suppose that was *my* fault.

Massenay   It wasn't *anybody's* fault –

Enter **Émile** *with another sandwich. Frosty silence. He dithers, trying to find the other little table.*

Massenay   For heaven's sake stop fiddling and faddling and put it over *there*!

Étienne   Yes, Monsieur. (*As he sets the table, he babbles.*) I didn't know which you wanted, so I brought salt, pepper, French mustard, English mustard . . .

Massenay   Fine! Marvellous! Brilliant! Go, go, go!

Étienne   Yes, Monsieur.

Exit. The scene picks up at the level it was before he entered.

Massenay   I'm not blaming anyone. I'm saying if it happened with me, it could happen with anyone.

Francine (*to* **Chanal**)   Did you hear what he said?

Chanal   Massenay . . .

Massenay   It's easy to talk. But it's what's in here (*Tapping his head.*) that counts. And what's in here says that if a wife lets it happen once . . . Ha!

Chanal   You really mean this?

Massenay   Of course I mean it. She goes out every single day.

Chanal (*trying to placate him*)   She did in my time.

Massenay   There you are then! We all know what she was doing in your time. Well? D'you blame me for being suspicious? Was I to wait till she *told* me?

Francine   Oh!

She goes and stands by **Chanal**.

Francine   After all I did for him! To think . . .

She touches **Chanal**'s *arm.*

Francine   I was married to a decent, honest man. And

to satisfy that beast, I trampled this decent, honest
man . . .

She taps him on the chest . . .

Trampled him . . .

In the stomach . . .

Trampled . . .

Again . . .

Trampled . . .

Again.

Chanal (*both mentally and physically uncomfortable*) Please
leave me out of it . . .

Massenay *advances on them. He uses* **Chanal** *as a punching-
ball to emphasise his points, just as she did.*

Massenay Why? That's all I want to know. Why did
you trample him?

Francine I trampled him because I *loved* you!

This accompanied by punching.

Massenay *Loved* me?

Francine *Loved* you!

Massenay Really! (*To* **Chanal**.) She says she *loved* me.

He breaks away. **Chanal** *escapes and sits.*

Chanal I *hate* this kind of conversation.

Francine (*who hasn't finished*) Yes, *loved* you! And look
where it's got me. (*She is now lecturing.*) We women, we
make the same mistake, always. We take as lovers men we
love. Instead, we should take men who're in love with *us*.

Chanal Or none at all.

Francine I chose you, and I was wrong. I should have

chosen . . . Coustillou. Yes, Coustillou adored me. (*To*
Chanal.) Didn't he? He did everything for me. *He'd*
never turn on me, turn on me . . . ohhh!

Massenay   If it's Coustillou you want, have him! He's
always here. He's yours!

Francine   Don't worry. I will if I want to.

Massenay (*to* **Chanal**, *beside himself*)   You heard her!
Your wife! You heard her!

Francine   And whose fault will it be? If all a woman
hears, day in day out, is that she must have a lover, don't
you think she ends up *looking* for one?

Massenay (*nose to nose with her again*)   You mean you go
looking for them?

Francine   How dare you?

Massenay (*with some difficulty: his emotion, and the words
themselves, make it difficult to say*)   Hussy! Slut!

Francine   Say that again!

Chanal, *absolutely furious, picks up one of the salvers and bangs
it hard on the floor.*

Chanal   Stop that! How dare you! How dare you call
my wife a hussyslut?

Massenay   Whose wife a hussyslut?

Chanal   Ah. *Your* wife a hussyslut. How dare you?

Massenay   D'you mind? Did *I* interfere, when she was
married to you and had all those lovers?

Chanal   What lovers?

Francine   There was only one.

Chanal   Exactly: one.

Massenay   One too many.

Francine   Oh!

Massenay   In any case, this is *my* wife, not *your* wife, *my* business, not *your* business.

*He and **Francine** glare at each other, then stalk to opposite sides of the stage. **Chanal** sits between them, his head in his hands. He tries several times to speak, lifting his head, then drops it again in despair. Finally:*

Chanal   Little ones ...

Francine (*pointedly*)   You're absolutely right. Darling. I don't know why I lower myself to argue.

Massenay   Ha!

Chanal   Why don't you both sit down, eat your sandwiches ...

Francine   Of course, the sandwiches.

Chanal   While they're still cold.

Francine (*sitting to eat*)   I'm starving.

Massenay   I suppose she wants me to say it's my fault.

*He, too, sits to eat. They are either side of **Chanal**.*

Chanal (*trying to lighten the mood*)   Don't be such a bear.

Massenay   Me? What did *I* say? Did *I* say anything?

Francine   No, it was the cat.

Massenay (*munching*)   She's the one who lost her temper. Just because I summoned up all my courage, and asked, ever so gently ...

Francine   Gently!

Massenay   We're not allowed questions any more.

They eat, pointedly.

Chanal   Children ... little ones ... Life is so short ... you squander it ...

Either side of him, they lift eyes, arms and forks to heaven simultaneously.

It's pointless.

They glare at him.

No, pointless. If you sat down and had a rational, quiet conversation every time, instead of –

Massenay   Exactly. If I've said that once . . .

Chanal   All right, let's start with you. Suppose you asked quietly, calmly, 'My darling, where have you been?'

Massenay   I do.

Chanal   You don't. You say, (*Roaring.*) 'Darling, where have you been?' If you'd said, (*Sugar-sweet.*) 'D'you realise it's three o'clock?', she'd have answered, 'I'm sorry, darling' – you see, two love-birds, cooing together? – 'I went to a funeral. The Duchaumel funeral.'

Massenay (*taken aback*)   The Duchaumel funeral?

Francine (*crisply*)   Exactly.

Massenay   That was today?

Francine   I'll give you three guesses.

Massenay   Oh lord, I forgot.

Francine   Ha!

Massenay   Did anyone . . . did anyone notice?

Francine   Of course they didn't notice.

Massenay   How embarrassing.

Chanal   You see? It's easy. Now . . . get up.

Massenay   What?

Chanal   Get up.

He tries to take the tray so that he'll stand up.

Massenay   I haven't finished.

Chanal (*snatching it*)   You have. Time to kiss and make up.

Massenay   You're joking.

Chanal   No, no . . .

He pulls him centre stage, like a reluctant child, then goes back for **Francine**.

Chanal   You too.

Francine (*letting herself be led*)   I'll do it this time. But I warn you, one day he'll make me so *angry* . . .

Chanal (*humouring*)   Of course he will. Now then . . .

He pushes them together.

How about a great big kiss?

Francine *stands glacially still.* **Massenay** *pecks her cheek.*

Francine   He'll go too far one day.

Massenay (*to* **Chanal**)   You hear? You hear?

Francine   I'll be sorry afterwards, but it'll be too late.

Chanal   Children . . .

Massenay   Now you've warned me, I'll be watching.

Francine   You wouldn't see an affair if you fell over it. The husband's always the last to know. Isn't that right, Alcide?

Chanal   Please leave me out of it.

Francine   We'll see! We'll see!

She stalks L.

Massenay   Oh yes. We'll see!

He stalks R. Pause. Enter **Madeleine**.

Massenay What do you want?

Madeleine Madame asked me to bring this dress.

Francine Thank you.

Madeleine It wasn't in the wardrobe, Madame. You'd put it out for sponging.

Massenay (*as* **Francine** *takes the dress*) Just a minute. You're not going to put it on in *here*?

Francine (*unbuttoning her dress*) Whyever not?

Massenay *He's* here.

Francine He doesn't mind.

Chanal I don't really count.

Massenay Of course you count!

Madeleine After all, Madame's first husband.

Massenay Who asked your opinion?

Francine (*sweetly to her*) Never mind Monsieur. Thank you, Madeleine.

She takes off her blouse.

Massenay This is incredible.

Chanal You're jealous. Of me.

Massenay Of course I'm not jealous. This is the sitting-room. Never mind. Oh, never mind.

He sulks, elaborately. **Francine**, *assisted by* **Madeleine**, *removes her skirt.* **Chanal** *is there, amiably there. This very fact seems to infuriate* **Massenay**, *who suddenly springs on him and turns him through 180 degrees, to face the other way. Then, ashamed that this might be taken for jealousy, he starts playing the effusive host.*

Massenay My dear old fellow.

He puts his arm round **Chanal**'s *neck, so as to keep him turned away.*

Massenay   How *are* you? Dear old friend. How long is it now?

Chanal   A year.

He turns his head, with deliberate nonchalance. **Massenay** *turns it back.*

Massenay   Fancy that. Me, too.

Chanal   Well, well, well.

Same business.

Massenay   Well, well, well.

Chanal   You never can tell.

Massenay   That's just what I say.

Same business.

Chanal   You're cricking my neck.

Massenay   Am not.

Chanal   Are so.

Francine (*who has put on her skirt*)   Fasten me up, Madeleine.

Madeleine   I can't, Madame. I haven't got the fingers. If it was kneading *bread* . . .

Francine   Perhaps Monsieur . . .

Massenay (*to* **Chanal**)   She means *me*. Stay exactly where you are.

Francine   Not you. You're clumsy.

Massenay   Fine. Whatever you like.

He sulks.

Francine (*to* **Chanal**)   Please, darling.

Chanal   Of course, darling.

He buttons the skirt. **Massenay** *paces, sulks, loses his temper completely, finally runs and pushes him out of the way.*

Massenay   Enough! Enough!

All   Oh.

Francine   What are you *doing?*

Massenay *has grabbed the blouse and is trying to force it over her head.*

Massenay   Will ... you ... put ... this ... *on?*

Francine   Stop it, you'll tear it.

Massenay   Get your *head* in!

Chanal   I say ...

Massenay (*to* **Madelaine**)   You: go. Knead bread, do anything you like, just go.

Madeleine   Yes, Monsieur.

She gathers up the clothes and exit, fast.

Massenay   You're making me look an idiot.

Francine   You hardly need us for that.

Massenay   You're my wife. You'll do exactly as I say.

Francine   Be very careful.

Massenay   Why?

Francine   I've had just about enough, that's why.

Massenay   *You've* had enough? *I've* had enough.

Francine   Right. Remember: you're responsible.

Massenay   Don't start again. 'I'll take a lover.' Take one! See if I care! Take one and be done with it.

Francine   Don't worry, I will.

Massenay   Get on with it, then.

He goes to his study door. **Chanal** *chases after him.*

Chanal   You won't win. A woman's fury . . .

Massenay   Leave me alone!

Exit. He leaves the door open.

Chanal   What a Bluebeard. (*Following him off.*) Massenay
. . . Émile . . . old chap . . .

Doorbell, off.

Francine   Take a lover! Right! I'll take one! I'll take
one now.

Étienne *shows in* **Coustillou**.

Étienne   This way, Monsieur.

Exit **Étienne**.

Francine   Coustillou! (*Casting her eyes to heaven.*) Oh, thank
you, thank you.

Coustillou (*as articulate as always*). Eugh . . . mooh . . .
Mada . . . eugh . . . ooh . . .

Francine (*grappling herself to his arm*)   We have to talk.

Coustillou   Moooah . . .

Francine   You love me. Don't you?

Coustillou (*alarmed*)   No! I don't! No!

Francine   You don't?

Coustillou   I do. Yes. No. Eugh. I don't know what I
mean.

Francine   Never mind. All that matters is, I'm yours.

She pivots round on his arm till she's spread across his chest.

Do anything you like with me.

Coustillou   Pa . . . pa . . . Pardon?

Francine (*impatiently*)   Get on with it.

Coustillou   Ohh. Mooaaah.

He collapses on to the piano stool, so that **Francine** *is in his lap.*

Francine   What's the matter? Oh, you're not going to . . . This isn't the . . .

Coustillou   No, no. Francine, Francine. Oh, oh. You don't –

Francine   I do.

Coustillou   Mooah . . . mwah! Mwah! Mwah!

He showers her with kisses.

Francine   That's better. Don't stop!

Coustillou   I won't.

More kisses.

Francine   Yes, yes! More, more!

Enter **Chanal**. *Unseen by them, he takes in what's happening, throws his arms disgustedly in the air and goes back out to fetch* **Massenay**. *The lovers continue. Doorbell, off.*

Francine   Someone's at the door. Quick. This way.

Coustillou   What?

Francine (*pulling him to the door of her sitting-room*)   In here. Come *on*.

Coustillou   Yes. Eugh . . .

In his confusion he has knocked over a chair. He bends to pick it up.

Francine   Leave it! You can sort it later!

Exit.

Coustillou   Francine, oh Francine!

He follows her out, fast, still bent double. Just as the door shuts behind them, **Chanal** *appears like a bullet from a gun out of* **Massenay***'s sitting-room. He is dragging* **Massenay** *by the hand, like a reluctant child.*

Chanal   Come *on!*

Massenay   What is it?

Chanal   I told you before: a woman's fury . . .

Massenay   No, please. Not more about my wife.

Chanal   You'll thank me later.

Massenay   I won't. I won't.

He covers his ears. **Étienne** *opens the main door for* **Belgence***.*

Massenay   Belgence! I'm so glad to see you.

Exit **Étienne***.*

Chanal   You have to listen.

Massenay   Can't you see I've got a visitor?

Chanal   I'm telling you your wife's . . .

Massenay   What wife? I have no wife.

Chanal   That's exactly what I'm trying to tell you.

Massenay   Fine. Tell me later. Go in there. At once.

Chanal (*as he is pushed unceremoniously into* **Massenay***'s study*)   But . . .

Massenay *shuts the door behind him and goes smiling to greet* **Belgence***.*

Massenay   My dear Belgence, I'm so glad to see you. Where have you been hiding, all these months?

Belgence   Oh, you know . . .

Massenay   My wife . . . my ex-wife . . . d'you see her at all these days? How is she?

Belgence Oh, you know . . .

Massenay I was a fool, you know. I should never have
. . . We were so happy. How things have changed! For
her, too, I suspect. It was a blow to her, too. And now
she's all alone . . . (*Sighing.*) Aah. (*With an effort.*) Never
mind. What's done is done. Water under the bridge. (*False
joviality.*) Eh? Eh? What brings you here this fine morning?

Belgence That's just it. I'm getting married.

Massenay Please be careful. You never know what
might happen. If it turns sour. I mean, take me –

Belgence This won't turn sour.

Massenay Ha! We all think that. And then it's too late.
D'you know the woman, through and through?

Belgence Oh yes.

Massenay Can't be done.

Belgence It can. She's your wife.

Massenay What?

Belgence Your ex-wife. Sophie.

Massenay *leaps at him and shakes him like a cherry tree.*

Massenay You're marrying my wife?

Belgence (*half choked*) What of it?

Massenay (*pushing him away*) You're out of your mind.
Why did you come here? D'you want me to be best man?
Oh, no. Oh, no.

Belgence Don't tell me you *mind.*

Massenay Me? Mind?

Belgence You want to keep her a spinster always?

Massenay What? No! Do what you like. It's nothing to

me. None of my business. It's up to the pair of you, entirely.

Belgence   That's exactly what I said. But Sophie said . . . I should ask your permission first.

Massenay   Permission first?

Belgence   Permission. First.

Massenay   Who does she think I am, her father? Her mother? What's it got to do with me?

Belgence   That's exactly what I said. But she said, no permission, no wedding.

Massenay   You're joking.

Belgence   She knows we're old friends. She doesn't want to come between us.

Massenay   Very thoughtful.

Belgence   It's nothing to you. You said so. Why should you care who she marries, me or anyone?

Massenay   Fine. I'll write you a note. I'll give you a licence.

Belgence (*overjoyed*)   Thank you. I must rush and tell her. She's in a cab, downstairs.

Massenay (*eagerly*)   You mean . . . ? (*Catching himself, feigning indifference.*) A cab, you say? Downstairs, you say?

Belgence   I know! Come down and tell her in person. Save yourself writing.

Massenay   *Me* go to *her*? You're joking. Did *she* come to *me*?

Belgence   She said she couldn't.

Massenay   Whyever not?

Belgence   Because your *wife* was here.

Massenay   Francine? Ha! *She* fills the house with husbands. There's one in there, right now.

Belgence   You wouldn't mind?

Massenay   It's a special occasion.

Belgence   If I'd realised . . .

Massenay (*trying to stay light*)   I mean, why don't you . . . Why doesn't she . . . ? I mean if she wants to . . .

Belgence   What a friend you are!

Massenay   Well, you know me.

He rings.

Belgence   This is marvellous. (*Seriously.*) Oh . . . when she comes, when you talk to her, if you could see your way . . . flatter me a little . . . mention my good qualities . . .

Massenay   Which ones are those?

Belgence   Coming from you, it'd have *authority*.

Massenay   I'll see what I can do.

Enter **Étienne**.

Étienne   Did you ring, Monsieur?

Massenay   Telephone the concierge. There's a lady in a cab downstairs. Ask him to tell her Monsieur Belgence would like her to come upstairs.

Étienne   Yes, Monsieur.

Exit. **Massenay** *is standing with his back to the study door.* **Chanal** *comes out, and taps him nervously on the shoulder.*

Chanal   Excuse me.

Massenay (*rounding on him*)   I . . . will . . . not . . . talk . . . about . . . my . . . wife.

Chanal   It isn't that. Just listen.

Massenay   Oh, for heaven's sake. What?

Chanal   The thing is . . .

Massenay *has moved, so that* **Chanal** *and* **Belgence** *can see each other. They incline their heads as strangers do.*

Massenay   Let me introduce you. (*To* **Belgence**.) Monsieur Chanal, my current wife's ex-husband.

Belgence   Monsieur.

Massenay (*to* **Chanal**)   Monsieur Belgence, my ex-wife's future husband.

Chanal   Congratulations.

Belgence   Thank you.

Pause. Then **Massenay** *is back where he was before the etiquette.*

Massenay   Well, what is it?

Chanal (*piteously*)   I'm in there. There's nobody.

Massenay   Read a magazine.

Chanal   I would, but have you any cigarettes? I've forgotten mine.

Massenay   You know I don't smoke. There's a box of cigars in there. You gave them to me. Your wedding present.

Chanal   Thank you. No, don't worry, I'll find them. (*To* **Belgence**.) Monsieur.

Belgence   Monsieur.

Exit **Chanal**.

Massenay   Belgence, I'm sorry.

Belgence   No, no. I'm overwhelmed.

Massenay   Pardon?

Belgence   I know you're still cross with Sophie.

Massenay   Me?

Belgence   No, no, you are. She doesn't deserve it, really. *She's* not cross with *you.*

Massenay   Funny way of showing it.

Belgence   You don't understand. She was young. Her head full of daft ideas. Fidelity in marriage . . . they told her that applied to husbands.

Massenay   They didn't.

Belgence   If I'd ten francs for every time she's said how sorry she was she'd been so hard on you –

Massenay   (*pricking up his ears*)   What? (*Feigning indifference.*) Ah.

Belgence   I'd be a millionaire.

Massenay   You're joking.

Belgence   Scout's honour.

Étienne   (*showing in* **Sophie**)   In here, Madame.

Belgence   Ah!

Massenay   (*rushing to her, exalted*)   You came!

Sophie   The concierge said . . .

Massenay   You really said it? You were sorry. If you'd known you wouldn't have . . .

Sophie   What are you talking about?

Massenay   Belgence told me. Himself. Just now.

Belgence   I thought he was still cross. I just said . . . you were sorry you were so hard on him before.

Sophie   What? Why did you tell him – ?

Massenay   You did? You did?

Sophie   I certainly didn't mean that *he* could –

Massenay *Why* did you say it, if you didn't mean it? *Why* did you?

Belgence (*seeing the way the wind is blowing*) I say . . .

Sophie You know very well why.

Massenay I didn't deserve it. A moment's indiscretion. Meaningless. Did you think how *miserable* you'd make me?

Belgence I say, Massenay . . . Massenay . . .

Massenay Stay out of this. (*To* **Sophie**.) You *knew* I loved you.

Belgence Hey!

Sophie Oh, you loved me?

Massenay Of course I loved you. I did.

Belgence Look, do you mind?

Massenay I said, stay out of it.

Belgence But just a minute . . .

Sophie You loved me so much you went looking for other women.

Massenay That's not important.

Sophie Not for a man. But what about me? I loved you.

Belgence Oh!

Massenay You can't have done. Or if you did, you cured yourself.

Sophie Who says I did?

Massenay You're marrying Belgence.

Belgence Thank you.

Sophie What does that prove? He knows I like him, but he knows I don't love him.

Massenay (*overjoyed*) That's *right*! (*Superbly.*) And, that being so, you've no right at all to marry him.

Belgence What d'you mean, no right?

Massenay Exactly what I say: no right.

Belgence Now just a minute. I didn't get her up here so that you could say she has no right.

Massenay Of course you didn't. But I have to. Your happiness is at stake.

Belgence *My* happiness?

Massenay Naturally. And you're lucky we found out today.

He goes and puts his arm round **Sophie**'s *waist.*

Massenay Found out how much in love we are.

Belgence (*opening his mouth soundlessly, like a beached fish*) Mp.

Sophie Oh, Émile.

Massenay Yes, we're still in love. And sooner or later, when two people love each other, fate has a habit of throwing them together. Dear friend that you are, we simply couldn't risk hurting you.

Belgence But –

Massenay Obviously, you're heartbroken.

Belgence I am.

Massenay It was the only way. Better be heartbroken now, get over it, than have it hanging over you some time in the future.

Belgence But couldn't you have –

Massenay I know what you're going to say. We should have sacrificed ourselves for you, for friendship. Of course we should, had it only been possible. But we had to deny ourselves. It would have been selfish, selfish.

Belgence   Pardon?

Massenay   Don't you agree, darling?

Sophie   Oh darling, why are you still shackled?

Massenay   I'll burst the shackles. I love you, you love me, we love each other, I'll divorce Francine and we'll remarry.

Sophie (*in his arms*)   Oh, Émile.

Belgence   No, no, no, no, no, no, no.

Sophie   Did you say something?

Belgence   No. Just no. I mean, no, I'd better go.

Sophie   If you feel you have to.

Belgence   Yes.

But he sits, defeated, on the piano stool.

Massenay   After all, you came of your own free choice.

Belgence   If I'd realised . . .

Sophie (*rounding on him*)   Thanks! Thank goodness I found out in time.

Belgence   Found what out?

Sophie   The kind of man you are. Jealous, a dictator, brutal. Look at Émile: not a jealous bone in his body.

Massenay   You know me . . .

Sophie   Émile, jealous? Impossible!

Belgence (*piteously*)   You're stealing my wife.

Massenay   Excuse me. *I* married her first.

Sophie   He did.

Massenay   To think I was ready to sacrifice myself for

this man's happiness. Now it's our happiness, and listen to him.

Sophie I'm glad I found out in time.

Belgence (*humbly*) I'm sorry.

Sophie Never mind. You can't help the kind of man you are. I'm just pleased I found out before it's too late. Émile, I have to go.

Massenay Don't be long.

Sophie Oh, no. (*To* **Belgence**, *different tone*.) You'll drop me off?

Belgence You don't mind?

Sophie Good heavens, you *are* our friend. *Our* friend.

Exit.

Belgence Really?

Massenay (*jovially punching him*) Don't be silly.

Belgence (*recoiling*) No . . .

Massenay Up to you.

Belgence I . . . I just wish you'd *told* me.

He rushes out.

Massenay No pleasing some people. Chanal! Chanal!

Enter **Chanal**.

Chanal What is it?

Massenay Dear boy, you see a man who loves his wife passionately, devotedly.

Chanal Francine?

Massenay Don't be ridiculous. Sophie, Sophie, Sophie.

Chanal What?

Massenay   Francine! I'm divorcing Francine.

Chanal   Ah. Well, the way things were going . . .

Massenay   What's that mean? What things?

Chanal   Well, obviously: Coustillou.

Massenay   What about Coustillou?

Chanal   Good heavens, he was showering her with kisses.

Massenay   Coustillou? You're joking.

Chanal   You'll see for yourself.

Massenay (*who doesn't believe a word of it*)   Well, so much the better. I want a divorce. Best thing all round. Francine's always wanted Coustillou, now she can have him. And I . . . I remarry the wife I love.

Chanal   You can't do that.

Massenay   Whyever not?

Chanal   It's . . . bigamy.

Massenay   Of course it's not bigamy. The law of nature, the imperative of nature, who can stand against it? Two hearts beating as one . . . Sh! Francine!

Enter **Francine**.

Francine   It's done. I've chosen one. A lover.

Massenay   Really?

Francine   You left me no choice. It's settled. Tomorrow, he'll be mine.

Massenay   Thanks for warning me.

Francine   You don't believe me.

Massenay   I do.

Francine   It's true.

Massenay   And this lover's name is – ?

Francine   I'm not telling. You wouldn't believe me, anyway.

Massenay   Whatever you say.

Chanal (*aside to him*)   She means it. It's Coustillou.

Massenay   You're joking.

Chanal   If he comes in like a normal person, will that convince you?

Massenay   Don't be ridiculous.

Chanal   Just wait and see.

Étienne   Monsieur Coustillou.

He ushers in **Coustillou**, *who is entirely relaxed, very man-of-the-world, full of the joys of spring.*

Coustillou   Now, now, Étienne. No need to tell them who I am. Massenay, good morning! How are you this morning? What *about* this weather? Birds carolling, sun shining, I was taking a constitutional, I said to myself, 'I know, I'll drop in on Massenay. Dear old Massenay!' What's wrong with you?

Massenay   He's normal.

Coustillou   Chanal! My dear old fellow! Nice to see you, after all this time.

Chanal   You're normal.

Coustillou (*going gallantly to* **Francine**)   Madame, I left the best till last. How are you? Since yesterday, how are you?

Francine (*aside*)   Stop being so *normal*. You're being *normal*.

Coustillou (*aside*)   My God, so I am. (*He makes a pathetically bad attempt at his earlier manner.*) I . . . eugh . . .

hoo ... um ...

Massenay   We know what's going on.

Coustillou   No ... hoo ... erg ... My dear, er ...

Massenay   Massenay.

Coustillou   ... Massenay, I ... moo ...

Massenay   What's wrong with you? You were fine when you came in just now.

Coustillou   I? Moo? I've been taking lessons. They seem to be working.

Massenay   That's obvious.

Chanal (*aside*)   This is ridiculous.

Coustillou   À propos, my dear fellow, I've an idea to put to you.

Massenay   What idea?

Coustillou   Dear friend ... I think we live far too far from one another.

Francine, **Chanal**, **Massenay**   Ah!

Coustillou *continues, oblivious to the fact that* **Massenay** *knows exactly what's going on, and has an agenda of his own.*

Coustillou   You've a ground-floor apartment lying vacant. What would you say if I asked to rent it?

Massenay (*feigning amazement*)   You?

Francine (*aside, bewildered*)   What's he *playing* at?

Massenay   My dear fellow! Nothing could be better! I've got the lease here. Just a minute ...

He takes **Coustillou** *to the table, and starts writing.*

Chanal (*aside*)   What do *I* get out of this?

Massenay   What date shall I put?

Coustillou Today. I'll move in tonight, and start tomorrow.

Massenay Start tomorrow, eh? (*Pretending there's a problem.*) There's just one thing: I have to leave for Calais tomorrow evening. Two days away.

Coustillou, **Francine** Ah!

They look at one another. **Chanal** *tries to warn* **Massenay**, *who pretends not to notice.*

Massenay Never mind. You don't need me. Just ask the concierge.

Coustillou Don't worry, I'll see to it.

Massenay I'll just finish this.

Coustillou Thank you.

Chanal (*aside*) The idiot.

Coustillou (*aside to* **Francine**) Tomorrow night.

Francine (*aside*) Try to stop me!

Chanal (*looking over* **Massenay**'s *shoulder*) What are you writing? That's not a lease.

Massenay Read it.

Chanal *breaks away to read.*

Coustillou Is that the lease?

Massenay (*Machiavellian*) Oh yes. Oh yes.

Coustillou (*to* **Francine**) That's it.

Chanal (*reading*) 'My dear Inspector Planteloup . . .'

Massenay *snatches it out of his hands.*

Massenay Don't read it aloud, you fool.

Chanal What are you playing at?

Massenay You did it for me, I'm doing it for him. I'm

doing it for you.

Chanal   Doing what?

Massenay   Remember? 'Marriage is like standing on the bridge of a great ocean liner. The pilot comes aboard. You point him to the wheel, and say . . .'

Chanal   I've heard this before somewhere.

Massenay   Exactly. *I* divorce *her*, *she* marries *him*, you install yourself down*stairs* . . .

Chanal   And you say –

Massenay   'There you are, old boy. She's all yours. Take her.'

Final curtain.

A Flea in Her Ear

La Puce à l'oreille

Characters

Victor-Emmanuel Chandebise
Raymonde, *his wife*
Camille, *his nephew*
Tournel
Doctor Finache
Don Carlos Homénidès de Histangua
Lucienne, *his wife*
Étienne, *the manservant*
Antoinette, *his wife, the cook*
Ferraillon, *hotel manager*
Poche, *drunken porter*
Rugby, *English guest*
Baptistin, *Ferraillon's doddery old relative*
Olympe, *Ferraillon's wife*
Eugénie, *the maid*

The action takes place in Paris in summer: Acts One and Three in Chandebise's apartment, Act Two in the Hotel Casablanca.

Note Chandebise and Poche are played by the same actor. Camille has no roof to his mouth, and is unable to pronounce any consonants unless he inserts an artificial palate into his mouth.

The original French title, *La Puce à l'oreille* (literally 'The Flea in the Ear'), has nothing like our English connotation of 'I gave him a flea in his ear'. It is slang for a sudden notion or *idée fixe*: a good English translation might be 'A Bee in her Bonnet'.

Act One

Chandebise's *elegantly furnished drawing-room. Rear C, wide bay with double door to the hall outside (which we imagine leads to the front door of the apartment and the main stairwell of the building). R and L of this, single doors to other parts of the apartment. Downstage L, window; downstage R, door. Fireplace, sofa, chairs, table and chairs, writing-desk. In the hall (visible when the main doors are open: table with* telephone. *As the curtain rises,* **Camille** *is standing by the writing-desk, reading a document which he has taken from one of the drawers. After a moment,* **Antoinette** *creeps in, tiptoes up behind him, takes his head in her hands from behind and gives him a quick kiss.*

Camille (*startled*) For heaven's sake! [*We hear 'O-E-E-AKE'. He will speak like this, vowels only, throughout this act.*]

Antoinette It's all right, they're out.

Camille I see.

Antoinette Come on, then. Come on!

Camille *looks at her for a moment, then gives her a long kiss. As if on cue, enter* **Étienne**, *ushering in* **Finache**.

Étienne This way, Doctor.

Antoinette *and* **Camille** Oh!

They dart apart. **Camille** *bolts out R.* **Antoinette** *leaps L.*

Étienne What are you doing here?

Antoinette Me? Dinner. Dinner menu.

Étienne They've gone out. You know they've gone out. Get back to the kitchen. No cooks in the drawing-room.

Antoinette But it's –

Étienne Hup, hup, hup!

Exit **Antoinette**. **Finache** *sits.*

Finache   You're very firm with her.

Étienne   All husbands should be. If you don't wear the trousers, they do. I'm not having that.

Finache   Bravo.

Étienne   She's a tigress, Doctor. Loyal . . . but jealous. A tigress. Creeps about the house, spies on me. It's incredible.

Finache   Incredible.

Étienne   I am in charge.

Finache   Of course. (*Rising.*) Well, if Monsieur isn't here . . .

Étienne   That's all right. I'm here. I'll talk to you.

Finache   How thoughtful. But I'd hate to –

Étienne   I've nothing else to do.

Finache   Oh, in that case . . . You don't know when he'll be back, Monsieur?

Étienne   Twenty minutes, at least.

Finache   H'm. (*He takes his hat from the table and puts it on. Goes upstage.*) Well, look, I'd love to stay, but –

Étienne   Oh, Monsieur . . .

Finache   No, no. We must be disciplined. I've a patient down the road. I can just polish him off.

Étienne (*scandalised*)   Monsieur!

Finache   Good grief, I don't mean that. I hang on to my patients. Bread and butter. I mean, I'll see him and be back in twenty minutes.

Étienne   That's quite all right . . .

Finache   How kind.

False exit.

That reminds me. If Monsieur comes back before I do ... (*He takes out a note.*) please give him this. Tell him I've examined the client, he's in perfect health and he's an excellent risk.

Étienne (*unconcerned*)   Fine.

Finache (*playing to him*)   I know what you mean.

Étienne (*shrugging*)   *Comme ci comme ça.*

Finache   Exactly. But business is business. Boston Life Assurance, Paris Branch, Paris and District, he had to know, your employer.

Étienne (*familiarly*)   The boss, I know.

Finache   Ahem.

Étienne   Oh, excuse me.

Finache   No, no. It's up to you. Tell him his ... matador's in tiptop shape. What's the fellow's name? Don Carlos Homénidès de Histangua.

Étienne   Histangua. I knew I'd heard it before. His wife's in there, in the dining-room. She called to see Madame.

Finache   What a small world! This morning I examine the husband, this afternoon his wife's in the dining-room.

Étienne   Yesterday they were both in there. Having dinner.

Finache   There you are, then.

Étienne *sits.*

Étienne   By the way, Doctor –

Finache   Don't mind me.

Étienne   That's all right. The thing is, I was saying to my dear lady just this morning –

Finache   Madame Chandebise ... ?

Étienne   No, no. My wife.

Finache   Your better half.

Étienne   Tut.

Finache   Sorry.

Étienne   The thing is, if one has ... Do sit down.

Finache   Sorry. (*He sits.*)

Étienne   What I mean is, if someone has ... pains ...
recurring pains, you know ... here, and here ...

Finache (*leaning forward in his chair*)   Aha. It might be ...
how can I put this? ... ovaries.

Étienne   Ovaries. That's what I've got, then. Ovaries.

Finache   They ought to come out.

Étienne (*jumping up*)   Oh, no. They're mine and I'm
keeping them.

Finache   I don't want them.

Étienne   You could have fooled me.

Enter **Lucienne**.

Lucienne   Étienne ... (*She sees* **Finache**.) Oh, excuse
me. (*To* **Étienne**.) You did say Madame was coming
back?

Étienne   Yes, Madame. She told me: 'If Señora ...
Señora ... uh ...'

Lucienne   Homénidès de Histangua –

Étienne   That's right. 'Comes round –'

Finache   'Comes visiting ...'

Étienne   Thank you. (*To* **Lucienne**.) 'Don't let her go.
I have to see her.'

Lucienne   She said the same in her note. So why isn't

she . . . ? Never mind, I'll wait a little longer.

Étienne   Thank you, Madame. We were just saying,
Monsieur and I . . .

Finache   Monsieur . . .

Étienne (*introducing him*)   Doctor Finache. Consultant-in-
chief to the Boston Assurance Company. He was telling
me, he saw Madame's husband just this morning.

Lucienne   Did he really?

Finache   I did indeed, Madame. I examined him in
person.

Lucienne   Whatever for?

Finache   Insurance. A formality. Madame, I congratulate
you. What a husband! What a figure! What physique!

Lucienne   Thank you, Monsieur.

Finache   It's a privilege, a husband like that.

Lucienne   It's exhausting.

Finache   A small price —

Étienne (*with a sigh*)   That's what Madame Plucheux
keeps saying.

Lucienne   Madame Plucheux?

Étienne   My wife. My . . . better half. What she could
do with a husband like Madame's husband here . . .

Finache   Nothing easier. If Madame agrees, if Señor de
Histangua agrees . . .

Étienne   Steady on.

Lucienne (*playing along*)   No, no, Doctor, no, no, no.

Finache (*laughing*)   I'm sorry, Madame. It's Étienne here,
my good friend Étienne. I don't know what I'm saying.
(*He fetches his hat.*) I really must go, if I'm to be back in

twenty minutes. Delighted to meet you.

Lucienne   Charmed.

Finache   Of course.

He starts to go. **Étienne** *accompanies him.*

Étienne   What we were saying earlier, Doctor. If I bend like this ... my ovaries ...

Finache   Senna pods, my dear fellow. Senna pods. That'll calm 'em.

Exeunt.

Lucienne   What a man. (*Looking at her watch.*) Ten past one. 'I have to see you' – this can't be what she meant. Oh ...

She sits and flicks through a magazine. Enter **Camille**, *on his way to return the paper to the writing-desk.*

Camille   Oh! Excuse me.

Lucienne   Monsieur.

Camille   Are you wanting the Director of the Boston Assurance Company?

Lucienne (*not with him*)   I'm sorry?

Camille   I said: are you wanting the Director of the Boston Assurance Company?

Lucienne   I'm sorry: I just don't follow.

Camille (*even more carefully*)   I just asked, are you wanting the –

Lucienne   No, no. French. Française. Französisch.

Camille   Me too. Me too.

Lucienne   You'll have to ask Étienne. I'm waiting for Madame Chandebise.

Camille   Oh. Sorry. (*He retreats towards the writing-desk.*) I asked because if it had been Monsieur Chandebise, the Director in person –

Lucienne   Yes. That's right. Oh yes.

Camille *reaches the desk, puts his paper in the drawer, shuts it and makes his escape.*

Camille   Terribly sorry.

Exit.

Lucienne (*staring after him*)   Not a Martian, surely.

Enter **Étienne**.

Étienne   Is everything all right, Madame?

Lucienne   Thank goodness. Listen. There was a man in here just now . . .

Étienne   A man?

Lucienne   Some kind of . . . wild man. I don't know what he said. O A E OO ANH INH. Something like that.

Étienne   Monsieur Camille.

Lucienne   From abroad?

Étienne   Sir's nephew. His brother's son. I know what you thought. He's got a problem. Can't say his consonants.

Lucienne   Is that it?

Étienne   It's hard at first. But I'm getting the hang of it.

Lucienne   He's giving you lessons?

Étienne   No, no. The more you hear, the more your ears get used to –

Lucienne   Yes, yes.

Étienne   Sir took him on as secretary. Amazing! A man who talks like a camel.

Lucienne All he has is vowels.

Étienne Oh no. I've seen him write. Consonants, everything. But you can't write always. Such a shame. Such an . . . unspoiled young man. D'you know, he's never had an affair.

Lucienne You're joking.

Étienne And neither have I.

Lucienne Well, good for him.

Étienne (*with a sigh*) I suppose so. Ah, here's Madame.

Enter **Raymonde**.

Lucienne At last!

Raymonde My dear, I'm so sorry. Thank you, Étienne.

Étienne Yes, Madame. (*To* **Lucienne**.) Excuse me, Madame.

Lucienne What? Oh.

Exit **Étienne**.

Raymonde I've kept you waiting.

Lucienne Hardly at all.

Raymonde I've been miles. Miles! I'll tell you in a minute. Lucienne, I sent you that note because . . . something awful's happening. My husband − an affair.

Lucienne Victor-Emmanuel?

Raymonde Exactly.

Lucienne Embarrassing.

Raymonde Just wait till I catch him.

Lucienne You mean you've no proof?

Raymonde Of course I've no proof. The swine. But still I'll catch him.

Lucienne   How?

Raymonde   I don't know. You decide.

Lucienne   Me?

Raymonde   You were my best friend at school. Ten years ago, but some things never change. Lucienne Vicard. Now you're Lucienne Homénidès de Histangua. But you're still my friend, my best, best friend.

Lucienne   Well, yes.

Raymonde   So in my . . . moment of need, who else should I turn to?

Lucienne   (*not too enthusiastically*)   Too kind.

Raymonde   So tell me, what's the best way?

Lucienne   Best way to what?

Raymonde   To trap my husband.

Lucienne   I don't know. Is that why you asked me to come?

Raymonde   Of course it was.

Lucienne   Thanks. Who told you he needed trapping, anyway? Perhaps he's the faithfullest of men.

Raymonde   He isn't.

Lucienne   You can't prove it.

Raymonde   And he can't hide it.

Lucienne   Exactly. Perhaps he isn't.

Raymonde   I'm not a baby. What would you say if your husband . . . I mean, a husband . . . on Tuesday completely changed his spots on Wednesday?

Lucienne   I'd say 'H'm!'

Raymonde   'H'm.' Exactly. A husband . . . a predictable, loving husband . . . so much so, I must admit, that just this February – no, March – I was beginning to think, 'Please, a cloud, a disagreement, a squabble, anything.' I even thought of a lover. To liven things up.

Lucienne A lover? You?

Raymonde Why not? I've got admirers. Devoted slaves. Well, one. Monsieur Tournel. You met him at dinner here last night. Didn't you notice how he ... how he ...? I thought women could always tell. I'm telling you, it was nip and tuck.

Lucienne Nip and tuck?

Raymonde My husband's best friend. It could have been meant. Well, maybe now it will be meant, now he's having an affair, my husband I mean.

Lucienne Listen, Raymonde –

Raymonde What?

Lucienne To start with, you adore your husband.

Raymonde I adore my husband – ?

Lucienne And second, what's the point?

Raymonde The point is, I'm furious. We're not talking about me taking a lover, we're talking about him ... him! It's just too much.

Lucienne (*fetching her coat*) It's the same thing entirely. Sauce for the goose ...

Raymonde You think I'm wrong?

Lucienne All I think is, you've got no proof.

Raymonde No proof. When a husband, for years, when he's been a ... a ... an engulfing torrent, and suddenly pfft! A desert, a Sahara ...

Lucienne It happens all the time. Rivers ... deserts ... It doesn't prove he's having an affair.

Raymonde Ha!

Lucienne It's like gamblers in casinos . . . one minute they're throwing it everywhere, the next, tuppence ha'penny.

Raymonde If only it *was* tuppence ha'penny. But nothing. Nothing!

Lucienne It still proves nothing. Except that he's . . . well, he's –

Raymonde *takes a pair of braces from her handbag and brandishes them at* **Lucienne**.

Raymonde All right then, what are these?

Lucienne What d'you mean, what are they?

Raymonde They're braces.

Lucienne I can see that.

Raymonde And d'you know whose they are?

Lucienne Well, his, I imagine. Your husband's.

Raymonde I knew you'd change your tune.

Lucienne Don't be silly. You've got a pair of braces. Of course I think they're your husband's. What else should I think?

Raymonde *puts the braces back in her handbag.*

Raymonde I suppose you can also explain why these braces arrived in the post at eight o'clock this morning.

Lucienne In the post?

Raymonde An urgent package. I opened it by accident.

Lucienne Pardon?

Raymonde When I was reading his post.

Lucienne You always read his post?

Raymonde   Yes.

Lucienne   Why?

Raymonde   To find out what it says.

Lucienne   Of course.

Raymonde   Of course.

Lucienne   So you opened his package, by accident.

Raymonde   By accident means it wasn't addressed to
me.

Lucienne   Of course.

Raymonde   Well, it's obvious, isn't it? If someone's
posting him braces, it's because he's left them behind
somewhere.

Lucienne   Aha.

Raymonde   Exactly. And d'you know where it was, this
'somewhere'?

Lucienne (*melodramatically*)   You interest me strangely.

Raymonde   The Hotel Casablanca. That's where.

Lucienne   What sort of hotel is that?

Raymonde   Can't you guess, with a name like that?

Lucienne   The Hotel Casablanca.

Raymonde *fetches a box from beside the door.*

Raymonde   They came in this. Look: the hotel name,
printed on the label. And here, in handwriting, 'Monsieur
Chandebise, 95 boulevard Malesherbes'. His name and
address.

Lucienne   Hotel Casablanca.

Raymonde   Now d'you believe me? A name like that, a
place like that, what else could be going on? Even I didn't
believe it at first. When he was so . . . so . . .

Lucienne Tuppence ha'penny.

Raymonde I thought, 'It's nothing. Don't be silly.' But this is something else. A nod and a wink.

Lucienne I see what you mean.

Raymonde I mean, if you just saw the place. It looks like every Saturday night you've ever heard of.

Lucienne You've been there?

Raymonde Just now.

Lucienne Pff.

Raymonde That's why I was so late.

Lucienne Ah.

Raymonde I had to know. 'There's only one way,' I thought. 'Go and ask the manager.' Ask the manager! Have you ever tried that? They stick together, all of them. They won't be budged.

Lucienne Rule Number One.

Raymonde D'you know what he had the gall to say to me? 'My dear Madame, if I blabbed the names of people who came to this hotel, you'd never come here again yourself.' He said that to me! Nothing doing. That ... ferret!

Lucienne You're far too polite.

Raymonde So it's up to us. The men are sticking together, we must do the same. I'm counting on you. A woman of the world. Tell me what to do.

Lucienne But I can't ... I mean I can't just ...

Raymonde One bright idea, that's all.

Lucienne Right. Um. Ah! Suppose you had it out with him?

Raymonde He'd lie. No one lies like a man – except a woman.

Lucienne (*suddenly*)   I know! This always works in plays.

Raymonde   What?

Lucienne   It's not exactly fair. But for a man . . . You get some perfumed notepaper, write a letter to your husband . . . burning, passionate . . . from another woman, of course – and end by suggesting a . . . rendezvous.

Raymonde   Rendezvous?

Lucienne   Rendezvous. You turn up as arranged – and if he turns up, you've got him.

Raymonde   Brilliant. Not very fair, but they're the ones that work. (*She goes to the writing-desk.*) We'll do it now. We'll write him a note.

Lucienne (*lightly*)   'Dear Victor-Emmanuel . . .'

Raymonde *has sat down to write. Now she jumps up.*

Raymonde   No good. He'll recognise my writing.

Lucienne   If you've written to him before . . . [*i.e.* . . . *of course he will.*]

Raymonde   He doesn't know your writing. You do it.

Lucienne   I can't. It's private.

Raymonde   I won't tell anyone. Are you my best friend or aren't you?

Lucienne (*weakly*)   You're tormenting me.

Raymonde   No, *we're* tormenting Victor-Emmanuel.

Lucienne   Oh, dear. (*Sitting to write.*) All right, where's the paper?

Raymonde   There.

Lucienne   Not that. It's got your address on it.

Raymonde   So it has. I know . . . I bought this card the other day ... for my dear little niece ... (*She finds a garish, hearts-and-flowers card.*)

Lucienne   He'll think it's from Goldilocks. He'll never come.

Raymonde   I suppose not.

Lucienne   Have you nothing chic, *soigné*?

Raymonde   What about this?

Lucienne   Just right. If the perfume's right ...

Raymonde   I've got the very thing. It came with a pink silk rose ... a free sample, came the other day. I was going to throw it out. Just a minute ...

She presses the bell, just as **Camille** *comes in, holding a piece of paper. He peers enquiringly round the room.*

Camille (*in his incomprehensible way*)   Oh, I'm sorry –

Raymonde   Camille. What is it?

Camille   It's all right. I was looking to see if Victor-Emmanuel was home.

Raymonde (*as naturally as if every word had been crystal clear*)   Not yet. What d'you want him for?

Camille   This letter to sign, some policies to look over. I didn't really mean –

Raymonde   He won't be long.

Camille   I might as well wait, then. Nothing else for it.

Raymonde   Whatever you say. (*She looks at* **Lucienne**, *who has been gaping at her throughout all this.*) What's the matter?

Lucienne   Nothing. Nothing.

Camille (*cheerfully to* **Lucienne**)   You see, Madame, I said she wouldn't be long. I said she'd soon be here.

Lucienne (*baffled, but hiding it*)   Oh yes, we did meet earlier.

Raymonde (*mischievously*)   That's not what he said. He said he said I wouldn't be long. I'd soon be here.

Camille   That's right.

Lucienne   Oh. Yes.

Raymonde (*introducing them*)   Monsieur Camille Chandebise, our cousin. Madame Carlos Homénidès de Histangua.

Lucienne   Delighted to meet you. I'm sorry I didn't catch what you said before. I'm hard of hearing.

Camille (*genially*)   No need to apologise, Madame. It's not your fault. I've a small speech problem.

Lucienne (*smiling awkwardly*)   Oh. Yes. (*To* **Raymonde**.) What did he say?

Raymonde   He said he has a small speech problem.

Lucienne   Really? Well, now you come to mention it . . .

Camille   You're very kind.

Enter **Antoinette**.

Antoinette   Did you ring, Madame?

Raymonde   Not for you, Antoinette. Three rings. Adèle.

Antoinette   Adèle's resting. I came instead.

Raymonde   Thank you. Go upstairs, would you, and bring me that perfume that came the other day. In the left-hand drawer.

Antoinette   Yes, Madame.

Raymonde   You can't miss it. There's a pink silk rose on the box.

Antoinette   Yes, Madame.

As she goes out, she makes a detour round the embarrassed
Camille, *looking him in the eyes, then pinches his bottom and
sails out as if nothing had happened.*

Camille   Ouch!

Raymonde *and* **Lucienne**. What?

Camille   Nothing. A touch of cramp.

Raymonde   Painful.

Camille (*rubbing his bottom*)   Agony.

Raymonde   We can see that.

Camille   I must get on. I've work to do. Madame ...
(*He bows to* **Lucienne**.)

Lucienne   Monsieur.

Camille (*at the door*)   Delighted to have met you.

Exit.

Lucienne   You understand every word he says.

Raymonde   Is that why you were staring?

Lucienne   Of course.

Raymonde   I'm used to him. It's easy. But you – fancy
pretending you hadn't noticed anything.

Lucienne   I was just being polite.

Enter **Antoinette** *with the perfume.*

Antoinette   Is this it, Madame?

Raymonde   Yes, thank you.

Exit **Antoinette**.

Raymonde   Now, let's get the letter written before
Victor-Emmanuel gets home.

Lucienne   Right. (*Pondering.*) Now, what sort of bait ....?

Raymonde   H'm.

Lucienne   This unknown woman . . . was it love at first sight, eyes met across a crowded room?

Raymonde   Oh, yes. What crowded room?

Lucienne   Were you at the theatre at all last week?

Raymonde   Yes. At that new Feydeau. With Monsieur Tournel.

Lucienne   Tournel?

Raymonde   I told you. Last night, at dinner. My would-be lover.

Lucienne   Better and better. Listen. (*Writing.*) 'Monsieur, I saw you last week at the new Feydeau . . .'

Raymonde   Mm. A bit cool, if it was love at first sight.

Lucienne   Cool?

Raymonde   Like writing to a bank manager. How about: 'Last week at the play I drank you in . . .' Something like that. And no 'Monsieur'.

Lucienne   You're good at this.

Raymonde   I'm just saying what I'd have written.

Lucienne   Right. (*She starts on a new sheet.*) 'Last week at the play I drank you in . . .'

Raymonde   'I couldn't tear my eyes away.' No coolness there.

Lucienne   It's how it is! (*Writing.*) 'There you were in your box . . . your wife, your friend . . .'

Raymonde   Tournel.

Lucienne   She wouldn't know that. 'The people next to me told me your name.'

Raymonde (*repeating as if in dictation class*)   'Told me your name . . .'

Lucienne (*writing*)   '... your name. So I knew who you were.'

Raymonde   This is easy!

Lucienne   'Since that moment of revelation, I've had no thoughts but of you.'

Raymonde   Too melodramatic?

Lucienne   Of course! That's how it's done.

Raymonde   If you say so.

Lucienne (*writing*)   'I tremble on the brink of adventure. Will you tremble with me? I'll expect you at five p.m. at the Hotel Casablanca –'

Raymonde   Won't that put him off, the same hotel?

Lucienne   Quite the reverse: it'll put him on. (*Writing.*) 'Hotel Casablanca, rue Kasbah. Ask for the room booked for Monsieur Chandebise.'

Raymonde (*dictating*)   'Don't fail me.'

Lucienne   'Don't fail me'! You're made for this.

Raymonde   I'm learning fast.

Lucienne (*writing*)   'Your devoted admirer.' There. Now the perfume.

Raymonde (*passing the opened bottle*)   Here.

Lucienne   Perfect. (*She sprinkles perfume over the note.*)

Raymonde   It's smudging the ink.

Lucienne   Oh no!

Raymonde   Now what?

Lucienne   Now what?

Raymonde   Begin again.

Lucienne   No! I've got it. (*Writing again.*) 'PS. Even as I write, tears spring unbidden to my eyes. Tears of joy, my love, hot tears of joy.' There. Where's the pink rose? There we are!

Raymonde   Why should you weep hot tears when you're trembling for adventure?

Lucienne   He won't ask that. (*Addressing the envelope.*) 'Monsieur Victor-Emmanuel Chandebise, 95 boulevard Malesherbes. Personal.' There. Now, we need someone to take this to the concierge.

Raymonde   I know: you!

Lucienne   What?

Raymonde   I can't send one of the servants: the concierge knows them. I can't go: he might ask the concierge to describe the lady. It has to be you.

Lucienne   It's slave labour.

Raymonde   You are my best friend.

Lucienne   Oh, if you say so. But really I –

Doorbell, off.

Raymonde   That'll be him. Quick, go out this way, door on the right, you're in the hall.

Lucienne   Till later.

Raymonde   Till later.

Lucienne *goes out.* **Raymonde** *hides the perfume bottle. The main doors open, and we see* **Chandebise** *talking to* **Étienne**. **Tournel** *is with him.*

Chandebise   The doctor said he'd be back?

Étienne   Yes, Monsieur.

Chandebise   Fine. (*To* **Tournel**.) Come in, come in. Give me five minutes, will you? Letters to sign.

Raymonde (*whom they haven't so far seen*)   That's right. Camille's in there with his tongue hanging out.

Chandebise   Good God, I didn't see you there.

Tournel   Good afternoon, Madame.

Raymonde   Monsieur Tournel. (*To* **Chandebise**.) I am here.

Chandebise   I met Tournel on the stairs. We came up together.

Raymonde   Oh.

Tournel (*taking some papers from his briefcase*)   I've brought details of the new clients.

Chandebise   I'll look at them in a moment. (*He hitches up his trousers.*)

Raymonde   What's the matter? Trouble with your braces?

Chandebise   Exactly.

Raymonde   Not the ones I bought you?

Chandebise   Yes, those.

Raymonde   They were all right before.

Chandebise   I've hitched them too tight.

Raymonde (*going to him*)   I'll help you.

Chandebise   It's all right. I can manage.

Raymonde (*tight-lipped*)   Whatever you say.

Chandebise (*to* **Tournel**)   Excuse me. I won't be a moment.

Tournel   That's fine. That's fine.

Chandebise *opens the inner door.*

Camille (*from inside*)   Ah, there you are.

Chandebise   What d'you mean, ah there I am? I've had a lot to do.

He goes in and shuts the door. At once **Tournel** *runs to* **Raymonde**.

Tournel   Raymonde, Raymonde, I dreamed of you all night.

Raymonde (*cutting him off*)   Not now. My husband's having an affair.

Tournel (*taken aback*)   What d'you mean?

Raymonde   These things are for idle moments, not times like this.

Tournel   But you told me . . . Raymonde . . . you said . . .

Raymonde   I may have done. Before the braces. But not now. Excuse me.

Exit.

Tournel   What have braces got to do with it?

Camille *appears at the inner door.*

Camille   Monsieur Tournel. My cousin's ready now.

Tournel   Pardon?

Camille   Monsieur Tournel, my cousin's ready now.

Tournel   I don't understand. Once more –

Camille   Just a minute. (*He takes a notebook and pencil, and writes, saying each syllable.*) Mon-sieur-Tour-nel-my-cou-sin's-rea-dy-now.

He hands the paper to **Tournel**, *who reads it.*

Tournel   'Monsieur Tournel, my cousin's ready now.' Well, why didn't you say so?

He gathers his papers and goes out.

Camille Fneuf! It's too much. I go out of my way to oblige him, and that's all I get: 'Well, why didn't you say so?' Fneuf!

Étienne *shows* **Finache** *in at the main door.*

Étienne He's here now, Monsieur.

Finache Jolly good.

Étienne I'll tell him you're here.

Camille (*who hasn't seen them*) It's grossly unfair. I say to him, extremely politely, 'Monsieur Tournel, my cousin's ready now.' 'Pardon?' he says. I say it again: 'Monsieur Tournel, my cousin's ready now.' He still doesn't get it. I write it down. 'Monsieur Tournel, my cousin's ready now.' And what do I get for my trouble? 'Well, why didn't you say so?' It's too much, too much, too much.

Finache Afternoon, Camille. Poetry?

Camille No, Doctor, complaining. I was complaining. What happened was –

Finache (*who doesn't follow*) Don't even try. (*New tone.*) Well, young fella-me-lad, how's life with you? Courting, are we?

Camille (*urgently*) Oh. Shh! No.

Finache I know what you mean. Your reputation. Camille, the saint, the monk.

Camille Please.

Finache The thing is, we doctors know all too well, the moment comes when even a saint has to step down from his pedestal. I mean, you know and I know, it's ridiculous to think that they still think –

Camille (*weak smile*) Oh, yes.

Finache You did as I suggested?

Camille Pardon?

Finache   The Hotel Casablanca.

Camille (*writhing*)   Shh.

Finache   There's no one here. Did you or didn't you?

Camille   Yes.

Finache   And what do you think?

Camille   Wow!

Finache   Exactly. Wow! There's nowhere better. Ah, well, I can see you're busy. Tell your cousin I'm here.

Camille (*delighted at the change of subject*)   Thank you. Thank you.

Finache   Just a minute. I nearly forgot. Your whatjimacallit.

Camille   What whatjimacallit?

Finache (*taking a box from his pocket*)   The one I said I'd get you. To help you speak like anyone else.

Camille   You mean you got one?

Finache   Of course I got one. It's a terrible affliction, congenital: a malformed oral vault. You speak perfectly normally, but the sounds don't bounce round and out as with anyone else, they get lost in your sinuses.

Camille   That's right.

Finache   And the answer's so simple. A whatjimacallit.

Camille   Let's see.

Finache (*opening the box*)   A palate of silver, dear boy, just like in a fairy tale.

Camille   I'll be able to speak normally?

Finache   Pardon?

Camille   I'll be able − ? Just a minute. (*He tries to insert the palate.*)

Finache Not yet. Soak it first, in warm water and boracic. You don't know where it's been.

Camille Oh. Right. All I was saying was, I'll be able to speak normally?

Finache What? Speak normally? You could audition for the National Theatre.

Camille I'll put it in water right away.

Chandebise (*off*) Camille.

Finache They want you.

Camille Tell them I won't be long.

Exit. Enter **Chandebise**.

Chandebise Camille.

Finache He won't be long. Something came up. Good afternoon.

Chandebise Finache. Good afternoon. What a coincidence. I was just talking about you.

Finache I came earlier. Étienne must have said.

Chandebise That's right, with the report on Histangua. A first-class risk.

Finache First-class. Here: the papers.

Chandebise Thanks.

Finache You said you wanted to ask me something.

Chandebise Advice, that's right. Something . . . personal. Quite unusual.

Finache Go on.

Chandebise I don't know how to begin. Er . . . you know my wife, my delightful wife?

Finache Delightful, yes.

Chandebise   And you know there's no more ... no more loyal husband than yours truly?

Finache   Really?

Chandebise (*piqued*)   What d'you mean, really? Really!

Finache   I didn't know.

Chandebise   I'm telling you. My wife's always meant everything to me. Everything. And I've always been to her ... in all modesty ... an upstanding man in every way.

Finache   Really?

Chandebise   There you go again. Really!

Finache   Well, I didn't know.

Chandebise   You do now. Upstanding. In every way.

Finache   I still don't see –

Chandebise   Of course you don't. That's the whole point. Did you see that play last year, *Anything to Declare*?

Finache   What?

Chandebise   That play. Did you see it? *Anything to Declare*?

Finache   Oh, really!

Chandebise   Well, did you or didn't you?

Finache   If you must know ... I wasn't alone. I didn't see it all.

Chandebise   There were ... little gaps.

Finache   Exactly.

Chandebise   Never mind. You must have seen enough to get the idea. Young man, new wife, honeymoon, teaching her the moves, customs officer, 'Anything to declare', mood completely broken.

Finache   I think I remember.

Chandebise The customs officer? He didn't break your mood.

Finache No fear.

Chandebise The point is, the effect on that poor young man. Every time he tried to snuggle up to his wife, take up where he left off, the same customs officer loomed up in his mind, the same question, 'Anything to declare' – and pfft.

Finache Embarrassing.

Chandebise Exactly. And that's what's happened between my wife and me.

Finache Really?

Chandebise Really. One fine morning – well, actually, it was night and it was pouring – about a month ago, I felt . . . you know . . . I suggested to Madame Chandebise, and she . . . you know . . . And then, how can I put it – ?

Finache A customs officer.

Chandebise Yes. I mean, no. It was more like . . . more like . . . I felt like a . . . like a . . . little tiny boy. A . . . little . . . tiny boy.

Finache Unfortunate.

Chandebise Of course, at first I wasn't worried. I mean, one has one's glorious past. Live to fight another day, that kind of thing.

Finache Quite right.

Chandebise But another day came, and I started thinking, 'Hang on. Suppose it's just like last time?' Wrong moment. Just when you need to gather all your . . . when you need to keep a clear head . . . Well, naturally, pfft. Just like the last time.

Finache My poor chap.

Chandebise   Poor chap's the word. I can't get it out of
my head. I never think 'Tonight, perhaps –'; I always
think (*Different tone.*) 'Tonight, perhaps –' and pfft.

Finache   You mean, even while you're –

Chandebise   I'm glad you find this funny.

Finache   What d'you want me to do? It happens all the
time. Every day. Auto-suggestion. You're a victim of auto-
suggestion. All you have to do is control it. Use it. Will-
power. To want is to get.

Chandebise   How d'you mean?

Finache   Don't say 'Tonight, perhaps –', say 'Tonight,
of course!' No self-doubt. Not an instant. Just don't think
of yourself. You can't think of yourself and of someone
else at the same moment. All you've just told me, you
should have told your wife, not me. Simply, clearly,
calmly, no beating about the bush. She'd probably have
laughed, you'd have laughed, you'd have laughed
together, you'd have felt a wave of . . . emotion . . . shared
emotion . . . passion, and Bob's your uncle.

Chandebise   Ah. Bob, you say?

Finache   And plenty of exercise. I'll give you an
examination. You spend too much time thinking, writing.

He puts his knee in the small of **Chandebise**'*s back, takes him
by the shoulders and pulls him upright.*

Finache   You stoop too much. That's why I made you
buy those American braces. I don't believe you've even
tried them.

Chandebise (*taking off his waistcoat to show his braces*)   I
wear them all the time. I've given away all my others. To
Camille. I really miss them. These look vile.

Finache   No one sees them but you.

Chandebise   Someone nearly saw them ten minutes

ago: my wife.

Finache   What a fuss you make.

Chandebise   Oh thanks. One humiliation after another.

Finache   You must be the king of self-pity. Take your waistcoat off, and I'll examine you.

Chandebise *starts to remove his waistcoat – just as* **Étienne** *shows in* **Lucienne**.

Lucienne   Tell Madame I'm here.

Chandebise (*struggling back into his waistcoat*)   Oops.

Étienne   Yes, Madame.

Exit.

Chandebise (*to* **Finache**)   Later. (*To* **Lucienne**.) Madame.

Lucienne   Monsieur.

Chandebise   How nice to see you. You've come to see Madame?

Lucienne   Come back. I had an errand to run. I was here earlier. I met this gentleman.

Finache   That's right.

Chandebise   No need to introduce you, then. Er . . . you didn't notice anything unusual?

Lucienne   About this gentleman?

Chandebise   No, no. My wife. I don't know what's wrong with her today.

Lucienne   I didn't notice.

Chandebise   Oh. Good.

Enter **Raymonde**.

Raymonde   There you are.

Lucienne   Hello again.

Raymonde (*aside to her*)   Done?

Lucienne (*aside to her*)   Any minute now.

Raymonde   Good.

Enter **Étienne** *with a letter on a salver.*

Étienne   Monsieur.

Chandebise   Mm?

Lucienne (*to* **Raymonde**)   Told you!

Étienne   A personal letter, Monsieur. The concierge just brought it.

Chandebise (*astonished*)   For me? Well ... Excuse me, ladies. (*He puts his spectacles on, reads the letter, recoils. Exit* **Étienne**.) Good heavens!

Raymonde   What?

Chandebise   Nothing at all.

Raymonde   A love letter?

Chandebise   No, no, no. Insurance ...

Raymonde   Ah. (*Furiously, aside to* **Lucienne**.) See what I mean? Come on!

Exeunt.

Chandebise   They're amazing, women! You'll never guess what this is.

Finache   What is it?

Tournel *appears at the inner door.*

Tournel   I'm still kicking my heels in here.

Chandebise   Oh, come in, come in. It's all right.

Tournel   What's all right? Afternoon, Doctor.

Finache   Tournel.

Chandebise   You won't believe this, either of you. I've
. . . got an admirer.

Tournel *and* **Finache**   You?

Chandebise   You needn't sound so surprised. Listen to
this. 'Last week at the play I drank you in.'

Tournel *and* **Finache**   You?

Chandebise   Me! She drank me in.

Finache   Oh, that admirer.

Chandebise   Yes, yes, yes.

Tournel (*who has taken the letter*)   'There you were in your
box . . . your wife, your friend . . .'

Chandebise   My friend. That's you. Nobody important,
'my friend', some . . . fellow or other.

Tournel   Thank you.

Chandebise   Every dog has his day. (*Reading.*) 'The
people next to me told me your name.'

Tournel   They do that.

Chandebise   'Since that moment of revelation, I've had
no thoughts but of you . . .'

Tournel *and* **Finache**   Really?

Chandebise   No thoughts but me. (*Slapping* **Tournel** *on
the back.*) Eh, Tournel, eh?

Tournel   She means it?

Chandebise (*waving the letter*)   She means it.

Finache (*taking the letter*)   She means it.

Tournel (*still unimpressed*)   It's very odd. (*To* **Finache**.)
Don't you find it odd?

Finache   Anything's possible.

Tournel   Just a matter of taste. That's what's so odd.

Chandebise   Do you mind?

Tournel   Just joking.

Chandebise   'I tremble on the brink of adventure. Will you tremble with me?' Silly child. Lucky child. Eh? Eh, Finache?

Finache   What d'you mean?

Chandebise   What I told you before.

Finache   Oh, that.

Chandebise   'I'll expect you at five p.m. at the Hotel Casablanca –'

Finache   What?

Chandebise   'Rue Kasbah.'

Finache   Oh, brilliant. She knows what she's doing. She's done this before.

Chandebise   What d'you mean? You mean, this hotel – ?

Finache   Exactly. I mean, I go there.

Chandebise   I'd never even heard of it.

Finache   Tournel'll tell you.

Tournel   Ah. I've heard of it, of course. But naturally, I've never –

Chandebise   My God!

Tournel *and* **Finache**   What?

Chandebise   She was crying.

Tournel *and* **Finache**   She wasn't.

Chandebise   She was. Look. Listen. 'P.S. Even as I

write, tears spring unbidden to my eyes. Tears of joy, my love, hot tears of joy.' Poor child. Look, she soaked it.

He waves the letter under **Tournel***'s nose.*

Tournel (*sniffing it*) Phooee.

Chandebise *and* **Finache** What?

Tournel What was it she was crying?

Finache Sh! Tears are private. We mustn't pry.

Chandebise Oh go on, laugh. I've an admirer – me. There we were, at the play, innocently watching the play, and all the time a woman was drinking me in.

Tournel It's amazing.

Chandebise You didn't notice?

Tournel Of course I noticed. I thought it was me.

Chandebise You. (*Suddenly.*) My God, what a fool I am. Of course it was.

Tournel *and* **Finache** What?

Chandebise It was you she was drinking in, not me.

Tournel Me?

Chandebise Well, obviously. And when she asked who was in the box, and they told her my name, she took you for me.

Tournel You think so?

Chandebise It's obvious.

Tournel But surely – ? Oh well, if you say so.

Chandebise Look at me. An admirer, me? But you, just look at you, it's what you're for! (*To* **Finache***.*) It's what he's for. (*To* **Tournel***.*) Bees round a honeypot.

Tournel No, really, no.

Chandebise   A honeypot. Just look at you.

Finache   You really didn't know?

Tournel   Well, I admit I'm . . . passable.

Chandebise   Passable! Women queue up to kill themselves for loving you.

Tournel   Just one.

Chandebise   See?

Tournel   And she's better now.

Chandebise   There you are, then.

Tournel   It's not definite, either. The evidence. She was eating mussels.

Chandebise *and* **Finache**   Mussels?

Tournel   Moules marinières. I'd given her up. She said she did it for love. But if you're poisoning yourself for love, you don't use moules marinières. Too . . . gourmet.

Chandebise   It's no use. Whatever you say, this letter is addressed to me, but it's meant for you.

Tournel (*to* **Finache**)   What do you think?

Finache   Me? Ha –

Chandebise   It's obvious. And since it's meant for you, you must go.

Tournel (*with pretended reluctance*)   I wouldn't dream of –

Chandebise   I can't today anyway. We're giving a dinner-party. The directors from Boston.

Tournel   No, no, I couldn't . . .

Chandebise   Of course you could. You can hardly wait.

Tournel   No, no, no.

Chandebise   Look at your nose. It's growing.

Tournel Oh well, if my nose is growing, I'd better say yes.

Chandebise (*slapping his back*) That's the way, you dog.

Tournel So long as I've time. (*To* **Finache**.) The fact is, I've something else just coming to the boil . . .

Chandebise (*popping up between them*) HaHA! Who with?

Tournel Ah. I can't tell you.

Chandebise Can't tell, won't tell! You dog, you.

Tournel Your unknown admirer will do in the meantime.

Chandebise (*hamming it*) She's all yours. Delighted to be of service.

Tournel (*the same*) Too kind, too kind. Give me the letter.

Chandebise Not a chance. What d'you need it for, anyway? You go to the hotel, ask for the room booked in my name. I'm keeping the letter. I don't get letters like this one every day. One day, I want my grandchildren – if I ever have any – to find it among my papers and say, 'What a man he must have been, Grandpapa!' All right, Finache, examine me.

Tournel What about the signatures?

Chandebise Two minutes, I'll be with you. Finache, we'll go in there, we won't be disturbed.

Finache Whatever you say.

Exeunt.

Tournel Two minutes. Two minutes, and then . . . I wonder who she is. 'I drank you in . . .'

Enter **Raymonde**, *hat on head.*

Raymonde Monsieur Chandebise not here?

Tournel   In there, with the doctor. Shall I tell him?

Raymonde   Don't disturb him. When you see him, tell him I've gone out with Madame de Histangua, and he's not to worry if I'm late back, I'll have dinner with a friend.

Tournel   I think he'll be late back too.

Raymonde (*sharply*)   What?

Tournel (*taken aback*)   He said he was entertaining the Boston directors, that's all.

Raymonde   He did, did he? Thanks for telling me. And now I'll tell you: he isn't. It's tomorrow, that 'entertainment'. I've seen the invitation.

Tournel   He's got the wrong day. I'll tell him.

Raymonde   No! He hasn't got the wrong day. Stop rushing about. He knows exactly what he's doing. It's an alibi. He'll come back tonight, say he got the wrong day. I know exactly what's going on.

Tournel   How can it be an alibi? Why should he tell me lies?

Raymonde   It's fair enough to lie to me?

Tournel   That's not what I meant. You're confusing me.

Raymonde   Don't be ridiculous. I know what you're doing. You know that if my husband has a mistress, you've nothing to hope for from me, so you're doing your best to persuade me he's the faithfullest of men.

Tournel   I'm not. I mean it.

Raymonde   Oh, do stop it.

Tournel   Raymonde . . . !

Raymonde   Pish, tush!

She slams the door in his face, and exit.

Tournel   Pish, tush! Really!

Enter **Camille** *from the kitchen, with a packet of boracic crystals and a glass of warm water.*

Camille   Monsieur Tournel ...! I'm sorry if I –

Tournel   Pish, tush! Ha!

Exit.

Camille   Sorry, I'm sure. (*He puts the glass on the table and unfolds the boracic.*) You've no idea how hard it is to find boracic in a house like this. (*He pours the boracic into the glass, then holds up the glass with one hand and the silver palate with the other, saying affectionately:*) There we are. Enjoy your bath!

He drops the palate into the glass, and puts the glass on the mantelpiece. **Étienne** *opens the outer door.*

Étienne   Señor Don Homénidès de Histangua.

Enter **Homénidès**. *He has a thick Spanish accent.*

Homénidès   Good afternoons.

Camille   Monsieur de Histangua.

Homénidès   Señor Chandebise he out?

Camille   He'll be here in a minute. He's with his doctor.

Homénidès   *Bueno, bueno.*

Enter **Finache** *and* **Chandebise**.

Camille   Here they are now.

Finache (*preparing to leave*)   Just do exactly as I told you.

Chandebise   Every word. I will.

Homénidès   My friend, good afternoons.

Chandebise   Señor, how are you?

Homénidès   Bright and breezy. You, Doctor, too?

Finache   Bright and breezy, yes. Excuse me, I'm in a rush.

Homénidès   Is no problem.

Finache   *Au revoir.*

Homénidès   Oh yes.

Finache (*at the door*)   And Chandebise ... Hotel Casablanca, happy landings. Pass it on.

Camille *jumps.*

Camille   Oh no!

He rushes out.

Finache   See you later.

Exit.

Homénidès   My wifes is here?

Chandebise   That's right. With mine.

Homénidès   This I guess. She say she come in my front.

Chandebise   Pardon? Come in your front?

Homénidès   Yes. You see her so?

Chandebise   Oh, come on ahead.

Homénidès   Is same thing. Same.

Chandebise   Shall I tell her you're here?

Homénidès   Is no need. I see her soon. I see your doctor this morning. Insurances.

Chandebise   He told me.

Homénidès   He make me pissings.

Chandebise   Pardon?

Homénidès Pss! Pss! Pss!

Chandebise Oh. Yes. They do.

Homénidès Why?

Chandebise What d'you mean, why?

Homénidès Why I piss for him?

Chandebise Well, naturally, to see if we can insure you.

Homénidès Is not me who insurings, is my wifes.

Chandebise You never told me that.

Homénidès I did. I say, I make insurings. For who, you didn't ask.

Chandebise No problem. Just ask Madame de Histangua to call at the company offices –

Homénidès To do like me?

Chandebise Ah, h'm.

Homénidès I forbid it. No. No, no, no.

Working himself up, he is now face-to-face with **Chandebise**.

Chandebise I'm sorry. Company regulations.

Homénidès (*puce*) Company regulations, I spit on them. For her I pissing. One for two.

Chandebise You can't do that.

Homénidès Ha! *Bueno*. No insurings. So.

Chandebise You're very protective.

Homénidès Protective I not. Is not dignified.

Chandebise I grant you that.

Homénidès Protective? Me, protective?

Chandebise (*soothingly*) You trust your wife. Of course you trust your wife.

Homénidès   Is no trust. Is sure. Is certain.

Chandebise   I don't follow.

Homénidès   (*brandishing a revolver*)   This you see?

Chandebise   Yes. Euh. Put it down. Careful. Yes.

Homénidès   Is no danger. Is precaution.

Chandebise   (*not reassured*)   Oh? Good.

Homénidès   I catch her with mans, I shoot his back, it come out back.

Chandebise   His back?

Homénidès   Her back.

Chandebise   Eh? Ah. You think they'd be . . . (*Gesture.*) Ah.

Homénidès   Theenk? I theenk? What you theenk I theenk?

Chandebise   Nothing. Nothing.

Homénidès   She know this. I tell her, wedding day, on steps of church.

Chandebise   How touching.

Homénidès   (*putting the gun away*)   She take no risks.

Enter **Tournel**.

Tournel   Ah, there you are.

Chandebise   Two minutes. I said, two minutes.

Tournel   I've other things to do.

Chandebise   It's all right. Get the papers ready. Half a second.

Tournel   (*not best pleased*)   Fine.

Exit.

Homénidès   Who he?

Chandebise   Monsieur Tournel.

Homénidès   Tournel?

Chandebise   A friend, a business colleague.

Homénidès   Ah.

Chandebise   A delightful fellow. Charming. He – oh, he's gone. Just one small failing – women.

Homénidès (*indulgently*)   Oh, peef.

Chandebise   He's in a hurry now because there's a woman waiting for him.

Homénidès   Haha.

Chandebise   When I say waiting for him, I really mean, waiting for me. (*He takes out the letter.*) She wrote me a letter, affair with passion.

Homénidès   *Es verdad?* Who her name?

Chandebise   I don't know. She didn't sign it.

Homénidès   Anonymous. I knowing heems.

Chandebise   That's right. She knows what she's doing. Married, probably.

Homénidès   How you knowing?

Chandebise   How I knowing? H'm. How I knowing? Well, you know, the style ... the tone ... they don't mess about. Here, see for yourself. (*He passes over the letter.*)

Homénidès (*highly amused*)   A husband there is? Is cuckolding?

Chandebise   You like that idea?

Homénidès   I like.

Chandebise   Fine.

Homénidès (*looking at the letter*)   Aee!

Chandebise   What?

Homénidès (*striding up and down, out of control*)   *Caramba. Hija de la perra que te parió.* [Heavens! What a daughter of a bitch.]

Chandebise   What's wrong with you?

Homénidès   My wife write thees.

Chandebise   I beg your pardon?

Homénidès (*leaping at his throat*)   Swine. Pig. Dog.

Chandebise   Ow. No. Hey.

Homénidès *holds him and fishes for his revolver.*

Homénidès   My dog. My beeg, beeg dog.

Chandebise   There's a dog as well?

Homénidès   He here.

Chandebise   Ah. Look. Really!

Homénidès *holds him against the table, cocks the revolver.*

Homénidès   My wife she write to you.

Chandebise   No, no, no, no, no, no. It's not your wife. All women write the same.

Homénidès   Is her. I recognise.

Chandebise   And it isn't me. Tournel. Tournel.

Homénidès   Tournel? He here just now? Fine. I keel him.

Chandebise   You can't do that. He's innocent. So far. I'll go and warn him.

Homénidès   Oh no, no, no, no. You leave. I keel.

Chandebise Oh come on, Histangua.

We hear the voices of **Raymonde** *and* **Lucienne**, *off*.

Homénidès My wifes I hear. You go in there. (*He menaces him with the gun towards the inner door.*)

Chandebise Histangua, my dear fellow . . .

Homénidès Your dear fellow, I keel you. Go, go, or else I shoot.

Chandebise If you'd only –

But **Homénidès** *pushes him out and locks the door. Enter* **Lucienne**.

Lucienne Ah, there you are, darling.

Homénidès (*mopping his brow, trying to calm down*) I here. *Si*, I here.

Enter **Raymonde**.

Raymonde Monsieur de Histangua. Good afternoon.

Homénidès Señora. I find you well? Your husband, well?

Raymonde Yes, thank you.

Homénidès You children, well?

Raymonde I don't have any children.

Homénidès Is all right. Is come, is come.

Raymonde *laughs nervously*.

Lucienne What's wrong with you?

Homénidès (*holding himself in check*) Nothing. Nothing.

Lucienne Well, I'm just going out with Raymonde. There's nothing you want me for?

Homénidès No. Go. Go. Go.

Lucienne Bye.

Raymonde   Goodbye, Monsieur.

Homénidès (*raging*)   Ha! Madame! Goodbye!

Lucienne   *Qué tienes, querido mió? Qué te pasa por que me pones una cara así?* [What's wrong, darling? Why are you behaving like this?]

Homénidès   *Te aseguro que no tengo nada.* [I tell you there's nothing the matter.]

Lucienne   *Ah, Jesùs! Qué caràcter tan insopotable tienes!* [Heavens, what a difficult man you are!]

Exit with **Raymonde**.

Homénidès   *Oh, sin vergùenza! Oh, la garça, la garça!* [The cheat, the liar, the bitch.]

Hammering at the locked door.

Be quiet, you, or else I shoot.

Silence. He prowls, reaches the other door, which opens to admit **Tournel**.

Tournel   Monsieur Chandebise . . . ?

Homénidès (*aside, through his teeth*)   The other one. Tournel. (*Aloud, smiling death's-head smile.*) No, Monsieur, is no here, no.

Tournel   Well, when he comes, tell him I've left the papers on the desk. He just has to sign.

Homénidès   Oh yes. Oh yes.

Tournel   I can't wait any longer.

Homénidès (*with strained affability*)   So go. So go.

Tournel   Oh. You mean – ?

Homénidès (*beside himself*)   If you stay I –

He has his hands trembling round **Tournel**'*s neck.*

Tournel   What have you in mind?

Homénidès (*getting control*)   Nothing. Nothing. Please go. Go, go.

Tournel   What a peculiar man. Good afternoon.

Exit.

Homénidès   I die of the heat. (*He sees* **Camille**'*s glass of water.*) Ah! (*He drains it greedily.*) Is better. (*He gets the aftertaste.*) Pouah. What it was, it was?

He puts the glass down. Enter **Camille**.

Camille   Monsieur de Histangua. All alone?

Homénidès (*leaping at him*)   You, you . . .! (*Calming himself.*) You come in the neeck. I go.

Camille   Oh.

Homénidès   And when I gone, this door – (*He points to the locked door.*) You open heem. I say you, open heem. Your master.

Camille   What master?

Homénidès (*furious again, striding about*)   *Oh, sin vergüenza, como podrìa imaginarone que mi mujer tuviese un amante!* [The cheat! How could I ever have imagined my wife would take a lover?]

Exit, whirlwind-like.

Camille   *Que mi mujer tuviese un amante!* You can't understand a word he says.

He goes to the locked door.

My master. What master?

He opens the door, recoils as **Chandebise** *appears, defeated.*

Camille   You?

Chandebise   Has he gone?

Camille   Who?

Chandebise   Ho . . . Homénidès.

Camille   Yes.

Chandebise   And Madame Homénidès?

Camille   That's right, with Raymonde.

Chandebise   Fine. And Tournel?

Camille   Just gone this minute.

Chandebise   Just this minute. My God, we've got to do something, now. Who can we send to warn them? Got it! Étienne.

Camille   Send where to warn who?

Chandebise   To the . . . to . . . the rue Kasbah. There! We're on a precipice. Catastrophe. Double murder.

Camille   Pardon?

Chandebise   I've just time. Before the Boston party. To get to Tournel's. My hat. My hat . . .

Camille   What *is* going on?

Chandebise   No time to explain. If Tournel turns up here while I'm out, just tell him, tell him, no rendezvous. His life depends on it.

Camille   His life?

Chandebise   Have you got all that? His life –

Camille   – depends on it.

Chandebise   Oh, catastrophe, catastrophe.

Exit.

Camille   What's wrong with them all today?

Enter **Tournel**.

Tournel   I left my briefcase . . .

Camille   Tournel!

Tournel   Ah, here it is.

Camille (*leaping on him, gabbling*)   In heaven's name, flee. Don't go there. Flee.

Tournel   What?

Camille   The rendezvous. The rendezvous. Flee for your life.

Tournel   Not now. I can't understand a word.

Camille   Tournel, Tournel –

Tournel   Not NOW.

Exit.

Camille *runs to the mantelpiece.*

Camille   My palate. Where's my palate? (*He sees the glass on the table.*) Ah. (*He puts the palate in his mouth, and rushes to the door.*) Tournel! Tournel!

Enter **Chandebise**, *with his hat on.*

Chandebise   Who are you chasing now?

Camille (*with absolute clarity*)   I'm chasing Tournel. The man's a pig-headed donkey. I told him what you told me to tell him, and he simply refused to listen.

Chandebise (*collapsing on the sofa in amazement*)   He can talk!

Camille (*racing after* **Tournel**, *as the curtain falls*)   Tournel ...! Tournel ...!

Act Two

*First floor of the Hotel Casablanca, rue Kasbah. Appropriate
decoration. The stage is split in two. L, approximately three-fifths of
the total area: landing reached by a staircase which continues to the
upper floors. Front L, against the wall, a desk. On pegs above it, a
uniform jacket and cap. Centre L, door to* **Rugby***'s room. Upstage
L, corridor leading to other rooms, the door to one of which is visible
to the audience. Between this door and the landing, a display-panel
of electric bells. R of the landing, partition-wall separating the
landing from the two adjacent rooms, the first of which is visible to
the audience. The partition ends downstage in a 'col-de-cygne':
swan's-neck curve. Centre R, door from the landing to the room.
Upstage R, door to the adjacent room, whose interior is not visible to
the audience. On the landing, against the swan's-neck of the
partition, a banquette. In the room R, upstage, four-poster bed on a
carpeted, screened dais. R of it, forming one of the wings, window
opening on to a garden. Downstage R, door to the bathroom of this
suite; L, against the swan's-neck, a small table. At the side of the
bed, an electric bell-push, surrounded by concentric rings like a target.
This bell-push is to alert the hotel management when it's time to
operate the revolve. This revolve (which never goes full-circle, but
only 180 degrees L or R, alternately) swivels the bed and rear wall
to reveal, from the adjoining room, an identical bed and wall. As the
curtain rises,* **Eugénie** *is finishing cleaning the room R.*
Ferraillon *comes down the corridor L and goes to the door of
this room.*

Ferraillon Eugénie! Eugénie!

Eugénie Monsieur?

Ferraillon (*outside the door*) What are you doing?

Eugénie The room, Monsieur.

Ferraillon (*entering the room*) You call this doing?

Eugénie Yes, Monsieur.

Ferraillon What about the bed? You call that done? It

looks as if someone's in there already.

Eugénie   There could be.

Ferraillon   None of that! This place isn't a knocking-shop.

Eugénie   No, Monsieur.

Ferraillon   It's a respectable, posh hotel. Married people come here.

Eugénie   But not together.

Ferraillon   Watch your tongue. Are you judging my customers now? Make this bed again, and make it sharpish.

He goes on to the landing.

Eugénie   He makes me sick.

Olympe *comes up the stairs, with a pile of sheets.*

Olympe   Augustin, who's that you're talking to?

Ferraillon   That little baggage. I wish I'd had her in the service. Under me.

Olympe   Augustin!

Ferraillon   Not under me, under me. For heaven's sake. I see that all day, it makes me sick.

Olympe   It better had.

Baptistin *pants up the stairs.* **Ferraillon** *grabs him.*

Ferraillon   Ah, there you are. What time d'you call this? Where have you been? Propping up that bar again?

Baptistin   Me?

Ferraillon   It's five o'clock. Why aren't you in bed? You ought to be in bed. Don't you want this job?

Baptistin   I do, I do.

Ferraillon   Right, then, get to bed. Another of 'em! Good-for-nothing, useless. Why do I listen? Put up with them? Because I'm kind-hearted, that's why, because I won't chuck my own uncle on the streets. And how does he thank me? Neglects his post, goes sneaking from bar to bar –

Baptistin   You see –

Ferraillon   Shut up! Bars! They should close 'em down. In the name of Public Decency. Suppose we'd needed a sick old man? Who'd have done it? Not me, for one. I'd have had you then, all right: absent on duty, neglecting your post –

Baptistin   But I thought –

Ferraillon   Button it! Bedtime. March!

Baptistin *slinks into the bedroom up R.*

Ferraillon   What's wrong with him? Relatives! Take, take, take – they're all the same.

Rugby *surges out of the room L, immediately behind him. He speaks with a strong English accent.*

Rugby   I say. Anyone for me?

Ferraillon   What?

Rugby (*flaring up*)   I said, anyone for me?

Ferraillon and **Olympe** *are clearly baffled. He tries again, more calmly.*

Rugby   What I mean is, has anyone come for me?

Olympe (*in tortured, pidgin English*)   No, no, no anyone.

Rugby   Thanks for nothing! Ha!

He scowls back into his room.

Ferraillon   What did he say?

Olympe   He asked if he'd had any visitors. I think.

Ferraillon Why does he keep talking English? I talk French to him.

Olympe He doesn't understand.

Ferraillon That's no reason why I should learn English. 'Eniwunformee'. He's just trying to be funny.

Olympe Poor man. This is the third time he's come here, and each time the woman he said he'd meet has hopped it.

Ferraillon Can't blame 'em. 'Eniwunformee'. Who's turned on by that?

Olympe Now, now. I'll put these sheets in the cupboard.

Ferraillon Oh, no you won't. Eugénie!

Enter **Eugénie**, *with feather duster and broom.*

Eugénie Monsieur?

Ferraillon Haven't you finished that room yet?

Eugénie Oh, yes, Monsieur.

Ferraillon 'Oh, yes, Monsieur.' You've always finished them.

Eugénie And someone always messes them up again.

Ferraillon Never mind being clever. Take those sheets and put them in the cupboard.

Eugénie Me?

Ferraillon Well, who else? Me?

Eugénie Whatever you say. (*She puts down her duster and broom, and goes for the sheets, muttering.*) Dust that. Carry those. Make that.

Olympe Oh, by the way, don't give anyone that room. (*Indicating the room down R.*) It's booked. Monsieur Chandebise. You remember him.

Eugénie   I do. The one who (*Aping* **Camille**.) speaks like this.

Olympe   That's him.

Ferraillon   He's coming today?

Olympe   He sent this telegram. (*To* **Eugénie**, *who is listening in.*) All right, Eugénie?

Eugénie   Yes, Madame.

Olympe   I didn't mean, 'All right, Eugénie?' I meant, 'All right, Eugénie?'

Eugénie   Oh. Yes, Madame.

Olympe   Don't go that way. Use the back stairs. If guests arrive, you'll be in the way with that pile of sheets.

Eugénie   Yes, Madame.

Exit.

Olympe   Look: 'Book same room as before, five-ish, Chandebise.' It was that room.

Ferraillon   Better just check. Officer's inspection.

They go into the room down R.

Much better.

Olympe   Including the bathroom?

She goes into the bathroom.

Ferraillon   Better check the mechanism.

He presses the button L of the bed. The bed and rear wall swivel (see opening stage direction), revealing the identical, next-door bed. **Baptistin** *is lying in it, on his back and in a nightgown, moaning piteously.*

Baptistin   Oh, my aching bones. My aching bones.

Ferraillon   All right, all right, it's me. Don't wear yourself out.

Baptistin (*sitting up*) Trying to catch me, eh? Well, here I am. Hard at it.

Ferraillon So I should think. The money I pay you! (*He presses the button, and the bed and wall swivel back.*) Good.

Olympe *comes out of the bathroom.*

Ferraillon Where's Poche?

Olympe Chopping wood. In the cellar.

Ferraillon The cellar? You sent him to the cellar? You know what he's like, and you sent him to the cellar?

Olympe The wine's in sealed casks. No problem.

Ferraillon No problem? He was my corporal for three years. No problem? Week after week after week. Every Sunday, rivers of tears, repentance, vows for the future ... and every Monday morning, bim, bam! Back among the bottles where he started.

Olympe At least you could rely on him.

Ferraillon I could rely on him, all right. And he could rely on me. This foot, this one here ... he could rely on me.

Olympe What a man you are!

Ferraillon I kept him on his toes. And in any case, I liked him. Why else d'you think I gave him a job here afterwards? I like a man I can rely on.

Olympe What a man you are!

Enter **Poche**, *in overalls, and carrying a bundle of firewood. He is drunken and decrepit, but otherwise is the spitting image of* **Chandebise**.

Ferraillon Talk of the devil. Hey up, Poche.

Poche Sarge. There's a telegram.

Ferraillon Well, give it to me. (*He takes it, then looks at*

Poche, *who is gazing at him with doggy devotion.*) What a picture. What an oil-painting.

He opens the telegram. Enter **Eugénie**.

Ferraillon   'Book usual room.'

Olympe   He's keen on it.

Ferraillon   'Show in anyone who calls and asks for me.' Hear that, all of you? If anyone calls and asks for Chandebise, show them in there.

Eugénie   Yes, Monsieur.

Poche   Sarge.

Ferraillon   All right, all right, get on.

Exit **Eugénie**. **Poche** *stays rapt where he is.*

Ferraillon   What's wrong with you? Oh ... Squad, squad, atten ... SHUN! Face ... re-VERSE! On your ... WAY! (*He spins him round, and boots him towards the stairs.*) Look at him. You'd swear he enjoyed it. You'd swear he understands every word I say. (*Roaring.*) Out of it. Hup, la, hup, la, hup!

Exit **Poche**.

Olympe   He's beautifully trained.

Rugby *comes out of his room, behind* **Ferraillon** *as before.*

Rugby   Anyone for me?

Ferraillon (*jumping*)   Don't keep doing that.

Rugby   All I said was, anyone for me?

Ferraillon   No, no. Eniwunformee. Nono.

Rugby   Aoh. Thenks.

He goes back into his room.

Olympe   He's amazing.

Ferraillon   He's a jack-in-a-box.

Olympe   He certainly makes you jump.

Finache *comes up the stairs.*

Finache   Afternoon, General.

Ferraillon *and* **Olympe**   Afternoon, Doctor.

Finache   You've got a room?

Olympe   Any time for you, Doctor.

Finache   No one asking for me?

Ferraillon   Not yet, Doctor.

Finache   Thank God.

Ferraillon   Is everything all right, Doctor?

Finache   Perfect, thank you. Wait till you see her.

Olympe   It's you we haven't seen, Doctor, for – it must be a month now.

Finache   One spreads oneself, don't you know. Spreads oneself.

Ferraillon   One ought to be loyal.

Finache   I've known her for over a month.

Ferraillon   Not faithful to her, faithful to us. To here.

Finache   See what you mean.

Ferraillon   If gentlemen start being faithful to women, we might as well close down.

Finache   See what you mean. That reminds me. When I came in just now, it was like the Marie Celeste downstairs. No one on the desk.

Olympe   No Poche?

Finache   Not Poche – the handsome Gabriel.

Ferraillon   Gabriel. Of course, you won't know. We had to sack him.

Finache   Such a nice young man.

Ferraillon   You can say that again.

Olympe   To some of the clients, he was far too nice.

Finache   You don't say?

Ferraillon   It's a bit much, if a gentleman can't bring his lady friend here without her being poached by the staff. This is a respectable hotel.

Finache   Respectable –

Ferraillon   Discipline. Military discipline. It starts and ends with discipline.

Finache   *Mon général!* Where was it you served?

Olympe   Don't ask.

Ferraillon   I'm not ashamed of it. I was a sergeant in –

Finache   The Home Guard.

Ferraillon   And proud of it. (*To* **Olympe**.) Sweetheart, a room for the doctor? Number Ten, perhaps?

Olympe   Perfect.

She starts going up the stairs.

Finache   Isn't Five free?

Ferraillon   Unfortunately, no.

Finache   Oh.

Ferraillon   But Ten's exactly the same, on the floor above.

Finache   Oh, Ten, then.

Olympe   I'll see to it.

Ferraillon   Go on, then.

Exit **Olympe**.

Finache   What a wonderful wife.

Ferraillon   And what a woman!

Finache   I'm sure I've seen her before somewhere.

Ferraillon   Possibly. You remember . . . years ago now . . . in Montmartre . . . La Belle Castagna . . .

Finache   Castagna . . . hang on . . .

Ferraillon   Mistress of the Duke of Gennevilliers . . .

Finache   That dinner-dance . . . had herself served up, on a silver serving-dish . . . stark naked . . .

Ferraillon   (*smugly*)   My wife.

Finache   I . . . oh . . . congratulations.

Ferraillon   She fell for me while I was still in the service. Mind you, you should have seen me then: the uniform, the bearing . . . she's always had a soft spot for the military.

Finache   La Castagna.

Ferraillon   She wanted an affair.

Finache   Pardon?

Ferraillon   Not my style. In any case, she was a personality, a looker, had plenty in the piggybank. A catch. I insisted on marriage from the start.

Finache   Well done.

Ferraillon   Conditions, of course. From that moment on, no fancy-men, no lovers. I don't know about you, Doctor, but I won't have my women running after other men.

Finache   Absolutely right.

Ferraillon   One has one's standards. Then we opened this place.

Finache   Good thinking.

Ferraillon   We're happy here. A plain, decent life . . . a bit aside each week, for our retirement. That reminds me . . . what we were talking about the other week . . . life insurance.

Finache   I knew you'd come round to it.

Ferraillon   Why not? I'm forty-four, my wife's (*He coughs.*) fifty-two, more or less.

Finache   Couldn't be better. In any good marriage, there ought to be a gap.

Ferraillon   I suppose so. But shouldn't it be the wife who –

Finache   If not the wife, then the husband. It has to be one or the other.

Ferraillon   I see what you mean. What I was thinking was, insurance, in case of death –

Finache   Well, fifty-two, makes sense. And then if you –

Ferraillon   What d'you mean, if I – ? You're joking.

Finache   I think we can work something out. Pay us a visit.

Ferraillon   When?

Finache   You'll find me, every morning, between ten and eleven, at the offices of the Boston Life Company, boulevard Malesherbes.

Ferraillon (*writing it on his cuff*)   Boulevard Malesherbes. And ask for –

Finache   The Managing Director. I'll tell him to expect you.

Ferraillon   Thank you, Doctor.

Finache My pleasure.

Olympe *appears at the top of the stairs.*

Olympe Your room's ready, Doctor.

Finache (*bounding up the stairs*) Wonderful! Wonderful! I can't wait. As soon as someone asks for me, bring them right up, will you?

He disappears upstairs.

Ferraillon Love! There's nothing like it.

Rugby (*surging out behind him, as before*) Anyone for me?

Ferraillon Nothing like this one, either.

Rugby That's right. Anyone for me?

Ferraillon (*smiling through his teeth at him*) Take a running jump.

Rugby Say again?

Ferraillon Take a running jump.

Rugby Run-NING-jum?

Ferraillon That's right. You've got it! Look at me again, that's it, big trusting eyes. Now, you're sure you don't understand a word I'm saying? Fine, I'll say it again. Take a running jump.

Rugby Ningjum? Thenks awfully.

Ferraillon Any time.

Rugby *goes to the door of his room, just as* **Raymonde** *comes up the stairs. She is heavily veiled.*

Rugby I say!

Ferraillon Can I help you, Madame?

Raymonde Which is Monsieur Chandebise's room?

Ferraillon This way, Madame.

She tries to follow him, but **Rugby** *is in the way, circling, crouching, trying to see under the veil.*

Rugby   HaHA! This is more like it. Talk about gay Paree ... This one must be for me. (*Sensing that she isn't.*) Oh. Maybe not.

Hands in pockets, whistling, he goes into his room and shuts the door.

Raymonde   What's the matter with him?

Ferraillon   He's English.

Raymonde   And he's impertinent. Has anyone asked for the room yet?

Ferraillon   No. Hey! I am right. It was you that came this afternoon.

Raymonde   Pardon?

Ferraillon   It's all right, Madame. I'm honoured. I knew if I said nothing, Madame would be delighted, would soon be back. But not so soon ...

Raymonde   I hope you're not thinking what I think you're thinking.

Ferraillon   Oh, Madame! (*Showing her into the room.*) This way, Madame.

She goes in, hissing at him in annoyance as she passes. He follows.

This is the main room, Madame. Most comfortable, as you can see. The bed's –

Raymonde   That's enough, Monsieur. I won't be needing that.

Ferraillon   Oh. (*Aside.*) Other plans, I suppose. (*Aloud.*) The bathroom's this way, Madame. Hot and cold running water, washbasin, bath –

Raymonde   I don't intend to stay here.

Ferraillon Ah. One last thing, Madame. In case of trouble, this button –

Raymonde Yes, yes, thank you. I'll manage.

Ferraillon Pardon?

Raymonde Please go away.

Ferraillon As Madame wishes.

Raymonde Thank you.

Ferraillon *goes out of the door.*

Ferraillon (*to the audience*) What a funny woman.

Raymonde (*to the audience*) What an impertinent man.

Poche *comes down the stairs.*

Ferraillon Ah, Poche.

Poche Sarge?

Ferraillon Have you finished the wood?

Poche One more load, sarge.

Ferraillon Fine. Hup, hup! And when you've fetched it, please put on your uniform. (*He takes the jacket and hat from their pegs and gives them to* **Poche**.) The guests'll be here any moment.

Poche Sarge.

Bell, off. **Ferraillon** *looks at the display board.*

Ferraillon It's that Englishman. Go and see what he wants.

Poche Sarge.

He knocks at **Rugby**'s *door.*

Rugby (*off*) Come in.

Poche *goes into* **Rugby**'s *room. During all this,* **Raymonde** *has been inspecting the room R. She goes into the bathroom, just as*

Tournel *comes up the stairs.*

Tournel   Excuse me: the room for Monsieur
Chandebise?

Ferraillon   This way, Monsieur. Er . . . but . . . you
aren't Monsieur Chandebise.

Tournel   I'm standing in for him.

Ferraillon   Of course. The telegram said anyone using
his name. The lady's waiting, Monsieur.

Tournel   And how does she look to you?

Ferraillon   Monsieur? To me? It's how she looks to you
that —

Tournel   The thing is, I've never met her.

Ferraillon   Ah.

Tournel   And before I get involved, I need to know: is
she an old boot or isn't she?

Ferraillon   No fear of that. She's not very polite, but
she's pretty enough.

Tournel   Fair enough. It's not politeness I'm here for,
after all.

Ferraillon   This is the room, Monsieur.

He takes him into the room R. Meanwhile, **Poche** *comes out of*
Rugby*'s room.*

Poche   Right away, Monsieur. (*Aside.*) What on earth's
an 'Eniwunformee'? I'll bring him a brandy.

Exit.

Ferraillon   No one here? In there, perhaps. (*He knocks
on the bathroom door.*)

Raymonde (*inside*)   What is it?

Ferraillon   Madame's Monsieur's arrived.

Raymonde Thank you.

Ferraillon She's in there, Monsieur.

Tournel Good, excellent.

Ferraillon *Bon appétit*, Monsieur.

Exit.

Tournel Thanks. (*Looking round.*) Not bad. Clean, comfortable ... Look at that bell. (*He makes his hand a pistol, and pretends to shoot at the bell.*) Target practice, eh? I'll not get bored. Well now, how shall I ... ? Where shall I ... ? It ought to be ...

He lies on the bed and draws the curtains, so that he is completely hidden. Enter **Raymonde**.

Raymonde So there you are at la – Where is he?

Tournel Cooeee!

Raymonde (*to herself*) We'll see about cooee.

Tournel Cooooeeeee!

Raymonde *draws the curtains and slaps him.*

Raymonde Ha!

Tournel Ow!

Raymonde Someone else!

Tournel You!

Raymonde You!

Tournel If only you'd told me! (*Rubbing his cheek.*) What a lovely surprise.

Raymonde What are you doing here?

Tournel Me? Aha! Affair of the heart. Beautiful woman, saw me at theatre, drank me in, wrote me a note, so I, out of the goodness of my heart –

Raymonde   No, no, no, no, no!

Tournel (*trying to take her in his arms*)   It's all right. She's nothing. Gone. Forgotten. It's you I . . . My love, my darling, the gods are smiling down . . .

Raymonde   Let me go.

Tournel   Never!

Raymonde   That letter wasn't for you, it was for Chandebise.

Tournel   Your husband? With a face like his? Impossible. We were sitting next to each other. The writer made a mistake, that's all.

Raymonde   You don't understand. That was my letter.

Tournel   Yours?

Raymonde   Yes, mine.

Tournel   You write him love letters? Your husband?

Raymonde   I wanted to see if he was having an affair . . . if he'd turn up here.

Tournel   Aha! You refused to have anything to do with me because you thought he was having an affair. Well he isn't. He hasn't come. I've come instead. You see?

Raymonde   That's very true.

Tournel   D'you know what he said when he read that letter? 'What's wrong with the woman? Doesn't she know I'd never betray my wife?'

Raymonde   He didn't.

Tournel   He did.

Raymonde   How wonderful!

She throws herself at him and kisses his cheeks.

Tournel   Ah, Raymonde. (*He holds her round the waist while*

he declaims.) So there we are! How ashamed you must feel,
to have doubted such a fine, upstanding gentleman.
(*Embracing her hungrily.*) Oong, oong. Now you must realise
... Oong, oong ... that you must put all that behind
you. Ooong, oong. Never again! Oong, oong. In fact,
oong, oong, it's your bounden duty now, you must, oong,
oong, start a love affair yourself. Oong, oong, oong. For
his sake, oong, his sake!

Raymonde (*melodramatically*)   You're right. (*Kissing him.*)
Mm, mm, mm. I should never have distrusted him. Mm,
mm, how cruel of me, how cruel, mm, mm. Poor
Chandebise, mm, mm, poor, poor, poor Chandebise.
Mmmmmmmmmm.

Tournel   Forget him! Forget him, I say. Think of
nought but me.

Raymonde   I will! I will! For his sake.

Tournel   Oh, Raymonde, Raymonde, my darling, I love
you, I love you...

Raymonde   Fancy me thinking it was him saying
'Cooee' in here.

Tournel   If that's what you want, we'll do it for him,
for him.

Raymonde   Pardon?

Tournel   Cooeee. Raymonde. Coooooeeeee!

Raymonde (*resisting*)   Tournel! What are you doing?
Tournel! I can't.

Tournel   You must. You shall.

Raymonde   Tournel. Tournel. No.

Tournel (*steering her to the bed*)   Give way, my love. Let
passion rule. Give way, give way.

Raymonde   What are you doing? Where are you taking
me?

Tournel   To our bower, to bliss.

Raymonde   You're mad! (*She pushes him so that he sits on the bed.*) What on earth d'you take me for?

Tournel   Didn't you just agree with every word I said?

Raymonde   Of course. To be your lover. But not . . . your whore.

Tournel (*sitting on the edge of the bed*)   What else is there?

Raymonde   Shy looks . . . fluttering lashes . . . hearts pounding . . . fingers, fingers fluttering . . . And then, I give you, I give you –

Tournel   What?

Raymonde   My heart, my love.

Tournel   My hat!

Raymonde   What else can you have expected?

Tournel   What else? What else does any hot-blooded knight expect when he wins fair lady's heart? It's fate, don't you see? It's fate. We're being drawn together, irresistibly, magnetically . . . Fate conspires. Your husband throws us together. For 'twas he, 'twas he, who sent me hither.

Raymonde   My husband?

Tournel   The very same. You're outnumbered, Madame. The whole world craves that this shall be, except – except for you alone.

He tries to take her in his arms.

Raymonde   Tournel, calm down.

Tournel   D'you think I could ever rest content with downcast eyes, fluttering fingers, pounding hearts? When there's so much more, much more –

Raymonde   Tournel, really.

Tournel   What am I to do with hearts, and hands, and lashes?

Raymonde   Oh.

Tournel   Titbits! Delightful titbits. But I starve for you, I pine. I sit at table and beg the menu, and all I get is crumbs. Say good morning, run the errands, walk the puppy, ah no, ah no, ah no!

Raymonde   Tournel –

Tournel (*in full rhetorical flood*)   No-o-o-o-o-o-o-o! Since you seem ignorant of the very vestiges of the rules of love, my proud beauty, I see I must instruct you –

Raymonde   What d'you mean?

Tournel   What alternative have I? To stumble from here, broken, a figure of ridicule, a puppet whose strings are cut?

Raymonde   Tournel –

Tournel   No words! You're mine. You belong to me. To me!

He pulls her towards the bed.

Raymonde   Stop it, Tournel.

Tournel   No, no!

Raymonde *breaks free, falls to her knees beside the bed and reaches one hand to the bell-button.*

Raymonde   Stay away or I'll ring.

Tournel   They never come. Ring all you like.

He runs and bolts the door. Meanwhile, **Raymonde** *pushes the button, and the bed and wall swivel.*

Raymonde (*as she is swept out of sight*)   Aee!

Tournel *is too busy at the door to notice, but the swivelling is now complete, and only* **Baptistin** *is now present, in his* *nightgown and in the bed.*

Tournel   Aee! What good will it be, to cry 'aee'? You're mine, you're mine, you're mine!

He throws himself on the bed.

Baptistin   Oh my back, my aching back.

Tournel (*dumbfounded*)   What?

Baptistin   My back, my aching back.

Tournel   Who are you? Where did you spring from? What are you doing there?

Baptistin (*sitting up, doltishly*)   Eh?

Tournel   And Raymonde? Raymonde! Where is she?

He opens the room door and calls into the corridor.

Raymonde? No one.

He leaves the door open, and goes towards the bathroom.

Raymonde?

He disappears into the bathroom, as **Raymonde** *appears from the room up R, to which the swivelling bed has transported her.*

Raymonde   What's going on? Where am I? Tournel! I've had enough of this.

She disappears down the stairs. At once, **Rugby** *comes out of his room.*

Rugby   Boy! Boy!

Raymonde *rushes upstairs again, four by four.*

Raymonde   My husband! My husband!

She hurtles into **Rugby**'s *room.*

Rugby   I say. By Jove. Well done!

He hurtles after her and slams the door. **Poche** *comes upstairs.*

Poche   What an idiot. The brandy's gone. I gave it to Baptistin yesterday. Baptistin! Hey!

Baptistin (*sitting up in bed, pince-nez on nose, reading a newspaper*)   In here.

Poche   Oh, there you are. What have you done with the brandy?

Baptistin   Next door. On the washstand.

Poche   Right.

He goes into the room up R, just as **Tournel** *comes out of the bathroom of the room down R.*

Tournel   Empty. Where can she be?

He makes for the stairs, just as **Raymonde** *bursts from* **Rugby***'s room, trying to break free of him.*

Rugby   Please, darling, please don't go.

Raymonde   Let go. Will you let go?

Tournel   There she is.

By now, **Raymonde** *has broken free. She whirls on* **Rugby** *to slap his face, and* **Tournel**, *who has hurried over, gets it full face.*

Tournel   Again!

Rugby   I say!

Tournel *has grabbed* **Raymonde** *and is pushing her back to the room down R. He snubs* **Rugby** *in passing.*

Tournel   Goodbye, Monsieur.

Rugby *goes into his room, fuming, and* **Raymonde** *goes into hers, followed by* **Tournel**, *who shuts the door.*

Tournel   Oh, Raymonde, Raymonde.

Raymonde   I can't stand it. My husband's —

Tournel (*bored*)   Yes, yes.

Raymonde   Here.

Tournel (*as before*)   Yes, yes. (*Getting it.*) What? Not Chandebise?

Raymonde   Yes, Chandebise. Victor-Emmanuel, disguised as a porter. Why? Don't you see? To catch us in the act.

Tournel   No.

Baptistin (*sympathetically*)   My back, my aching back.

Raymonde   Eek!

Tournel   What?

Raymonde   Who's he?

Tournel   He who? Oh, he he. No idea. Some invalid. He came from nowhere. (*To* **Baptistin**.) What is it you want?

Baptistin   You did it.

Tournel   What?

Raymonde   Never mind. Make him go. Get rid of him.

Tournel   Right. (*To* **Baptistin**.) You heard. Go. Scat. Shoo.

Baptistin   You don't understand. If I'm in the way, just press that button. That'll do the trick.

Tournel   Oh, very funny. What d'you take me for?

He presses the button, and the bed swivels.

Raymonde   Really! That's the limit. Spectators, now.

Tournel   It's not my fault. All I did was –

They argue. Meanwhile, the other bed swings into place. **Poche** *is sitting on it, drinking from the brandy-bottle. He's not best pleased at being found out.*

Poche   Well? Well? What are you staring at?

Raymonde Aee!

Tournel Chandebise!

Raymonde Victor-Emmanuel!

Tournel (*on his knees, beseeching*) My dear chap, it's not what you think.

Raymonde (*the same, on the other side*) Please, please let me explain.

Poche You what?

Tournel Appearances are against us, but I promise you we're innocent.

Raymonde That's right. We never expected to meet each other.

Tournel If it hadn't been for that letter –

Raymonde The letter. My letter. My fault. I asked her to write it.

Tournel That's true, she did, she did.

Raymonde I'm so ashamed. I thought you were having an affair.

Poche Me?

Raymonde Oh, tell me you believe me. Tell me.

Poche Of course I do. (*Aside.*) Loonies. (*He laughs.*)

Raymonde (*terrified*) Victor-Emmanuel, no. Don't laugh like that.

Poche What's wrong with my laugh?

Raymonde I know what it is. You don't believe me.

Tournel That's obvious.

Raymonde How can I prove it?

Poche Excuse me. I can't stay here. I have to deliver

this brandy to Number Four.

He makes for the door. **Raymonde** *pulls him to face her.*

Raymonde   Victor-Emmanuel, what's wrong with you?

Poche   With me?

Tournel (*pulling him round the other way*)   Please, please, old man. At a time like this, not . . . brandy!

Poche   They need it in Number Four. This brandy, now.

Raymonde   Oh, stop it. Stop playing with me. Rage, scream, kick, hit me — anything but this dreadful calm.

Tournel (*the same*)   No, no, hit me, hit me.

Poche   Well, this is unusual. Madame, I assure you —

Raymonde (*piteously*)   'Madame'! Call me Raymonde. Oh, please.

Poche   Who, me?

Raymonde   Yes, yes. Raymonde, Raymonde.

Tournel   Call her Raymonde.

They're kneeling and supplicating. **Poche** *gets down on his knees, too.*

Poche   You don't understand. In my position . . . What I mean is, Madame . . .

Tournel   Stop calling her Madame. Call her Raymonde.

Poche   If you say so. What I mean is, Raymonde . . .

Raymonde   Say 'I believe you. I trust you.'

Poche (*obediently*)   I believe you. I trust you.

Tournel   At last.

Raymonde   Now kiss me, kiss me.

Poche   Pardon?

Raymonde Kiss me, prove you still love me.

Poche If you say so.

Still kneeling, he wipes his lips on his sleeve, puts his arms round her (without dropping the bottle) and kisses her on both cheeks. She's transfigured.

Raymonde Ah.

Tournel That's the way.

Raymonde Thank you. Oh thank you.

Poche (*smacking his lips*) Ve-ry tasty.

Tournel (*exalted*) Now me. Now kiss me, too.

Poche What?

Tournel To prove you believe me too.

Poche If you say so. (*Going to him.*) Too tall.

He climbs on the platform of the bed, and kisses **Tournel**.

Tournel Oh, it feels so good!

Poche I preferred Madame.

Raymonde Madame!

Poche Now, if you'll excuse me: the brandy. Number Four.

Raymonde Oh, no.

Tournel (*stopping him*) What is this game?

Raymonde Are you my husband or aren't you?

Poche Of course I'm not. I'm a porter, here.

Tournel What?

Raymonde Oh no! He's had a brainstorm.

Poche Brainstorm? Not likely. You're playing games. I'm Poche. Poche. If you don't believe me, ask Baptistin.

Tournel   Who?

Poche   The ill old fool.

He presses the button, and the bed swivels.

Baptistin   My back, my aching back.

Poche   Never mind that. Say who I am.

Baptistin   What d'you mean, say who you are? Have you forgotten?

Poche   Of course I haven't. She wants to know.

Raymonde   That's right. Er . . . who is this gentleman?

Baptistin   Who is he? Poche.

Tournel *and* **Raymonde**   Poche?

Baptistin   Poche the porter.

Poche   Told you.

Raymonde   You mean, that was true?

Ferraillon (*calling from the top of the stairs*)   Poche!

Tournel   Impossible. They're identical. They've set this up.

Ferraillon   Poche!

Poche   Sarge! Excuse me, the boss.

Raymonde (*pushing past him*)   Aha! The boss. Now we'll know for sure.

Tournel (*the same*)   Out of the way!

Raymonde   Monsieur! Monsieur!

Ferraillon   Madame?

Raymonde   Please tell us: who is this man?

She points to **Poche**, *who has followed them out.*

Tournel   Exactly.

Ferraillon   Him? Poche.

Poche   Told you.

Raymonde *and* **Tournel**   Poche.

Ferraillon (*advancing on him*)   Poche, yes, on the bottle as usual. Poche, Poche, Poche!

Each word requires a kick, and a little jump from **Poche**, *which* **Raymonde** *and* **Tournel** *can't help but echo.*

Poche, **Raymonde**, **Tournel**   Oh, oh, oh.

Poche   I told you.

Ferraillon (*snatching the bottle*)   You never stop, do you?

Tournel *and* **Raymonde**   Eh?

Poche   No, sarge, it's for Number Four.

Ferraillon   I'll give you Four. (*Same business as before.*) Four, four, four, four!

Poche   But boss –

Ferraillon   Now get out of it. Hop, hop, hop!

Poche   Yes, boss. (*To the others, as he vanishes down the stairs.*). I told you.

Ferraillon   Monsieur, Madame, what can I say? Our porter. A hopeless case.

Raymonde (*after a pause, shrugging*)   The porter. It was the porter.

Tournel   Raymonde . . .

Raymonde   What?

Tournel   We kissed the porter.

Raymonde   I've just said that.

Tournel   Did you? I must have missed it. I could have sworn it was him . . . Two peas in a pod.

Raymonde   If I hadn't seen those kicks, I still wouldn't be sure. But even if Victor-Emmanuel was trying to catch us out, he wouldn't have have stood there and let that man kick his –

Tournel   Lower back.

Raymonde   Exactly.

Tournel   No doubt about it.

Raymonde (*collapsing on the banquette*)   I can't take much more. I'm exhausted. Give me some water.

Tournel (*patting his pockets*)   Water, water . . .

Raymonde   Not in there.

Tournel   You're right. But where?

Raymonde   In the room.

Tournel   In the room. Right. (*To* **Baptistin**.) Where's the water?

Baptistin (*looking up from his paper*)   Bathroom.

Tournel   Thanks.

He goes into the bathroom. **Raymonde** *trails into the bedroom.*

Raymonde (*dolefully to* **Baptistin**)   The porter. Who'd have thought it? The porter.

Baptistin   It's a funny old world and no mistake.

He reads. She opens the window to breathe fresh air. In the meantime, **Eugénie** *has come down the stairs, meeting* **Poche** *on his way from the cellar with a bundle of logs. One falls.*

Poche   Pick that up for me, Eugénie.

Eugénie   Right-oh.

She picks up the log, and adds it to the others. She and **Poche** *are on the stairs.* **Raymonde** *closes the window of the room down R.*

Raymonde   I thought you were getting me some water.

Tournel . . . ?

She goes into the bathroom. **Camille** *and* **Antoinette** *come up the stairs, hand in hand.* **Camille** *is very happy. He has his palate in place, and speaks clearly.*

Camille   Dis way, iddle baby. Dis way. Time for byebyes. Don't oo love oo big, big Daddykins? Up we go! This way, darling. This way, they've booked our beddybyes.

Poche   Can I help you, Monsieur?

Camille   Yes, I – eugh! Victor-Emmanuel!

He hurtles into the room up R.

Antoinette   Monsieur!

She disappears into **Rugby**'s *room.*

Poche   Why do they all call me Victor-Emmanuel?

He goes upstairs. Exit **Eugénie**. **Raymonde** *and* **Tournel** *come out of the bathroom.*

Tournel   Feeling better now?

Raymonde   Yes. No. I don't know. There's too much happening. I think I . . . I think I'm going to –

Tournel   You mustn't.

Raymonde   It's not for fun.

Tournel   Of course it isn't. Lie down a moment, rest a moment. Here we are . . .

He takes her to the bed.

Raymonde   Just for a moment. (*She lies down – on* **Baptistin**.) Ah!

Baptistin   Ow!

Tournel   You! Why are you still here?

Baptistin   You brought me here.

Raymonde   I've had enough. (*Shaking* **Tournel**.) Make him go away. Don't argue. Make him go away.

Tournel   All right. (*To* **Baptistin**.) Good riddance, you.

He presses the button. The bed starts to swivel.

Raymonde (*furious*)   It's ridiculous, bursting into people's rooms, and – (*As the bed starts to swivel, as she's still standing on the step.*) Aee!

Tournel (*catching her*)   Here we are!

He's supporting her as the bed swivels completely, revealing **Camille**, *crouched on all fours on the other bed.*

Camille   Ah! Ah! You!

Raymonde *and* **Tournel**   Camille!

Camille   I'm sorry. It's the bed, the bed.

Raymonde   That's not Camille. I can understand him.

Tournel   It must be someone else.

Camille (*getting off the bed*)   I tell you it's the bed.

Raymonde   I've had enough. I'm going home.

Tournel   Me too.

They rush off, downstairs.

Camille   Tournel? Raymonde? What are they doing here? Oh God, if they recognised me . . . !

He goes on to the landing and shuts the door behind him.

Antoinette? Where is she? She went in here . . .

He bursts into **Rugby**'s *room.*

Camille   Hey!

Huge argument from **Rugby**'s *room. We hear the three voices, furniture being thrown about, glass breaking. It continues under what follows.* **Raymonde** *and* **Tournel** *rush upstairs as fast as they rushed down.*

Raymonde Étienne, now! Étienne, my God!

Tournel What next?

*They rush out along the corridor up L. The noise in **Rugby**'s room swells to a climax, the door bursts open, **Camille** is hurled out and **Rugby** storms after him.*

Rugby Clear orf! Clear orf, now!

Camille But Monsieur . . .

Rugby Right. You asked for this.

*He lands a haymaker, full in **Camille**'s face. And another.*

Camille Ow!

He loses his palate, with predictable results.

I say. Now I've lost it. Lost it!

*He tries to get down on all fours to find it. But **Rugby** will have none of that.*

Rugby Oh, no you don't. Come here.

He picks him up like a sack of coal.

Camille My thingumajig. I've lost my thingumajig.

Rugby Get in there!

He dumps him in the room down R.

Cheeky young blighter. Now then.

He bursts into his own room.

Did you miss me, darling?

*As soon as the door's shut, **Étienne** comes up the stairs.*

Étienne Hello? Anyone about?

He sees the palate, and picks it up.

Silver! Eugh, it's wet.

Enter **Eugénie**.

Eugénie   Did you call, Monsieur?

Étienne   Ah, Mamzelle. Look, I found this. I don't know what it's for, but it was down there.

Eugénie   It looks like buried treasure.

She shows it off to **Étienne**, *as if it's a brooch.* **Camille** *comes out of his room, bent double, searching.*

Camille   I've got to find my thingumajig. (*Still bent double, he bumps into* **Étienne**. *He straightens up, briefly.*) Euugh!

He bends again, and scuttles into the room down R. Neither **Étienne** *nor* **Eugénie** *has seen him.*

Eugénie   One of the guests must have dropped it. I'll put it in Lost-and-Found.

Étienne   Right. And by the way, has a woman been here, asking for Mr Chandebise's room?

Eugénie   Oh, yes.

Étienne   Where is she?

Eugénie   No, Monsieur, you can't.

Étienne   Don't be silly. Her husband'll be here any minute. A killer.

Eugénie   Aah!

Étienne   I've got to warn her.

Eugénie   If that's all you want, she went in there. (*She points to* **Rugby**'s *door.*

Étienne   Thanks.

He knocks.

Rugby (*off*)   Come in!

Étienne (*going in*)   Excuse me, Monsieur, I –

Rugby *and* **Antoinette** (*off*) Aah!

Étienne (*off*) My wife!

Another row breaks out, exactly like the first.

Eugénie What on earth do they do in there?

Antoinette *bursts out, dishevelled and half undressed.*

Antoinette Étienne! My husband! Aah!

She rushes downstairs. **Étienne** *hurtles out after her.*

Étienne Stop her! Stop her!

Rugby *grabs him and spins him round, pinning him against the wall.*

Rugby You bloody fool.

Étienne Ow.

Rugby I'm going to kill you. (*Banging him against the wall.*) See?

Étienne But she's my wife.

Rugby See? See?

Étienne Put me down.

Rugby Had enough? Right!

He goes into his room and slams the door.

Étienne First a cuckold, then a punchbag.

Eugénie You should have told me you were the husband.

Étienne D'you think I knew?

Eugénie *shrugs and goes to the stairs, where she meets* **Poche**.

Étienne You don't understand. Let me explain. Wait, wait . . . Euuugh! Monsieur.

Poche What now?

Étienne   Monsieur, all those logs.

Poche   Logs, what of it? Logs.

Étienne   Monsieur, I'm a cuckold. A cuckold.

Poche   No!

Étienne   Yes. And he's ... an Englishman!

Poche   Ah, Eniwunformee.

Étienne   He didn't tell me his name. Monsieur, you're here, you don't need me, do you mind if I go after her, the cheat, the baggage, and ...? Please, Monsieur.

Poche (*expansively*)   Go. Go.

Étienne   Oh, thank you, thank you. Come here, you. Wait!

He rushes out downstairs.

Poche   It's just that sort of day, today.

Lucienne (*off, downstairs*)   Mind where you're going!

A bell rings. **Eugénie** *looks at the display board.*

Eugénie   It's for you.

Poche   Right. Coming, coming ...

Exit. **Lucienne** *comes up the stairs.*

Lucienne   I could have sworn that was Étienne ...

Eugénie   Good afternoon, Madame.

Lucienne   Ah, Mamzelle. That man who nearly knocked me over just now – doesn't he work for Monsieur Chandebise?

Eugénie   He did ask for Monsieur Chandebise's room. It was baffling. He said he wanted to warn a woman she was in deadly danger, because her husband knew everything, and as soon as he saw her, bam! She was his own wife. Baffling.

Lucienne   You're making this up.

Eugénie   I saw it with my own eyes, Madame.

Lucienne   Oh, all right. Show me the room booked for Monsieur Chandebise.

Eugénie   This one, Madame. (*She points to the room down R.*)

Lucienne   I'll wait in there.

Eugénie   Yes, Madame. They said if anyone came, I was to let them in.

Lucienne   Thank you.

Exit **Eugénie**. **Lucienne** *goes to knock at the door.* **Camille** *comes out of the other room, bent double as before.*

Camille   I've got to find my thingumajig.

He searches, and comes up against **Lucienne**, *who doesn't see him.*

Lucienne   Why don't they answer?

Camille   Madame de Histangua! I've had enough of this!

He scoots for the stairs. **Lucienne** *opens the door and goes in.*

Lucienne   Empty. What's going on? Raymonde told me quite clearly, 'I'll catch him between five and ten past, five thirty at the latest.' Didn't she wait for me? Is she in here?

She goes to inspect the bathroom. **Camille** *pelts back upstairs.*

Camille   Victor-Emmanuel! Victor-Emmanuel!

He goes into the room up R. **Lucienne** *comes out of the other room.*

Lucienne   No one. Well, I can't wait all night.

She makes for the stairs, just as **Chandebise** *comes up them,* *dressed as in Act One.*

Chandebise There's no one to ask. Ah! You!

Lucienne Monsieur Chandebise!

Chandebise (*urgently*) You haven't see Étienne?

Lucienne Pardon?

Chandebise Étienne. Étienne. You haven't seen Étienne.

Lucienne No, why?

Chandebise Because I sent him to tell you — I couldn't come myself — urgent appointment — but it was tomorrow — so I came myself to —

Lucienne To what?

Chandebise Poor child! Falling head over heels — for me!

Lucienne Pardon?

Chandebise Oh, come, come, come. But why didn't you sign the letter?

Lucienne What letter?

Chandebise The one you wrote begging me to meet you here.

Lucienne Ah. (*New tone.*) How could you possibly imagine it was me who —

Chandebise Well, obviously: I showed it to your husband.

Lucienne What?

Chandebise He recognised your writing.

Lucienne What are you saying?

Chandebise And he's probably going to kill you.

Lucienne   Where is he?

Chandebise   He'll be here any minute.

Lucienne   Don't just stand there. Come on!

She hurtles for the stairs.

Chandebise   It's mad. It's mad.

He rushes after her, down the stairs. **Olympe** *comes along the corridor.*

Olympe   Eugénie! Eugénie! Drat the girl.

She's at the top of the stairs. **Chandebise** *and* **Lucienne** *hurtle up.*

Chandebise   It's him. Histangua! Help!

Lucienne   My husband! Help!

Olympe   What's going on?

Chandebise (*knocking into her*)   Get out of the way!

Olympe   Pardon?

Lucienne (*the same*)   Make room!

Lucienne *rushes into the bathroom of the room down R,* **Chandebise** *into* **Rugby**'s *room.*

Olympe   Madame . . .

Raymonde, *veiled, comes along the corridor, with* **Tournel**.

Raymonde   Do hurry. I won't be happy till we're away from here. (*Bumping into* **Olympe**.) Out of the way!

Olympe   Ah!

Tournel (*also pushing past*)   Make room! (*To* **Raymonde**.) Come on!

They run downstairs.

Olympe   What's going on? What on earth's going on?

Histangua (*off, downstairs*)   Where they are? I keel them! Yah!

Raymonde *and* **Tournel** (*off, downstairs*)   Aaah!

Olympe (*shouting down the stairs*)   What's going on?

Raymonde (*rushing up the stairs*)   Histangua! He's here! (*Bumping into* **Olympe**.) Get out of the way!

Olympe   Heuuh.

Tournel (*same business*)   He'll kill us all. Make room!

They rush off down the corridor L.

Olympe   What next? What next?

Homénidès *lopes upstairs, brandishing a revolver.*

Homénidès   Tournel. Woman in veil. My wifes. I find, I find.

Olympe   Where are you going, Monsieur?

Homénidès   To keel heem both. Make room. Make room!

He jostles past her, and off down the corridor.

Olympe   To keel heem both? Oh, help! Help!

Enter **Ferraillon** *and* **Eugénie**, *fast.*

Ferraillon   What is it? What's the matter?

Olympe (*breathless*)   He's mad. He's mad. He'll kill us all.

Ferraillon   What?

Olympe (*collapsing in* **Eugénie**'s *arms*)   Ah ... ahah ...

Eugénie   Monsieur! Monsieur!

Ferraillon (*rushing to help*)   Here. Let me ... In here ...

They go to the only room not so far used.

Give her some smelling salts.

Eugénie Yes, Monsieur.

Ferraillon *shuts the door and leaves them to it. He becomes aware of the furious row going on in* **Rugby***'s room.*

Ferraillon Now what?

Rugby*'s door bursts open.* **Rugby** *is trying to throw* **Chandebise** *out,* **Chandebise** *is clinging to the door-frame like a limpet.*

Rugby. Out! Out!

Chandebise Will . . . you . . . put . . . me . . . down?

Ferraillon Oi! Stop it. Stop it!

At this precise moment, **Rugby** *dislodges* **Chandebise** *so violently that he sends him spinning down the corridor to collapse on the banquette.* **Rugby** *goes into his room, fuming, and shuts the door.*

Chandebise For heaven's sake . . . !

Ferraillon Poche. You blasted Poche.

Chandebise What did you say?

Ferraillon *grabs him and kicks him, as usual.*

Ferraillon I said this . . . and this . . .

Chandebise (*jumping with each kick*) Ow! What are you . . . ow!

Ferraillon Drunk . . . en . . . oaf!

Chandebise I beg your . . . ow! (*He breaks free.*) What the devil d'you think you're doing?

Ferraillon I beg your pardon?

Chandebise I'm Monsieur Victor-Emmanuel Chandebise, Director of the Boston Life Insurance Company, Paris Branch.

Ferraillon You've really had too much this time.

Chandebise You're going to be very sorry.

Ferraillon (*grabbing and kicking*) Oh, sorry? Like this . . .
and this . . .

Chandebise Ow! Ow!

Ferraillon And this . . .

Chandebise (*breaking free again; nose to nose with
Ferraillon*) I . . . will . . . not . . . stand . . . for . . . this!

Ferraillon Where did you get those clothes?

Chandebise What?

Ferraillon *grabs his jacket and starts wrenching it off.*

Chandebise Hey!

Ferraillon Keep still. Put your arm through there.

Chandebise You're out of your mind.

Ferraillon (*forcing him into the livery jacket and cap*) Get
this on. And this.

Chandebise I won't.

Ferraillon You will.

Chandebise I don't want to.

Ferraillon (*huge*) Don't want to? You horrible little man,
in this house you'll do exactly as you're told!

Chandebise (*crumpling*) Oh. Sorry.

Ferraillon Now, go to your room. Go on. Hup! Hup!
Hup!

Chandebise Yes. Yes. He's mad.

Ferraillon What did you say?

Chandebise Nothing.

Ferraillon Get down those stairs!

Chandebise   You're crazy.

Ferraillon   Whaaat?

Chandebise   I'm going.

He goes, all but falling down the stairs.

Ferraillon   I should think so! All that brandy. It's the last time, d'you hear me, the last time.

Eugénie *comes out. We hear* **Olympe** *panting inside the room.*

Eugénie   Monsieur!

Ferraillon   What now?

Eugénie   Madame's making funny noises.

Ferraillon   Oh, for ... Go to Number Ten, find Doctor Finache, ask him to hurry. Go on, go on.

Eugénie   Yes, Monsieur.

She runs upstairs.

Ferraillon   What next, what next, what next?

He goes in to calm **Olympe**.

Ferraillon   There, there, darling, what's the matter?

As soon as the door is shut behind him, **Poche** *comes in L. He has some letters, and is unfastening his apron.*

Poche   Off to the post.

He hangs the apron on its peg, and looks for his livery.

Hey! My coat, my cap. Who's had them? What's this they've left me?

He tries on **Chandebise**'s *discarded jacket and hat.*

They're not brilliant, but they'll have to do. It's only the post office, after all.

Bell.

Someone wants me. Coming! Coming!

He goes out, L, just as **Eugénie** *comes downstairs with* **Finache**.

Eugénie   This way, Doctor. Quick.

Finache   I didn't come here to work. What's wrong with her?

Eugénie   Nothing, really. A sort of eeheeheehee.

Finache   Pardon?

Eugénie   A sort of eeheeheehee. Or a brrrrrrrbabrrrrrrr. A prrrrffff!

Finache   Why didn't you say so before? A prrrrffff!

Eugénie   Something knocked her all of a heap. She went all upsy-daisy.

Finache   So I have to come down and see to her? You've got a soda siphon, haven't you? Well, use it.

Eugénie   But now you've come down all this way . . .

Finache   Oh, all right. Where is she?

Eugénie   This way, Monsieur.

She opens the door, and we hear **Olympe**'s *cries as before.*
Eugénie *shows* **Finache** *in and shuts the door behind them.*
Chandebise, *in* **Poche**'s *uniform, comes gingerly up the stairs.*

Chandebise   Has he gone? Madman! If that's how he treats his guests . . . Now then, my jacket . . . my hat . . . Didn't he hang them over here? Where are they?

He bends down to look. **Raymonde** *and* **Tournel** *enter, hurriedly.*

Raymonde   We've lost him. Quick, a taxi.

Tournel   Look: the porter.

Raymonde   That's right.

Chandebise (*still bent double*) Where the devil are they?

Raymonde Poche, a cab. Now.

Chandebise What?

Raymonde A cab.

Chandebise My wife!

Tournel Eh?

Raymonde My husband! It was him!

She rushes out.

Chandebise Tournel, too. Here. With her.

Tournel (*dazed*) It was him.

Chandebise (*leaping for his throat*) What are you doing here? What are you doing with my wife?

Tournel (*half-choked*) You know. You know.

Chandebise What d'you mean, I know?

Tournel We told you, five minutes ago.

Chandebise Told me? (*Shaking him.*) Told me what? Told me what?

Tournel Oh, come on. Come on.

Enter **Ferraillon** *in a fury.*

Ferraillon Not again! Not Poche again!

He drags him away from **Tournel**, *who rushes out.*

Chandebise The madman.

Ferraillon (*starting the kicking routine again*) Drunk! Drunk! Drunk!

Chandebise (*jumping, as before*) Ow! Ow! Ow!

Ferraillon Pig.

Chandebise Now that's enough.

Ferraillon   Want some more, do you?

Chandebise   No! Help! Madman! Help!

He runs upstairs. **Ferraillon** *pelts after him.*

Ferraillon   I'll give you madman, you drunk, you swine. Into your room. I'll lock you in. We'll talk about this tomorrow. Hup! Hup! Hup!

As soon as they've gone, **Rugby** *comes out of his room, furious.*

Rugby   This place is a medhouse. A medhouse.

He goes downstairs, leaving his door open. **Camille** *comes out of his room.*

Camille   I think the coast's clear. I'm off.

Lucienne *appears from her room.*

Lucienne   It's gone very quiet.

Camille   I must find my thingumajig.

He starts looking.

Lucienne   My husband must have gone.

They bump into one another.

Camille   Madame de Histangua!

Lucienne   Monsieur Camille! Don't leave me. Stay with me. My husband's here. A gun. He's killing everyone.

Camille   My God!

Lucienne   Don't leave me. Please!

Camille   No. Oh, no.

Homénidès (*off*)   Where are they?

Camille   It's him! Come on!

They rush to the stairs, but bump into **Rugby** *who is coming up.* **Camille** *rushes into the room down R, shuts the door and leans on it to block it.* **Lucienne** *rushes into* **Rugby**'s *room, much to his delight.*

Rugby Now that's more like it!

He hurries after her. **Homénidès** *rushes down the stairs.*

Homénidès Where are you? I find, I keel. Where is he, room of Chandebise? Why no one here, in all hotel?

He hurries on downstairs. Enter **Poche**, *L.*

Poche There's still someone shouting.

Lucienne *runs out of* **Rugby's** *room.* **Rugby** *chases her.*

Lucienne Will you leave me alone?

Rugby Not again!

He sulks back into his room.

Poche That told him.

Lucienne (*rushing to him*) Oh, Monsieur Chandebise –

Poche Eh?

Lucienne Heaven must have sent you. Save me! Hide me!

Poche But why, Madame?

Lucienne (*all but sobbing on his breast*) My husband's after me. He wants to kill me.

Poche What did you say?

Lucienne Oh, save me, save me.

Poche (*putting his arm round her*) There, there. This way.

He supports her to the stairs, and they start down together.

Homénidès (*from below*) Ah, there you are!

Lucienne It's him! Oh, no!

She runs and hammers on **Camille's** *door.*

Lucienne Let me in! Let me in!

Camille (*pushing from inside*)   No entry! No entry!

Poche   Hurry up.

She rushes towards **Rugby***'s room.*

Poche   Not there! The Englishman!

Lucienne   Where, then? Where?

Poche   There!

He takes her into the room up R. **Homénidès** *appears, with gun.*

Homénidès   No hide. I see you. Both.

Eugénie *comes out of* **Olympe***'s room.*

Eugénie   Can I help you, Monsieur?

Homénidès   Monsieur Chandebise's room? Monsieur Chandebise's room?

Eugénie   It's that one, there.

Exit, L.

Homénidès (*hammering on* **Camille***'s door*)   Open heem! Open heem!

Camille   No one at home.

Homénidès   I cry you, open heem, one, two, three!

He bursts in and leaps for **Camille***'s throat.*

Homénidès   My wifes, where she is, my wifes? I keel her, yais?

Camille   I don't know. I haven't seen her. Look! (*He turns out his pockets.*)

Homénidès   I find her, I keel her. I shoot her, so!

He aims and fires at the target bell-button. The bed swivels, to reveal **Lucienne** *and* **Poche***.*

Lucienne   Aee!

She runs for it, followed by **Poche**.

Homénidès At last!

He runs after her, firing the gun. Everyone dashes out and grabs him. In the mêlée, he goes on firing as the curtain falls.

Act Three

Chandebise's *house, as in Act One.* **Antoinette** *hurries in. She has put her cook's uniform back on and is fastening her dress. Her apron and cap are in one hand, and she's flustered.*

Antoinette He'll be back any minute. Étienne. I'll never have time. Oh ... more haste, less speed. Ow!

Étienne (*off*) Antoinette! Antoinette!

Antoinette Ah!

She bolts the door.

Étienne (*closer*) Antoinette!

Antoinette (*struggling with her cap and apron*) Oh God ...

Étienne (*outside the door*) Antoinette! (*Rattling the handle.*) Open up. She's locked herself in. Just wait where you are ...

His voice fades as he goes L.

Antoinette Hurry ...

She finishes dressing, unbolts the door and tiptoes out into the room down R. At the same moment, **Étienne** *bursts in by the door upstage L.*

Étienne Antoinette! Where's she hiding? Antoinette!

Antoinette (*serenely, at the door down R*) Is that you doing all the shouting?

Étienne Of course it's me. What d'you mean, locking the door like that?

Antoinette (*innocently*) Sorry?

Étienne I said, why did you lock the door?

Antoinette (*magnificently unruffled*) I didn't lock the door.

Étienne For heaven's sake!

He goes angrily to the door and turns the handle. The door opens.

What?

Antoinette Finding doors hard all of a sudden?

Étienne This one's never easy. And it's not the point. The point is, what were you doing ten minutes ago at the Hotel Casablanca?

Antoinette Where?

Étienne The Hotel Casablanca.

Antoinette What on earth is that?

Étienne What d'you mean, what on earth is that . . . ? I saw you there.

Antoinette Me? There? You saw me, there?

Étienne That's what I said.

Antoinette I haven't left this house.

Étienne Pull the other one.

Antoinette I'm telling you.

Étienne You haven't left this house. Now I've heard everything. I knew you'd have an excuse, some brilliant reason − but not 'I haven't left this house'.

Antoinette You wouldn't want me to tell lies, do you?

Étienne I saw you. With these eyes.

Antoinette What's that got to do with it?

Étienne Pardon?

Antoinette Whatever you saw or didn't see, I was here.

Étienne You were there. I caught you. Half undressed, in the arms of an . . . an Englishman.

Antoinette Me?

Étienne Yes, you. He tried to beat me up.

Antoinette   An Englishman? H'm . . . No, impossible. I don't speak English.

Étienne   Oh, brilliant! What you were doing, it's the same in any language. No need for words. You weren't in the arms of an Englishman?

Antoinette   I never left this house.

Étienne   All right, you never left. We'll see about that.

Antoinette   Now where are you going?

Étienne   To ask the concierge.

Antoinette   Ask him what?

Étienne   Whether you went out or not.

The next two speeches are simultaneous.

Antoinette   Don't be so silly, Étienne. The concierge. Don't drag him into this. D'you want to look a fool?

Étienne   Haha! Weren't expecting that, were you? You thought you'd got me, and now we'll see about that.

Antoinette   Étienne, be sensible.

Étienne   Leave me alone.

Antoinette   Oh, do what you like!

She folds her arms and sits, facing the audience. **Étienne** *flings open the main doors, goes into the hall and picks up the phone.*

Étienne   Hello. Monsieur Ploumard? It's me. Listen, I know this may sound strange, but . . . What time did my wife go out today? Hn. Hn. What d'you mean, she didn't? Of course she did – you didn't see her, that's what you mean . . . Hn. Hn. She was here, having a bite with you? Hn. Because everyone else was out, she came down and had a bite with you . . . ? Hn. Hn. Hn.

Antoinette (*to the audience*)   Five francs, that cost me.

Étienne   I'm amazed. I . . . no, no. Thanks. Thanks very much.

He hangs up and comes back.

Antoinette Well?

Étienne Oh, leave me alone. I think I'm going mad.

Antoinette You're not going mad, you're just a fool. You're jealous.

Étienne Get into the kitchen. We haven't finished this.

Antoinette Whatever you say.

Exit. **Étienne** *is about to follow, when the bell rings.*

Étienne Coming! (*To the audience.*) If it isn't her, it must be me.

Bell, off.

I said I'm coming.

He goes into the hall, and ushers in **Raymonde** *and* **Tournel**.

Raymonde Didn't you hear the bell?

Étienne I was on my way, Madame.

Raymonde Where's Monsieur? Still out?

Étienne Yes, Madame.

Raymonde Fine. Thank you.

Étienne Yes, Madame.

He goes to the door, brooding. As he passes **Tournel**, *he mutters to himself:*

It's incredible.

Tournel Pardon?

Étienne Oh, not you, Monsieur.

Tournel Thank you.

Exit **Étienne**. **Tournel** *hovers in the doorway.*

Tournel Well ... look ... now you're home ... I think
I'll be —

Raymonde You're not going, are you?

Tournel Oh.

Raymonde You can't just leave me. What'll he be like
when he gets back? You saw what he was like just now,
when he saw us in the hotel. The second time. I thought
he was going to kill you. What if he starts all that again?

Tournel That's why I'd better stay?

Raymonde I don't want to be the only one.

Tournel Oh, all right.

Raymonde You don't sound very keen.

Tournel You know how it is ...

Raymonde I know how men are. Do anything, own up
to nothing.

Tournel There's nothing to own up to. Nothing
happened.

Raymonde No thanks to you! In any case, Victor-
Emmanuel doesn't know nothing happened. He was there,
he saw, he guessed. You could tell by his face, he guessed.

Tournel What I don't understand is, why it took him
so long.

Raymonde What d'you mean?

Tournel Well, the first time, when he was on that bed,
with that bottle ...

Raymonde That's right.

Tournel He didn't seem to care then. Seemed happy
enough then.

Raymonde When he kissed us. Both.

Tournel And then the next time we see him, in uniform, he goes for our throats. It shouldn't be like that. In affairs like that, you never stop to think. You see; you act.

Raymonde That's right. What's going on?

Bell, off.

It's him.

Tournel That was quick.

Lucienne (*off*) Is Madame back yet?

Étienne (*off*) Yes, Madame.

Raymonde Lucienne.

She goes to the main door.

Come in.

Enter **Lucienne**.

Lucienne Raymonde. It was dreadful. Awful.

Raymonde I know.

Lucienne My legs were like this. (*She makes jelly-legs.*)

Raymonde *and* **Tournel** (*sympathetically*) Oh.

Lucienne I can't go home. I daren't. (*Change of tone.*) Monsieur Tournel. I'm sorry . . .

Tournel That's quite all right.

Lucienne I'll go away. Anywhere. I'll hide. I can't face him. He's like a wild beast —

Raymonde A hurricane. He saw us at the hotel, Monsieur Tournel and me . . . started chasing us with a revolver . . . I mean, why should he want to kill us?

Tournel I wondered that.

Lucienne He chased you too?

Raymonde Like a whirling dervish, a demon.

Lucienne I thought I was done for. Fortunately, I met your husband. He saved me. If he hadn't been there, I'd have fainted, and then what might have ...?

Raymonde You mean Victor-Emmanuel –

Lucienne Yes. He was odd, as well.

Raymonde You're joking.

Lucienne I can't understand it. The stress of events. He was like a different person.

Raymonde We noticed that.

Lucienne Ten minutes before, when I saw him first, he was perfectly calm. Warned me about my husband, suggested I escaped while I could. Then paf! Everyone chasing everyone. We ran down the stairs, someone came, we ran up again. He said, 'Who's the Red Indian? A friend of yours?' A friend? My husband! I said, 'You know who it is. It's my husband.' He said, 'Never seen you before in my life. Who are you?' Oh, my God! That was it! The moment when he ... when his mind ... Paf! Just like that.

Raymonde (*to* **Tournel**) Just like with us.

Lucienne He was gabbling. He wasn't Chandebise, he was the porter, the hotel porter, fetching wood, someone stole his uniform ...

Raymonde It's crazy.

Tournel Crazy.

Lucienne Then he tried to ... to ...

Raymonde *and* **Tournel** Yes?

Lucienne You know. I said, 'Don't be silly, Chandebise.' 'Poche,' he said. 'Poche.' Just like that. 'Poche.'

Raymonde (*to* **Tournel**)   That's it exactly. 'Poche.'

Tournel   That proves it.

Lucienne   I'd had enough. I pushed him out of the way, I ran. What is going on?

Raymonde   That's right. Has he really gone crazy, or is it a trick, some trick? It's baffling.

Tournel (*gloomily*)   It makes no difference.

Lucienne *and* **Raymonde**   Pardon?

Tournel   After a day like today . . .

Raymonde   Is that all? I thought you were going to say —

Tournel   I wasn't.

Raymonde   Ah, well. What do we do next?

Tournel   Search me.

Lucienne   One husband's out for blood.

Raymonde   And the other's off his head.

Tournel   What do we do next?

All three   What do we do next?

They huddle. Bell, off. They have a whispered conference.

Lucienne   Someone there.

Raymonde *and* **Tournel**   Yes.

Tournel   It could be . . . Chandebise.

Raymonde   He's got his own key.

Tournel   He might have forgotten it.

Raymonde   That's right.

Tournel   I remember once, last winter, it was snowing . . .

Raymonde　Not now. Later.

Tournel　Charming.

He sits, sulkily.

Lucienne　Why don't they open the door?

Raymonde　That's right. When the bell rings —

Tournel　It's because there's someone there.

Raymonde　You're right.

Tournel　Of course I'm right.

Enter **Étienne**.

Étienne　Madame! Madame!

Raymonde　What is it?

Étienne　Oh, Madame.

Raymonde　What?

Étienne　It's Monsieur.

Tournel *and* **Lucienne**　Ah!

Raymonde　Yes?

Étienne　It's Monsieur and it's not Monsieur. I opened the door. He came in. He said — (*Imitating* **Poche***'s drunken manner*) — 'Is this Monsieur Chandebise's house?'

The others　What?

Étienne　I thought he was joking. I said, 'Heeheehee,' like that, 'Heeheehee, Monsieur Chandebise's house.' But he wasn't laughing. He looked me in the eye and said, 'Tell him it's about the uniform.'

The others　Pardon?

Étienne　Oh, Madame ... Madame ... Monsieur ...

Raymonde　I've had enough of these games. Where is he?

Étienne In the hall, Madame. Waiting.

Raymonde Waiting?

Lucienne *and* **Tournel** In the hall?

Raymonde It's ridiculous.

She throws open the main doors, to reveal **Poche**, *still wearing* **Chandebise**'s *jacket and hat, sitting on the edge of a chair like someone in a dentist's waiting-room. When he sees them all, he grins a death's-head grin.*

The others (*recoiling*) Ah!

Raymonde What exactly are you playing at?

Poche (*getting up*) Pardon?

Raymonde Sitting there. In your own hall. Like . . . an undertaker.

Poche Madame?

The others (*astounded*) 'Madame'?

Raymonde What d'you mean, 'Madame'? Come in here.

Poche (*nervously*) I was hoping . . . Monsieur Chandebise . . .

Tournel *and* **Lucienne** What?

Raymonde What did you say?

Étienne You see what I mean, Madame?

Poche (*prodding him roguishly*) I remember you. You were in the hotel just now.

Étienne That's right.

Poche The cuckold.

Étienne Ah. Well . . .

Raymonde What's he talking about?

Poche   You were there too, Madame. I remember you. Those kisses. (*Advancing on her.*) Hello again, Madame.

Raymonde (*hiding behind* **Tournel**)   What's he playing at?

Tournel   Now, now, old chap . . .

Poche   You too! I remember you, too. The gigolo . . .

He advances as if to kiss him.

Tournel   Steady on. Victor-Emmanuel.

Poche   No, Poche. Poche.

Lucienne   He's doing it again. 'Poche, Poche.'

Poche   Madame! You too. The squaw. The Red Indian's . . . Oh, Madame, what a carry-on.

Lucienne   Yes . . .

She joins the others, in a huddle as before.

Poche   Heeheehee. It's amazing. Heeheehee. They all live in the same house. Heeheehee.

The others (*sotto voce*)   Listen to him.

Poche   Hey. What's wrong with you all?

The others   Nothing. Nothing.

Poche (*to the audience*)   Mind you, they are quite nice. For lunatics.

Raymonde   What is the matter with him?

Lucienne   Can't you call a doctor?

Étienne (*seizing his chance of escape*)   I could ring Doctor Finache, Madame . . .

Raymonde   If you want to.

Étienne   Yes, Madame.

He makes for the door. **Poche** *catches him.*

Poche   You going?

Étienne   Yes, please, Monsieur.

Poche   Well, if you see Monsieur Chandebise, don't forget my message.

Lucienne (*to the others, sotto voce*)   D'you hear that?

Étienne   No, Monsieur.

Exit.

Tournel   What on earth's got into him?

Raymonde   It's not a trick. It's real.

Poche (*moving to explain*)   It's about my uniform . . .

Lucienne *and* **Tournel**   Of course it is.

Raymonde   For heaven's sake, stop it.

Poche   Eh?

Raymonde   If you're not feeling well, say so and we'll see to you. If you're playing games, I'm telling you: stop now.

Poche   Ah.

Raymonde   We made everything clear before. In the hotel. There's nothing between Tournel and me. Nothing. Madame de Histangua will bear that out.

Lucienne   Nothing.

Raymonde   What more d'you want, for heaven's sake?

He looks at her.

Oh, I see. Well, in that case, Monsieur Tournel will be happy to oblige.

She pushes **Tournel** *to face him.*

Tournel   Who, me?

Poche (*almost knocked flying*)   Ow.

Raymonde You see! You can believe us or not. But whichever it is, act like a grown-up. Stop playing the fool.

Poche Who, me?

Raymonde One minute you're kissing us, the next you're at our throats. Well, Monsieur Tournel's throat.

Poche (*to* **Tournel**) I'm at your throat?

Tournel Yes.

Raymonde Why? That's all we want to know. D'you believe us or don't you?

Poche Of course I believe you.

Raymonde Give us another kiss, then, and let's have done with it.

Poche As many as you like.

He wipes his lips on his sleeve and advances on her. She pushes him away.

Raymonde Erg!

All Now what?

Raymonde Have you been drinking?

Poche Pardon?

Raymonde You stink of brandy.

Poche Do I?

Raymonde *grabs his chin and drags him so that* **Tournel** *can smell him.*

Raymonde He has, hasn't he?

Tournel (*reeling back*) Phew!

Raymonde Hasn't he?

Tournel Like a fish.

Raymonde So you're drunk, too? On top of everything else?

Poche I've had a drop or two. A lil drop. Medicinal.

Raymonde He's . . . plastered!

Poche Hey, less of that. Who d'you think you . . . ? A lil less o that . . .

Raymonde Oh, go and sleep it off.

Poche What?

Tournel This way. Victor-Emmanuel, this way.

Poche (*yelling at him*) It's Poche! Poche! Poche!

Each 'P' is an alcoholic blast in **Tournel***'s face.*

Tournel Oh, Poche, then. Poche. If you insist.

Poche *staggers towards* **Lucienne**, *who retreats*.

Lucienne No.

Poche I do insist. We'll have no more of this. If we have any more of this, I'll get very, very cross.

Raymonde You're disgusting.

Étienne *shows in* **Finache**.

Étienne Madame, here's the doctor.

All Ah.

Finache (*to* **Raymonde**) What's wrong? I got to the door, and Étienne was just trying to phone me. (*To* **Poche**.) There you are, Chandebise.

Poche (*looking behind himself*) Where is he, Chandebise?

Finache Very funny. (*To* **Raymonde**.) What's wrong?

Raymonde What's wrong? Look at him: plastered.

Finache He can't be.

Étienne Not Monsieur.

Tournel *and* **Lucienne**   He is.

Poche   I am?

Raymonde   Smell his breath. Go on.

Finache (*going to* **Poche**)   You haven't really been . . . ?

Poche   Me? Pfffffff!

Finache (*recoiling*)   Pfaugh.

Poche   Ver' funny.

Finache   He has. He is.

Raymonde   You see?

Étienne (*to* **Poche**, *scandalised*)   Monsieur!

Poche   Wassammarrer?

Finache   Look, old chap, however did you get in a state like this?

Poche   Right. (*Squaring up to him.*) Take off your coat.

Finache   Pardon?

Poche   I'm no drunker'n you are.

Finache   All right. Calm down.

Poche *goes round the company, cowing them one at a time, till they form a dejected line, up and down which he marches.*

Poche   Ver' funny. You think you're ver' funny. All of you. I don' even know your names. I came for Monsieur Chandebise. I'll see Monsieur Chandebise. Where are you hiding him?

Finache   My God.

Raymonde   That's what's wrong.

Lucienne   One minute he's normal, the next –

Tournel   It started this afternoon.

Finache Did it . . . ? H'mmm . . .

Poche What is it? Who you looking at? Whadd'you take me for? I've had enough of this.

Finache That's right, there, there.

All There, there.

Poche Where?

He stalks to a chair and sits. The others hold a whispered conference.

Raymonde He's impossible.

Tournel Impossible.

Lucienne *and* **Étienne** That's right.

Finache It's new to me. Has it happened before?

Raymonde Of course not. (*To* **Étienne**.) Has it?

Étienne (*to* **Finache**) No, Monsieur.

Finache Hallucination, amnesia, obliteration of the self . . . I've only seen it twice before.

All Ah?

Finache Terminal alcoholics.

All Ah.

Finache The next stage: delirium tremens.

All Oh.

Poche, *still furious, slams his hat down on the table.*

All Ooh!

Raymonde It's ridiculous. He doesn't drink. A glass of wine once or twice a week.

Tournel Even then, he leaves most of it.

Étienne I usually finish them. I can't bear waste . . .

Lucienne Surely that wouldn't be enough −

Finache It's not how much you drink, it's natural propensity.

Tournel I knew it.

The others Pardon?

Finache Natural propensity.

Tournel They don't understand medical language. Natural propensity . . . in his case, to be an idiot.

Finache (*nodding agreement until the last word*) Yes . . . yes . . . No!

Tournel Isn't it? Sorry.

Finache Natural propensity: the amount each individual metabolism can absorb. One person can drink a bottle of spirits a day: nothing. Another, half a glass − alcoholic.

Poche (*to the audience*) They're still doing it.

Finache It's the latter group who run the gravest risks. Because they don't suspect. A glass once or twice a week − what's wrong with that? Then one day: poom! And there you have it.

He gestures at **Poche**. *They all gaze at him as if he's an exhibit.*

All Ahaaaah.

Poche Enjoying yourselves?

All Oh.

Poche (*getting up, ramming his hat on his head*) You don't get it, do you? Stop this and stop it now, or there'll be big, big trouble. Ver'.

Finache Look, old chap . . .

Poche I said what I said and I said it.

Finache It's all right. There, there. (*To the others.*) Bad temper: sure sign.

Poche   What did you say?

Finache   Nothing. Hold out your hand.

Poche   Whadd'you mean?

Finache   Like this, look! (*He holds his arm out stiffly in front of him, the way people do.*)

Poche   Like this? (*He holds out his arm.*)

Raymonde   Look, it's trembling.

All   Oh.

Finache   Exactly. A symptom. We doctors call it, alcoholic shake.

Poche (*dancing with fury*)   Aah! Aaah! Aaaaaah!

All (*terrified*)   Oh!

Poche   That's it. That's it. That's it.

Finache   Calm down. For heaven's sake, calm down.

Poche   You're doing this on purpose, aren't you? (*To them all.*) Aren't you?

All   No, no, no.

Raymonde   Calm down, darling.

Poche   Get stuffed!

Raymonde   What did he say?

Finache   They don't know what they're saying. They're not in control. Go over there. You're exciting him.

Raymonde   Me, exciting him? Did you hear what he said to me?

Finache (*manoeuvring them to the door L*)   He's over-excited. Leave him alone with me. And Étienne. We'll try to get him to bed.

Raymonde   You'd better. Because if you don't −

Finache   All right, all right. Tournel, please . . . (*To*
Lucienne.) Madame . . .

Lucienne   What a dreadful thing to happen, at his age.

Tournel   I remember, twelve years ago, summer it
was . . .

Raymonde   Not now, for heaven's sake!

Exeunt.

Finache (*approaching* **Poche**)   Now then, old chap . . .

Poche   Good job you got rid of them. Because if you
hadn't . . .

Finache   Anyone could see that.

Poche   What's wrong with them all? Touched in the
head?

Finache   Touched, that's it.

Poche (*to* **Étienne**)   You see? Touched.

Étienne   Yes, yes, touched.

Poche   You could have told me. A lil hint. 'The whole
lot of them are bats' − something like that.

Finache *takes his wrist to feel his pulse.*

Poche   Hey. What now?

Finache   It's all right. It'll help you.

Poche   I needn't have got so cross. What you do, with
fruitcakes, you agree with everything they say.

Finache   That's odd. Your pulse.

Poche   What about it?

Finache   It's hardly there at all. (*To* **Étienne**.) It's
hardly there at all.

Poche Of course it isn't. What d'you take me for, repulsive?

Finache Repulsi — oh, a joke. Hahahahaha. (*To* **Étienne**.) You too.

Étienne Oh. Hahahaha.

Poche See, even he's laughing. Mr Bowler Hat.

Finache Yes, yes, yes, yes, yes, yes. Well, now we've all had a good laugh, it's time to be serious.

Poche What d'you mean?

Finache I mean, speaking as a friend . . . You know me . . .

Poche No I don't.

Finache Ah. Hahahaha. All right, I'm the doctor. I look after people. Plasters, thermometers, bed-rest, poultices —

Poche All right, you're a doctor. Who's arguing?

Finache Exactly. And as a doctor, I can tell . . . just by looking . . . you're very tired.

Poche Am I?

Finache Very, very tired. (*To* **Étienne**.) Isn't he?

Étienne Very.

Poche And you're surprised? Up at five, sweep, dust, polish —

Finache That's right.

Étienne That's right.

They look at each other in commiseration, as if to say 'Poor chap'.

Finache So, if someone's tired, the best thing to do is go to bed and sleep.

Poche What? No, no, no, no, no!

Finache (*hastily*)   Of course not. What a silly idea. But at least take off that jacket. It looks really uncomfortable. Étienne will get you a dressing-gown.

Poche   I want my uniform.

Finache   Of course you do. Of course you do. Étienne!

Étienne   Yes, Doctor.

Exit R.

Finache (*putting his arm round* **Poche**)   There's a lovely bed in there . . .

Poche   What is all this?

Finache   You could stretch out . . .

Poche   Stop pulling me. You're making me seasick.

Finache   Nighty night, sleep tight −

Poche (*breaking free*)   But what about Monsieur Chandebise?

Finache   Chandebise. Ah. If Chandebise says anything to you, be sure to tell me.

Poche   All right.

Enter **Étienne**.

Étienne   One dressing-gown.

Finache   That's right. Take off your coat.

Poche (*letting them take off his jacket*)   Nothing else. Don't think you're going to −

Finache   Don't worry about a thing. Oh, look, isn't this lovely dressing-gown?

Poche (*tying the belt*)   I'll say. I feel like a real missionaire.

Finache   You see?

Poche   It's comfier than that uniform.

Finache   Of course it is. Now then . . . something tells me . . . a little bird tells me you must be thirsty.

Poche   Clever little bird.

Finache   That's right! I'm going to give you something to drink. It may not be very nice, but you still have to drink it, all in one.

Poche   A stiff one.

Finache   Eh? Oh. Exactly.

Poche   Go on, then.

Finache   Fine. (*To* **Étienne**.) Ammonia drops.

Poche (*who can't hear them*)   A lil stiff one, eh . . .

Finache   Dissolve them in water. Then make sure he drinks them.

Étienne   Yes, Doctor.

Finache   Then, when he's sobered up . . . I'll write you a prescription.

Étienne   Yes, Monsieur.

Finache   Have you something to write with?

Étienne   In the writing-desk, there.

Finache   Splendid. While I'm doing that, you put him to bed.

Étienne   Yes, Doctor. (*To* **Poche**.) Monsieur, if you'd . . . why don't you . . . lean on me.

Poche (*as* **Étienne** *leads him out*)   Thass very kind of you.

Étienne   Too kind, Monsieur, too kind.

Poche   Such a shame.

Étienne   Monsieur?

Poche About your wife.

Étienne No, no. She was with the concierge. She was. She was.

Poche Whatever you say.

Exeunt. **Finache**, *meanwhile, has opened the writing-desk.*

Finache What a smell? It's this paper. Phew! (*He drops it.*) Whoops. (*He picks it up, puts it in the pad of writing paper and back in the desk.*) Ah. Someone's coming. Camille.

Enter **Camille**, *out of breath.*

Camille Well, thank you, Doctor. That hotel of yours. What a time I've had.

Finache What? Speak more slowly.

Camille What a time I've had.

Finache For heaven's sake, put in your thingumajig. What d'you think I brought it for?

Camille I can't. I've lost it.

Finache Pardon?

Camille The Englishman gave me such a punch, I lost it. (*He mimes.*)

Finache Ah! An Englishman punched you.

Camille And that's not all. It was a nightmare. Everyone was there. In the hotel. Tournel, Raymonde, Victor-Emmanuel, with logs. Logs on his back. Why? Madame de Histangua. Her husband, with a gun. Bang! Bang! Shooting. What a business! I'm fed up. What a business!

He slumps. Enter **Antoinette**.

Antoinette Madame says, please, how is Monsieur?

Finache Better than he was. Yes, tell her that: better than he was. No. I'll tell her myself.

Camille   What's going on?

Finache   Nothing. Chandebise isn't feeling well.

Camille   Is that all?

Enter **Étienne**.

Étienne   He's in bed, Monsieur.

Finache   Jolly good.

Étienne   Evening, Monsieur Camille.

Camille   Evening, Étienne.

Finache   Go and see to the drops while I tell Madame.

Étienne   Yes, Doctor.

He goes out by the main doors, leaving them open. **Finache** *and* **Antoinette** *go out L.*

Camille   I've had enough. Quite enough. I feel like a feather. A speck of down, blown in a hurricane.

Knock on the door, R.

Come in.

Enter **Poche**, *still wrapped in the dressing-gown.*

Poche   Scuse me . . .

Camille   Victor-Emmanuel!

Poche   (*severely*)   Someone else I saw at the Hotel Casablanca.

Camille   (*aside*)   Oh no! (*Aloud.*) I'll explain. I was there. It was because I . . . There was someone who . . .

Poche   What're you eating?

Camille   Pardon?

Poche   Spit it out. Don't mind me, spit it out.

Camille   I haven't anything in my mouth. I was saying,

there was someone who ... euh ... insurance, needed
insurance ...

Poche   Oh, stuff all that.

Camille   Eugh?

Poche   None of my business, is it? I'm dying of thirst in
there. They said they were getting a drink. Where is it,
that's what I want to know.

Camille   Who said?

Poche   Hoo heh?

Camille   Who said?

Poche   Hoo heh? Oh, who said? The doctor.

Camille   It's clearly an oversight. I'll just go and −

Poche   Thirsty, yes. Thirsty.

Camille   I'll see to it.

Poche   Good.

Exit, into the room R.

Camille   That's a relief. I thought he'd guessed. He
took it very well. I thought. Very well indeed. All these
years, I've misjudged him. I thought he was puritanical,
but he's not at all. (*Etc: ad lib to cover the quick change.*)

Enter **Chandebise** *by the main doors, rear, in* **Poche**'s
uniform.

Camille   Aah!

Chandebise   What on earth's the matter?

Camille   Oh God. No, no. There ... (*Pointing down R.*)
and then there ... (*Pointing to the rear doors.*)

Chandebise   I don't understand.

He advances on **Camille**, *who scuttles away, putting chairs, tables
etc. between them.*

Camille   Get away. I'm seeing things. I'm seeing things.

Chandebise   Camille, for heaven's sake . . .

Camille   Get away! Get away! Oh no! Oh no!

*Exit, R (into **Poche**'s room).*

Chandebise   What's wrong with everyone today? Phew, that hotel! Hey, my jacket. Thank goodness. (*He starts changing.*) Even the concierge didn't recognise me.

Camille *rushes out R, bumping into **Étienne**, who is going in the opposite direction.*

Camille   Étienne. I'm seeing things. Seeing things.

Exit L.

Chandebise   Here we go again.

Étienne   What's wrong with Monsieur Camille?

Chandebise   Ah, Étienne. Just what I was wondering.

Étienne   Ah! You know who I am, Monsieur?

Chandebise   Of course I know who you are. Any reason why I shouldn't?

Étienne (*hastily*)   No, Monsieur.

*Enter **Camille**, **Finache**, **Raymonde**, **Tournel** and **Lucienne**.*

Camille   There, you see. I said there were two of him.

All   Heugh!

Camille   Two of them. I'm seeing things. Seeing things.

Exit through the hall, R.

All   What's wrong with him?

Raymonde   It's all right, darling. We wondered if —

Chandebise   You? You, here? (*To **Tournel**.*) Not to mention you . . .

Raymonde *and* **Tournel**   Pardon?

Chandebise *grabs him by the neck and starts shaking him.*

Chandebise   Explain yourself. What were you up to, eh? Eh? When I caught you in that . . . in that . . .

All   Oh, no.

Raymonde   Not again.

Tournel   I've explained a hundred times.

Chandebise   Oh, you have? You've explained? And you think I'm fooled? You're wrong. Now, out.

Raymonde   Darling . . .

Chandebise   You, too. Out.

Lucienne   Monsieur Chandebise . . .

Chandebise   I do beg your pardon. I didn't see you there. Excuse me a moment. (*To the others.*) Out, out, out!

Finache (*trying to pull him to the room R*)   Lie down again. Lie down. You've lost control. Come back when you feel a little better.

Raymonde   When he feels better? What about me? When I feel better?

She stalks out, followed by **Lucienne**.

Finache   Now see what you've done. (*To* **Tournel**.) If you wouldn't mind . . .

Tournel   He's really gone. He's really, really gone.

Exit after the women. **Étienne**, *too, has made himself scarce.*

Finache   Now then, Chandebise, old man −

Chandebise   I'm so sorry. I do apologise. I let myself go for a moment. I lost control.

Finache   Don't worry. It lets off steam. You'll feel all the better for it.

Chandebise (*still trembling*) You think so?

Finache Of course. Look how much better you are already. Knowing who people are . . . where we are now . . .

Chandebise What are you talking about?

Finache You're better already.

Chandebise You're in this as well.

Finache Pardon?

Chandebise Knowing who people are, where we are now. Do I normally not know who people are, is that what you're saying?

Finache No, not exactly, no . . .

Chandebise I lost my temper for a moment, not my marbles.

Finache Oh, yes, yes, yes, of course you did. Didn't! I think you really ought to lie down again.

Chandebise Again?

Finache Why on earth did you put your jacket back on?

Chandebise Did you prefer me as a flunkey?

Finache A flunkey. Ah . . .

Chandebise You think it's fun dressing up as a flunkey?

Finache (*aside*) Ay-ay-ay-ay-ay.

Chandebise And not any old flunkey, but a flunkey there . . .

Finache (*aside*) It's hopeless.

Chandebise The Hotel Casablanca. I never want to hear that name again as long as I live.

Finache You went there, then?

Chandebise Went there!

Finache You shouldn't have.

Chandebise I know that now. A scrum in this room, a brawl in that room, a madman on the desk. My clothes, stolen. Porter's uniform! Shoved in yet another room. Locked in! Out the window. Down the drainpipe. Not to mention Homénidès. Homénidès! Don't mention that hotel to me again.

Finache (*aside*) Tsk, tsk, he's really bad.

Chandebise I'll be revenged on the whole pack of them.

Enter **Étienne**, *with a glass of water and some drops, on a tray.*

Étienne Here we are.

Chandebise What do you want?

Étienne Nothing, Monsieur. The doctor asked −

Finache That's right. I did.

Chandebise Fine. Fine.

Finache Thanks.

Étienne If you'd see to it, Doctor . . .

Finache No problem.

He puts drops into the water.

Chandebise Something the matter?

Finache No, no. Here, drink this.

Chandebise Me?

Finache It'll calm your nerves. After all you've been through.

Chandebise How thoughtful! Thank you. (*He takes the glass.*)

Finache Make sure you drink it all at once.

Chandebise No problem.

He drinks a bit, then rushes to the window, hurls it up and spits.

Pouah!

Finache I told you to drink it all at once.

Chandebise What are you trying to do to me? Is this another joke?

Finache Come on, old chap.

Chandebise Oh, go to – Out of the way!

Finache Where are you going?

Chandebise To wash the taste away.

Exit, R. Bell, off.

Étienne Someone at the door.

He goes to answer it.

Finache He wasted the whole thing.

Ferraillon (*off*) Monsieur Chandebise?

Étienne (*off*) This way, sir.

Finache He's all we need.

Ferraillon (*at the main door*) Doctor Finache.

Finache How nice to see you.

Ferraillon I hate to disturb you.

Finache Is it about the insurance?

Ferraillon Oh, I wouldn't intrude for that. I'll make an appointment for that. No, I've brought something we found in the hotel, something belonging to Monsieur Camille Chandebise. (*He takes out the palate.*)

Étienne   That's right. I found that.

Ferraillon   Ah. (*Recognising him.*) Monsieur . . . ?

Étienne   Étienne. I work for Monsieur Chandebise.

Ferraillon   Charmed, I'm sure.

Finache   Show me a minute. Yes, it's Camille's palate. So he lost it in the − ? How did you know it was his?

Ferraillon   His name and address, engraved.

Finache   Oh, yes. 'Camille Chandebise, 95 boulevard Malesherbes.' That's very bright of him.

Ferraillon   And very useful, if he forgot his visiting cards.

Finache   He'll be very pleased. I'll take it to him.

Antoinette (*hurrying in*)   Doctor, Doctor, I don't know what's the matter with Monsieur Camille. I found him just now stark naked, in the bathroom, taking a shower.

Finache   What of it?

Ferraillon   On Thursday?

Finache   I know what it is. You call to see him, he takes a shower. Really. Antoinette, where's the bathroom?

Antoinette (*pointing off the hall, R*).   This way, Doctor.

Finache   What's wrong with everyone today?

He and **Antoinette** *go.* **Ferraillon** *comes downstage.*

Ferraillon   A shower on a Thursday. No sense in that.

He finds **Poche**'s *uniform jacket and cap, discarded by* **Chandebise**.

Ferraillon   Just a minute. Poche's uniform. What's it doing here? Is my porter somewhere here?

Étienne   Of course not. Why should he be?

Ferraillon   It's very odd.

Enter **Chandebise**.

Chandebise   What a disgusting taste.

Ferraillon   Poche!

Chandebise   The madman!

Ferraillon *chases him round the furniture.*

Ferraillon   What the devil are you doing here?

Chandebise   Ah. Ha. Ha. Haaaa.

Ferraillon (*catching him*)   Dropping my uniform all over town.

Chandebise   Ah. Ha. Aaah.

Étienne (*trying to separate them*)   Monsieur! What are you doing?

Ferraillon   You keep out of it.

Chandebise (*breaking free*)   Grab him!

Exit. Now **Ferraillon** *and* **Étienne** *are struggling.*

Ferraillon   Put me down!

Étienne   That's Monsieur Chandebise. The boss.

Ferraillon   Of course it's not. It's Poche.

Door slams, off.

After him!

Étienne   No! No!

Exeunt. Pause. Then **Chandebise** *sticks his head round the door L.*

Chandebise   Has he gone? Phew! Thank God I thought of slamming the outside door. He'll think I'm halfway down the stairs. Phew!

Étienne (*from the hall*)   Not now, Monsieur!

Homénidès (*from the hall*)   I said, let me past!

Chandebise   Now what?

Homénidès *bursts in, with a box of duelling pistols.*

Chandebise   You!

He tries to get away.

Homénidès   Stay where you are.

Chandebise   Look, old chap . . .

Homénidès   Old chap? Is no more old chap. You slip
me before. I find you now. And if arrested I not been, I
show you revolver, revolver, no? Policeman he confiscate.
Or else I show.

Chandebise   Aren't our policemen wonderful?

Homénidès   So . . . these I bring.

Chandebise   What?

Homénidès   Fear nothing. I not keel you like a dog. I
keel like dog in hot blood only. When I catch you in,
what you say in French, 'ze dog in ze manger'.

Chandebise   Ah. Yes.

Homénidès   To keel now, would be murder. I no want
that.

Chandebise   Me too. I no want that.

Homénidès   So here we have, two pistols. One loaded
is, the other blank.

Chandebise   I'll have the first one.

Homénidès (*hugely*)   Bahaaaah!

Chandebise *jumps back.* **Homénidès** *takes out a piece of
chalk.*

Homénidès This chalk I take. Your heart I chalk.

He draws a circle on **Chandebise**'s *chest.*

Chandebise (*rubbing hard*) You can't do that.

Homénidès (*chalking himself*) The same I me.

Chandebise It'll never catch on.

Homénidès Each one he pistol take. Barrel on other he front. Poom! Poom! One stand — he have good gun.

Chandebise What about the other one?

Homénidès Bahaaaah! In Espain, we call it yoo-ell.

Chandebise Oh well, in Espain . . .

Homénidès You shoose.

Chandebise What?

Homénidès I say, you shoose!

Chandebise No, no, thanks. It's late. I never fight duels this late.

Homénidès If you no shoose, you die.

Chandebise You're not joking. Oh, my God. Help!

Exit, L.

Homénidès Come back!

Exit after him.

Chandebise (*off*) Help, someone, help!

Homénidès (*off*) I find you. Wait!

Chandebise *rushes in.*

Chandebise Help!

He crosses the stage and goes into the room R, then dashes back again.

I'm in there. I'm asleep, in there! I'm seeing things. I'm seeing things.

Homénidès (*off*)   Where you are? I hear.

Chandebise   Aaaah!

Exit by the main door. Enter **Homénidès** *L.*

Homénidès   I tell you, wait. I come.

He runs to the main door and finds it locked. He rattles it angrily.

Chandebise (*off, running L*)   Please, someone, help!

Homénidès   Ah, there you are.

He tries the door L. It's now locked as well.

What game you play? What silly game you play? Open!
At once! Be opening this door.

Enter **Poche**, *in the dressing-gown, from the room R.*

Poche   Who's doing all this shouting?

Homénidès   Ah, there you are. One gun you take.

Poche   The Redskin. Aeee!

Homénidès   I keel you now.

Poche   Help!

Chase. **Poche** *scrabbles round all the doors in turn, and finds them
locked. At last he comes to the window which* **Chandebise**
opened earlier.

Poche   Ahhh! (*He jumps out.*)

Homénidès   Poor devil. He keel himself. (*He looks out.*)
No, he safe. I keel him: good. Oof, is hot work, chasing.

He sees on the table the remains of the drink, drinks, spits.

Pouah! What foulness is drinking heem in France. My
mouth I wipe. Paper I find, I find.

He goes to the writing-desk, takes out the scented paper.

Hooah. What perfume is! What writing! My wifes is perfume. My wifes is writing. 'Last night at the theatre I drank you in . . .' Is the same. Why two letters? This one here, the other one . . . ? I find her, I ask, I ask.

He runs to the door L and beats on it.

Open! I cry you open!

Tournel *opens the door.*

Tournel   What's all the noise about?

Homénidès   Tournel! Aha!

He drags him into the room.

Tournel   The madman.

Homénidès   This letter.

Tournel   Put me down.

Enter **Raymonde**.

Tournel   What on earth's going on?

Homénidès *drops* **Tournel** *and goes to her.*

Homénidès   This lètter, I find heem in your papers. Why?

Raymonde   I beg your pardon? Who said you could search my papers?

Homénidès   I asking first. Wife's writing is. My wife's writing is. You tell me: why?

Raymonde   Ah . . .

Homénidès   To write her love-letterings, is here she comes?

Raymonde   Of course it is! And that proves everything. She's innocent. Entirely innocent.

Homénidès   *Què? Como?*

Raymonde   Exactly. Kaycomo. If there was the slightest thing going on between your wife and my husband, d'you think she'd come here to write about it?

Tournel   Not done, old man. Not done at all.

Homénidès   *Nombre de dios.*

Raymonde   Oh, you don't? All right, then, here she is. Ask her yourself.

Enter **Lucienne**. **Homénidès** *runs to her.*

Homénidès   Now at once you telling me –

Lucienne   My husband!

Homénidès   Don't go. Please. Just one word, you give me peace. This letter, this letter.

Lucienne   What letter? (*Seeing it.*) Aee!

Homénidès   I find heem. Why you write heem? Why?

Lucienne (*looking at* **Raymonde**)   It's a secret.

Raymonde   Go on, tell him. Just one word, you give him peace.

Homénidès   Oh, *si.*

Lucienne   It's all right?

Raymonde   Go on.

Lucienne   Thank you. (*To* **Homénidès**.) What an Othello you are! (*To* **Raymonde**, *pointing to him.*) *Qué tonto!* (*To him.*) *Raimunda créia tener motivo de dudar de la fidelidad de su marido.* [Raymonde thought she had proof of her husband's unfaithfulness.]

Homénidès   *Como?*

Lucienne   *Estonces para probarlo decidío darle una cita galante ... al la cual ella también asistiría.* [To find out for sure, she arranged a rendezvous for him and made sure she'd be there.]

Homénidès (*impatiently*)   *Pero, la carta, la carta!* [But, the letter.]

Lucienne (*losing her temper*)   *Eh! La carta! La carta! Espera, hombre!* (*Controlling herself, stressing all the 'i' sounds.*) *Si ella hubiese escrito la carta a su marido, esto hubiera reconcido su escritura.* [The letter! Wait, man! If she'd written to her husband herself, he'd have recognised her writing.]

Homénidès (*eagerly*)   *Despues, despues.* [Go on.]

Lucienne   *Entonces ella me ha encargado de escribir en su lugar.* [So she asked me to write it for her.]

Homénidès   *No? Es verdad?* (*To* **Raymonde**.) *Es verdad?* [Is this true?]

Raymonde   Pardon?

Homénidès   *Es verdad to que ella dice?* [Is what she says true?]

Raymonde   Oh, *verdad*, every word, *verdad*. (*She shrugs to the audience.*)

Homénidès. *Ah, señora, señora, cuando pienso que me he metido tantas ideas en la cabeza!* [Madame, madame, when I think of the ideas I had in my head ...]

Raymonde   Oh, it's quite all right. Really. No trouble at all.

Homénidès (*to* **Lucienne**)   *Ah! Que estupido, estupido soy!* (*To* **Tournel**.) *Ah, no soy mas que un bruto! Un bruto! Un bruto!* [What a fool I am. I'm no better than an animal.] (*On each 'bruto' he thumps himself contritely on the chest.*)

Tournel (*thumping him too*)   We've been telling you that all afternoon.

Homénidès (*to* **Lucienne**)   *Ah, querida, perdoname mis estupideces.* [Darling, please forgive my stupidities.]

Lucienne   *Te perdono, pero no vuelvas a hacerlo.* [All right, but you don't deserve it.]

Homénidès   *A, querida mia, ah, yo te quiero!* [Darling, I love you!]

They sit down, hand in hand.

Raymonde (*to* **Tournel**)   Don't people get on well, in Spanish?

Enter **Finache**, **Camille** *and* **Chandebise**, *fast.* **Camille** *is dressed in a bath-towel, and still hasn't got his palate.*

Finache   You're crazy. Both of you. It's impossible.

Camille   I saw him at the same time, there . . . and there.

Chandebise   And I saw . . . myself. In there, asleep on my bed.

Finache   You did, did you?

Homénidès (*from the sofa*)   *Qué? Qué?*

Camille   You again!

Homénidès   No. Is all right. I calm. This letter, is no my wifes he write. (*To* **Chandebise**.) Is yours.

Chandebise (*to* **Raymonde**)   Is you? I mean, it was you?

Raymonde   I've been telling you all afternoon.

Chandebise   Me?

Tournel   And each time, we kissed and made up. Each time.

Chandebise   What's he talking about?

Homénidès   And just for that, I make you yump out the window.

Chandebise   Pardon?

All   Yump?

Homénidès   Not pleased at all I was.

Chandebise You made me jump out of the window?

Homénidès Of course. You come out of here ... (*The door, R.*) and hop! You yump.

Chandebise You see? You see? He saw it too! We're all seeing things. What you saw, what yumped out of the window, was what I saw, asleep in my bed.

Camille And what I saw, here and here.

Chandebise That's right. That proves it. I never jumped out of any window.

Homénidès What is thees you say?

Finache (*holding his head in his hands*) I don't understand this. I don't understand at all.

Tournel It's witchcraft.

Étienne *shows in* **Ferraillon**, *who is holding the dressing-gown.*

Ferraillon Excuse me ...

Chandebise The madman!

He hides under the table. Everyone talks at once.

Finache *and* **Camille** Ferraillon!

Raymonde From the hotel.

Tournel Casablanca!

Ferraillon I was on my way out, when my porter fell on my head. He came from that window, there.

All What?

Tournel, **Camille**, **Homénidès** The porter!

Ferraillon And he was snitching this dressing-gown.

Raymonde That's my husband's dressing-gown. It's yours, Victor-Emm — where is he? Victor-Emmanuel ... ?

They all start searching.

All   Victor-Emmanuel? Chandebise . . . ?

Ferraillon *finds* **Chandebise** *under the table.*

Ferraillon   Aha!

All   What?

Ferraillon   It's him again. It's Poche!

He drags him out.

All   Poche? Poche?

Chandebise   Ahah. Ahaaaaah.

Ferraillon (*back to the kicking routine*)   You drunk, you thief, you swine.

All   Hey.

Raymonde   Just a minute. That's my husband.

Ferraillon   Pardon?

Chandebise   He's a madman. He does it every time he sees me.

Ferraillon   This is your husband?

Raymonde   Yes. Monsieur Chandebise.

Ferraillon   He can't be. He's the double of my porter, Poche.

All   Your porter, Poche?

Ferraillon   The one who just jumped out of that window.

All   Ah.

Chandebise   I think I understand. The man I saw in bed just now and took for me −

All   Was Poche.

Raymonde The one we saw in bed at the hotel, with the brandy –

Tournel The one who kept kissing us –

All Was Poche.

Lucienne The one who tried to drag me to the bar –

Camille And who was carrying all those logs of wood –

All Was Poche.

Chandebise Poche! All of them were Poche. I'm sorry he yumped. I'd have liked to meet him, Poche.

Ferraillon That's easy. Just pay a call at the Hotel Casablanca.

Chandebise Never again.

Raymonde Not even for the beauty who drank you in?

Chandebise Oh, very funny. What a silly trick to play!

Raymonde What else could I do? After what was happening, I had to find out if –

Chandebise What d'you mean, after what was happening?

Raymonde Well, after . . . (*She whispers in his ear.*)

Chandebise But that was nothing.

Raymonde That's what I mean.

Chandebise But it wasn't –

Raymonde It gave me a bee in the bonnet, that's all.

Chandebise I'll show you bonnets, bees. You wait till tonight. I'll show you bees.

Raymonde Really?

Chandebise Well, I'll do my best.

Camille (*stepping forward*) I think I can explain what's been going on –

All   Not now! Not now! Not now!

Final curtain.

Jailbird

Gibier de potence

a farce in one act

Characters

Pépita, *the music-hall singer 'Sheherazade'*
Plumard, *a herbalist, her husband*
Taupinier, *Pépita's admirer*
Lemercier, *alias Grumpard, a schoolteacher*
Mariette, *the maid*
Dubrochard, *special constable*

Note   In the original, Dubrochard was accompanied by two constables, who did not speak.

The drawing-room of **Pépita**'s *and* **Plumard**'s *house in Paris. Centre back, door to the hall. Upstage L, fireplace; upstage R, door to other parts of the house. Centre R, door to a closet; centre L, door to other parts of the house. Elegant furniture in the latest style, including a writing-desk. On the mantelpiece, a metre ruler (rigid); beside the fireplace, a child's hoop adorned with little bells.*

As the curtain rises, **Pépita** *is sitting in an armchair reading the paper, and* **Plumard** *is at the writing-desk finishing a letter.*

Plumard '. . . and you'll recognise him by his appearance of total imbecility. Signed, a well-wisher.' That ought to do it. He's in for a great big shock.

Pépita Oh no!

Plumard What is it?

Pépita She's dead.

Plumard Who's dead?

Pépita That poor girl, the victim of Suresnes.

Plumard Oh, her.

Pépita You're always the same. Heartless. If it isn't you who's died.

Plumard We're like that, we men: robust. We have to be.

Pépita No you haven't.

Plumard Excuse me, I think I know more about what men have to be than you know about what men have to be.

Pépita Of course you do. (*Aside.*) A music-hall singer, a doddering old herbalist: of course he does.

Plumard There are some things women just aren't *made* to know.

Pépita (*reading*) 'After a night of searing agony, during which every drop of blood in her body turned . . .'

Plumard   Turned?

Pépita   Like milk.

Plumard   Three pinches of chicory, four of watercress, that would have saved her.

Pépita   I was reading the paper, not asking for a prescription.

Plumard   Of course you were. But you know us medical people: never off duty . . .

Pépita   Medical people? You're a herbalist. An old herbalist. A sort of glorified witch-doctor.

Plumard   Even witch-doctors have professional standards, my darling.

Pépita   Whatever you say. (*Reading.*) 'As soon as the poor wretch was dead, they seized their chance and buried her.' It's awful.

Plumard   What d'you expect? As soon as she was dead . . . that's life.

Pépita   They still haven't found him: the murderer. No, they must have done. As soon as Taupinier gets here, I'll send him for an evening edition.

Plumard   Ha! Taupinier's coming, is he?

Pépita   What's wrong with Taupinier? What have you got against Taupinier?

Plumard   Nothing. (*Aside, as she shrugs and goes on reading.*) Except that he's after my wife, the swine. Every time he calls, she sends me out. 'Take the hoop and play with Baby.' Six months, it's been going on. Don't think I haven't noticed. I'm not one of those husbands who notice nothing. I knew from the start, well, from this lunchtime. I was reading *Othello*. Play, by some Englishman. Writes very good French, for an Englishman. I knew it at once! 'Pillows,' I thought, 'yes, pillows.' Then

I thought, 'No, too English.' I decided on something more French, more lingering. So I grabbed a pen and wrote straight to the police. (*Reading us his letter.*) 'Come to 7 rue des Anes, Monsieur and Madame Plumard, at five o'clock this afternoon. That swine'll be there, that blackguard, that villain. And you'll recognise him by his appearance of total imbecility. Signed, a well-wisher.' A bit melodramatic, but I don't care. Now, it's five to four. One hour five minutes, then heh, heh, heh, heh.

Doorbell, off. Enter **Taupinier**.

Taupinier   Afternoon.

Pépita   Ah! Lovely to see you. Run down to the shop and buy an evening paper. Then go to the police station . . .

Taupinier   It's go, go, go with you. Never mind. I flit, hither, thither, I swoop like a swallow . . .

He goes to the door.

Plumard (*muttering*)   Get on with it.

Taupinier (*coming back*)   I nearly forgot. What am I to do at the police station?

Pépita   Ask if anyone's handed in my brooch. My diamond brooch . . . you know . . .

Plumard   *I* know. Your darling diamond dogshead. Woofles.

Taupinier   Oh, that brooch. So many memories . . .

Plumard   Pardon?

Pépita (*quickly*)   Memories of my father. He wore it, often.

Plumard   Your father wore a brooch?

Pépita   At functions. Only at functions. They never made him a Mason . . .

Plumard One can see why.

Taupinier Well, excuse me.

Plumard (*grabbing the tails of his coat*) Don't be long. You haven't got all day. You've time. It's only just four. You've got an hour.

Taupinier (*baffled*) Till when?

Plumard Till five. I mean, we look forward to seeing you then, at five.

Taupinier Till five, then. Till five.

Exit.

Pépita Isn't he charming?

Plumard Charming's not the word. (*Aside.*) He's in for such a shock.

Enter **Mariette**.

Mariette Madame, there's a gentleman. Asks if you're at home. Monsieur Lemercier.

Pépita Never heard of him. Show him in. Ask him to wait. I'll just straighten my hair. And so will Monsieur.

Plumard What will Monsieur do?

Pépita Comb his hair. What's left of it.

Plumard Yes, darling.

Exeunt. **Mariette** *shows in* **Lemercier**. *He has an umbrella in one hand and a pet-basket in the other, containing a small dog.*

Mariette This way, Monsieur.

Lemercier You did say the right name? Lemercier?

Mariette Yes, Monsieur.

Lemercier Thanks.

Exit **Mariette**. **Lemercier** *mutters to himself.*

Lemercier, good. Not Grumpard. Must get things right. At home, in the classroom, it's Grumpard, Latin teacher. In Paris, on the razzle, it's Lemercier, man-about-town. Grumpard can't go calling on actresses, singers . . . but Lemercier can. Oh, Sheherazade, Sheherazade . . . Oh, those Arabian Nights . . . brrrr-ha-hey! What a stroke of luck, at the theatre last night. 'Poor Sheherazade,' they were saying − I couldn't help overhearing, since I *was* listening − 'Poor Sheherazade. She's broken-hearted. She's lost her Woofles, and she's almost beside herself.' Beside herself! That's where I intend to be. (*To the dog in the basket.*) Oh yes, ickle Woofles, did you know when I bought you just now in the flea-market, your name was Woofles? It is now, it is now. Oh, Sheherazade, she'll be so grateful, Sheherazade . . . Someone's coming!

Enter **Plumard**.

Lemercier Who's this?

Plumard (*bowing*) Delighted, delighted.

Lemercier (*bowing back*) The feeling's entirely mutual. (*Aside.*) Who *is* he?

Plumard Please do sit down.

Lemercier Just what I was going to say.

They sit. Pause.

Excuse me . . . I don't want to seem . . . It's just that . . . Are you the manager?

Plumard Pardon?

Lemercier The manager. Her manager. They all have managers. Are you the manager?

Plumard I most certainly am not. I'm Monsieur Plumard.

Lemercier Plumard. Monsieur Plumard. Ah. (*Getting up to go.*) This isn't . . . she doesn't . . . Sheherazade . . .

Plumard This is where she lives, yes. Sheherazade. My wife.

Lemercier You're Monsieur Sheherazade?

Plumard Plumard. I told you.

Lemercier Ah. Unusual. Most wives have the same name as their husbands. Take mine, for instance. She's Madame Grumpard, I'm Monsieur . . . Lemercier. (*Aside.*) Whoops.

Plumard (*getting up*) I think I can explain. Please do sit down.

Lemercier Just what I was going to say.

They sit, as before.

Plumard I'm a herbalist, Monsieur. Or was, at least. One day, Mamzelle Sheherazade asked me to call at the theatre. She was feeling a little . . . strained. Next morning, thanks to my advice, she was right as rain. I recommended: doing nothing at all.

Lemercier Fine, if you don't overdo it.

Plumard As I say, next morning she was right as rain, and to cut a long story short, two weeks later we were married. And five months later, Monsieur, I was a father! A bouncing baby boy, full-size and perfect in every way.

Lemercier Amazing.

Plumard Astounding. Such a rare case, I wanted to write to the Academy of Medicine, but Madame said no. I'd have loved to hear how they explained it. As I say, astounding.

Lemercier And as Horace says, '*Parturiunt montes . . .*'

Plumard Does he really? (*Aside.*) Some foreign friend of his. (*Aloud.*) So now you see. Mamzelle Sheherazade is Madame Plumard. I made her keep her name for professional purposes. I mean, imagine a name like

Plumard on theatre bills!

Lemercier   Oh, yes. Is Madame, ah, Plumard at home today?

Plumard   She'll be here directly. (*Aside.*) What a delightful man. I feel I could tell him *anything*.

Lemercier   D'you mind if I put on my overcoat? This time of year, whenever I take it off, I freeze.

He takes his coat from the dog-basket, which it's been hiding.

Plumard   A dog!

Lemercier   It's a surprise. Don't tell her!

Enter **Pépita**.

Pépita   Monsieur, I'm sorry to keep you waiting.

Lemercier (*hiding the basket*)   Just what I was going to say.

Pépita   Do sit down.

Lemercier   Just what I was going to say, again.

They sit. Same business as before.

Pépita   Now, Monsieur . . . ?

Lemercier   Oh, yes. (*Aside.*) My God, she's beautiful!

Pépita   Yes?

Lemercier   Dear Madame, I came to lay at your feet –

Pépita   A song? Of course! You're a young composer.

Lemercier   Well, I am *young*. I've been young for years. But I'm not a composer. No no, it's this darling little doggy.

He reveals the basket.

Pépita   A doggy!

Lemercier   I'm sorry to hand him over so . . . *unsubtly*. I did hide him in a big, big box of chocolates, but he ate them all. And the box.

Pépita It's very kind of you, Monsieur. But I don't quite −

Lemercier Don't you see? Woofles!

Pépita Woofles?

Lemercier Woofles. You lost him, I found him, Woofles.

Plumard Ha! Woofles! *That?*

Lemercier He isn't?

Pépita Oh, no, Monsieur. My Woofles is a doggy's head.

Lemercier Decapitated?

Pépita Diamonds.

Lemercier Diamonds. Ah. Excuse me ... d'you mind if I ...? My overcoat. I don't know about you, but in this weather I'm always either too ... or too ...

Pépita So this Woofles isn't my Woofles after all.

Lemercier I quite see that. Of course, I quite see that. But it is the thought that counts.

Pépita Oh yes, Monsieur.

Lemercier *Errare humanum est.*

Pépita I don't speak Swedish, sorry.

Lemercier That's a relief. I don't either.

Plumard Don't be embarrassed. Thousands of people don't. This reminds me of a day last week. Last Friday. I was fishing. In the river. Nothing. Then all at once, a bite! 'Aha!' I said to myself. 'A pike!' It was a toupée.

Lemercier A toupée?

Plumard A hairpiece. A wig. Someone's hairpiece.

Lemercier I don't see the connection . . .

Plumard I didn't say there was a connection. I said it reminded me . . . (*Aside.*) Pedant!

Lemercier Madame, I'm so dreadfully sorry . . .

Pépita (*smiling sweetly*) Not at all, Monsieur.

Plumard We're the ones who're sorry. For your sake. I mean, there *was* a small reward. We'd have given you it gladly. But since you brought a dog, not a dog, you do understand . . . I mean, under the circ –

Pépita Darling.

Plumard Yes, darling?

Pépita Go and play with Baby, there's a darling.

Plumard *goes with great dignity to the door, then says aside:*

Plumard I'm going, because I don't want to look a fool. But just wait till five o'clock. He's in for such a shock!

Exit.

Pépita I do apologise for my husband. He's a joker, he likes to make jokes.

Lemercier A man of infinite jest and fancy. Yes. He doesn't look it, but he is.

Enter **Taupinier**.

Taupinier Sorry I took so long. It's not been handed in.

Lemercier (*aside*) Another of 'em!

Pépita (*introducing them*) Monsieur Taupinier . . . Monsieur Lemercier . . .

Taupinier Delighted.

Lemercier   Just what I was going to say.

Taupinier   My father knew a Monsieur Lemercier. His
dustman. You're not by any chance . . . ?

Lemercier   Not as such.

Taupinier   No, you're right. If you were, you'd be dead
by now. You were poorly even when I knew you. What a
pity: we could have talked over old times.

He takes **Pépita** *apart to talk to her.*

Lemercier   The loss is mine, Monsieur. (*Aside.*) Time I
was going. (*Aloud.*) Madame, it's time I . . . Delighted to
have met you, *o formosa puella.*

Pépita   You say the nicest things. Goodbye, Monsieur.

Lemercier   Not in the least. Er . . . I'll take my dog.
Come on, Woofles.

He gathers everything but his umbrella, and exit.

Taupinier   Who on earth was that?

Pépita   Some idiot. Never mind. Did you get the paper?

Taupinier   Yes. Here.

Pépita   Quick! Ah! (*Reading.*) 'The crime at Suresnes.
Description of assassin. The ass —'

Taupinier   An ass, was he?

Pépita   Don't be silly. Listen. 'The assassin was the
victim's ex-lover. Name: Lemercier.' Oh, my God! 'He
vanished last night, and no one knows his present
whereabouts.' Oh no!

Taupinier   He couldn't be . . . !

Pépita   Of course he could. They're clever, assassins.
Fiendish.

Taupinier   You are silly.

Pépita (*reading*) 'We publish this description, in case it jogs anyone's memory. Police are on the lookout for a man in his early forties, with chestnut hair.' I told you!

Taupinier Our Lemercier's was white.

Pépita Of course it was: guilty conscience. People often turn white overnight. Or perhaps, a wig.

Taupinier (*impressed*) You're right.

Pépita This is terrible. (*Reading.*) 'Chestnut hair, brown eyes.' My God, I never noticed what colour his eyes were. Did you?

Taupinier No, I forgot.

Pépita 'Nose, ordinary; mouth, ordinary; teeth all present except for third left-side molar.' A clue! Third left-side molar. 'Height, one metre sixty-six.' How high is that?

Taupinier My God: *his* height!

Pépita 'Strawberry mark on right thigh.' The *right* thigh! 'Red flannel underwear.' This is going to be hard to check. My God, to think I had a murderer here, in my own front room!

Doorbell.

Taupinier Someone's at the door.

Pépita It's all right, I'm out. My God, look: his umbrella. It may be a clue. Here, quick!

They open the umbrella and peer into it.

Taupinier Looks harmless enough to me.

Enter **Lemercier**.

Lemercier I'm sorry, but I think I left my —

Pépita *and* **Taupinier** (*jumping*) It's him!

Lemercier My umbrella. Goodness. Is it raining in here?

Pépita   Yes, er, no. We were going for a walk. It's been terrible weather now for *weeks* . . .

Taupinier   Never go without an umbrella.

Lemercier   Just what I was going to say. That's why I came for mine.

Pépita (*stopping him before he takes it and goes*)   You're very kind, but we couldn't dream of letting you go out in weather like this. Please do sit down.

Lemercier   Just what I was going to say.

He takes a chair C, and sits.

Pépita (*aside to* **Taupinier**)   It's him. Brown eyes.

Taupinier   And an ordinary nose.

Pépita   And just look at his mouth!

Lemercier (*aside*)   What are they staring at? Ah! Got it! (*Aloud.*) I understand.

Pépita *and* **Taupinier** (*jumping*)   Ah!

Lemercier   You're obviously wondering what's happened to Woofles. I got rid of him.

Pépita   You murdered him?

Lemercier   Good heavens no. I gave him away.

Pépita   Gave him away?

Taupinier   How heavy was he?

Lemercier   Oh, light. No, no, I didn't give him a weigh, I gave him away. To the little girl downstairs. She wanted a Woofles, I had a Woofles, she was delighted. Her mother wasn't: she preferred the cat.

Taupinier   What cat?

Lemercier   Any cat! Ha, ha, ha.

Pépita *and* **Taupinier**   Ha, ha, ha.

Pépita   It was very thoughtful of you.

Taupinier (*to her*)   He's an idiot.

Lemercier (*getting up*)   Now, Madame, if you don't mind
... the time has come ... (*He takes off his overcoat.*) ... to
take off my coat. This weather!

Pépita   Not at all. Put it over the chair, there. (*To*
Taupinier.) This is your chance. Measure him.

Taupinier   What?

Pépita   See how tall he is.

Taupinier   How can I?

Pépita   Try.

Taupinier *fetches the metre rule and starts following*
Lemercier *about, trying to measure him without being noticed.*

Lemercier (*folding his coat to put it neatly over the
chairback*)   In this weather, you understand, one can't be
too –

He turns; **Taupinier** *hastily begins twirling the ruler like a
dancer's cane.* **Lemercier** *shakes his head in surprise, then turns
back. At once* **Taupinier** *starts trying to measure him again.*

Lemercier   As I was saying, you just can't be too –

He turns. **Taupinier** *at once pretends to be measuring the table.
In his haste to be nonchalant, he sweeps* **Lemercier**'s *hat from
the table to the floor.*

Lemercier   My hat!

He bends to pick up his hat. **Taupinier** *dashes behind him to
measure him. But he can only measure him bending, as*
Lemercier *straightens up at once.*

Taupinier (*to himself*)   No, no. Taller than that.

Lemercier *gives him a hard stare. He goes and pretends to measure the wall.*

Taupinier The wall. Taller. A taller wall . . .

Lemercier (*aside*) Some kind of builder . . .

He finishes hanging up his coat. **Pépita** *and* **Taupinier** *have a whispered conference.*

Pépita Well?

Taupinier He won't stand still.

Lemercier (*aside to himself*) What are they doing?

Taupinier You talk to him. Distract his attention.

Lemercier (*to himself*) They're up to something.

Pépita So you gave Woofles to the little girl downstairs?

Taupinier *creeps up behind him to measure him, but at the key moment,* **Lemercier** *sits down in a chair.*

Lemercier What else could I do?

Taupinier *suddenly realises that* **Lemercier** *is staring at him. He makes fencer's passes with the rule, dances about – and treads accidentally on* **Lemercier**'s *foot.*

Lemercier Ow!

He hops about. Meanwhile:

Taupinier It's hopeless.

Pépita We'll try something else. Yawn.

Taupinier Pardon?

Lemercier Pardon?

Pépita *and* **Taupinier** Nothing!

Pause.

Pépita (*aside to* **Taupinier**) Yawn, I said.

Taupinier   I don't want to yawn.

Lemercier (*trying to attract attention*)   Excuse me . . .

Pépita   That way we'll see his tooth. The one that isn't there.

She takes a chair and sits on one side of **Lemercier**.
Taupinier *does the same on the other side. Business:*
Taupinier *leans towards* **Lemercier**, *who leans away towards*
Pépita. *She leans towards him, and he leans away towards*
Taupinier. *They do this at least twice. Then they sit awhile bolt upright. Pause.*

Lemercier   All I meant was . . .

Pépita *yawns, hugely.* **Lemercier** *tries* **Taupinier**.

Lemercier   All I meant was . . .

Taupinier *yawns hugely.* **Lemercier** *tries* **Pépita** *again.*

Lemercier   I have to be very –

Pépita *yawns as before.* **Lemercier** *tries* **Taupinier** *again.*

Lemercier   Very careful. I have to be very –

Taupinier *yawns.*

Lemercier   I'm sorry if this is boring you.

Taupinier   Not at all. Do go on.

He yawns. **Lemercier** *tries to continue, but wherever he turns, they're yawning.*

Lemercier   It's a complicated medical history . . . a complicated – (*Yawning.*) Now I'm doing it.

He yawns vastly. They jump up to peer into his mouth, but he quickly covers it with his hand.

I'm so sorry.

He picks up his chair and moves upstage, muttering:

They started it.

The others have another conference.

Taupinier Now what? The strawberry mark?

Pépita Right thigh.

Lemercier I really think I ought to be −

Taupinier (*aside to* **Pépita**) How on earth do we − ?

Pépita *I* don't know. Try, anyway.

Lemercier *goes to put on his coat.*

Pépita You're not going, Monsieur?

Lemercier No, no, no, no. I was feeling a little cold, that's all.

Pépita Perhaps you'd like something to eat?

Lemercier Between meals? No thanks.

Pépita Some fruit, perhaps?

Taupinier Strawberries. I can always eat strawberries, any time.

Pépita You must like strawberries.

Lemercier I like them, but they don't like me. I had some once, out of season, in February, just like today − and they settled on my stomach.

Pépita (*aside to* **Taupinier**) Did you hear that?

Taupinier He's given himself away.

Lemercier (*aside*) They're at it again.

Pépita Now we're getting somewhere. Tell him you're cold.

Taupinier (*to* **Lemercier**) Don't you find it cold in here?

Lemercier Yes. Madame, if you don't mind . . . my overcoat . . .

He starts taking it off.

Taupinier You're cold, and you're taking it off?

Lemercier I could catch a chill.

Pépita It's not coats that stop chills, it's underwear.

Lemercier The only thing.

Pépita And they make it so pretty nowadays.

Taupinier Stylish, even.

Pépita All colours.

Taupinier White.

Pépita Blue.

Taupinier Green.

Pépita Yellow.

Taupinier Red-white-and-blue. They do. For patriots.

Lemercier For patriots, of course. (*Aside.*) Why am I *saying* this?

Pépita I wonder, Monsieur … I don't want to pry … but if you could … I mean, if you wouldn't mind … What colour is your vest?

Lemercier Pardon?

Taupinier Answer! At once! Don't shilly-shally!

Lemercier What an odd conversation. My dear Madame —

Taupinier Don't wriggle. Confess!

Pépita (*aside*) If he says red, he's caught.

Lemercier Well, for heaven's sake. Yellow.

Pépita (*aside to* **Taupinier**) I told you! It's him! He's lying!

Taupinier So he is.

Pépita We've all the evidence we need.

Taupinier Just look at him, anyway. That shifty eye. No, that one. Look.

Lemercier (*aside, putting on his coat*) I'm off.

Pépita He's going.

Taupinier He must have washed off the blood.

Pépita Have you noticed how he keeps fiddling with that overcoat? On, off, on, off . . .

Taupinier Not used to drawing-rooms. You can always tell.

Lemercier (*aside*) I've had enough. (*Aloud.*) I'm sorry, I'm in your way.

Pépita Not at all.

Taupinier Hardly even noticed you.

Lemercier (*aside*) It's turning ugly. Where on earth's Plumard?

Pépita (*to* **Taupinier**) We've got to move fast. You keep him talking; I'll fetch the police. (*To* **Lemercier**.) Excuse me, Monsieur. I leave you with Monsieur.

Exit.

Taupinier (*aside*) Alone with a murderer! Don't panic . . .

Lemercier (*aside*) Alone with an oaf! How *could* she . . . ?

Taupinier (*aside*) He mustn't suspect.

He hums nonchalantly.

Lemercier (*aside*) Humming, now! He needs a lesson, and no mistake.

Taupinier (*aside, looking at him*) I've never seen a murderer as close as this . . .

Lemercier (*advancing on him*) Excuse me, Monsieur, but what exactly are you staring at?

Taupinier (*retreating*) Ah. I . . .

Lemercier I can't *abide* people of your kidney.

Taupinier (*aside*) My kidney? Why's he talking about my kidney? Oh, there's only one thing for it.

He marches up to **Lemercier**, *breathing hard to give himself confidence.*

Taupinier Shuf, shuf, shuf, shuf, shuf, shuf, shuf, shuf . . .

Lemercier Now he thinks he's a train.

Taupinier I'm not who you think I am at all. You think I'm an honest man, a decent, ordinary, boring, everyday sort of man. No, no, no. Ha, ha, ha. I'm a criminal, a criminal.

Lemercier (*starting*) What?

Taupinier As big a criminal as you. Bigger. I murdered my father. I murdered my mother. I murdered my brother . . . my sister . . . the window-cleaner . . . (*Aside.*) Say something, or I'll kill the whole neighbourhood. (*Aloud.*) As soon as that was done, I murdered –

Lemercier (*aside*) What's wrong with him?

Taupinier Oh, never mind. I took up mass murdering, that's all.

Lemercier (*aside*) And she leaves me alone with him! It's some kind of trap.

He backs away, picking up a chair to defend himself with.

Taupinier I hate everything, everyone. Except crime, of course . . . and criminals . . . That's why I . . . (*Aside.*) I've got to go through with this . . . (*Aloud.*) . . . I'd like to shake your hand.

He advances on **Lemercier**, *holding out his hand.* **Lemercier** *defends himself with the chair, and* **Taupinier** *is left shaking one of its legs.*

Lemercier (*aside*) What's he talking about?

Taupinier I know, you see. I know you're a criminal. Dyed, double-dyed, oh triple-dyed . . .

Lemercier What? Me? Ah! (*Aside.*) Better humour him. (*Aloud.*) You're right, Monsieur!

He bangs down the chair − on **Taupinier**'s *foot.*

Taupinier Aee!

Lemercier (*holding out his hand*) I'm delighted to shake your hand . . . the hand that dipped itself in the blood of so many victims. We're soul-mates . . . soul-mates . . .

Taupinier Soul-mates . . .

They shake hands.

Lemercier (*aside*) What a fiery hand!

Taupinier (*aside*) What an icy hand!

Lemercier As you probably know, I've committed hundreds of heinous crimes.

Taupinier Good heavens, yes. Everyone knows. You're famous.

Lemercier I've been in the crime business for years.

Taupinier Me too. My whole life.

Lemercier Not more than me.

Taupinier Perhaps.

Lemercier Oh, really?

Taupinier I was still in nappies when I started. One day, infuriated past bearing by the fact that my nanny thought more of her soldier friend than she did of me, I bit her to death. The soldier died soon after.

Lemercier You bit him too?

Taupinier Broken heart.

Lemercier (*aside*) My God, what a monster. (*Aloud.*) That's nothing. My, er, first exploits began much earlier.

Taupinier They didn't!

Lemercier Before I was even born, Monsieur. Two of us there were, in my mother's womb. Me, my twin brother. I snarled at him, 'This womb isn't big enough for the both of us,' and I kicked his little head in. Bam! Bam! (*Aside.*) Oof!

Taupinier My dear fellow . . .

They shake hands again. Pause.

Lemercier I knew we'd be friends. Soul-mates. We can tell each other everything. And that reminds me: what brings you here, dear friend?

Taupinier (*tapping his nose*) There you have it.

Lemercier A crime, eh? You've . . . business . . . on the go?

Taupinier Murdering business. Murdering . . . Plumard!

Lemercier (*staggered*) Plumard!

Taupinier You're sorry for him?

Lemercier Sorry for him? Sorry? What does that mean, sorry? There's no such word as sorry.

Taupinier Oh, sorry. No.

Lemercier I tell you what: I'll help you. We'll murder him together.

Taupinier   Thanks very much.

Lemercier   My pleasure. (*Aside.*) It's easier than I thought, this murdering. (*Aloud.*) Just one question: why are we murdering him?

Taupinier   Because I love his wife.

Lemercier   Sheherazade?

Taupinier   I'm mad for her.

Lemercier   Mad?

Taupinier   Yes, mad, d'you hear, mad.

Lemercier (*carried away*)   Mad, crazy, demented, raving, frantic, wild, berserk, insane . . .

Taupinier   You sound just like a teacher.

Lemercier   I am! I am!

Taupinier   A teacher?

Lemercier (*hastily*)   Of murderers. In murderer-school. (*Aside, collapsing in a chair.*) This is harder than I thought.

Taupinier (*collapsing in another chair*)   They teach it in school now! What next?

Enter **Plumard**. *They don't see him: each is wrapped in his own thoughts.* **Plumard** *doesn't see them. He locks the door and pockets the key.*

Plumard (*aside*)   Got him. He can't get out. The police are downstairs. I'll go in there, heh, heh, heh, and watch.

He tiptoes to the door L, and exit.

Lemercier (*aside*)   Thank goodness he thinks I'm a murderer, or else he'd murder me.

Taupinier (*aside*)   If he didn't think I was a murderer, I'd be salami.

Noise, off.

Both   Aee!

Dubrochard (*off*)   Open, in the name of the law.

Both   The police!

Dubrochard (*off*)   Open up, or I break it down.

Lemercier *and* **Taupinier** *rush and cling to one another.*

Both   Don't panic. (*Pause.*) Run for it!

They rush out, one L, one R.

Dubrochard (*off*)   I shall count to three. One, two . . .

Plumard *comes out of hiding and goes to open the door.*

Plumard   I can hardly wait . . .

Enter **Dubrochard**.

Dubrochard   Don't try to escape.

Plumard   Pardon?

Dubrochard   Arrest, my lad. You're under arrest.
Anything you say . . . You're mine, lad, mine.

Plumard   Who are you?

Dubrochard   Dubrochard. Special constable. Grocer by
profession. Fine teas and coffees. Where d'you get your
beans?

Plumard   Pardon?

Dubrochard   Beans, lad, beans. Where d'you get your
beans?

Plumard   Jar in the kitchen. Why?

Dubrochard   Joker, hey? That does it. Come with me.

Plumard   You're joking.

Dubrochard   Never joke on duty. Handcuffs, caution,
hup!

Plumard You've got the wrong man.

Dubrochard Nonsense. Full description. 'Appearance of total imbecility.' No doubt about it.

Plumard Hey!

Dubrochard Don't believe me? Look in a mirror.

Plumard I tell you I'm an upright citizen.

Dubrochard No speeches. No politics: on duty.

Plumard For heaven's sake!

Dubrochard Religion, too? On duty: no religion.

Plumard That does it. I'm going to have words to say.

Dubrochard Confession, eh? One minute. Notebook . . . pencil . . .

Plumard You've got the wrong man. He's in there. He's gone in there.

Dubrochard None of that. Talk, can't you, talk!

Plumard All I mean is —

Dubrochard Sh!

Plumard You told me 'Talk'.

Dubrochard Investigate.

He goes to the door, R.

Open, in the name of the law.

Taupinier *sticks his head out.*

Taupinier Not this side, that side.

Dubrochard Embarrassing. Sorry. Free beans, any time care to call . . .

He goes to the door, L.

Open, in the name of the law.

Lemercier *sticks his head out.*

Lemercier Not this one, that one.

Dubrochard Sorry. Embarrassing. Just a minute . . .
You're both under arrest.

Lemercier *and* **Taupinier** What have *we* done?

Dubrochard I'll ask the questions.

Enter **Pépita**.

Pépita What's all this racket?

Taupinier Save me, Madame. They think I'm a
murderer.

Pépita You? Good grief, *he's* the murderer.

Lemercier Me?

Dubrochard You admit it, do you? I'll write that
down. Name?

Lemercier *Di deaeque omnes* . . .

Dubrochard Not first names, surname.

Lemercier Grumpard.

Dubrochard No need to be rude.

Lemercier No, no: Grumpard. My name, my name.
I'm a Latin teacher.

All Ooh!

Pépita He is not. He's Lemercier, the murderer.

Dubrochard Another of 'em! We arrested one
Lemercier this morning.

All What?

Lemercier I tell you I'm not Lemercier.

He shows them inside his hat.

Look, this label: I'm Grumpard. Lemercier's a false name.

Dubrochard I'll write that down.

Taupinier Just a minute. All those crimes you were telling me . . .

Lemercier I made them up. To put you off the scent.

Taupinier That's funny. So did I.

Both My dear fellow.

They shake hands.

Dubrochard Look here, if *you're* not the criminal, and *you're* not . . . Who is?

Pépita There isn't one.

Dubrochard Aha! Embarrassing. Wrong house . . .

Lemercier If you'll excuse me . . . I've got a class waiting.

Dubrochard (*wildly*) And I've got coffee beans. Grocer business, no more police business, greenyah, greenyah, greenyah.

Curtain.